Back Stories

Back Stories

U.S. NEWS PRODUCTION AND PALESTINIAN POLITICS

Amahl A. Bishara

Stanford University Press
Stanford, California

Stanford University Press
Stanford, California

Library of Congress Cataloging-in-Publication Data

Bishara, Amahl A., 1976- author.
  Back stories : U.S. news production and Palestinian politics / Amahl A. Bishara.
    pages cm
  Includes bibliographical references and index.
  ISBN 978-0-8047-8140-4 (cloth : alk. paper)--ISBN 978-0-8047-8141-1 (pbk. : alk. paper)
  1. Journalists, Palestinian Arab--West Bank. 2. Journalism--Political aspects--West Bank.
  3. Journalism--Objectivity--United States. 4. West Bank--Press coverage--United States.
  5. Gaza Strip--Press coverage--United States. 6. Palestinian Arabs--Press coverage--United
  States. 7. Al-Aqsa Intifada, 2000---Press coverage--United States. 8. Arab-Israeli conflict--
  1993---Press coverage--United States. I. Title.
  PN5449.W46B57 2012
  070.4089'9274--dc23   2012031153

Typeset by Bruce Lundquist in 10/14 Minion

To my parents,
June and Ghassan Bishara

As you express yourself in metaphor, think of others
(those who have lost the right to speak).

Mahmoud Darwish, "Think of Others"

CONTENTS

LIST OF ILLUSTRATIONS

ACKNOWLEDGMENTS

A book that centers on recognition of unacknowledged labor should have fine acknowledgments indeed. Fully voicing the ways in which this project depended on the contributions of others will be impossible, in part because I am unable to name the journalists from whom I learned so much. Still, I want first to express my deep gratitude to the journalists with whom I worked, especially the Palestinian journalists. They shared with me their insights about their profession, the second Intifada, and the international politics of Palestine, and they trusted me to accompany them on the job and spend time with them after hours. In addition to all of this, they produce the news that I rely upon every day to follow events in the Middle East. My gratitude to them expands each time I see a powerful image from Gaza or Bethlehem, and each time I read an incisive article. I hope that this book honors these journalists' work by uncovering for a broader audience the routes knowledge travels before it is published, and by introducing some of these journalists' ideas into new circuits and conversations. I also thank the people who shared with me their interpretations of U.S. news articles discussed in this book's interludes for lively and insightful conversations.

I owe a special debt to those who have done work to promote freedom of expression in the Middle East. As with the journalists, I have benefited from their work in two ways: not only has their research provided a starting point for my own analysis on violence against journalists, but also their advocacy for journalists in the occupied territories and beyond has helped to ensure that journalists are able to do their work. I especially thank Joel Campagna and the Committee to Protect Journalists for allowing me to work with them and to make the documentary *Across Oceans, Among Colleagues* about their advocacy early in my research period.

This project had its start at New York University, where generative conversations about anthropology of media, contemporary ethnography, and the Middle East helped me to design this project. Had I been anywhere else, I am sure that this project would have taken shape in a less creative manner, if it had taken shape at all. I am grateful to Lila Abu-Lughod for modeling ethnographic writing that makes the most of every phrase and for inspiring me to meet the special responsibilities and challenges of contemporary Middle East ethnography. Faye Ginsburg motivated me to begin thinking about what the "indigenous" media of Palestinians might be (news, of course!), and she encouraged creative and bold approaches to writing about and making media. She and Fred Myers also helped me to think about materiality of media and the politics of culture in global contexts. Steven Feld inspired attention to the affective and embodied dimensions of politics, place, and media production. Michael Gilsenan urged close readings and a consideration of my relationship with texts. Zachary Lockman helped me to be more precise in my writing—a constant effort—and oriented my thinking on the field of Middle East studies. Terrific colleagues, including Shanti Avirgan, Jessica Cattelino, Kristin Dowell, Aaron Glass, Sherine Hamdy, Graham Jones, Eleana Kim, Ricardo Montez, Brooke Nixon-Friedheim, Naomi Schiller, Nina Siulc, and Jessica Winegar, read and shared grants and chapters, collaborated with me in producing *Across Oceans, Among Colleagues*, and helped me to navigate the travails of field research. Cheryl Furjanic and Jeff Himpele taught me how to use a camera and how to tell a story in film, skills that were invaluable for my fieldwork and continue to be a gift. I am thankful for support of this project from the Fulbright-Hays Doctoral Dissertation Research Abroad grant, the National Science Foundation Graduate Research Fellowship, the McCracken Graduate Fellowship from New York University, the Lichtstern Research Award from the University of Chicago Department of Anthropology, and a Faculty Research Award from Tufts University.

As I continued to develop this project, I benefited from the company of many colleagues reading and thinking about this material alongside me. I am grateful to Thomas Abowd, Julie Chu, Hilary Dick, Paja Faudree, Zeynep Gürsel, Andrew Graan, Jessica Greenberg, Rosemary Hicks, Rich Jankowsky, Margaret Litvin, Robin Shoaps, and Winifred Tate for their readings of chapters from this book. During a sojourn in Chicago, I benefited from comments from Jean and John Comaroff, William Mazzarella, and Michael Silverstein. I am tremendously grateful to Hussein Agrama, Summerson Carr, Jessica Cattelino, Ken Garden, and Sarah Pinto for their patience in reading several drafts as I waded through revisions! Daniel Listoe was a patient, perceptive, and generous editor. I am grateful for the intellectual fellowship I have found at Tufts and beyond in valued friends and colleagues, especially Stephen Bailey, Ken Garden, David Guss, Margaret Litvin, Deborah Pacini Hernandez, Sarah Pinto, Rosalind Shaw, Cathy Stanton, and Jonathan Wilson. Duncan Pickard and Zachary Sheldon were incisive research assistants. A few colleagues have been important interlocutors during both fieldwork and the writing process: Michael Kennedy, Peter Lagerquist, Julie Norman, and most especially Lori Allen, who has with forbearance and acuity read much of this manuscript multiple times. She, Jessica Cattelino, Sherine Hamdy, Sarah Pinto, Winifred Tate, and Jessica Winegar have helped me think and rethink what it means to do ethically grounded and ethnographically rich anthropology in times of crisis, and to still have fun doing it! I am very grateful to my two anonymous reviewers for their discerning and motivating comments. I also thank everyone who has worked with this manuscript at Stanford University Press, including Mariana Raykov and Jeff Wyneken, and especially Kate Wahl, whose advice on refining the manuscript and hands-on work in making a book have been invaluable.

In the field, I was fortunate to have many homes. The Bisharas of Tarshiha, especially Bassam and Violette Bishara, made me feel like a part of their households with a warmth I never could have imagined. In Jerusalem, I drew encouragement and nourishment from the Qupty family. In 'Aida Refugee Camp, the amazing Al-Azza family took me in and gave me a new vantage point on Palestinian life, and then the excellent Al-Azraq family did it all over again. I thank my inspiring cousins, including Yvette Qupty, Jada Carlson, and Basim, Ghousoon, Janan, Rana, and Suhad Bishara, and those who became like siblings, Khawla, Majeda, Fatima, and Nasser Al-Azraq, and Nisreen, Nidal, Afaf, and Shifa Al-Azza, for their kindness and generosity, and for sharing with me their ideas about politics and representation. Thanks to Salah and Rasha Ajarma for their unending resourcefulness, Saed Abu-Hijleh for his magnanimity, and Mohammad Al-Azza for the fantastic images. Surely one of the greatest Palestinian pleasures is feeling in the groove with families and friends one loves, sitting on the veranda or around a space heater (or drum, or computer). It is perhaps one of the qualities of this pleasure in collectivity that makes it impossible to name all of the people with whom one shares this experience, but you know who you are, and I do too.

My parents, June and Ghassan Bishara, set me on the path to caring about the world (and the news!) and loving learning and writing. I cherish the encouragement, ideas, and love that they have shared with me from the beginning. I appreciate my dear friends Carolyn Fast, Jennifer Couzin-Frankel, Judy Rader, and Jay and Amy Schlesinger for their unflappable good cheer and smart support. Life while book-writing must go on, and I thank my daughter's (nonfamilial) caregivers for helping to make that happen: Pam Hawkesworth, Muhdiya Al-Azraq, and Nirmala and Ramesh Sharma. I am grateful to Zaha for her effortless joy and curiosity, and for including among her first sentences, "Put that down!" with reference to my laptop. Finally, I thank my partner in all things, Nidal Al-Azraq, for all that he has done to help me make this book, only fragments of which can be captured here: his keen observations and reorienting interpretations, his methodological magic-working, his taking care of our daughter, and, always, looking out for me.

A NOTE ON TRANSLITERATION

I have used a modified version of the *International Journal of Middle East Studies* system for transliterating Arabic that, for clarity across multiple publication formats, eliminates diacritics other than ' for *ayin* and ' for *hamza*. Occasionally, I have transliterated a phrase to retain its sound when spoken, or written a word according to its standard English transliteration. I hope this system will be accessible for those who do not speak Arabic and clear for those who do.

Back Stories

INTRODUCTION

You could say my field arrived at my doorstep every morning, back in the time when most people who regularly read the newspaper had home delivery. But it was at Dulles International Airport near Washington, D.C. that I truly felt a beginning for my fieldwork on U.S. journalism during the second Intifada. I was awaiting the arrival of Mazen Dana, a cameraperson for the Reuters news agency who was based in the West Bank city of Hebron. Mazen was coming to the United States to receive a freedom of the press award from the Committee to Protect Journalists (CPJ), a New York-based organization. I was making a short documentary—my first—about CPJ and Mazen's work. It was November 2001, just months after the Al-Qaeda attacks of 9/11, and the airport was a place of some anxiety for Arabs and those hoping to receive them. The embrace between Mazen Dana and Joel Campagna, CPJ's Middle East director, exuded momentary relief. But no one was really at ease. As we drove home from the airport, Joel and Mazen talked about the news of the day. The United States had just bombed Al-Jazeera's office in Kabul as part of the war in Afghanistan.

Mazen Dana was an unusual candidate for CPJ's award. The organization usually honors journalists from around the world who investigate, write, and publish stories about corruption, conflict, or human rights abuses. Mazen did not write, edit, or publish. He had worked in his hometown for over a decade carrying a heavy video camera on his shoulder day after day to report on some of the most pernicious violence in the Israeli-occupied Palestinian territories of the West Bank and Gaza Strip.[1] In the year before Mazen received the award, as CPJ recounted,

> Dana was shot in the leg with a rubber-coated bullet while filming Palestinian youths throwing rocks at Israeli soldiers. Two months later, Jewish settlers beat

him unconscious while he tried to film a conflict. The next day, an Israeli police officer smashed Dana's head in the rear door of an ambulance while he was filming the evacuation of a Palestinian youth wounded in clashes. Dana was shot again last October, in the same leg, two days in a row.[2]

His story called attention to the often grueling work of gathering the images that flow behind a correspondent's televised report. Mazen's work made evident that journalism is not only about ideas and analysis, the lone reporter and a notebook, but also about physical labor and risks. These are some of the underrecognized dimensions of journalistic labor.

A few days after his arrival, Mazen, Joel, and I were at the Waldorf-Astoria hotel in New York City for the awards ceremony. Hosted by Tom Brokaw, then the anchor of *NBC Nightly News*, the dinner gathered about a thousand journalists to recognize Mazen and the other awardees. It was a critical time for American journalism. As Ann Cooper, then CPJ's executive director, told me that evening, "All of these American journalists [have come] together after a couple of months covering really the story of their lives."[3] A day before the dinner, four journalists had been ambushed and killed by gunmen in Afghanistan. For now, the journalists in the Waldorf-Astoria's great ballroom were far from the front lines, but in the coming years, many would encounter such dangers firsthand, and their relationships with journalists from the places they covered would be crucial.

The audience watched a video of Mazen being shot by Israeli soldiers, beaten by Israeli settlers, and hit by errant Palestinian stones directed at Israeli soldiers. In our New York formal attire, we saw him wiping his bloodied lip and heaving a belabored breath as he was wheeled into an ambulance. Then Mazen appeared before us, smaller in real life than on the screen, wearing a suit. Mazen's speech, delivered in Arabic and translated into English by Joel, drew heavily on themes of professional identity, emphasizing what he shared with his audience rather than what separated them:

> I am happy to be here and proud to receive this prestigious award from the Committee to Protect Journalists. It is the result of fourteen years of continuous sweat and toil.
>
> It gives me strength to know that our colleagues around the world are supporting us in the quest for truth against those who seek to stifle it. . . .
>
> Being here, I leave behind my colleagues of whom I am very proud and who are no less courageous and deserving of this award, especially my close Reuters colleague Nael Shiyoukhi who has worked by my side for eight years.

Words and images are a public trust and for this reason I will continue with my work regardless of the hardships and even if it costs me my life.

Yesterday, a tragedy befell four of our colleagues in Afghanistan. This tragedy illustrates just how costly uncovering the truth can be. The bitterness of this event is only alleviated by the knowledge that journalists around the world continue to strive for the truth. And your support for us on the front lines gives us hope.[4]

Mazen received a standing ovation from the assembled journalists, the longest of the evening.

This book is an ethnography of U.S. journalism during the second Intifada and its aftermath. The second Palestinian Intifada, an uprising against Israeli occupation that started in 2000, is a vital context for the study of journalism; likewise, journalism is an important lens through which to understand the second Intifada. This ethnography examines two dynamics that are generally obscured by the time news texts arrive in the United States. First, this book builds on a robust literature about knowledge production that recognizes that facts and knowledge do not exist preformed in the world, but rather are created through individual and collective labor, in specific cultural, political, and ethical contexts. This book analyzes epistemic practices, or the practices related to knowledge and its production, in circumstances shaped by geopolitical hierarchies and outright military conflict. The everyday realities of news-making in the Israeli-occupied Palestinian territories of the West Bank and Gaza Strip necessitate collaboration between the foreign correspondents, who usually receive authorial credit, and the Palestinian translators, reporters, fixers, guides, and photojournalists who gather information and record images. Palestinians are integral to the production of U.S. news in the occupied territories, even though they are only occasionally recognized as authors of U.S. news, and though they rarely shape its narratives. Beyond the issue of recognizing Palestinian labor, looking at Palestinian journalists' work encourages a reexamination of objectivity and distance as key values and stances of knowledge production in journalism and beyond. Palestinian journalists also employ a wide range of skills necessary for knowledge production, only some of which are conventionally acknowledged. This book asks what we can learn about knowledge production, violence, and state authorities when we place Palestinian journalists at the center of an inquiry about journalism.

Second, because foreign correspondence was so pervasive as an on-the-ground practice during the second Intifada, the production of news itself—

apart from journalistic texts—has had a critical political and social impact as well. So many people harbored hopes from encounters with the media or nursed grievances following such encounters. Seeing journalists working in their cities, villages, and refugee camps helped Palestinians to imagine the world beyond the occupied territories, and it also prodded people to think about how they represented themselves to other Palestinians. This book considers what we can discern about logics of protest and statecraft by studying interactions among activists, officials, journalists, and other members of the public.

These questions were in the back of my mind during Mazen's visit, but more simply I wanted him to enjoy his time in two American cities I knew well. Joel showed him around Washington and New York. They visited the White House and the United Nations. They shopped. I went with them to the Brooklyn Bridge and took a picture of them as they held a handwritten greeting to Mazen's soundperson, Nael Shiyoukhi (Figure 1). Mazen and Joel had a warm

Figure 1   2001 International Press Freedom awardee Mazen Dana and Committee to Protect Journalists Middle East director Joel Campagna. They hold a greeting to Mazen's soundperson Nael Shiyoukhi as they pose on the Brooklyn Bridge in November 2001. *Source*: Amahl Bishara.

rapport, established during Joel's visits to the West Bank and solidified over their many phone calls over the years about incidents in Hebron. Joel was visibly pleased to be the host this time around. Both were welcoming to me as well. Mazen offered to carry extra equipment and gave me, a novice documentarian, advice on working with video ("Always, always remember the white balance!").

Mazen's visit illuminated the various ways that people with overlapping epistemic and political projects can connect with each other: the formal professional acknowledgment of Mazen's ovation at the Waldorf-Astoria; the camaraderie between Joel, the human rights worker, and his subject Mazen, the journalist; Mazen's quiet but persistent recognition of his soundperson, Nael; their extension of this epistemic fellowship to me, a young researcher and filmmaker. CPJ produces and is fueled by the networks that grow around the category of the journalist and the value of press freedom. A human rights organization established in 1981 by a group of U.S. foreign correspondents who sought to support their foreign colleagues working in restrictive conditions, CPJ's mission is to "promote press freedom worldwide by defending the rights of journalists to report the news without fear of reprisal."[5] Their work takes for granted the idea that journalists of different nationalities must collaborate in order for press freedom to flourish globally. CPJ relies on journalists around the world for information about attacks on the press. Those same journalists depend on CPJ to put pressure on their governments when they face trouble.

The camaraderie among Joel, Mazen, and me is also an important reminder that throughout my research on journalism I, as an anthropologist, *write alongside* other writers and media makers. This is not quite what Laura Nader has called "studying up,"[6] although I was, generally speaking, professionally junior to the journalists I worked with when I did this research. It is more akin to what Ulf Hannerz, also writing about journalists, termed "studying sideways," writing about a parallel craft.[7] Indeed, anthropology bears many similarities to journalism, and like other anthropologists who have studied journalism, I believe anthropologists can benefit from a reflexive approach to our own work in light of a study of journalism.[8] But writing alongside implies more than just a similarity of practice. I regularly depend on journalists for perspectives on the world, which they offer me. I start my days reading their words and listening to their voices, whether they fascinate me or frustrate me. Writing alongside is a kind of ethnography that involves recognizing one's indebtedness to other knowledge producers while at the same time maintaining a critical stance toward institutions, the broader cultural norms that situate them, and individuals within these institutions, too. It can also involve epistemic fellowships: collaborations in knowledge production in which people with different disciplinary or professional backgrounds and different epistemic standards, styles, and ultimate goals can say certain things together, even if they disagree on other topics.[9] Mazen, Joel, and I each sought to share with our own audiences something about freedom of the press, especially in contexts of struggle as during the second Intifada, though this is not the only goal any of us have had.

I am also interested in analyzing practices of collaboration *within* the field of journalism, especially among journalists of different nationalities. Developments in the Israeli-Palestinian conflict and the wars in Iraq and Afghanistan have rendered such journalistic collaboration more vital than ever. For example, for years when parts of Iraq lacked basic security, U.S. journalists there who did not look Arab or speak Arabic were unable to do much of their own reporting, and so they relied on Iraqi (and other Arab) reporters, fixers, and camerapeople to be their eyes and ears.[10] Usually without knowing it, we in the American public relied on these Arab journalists too. In the West Bank, foreign correspondents and other internationals do not face the same general threats to their lives as did journalists in Iraq. Still, staying safe and managing Israeli restrictions demand special expertise. Similar dynamics of collaboration are at work in the West Bank because most U.S. journalists require linguistic and cultural interpreters and guides. These forms of collaboration remain hidden in journalism's public texts.

Thus the first major aim of this research project has been to elucidate exactly what Palestinian journalists contribute to the production of U.S. news in terms of information, images, and pure sweat and blood. In dominant spheres in the United States and elsewhere, Palestinians are *epistemic others*, regarded as constitutively different in how they relate to knowledge: less capable and less trustworthy. This is a corollary of broader orientalist presuppositions of an essential difference between Arabs and Euro-Americans.[11] Palestinians are outside the bounds of the U.S. public sphere, not only geographically but because they are non-Westerners, Arabs during the "War on Terror," and on top of that stateless during an era when, as Hannah Arendt has famously observed, "being citizens of some commonwealth" grants "that tremendous equalizing of differences" that accords one rights and recognition.[12] Scholarship on the need for Palestinians to demand "permission to narrate,"[13] and on their alternative ways of making history as stateless people,[14] has examined the issue of knowledge production from a position of statelessness. Critical studies of knowledge production in Israel highlight the ways in which state power facilitates the production of knowledge that supports the nation-state.[15] This study, complementarily, looks at how Palestinians help to constitute the building blocks of Americans' public sphere—basic journalistic texts and images—even if they have not yet attained permission to narrate in these spheres.

In doing so, it also considers the topic of epistemic others from another angle. Palestinians—especially those living in the occupied territories—generally do inhabit an epistemic difference. They have different kinds of knowledge as well as different perspectives about knowledge compared to American journalists or the news-reading public, albeit not for reasons orientalists might imagine. Many Palestinian journalists see little conflict between their duty to report objectively and their duty to tell people about the injustice of occupation, because this is the primary "story" they have been hired to cover over the last decades. In most cases, legal barriers prohibit these journalists from doing reporting in Israel that might provide "balance" to this narrative. Even more fundamentally, Palestinians are less likely to conceive of political knowledge as a reified body of knowledge set apart from their lives. Both because of how the U.S. public sphere sees them and because of their actual epistemic difference, their contributions to journalism open important questions about journalistic values. In understanding their work, we can probe assumptions about who can (and does) participate in dominant public spheres, and on what terms. We can trace the contours of transnational public spheres[16] in an era of media conglomeration, when knowledge is often presumed to be something indistinguishably "global." Mazen's statement at the Waldorf-Astoria that "words and images are a public trust" rings true—but determining who is or should be in that public is a highly political issue.

Aside from my hours in the editing room with footage of Mazen's visit, I did not see Mazen again. In August 2003, weeks before I was bound to make my own arrival at Ben Gurion International Airport in Tel Aviv for my fieldwork, I opened a Yahoo! webpage to find the headline, "British Journalist Killed in Iraq." When I clicked on the headline, I saw a familiar press photo of Mazen in a leather jacket in front of what looked like London greenery. Later headlines corrected the mistake of confusing Mazen's national identity with the national base of his news organization, but nothing would change the fact of Mazen's death. U.S. soldiers had shot him as he was working just outside Abu Ghraib prison. Although his crew had alerted the guards to their presence in the area, U.S. soldiers said that they thought his camera was a rocket-propelled grenade launcher. He fell to the ground while his camera was rolling. Next to him was his soundperson and best friend Nael Shiyoukhi.

The first years of the twenty-first century have been dire for global press freedom. Not only have unstable or authoritarian states impeded journalists' work, but democratic states claiming to be motivated by national security have as well. The U.S. wars and occupations in Iraq and Afghanistan have presented ominous challenges to journalists.[17] Israel, known to many as the only democracy in the Middle East (though this claim deserves to be problematized on several accounts), has been cited by free press organizations for its restrictions on journalists in the occupied territories.[18] In creating a global index of press freedom, Reporters Without Borders has taken to examining separately how the United States and Israel deal with press freedoms within their recognized borders and in territories they control. In 2003, for example, the United States and Israel, respectively, ranked 31 and 44 on the index "at home," but 135 and 146 for territories they controlled.[19] Investigating the occupied Palestinian territories as they are implicated in Israeli and even U.S. democracies urges an inquiry into the "margins of the state."[20] A second major aim of this book, then, is to examine the relationship between press freedom and violence on the fringes of recognized democratic systems, where the necropolitical, or "the subjugation of life to the power of death,"[21] can be as relevant as the electoral.[22] Following an anthropological tradition of using ethnography to expand on concepts of human rights,[23] I argue that to fully identify limitations on freedom of the press, we need to go beyond the usual (and indeed, undeniably important) categories of restrictions on the press that a human rights organization might catalogue—like censorship, newspaper closure, and journalists' beatings and arrests—to look more expansively at conditions that promote or inhibit the production of news. Journalists' work, like that of other knowledge producers, is not only mental; it is also embodied, and in this sense material conditions like the ability to move freely have a profound effect on journalists' abilities to work. In this book, I seek to uncover some of the manifold and often pernicious connections between violence, broadly defined, and speech.

When I arrived in Israel and the West Bank a few weeks after Mazen's death, one of my first stops was to visit his family in Hebron. I met Mazen's wife and four young children, as well as his extended family. They welcomed me with an immense platter of *mansaf*, a Hebron specialty of lamb, yoghurt, and rice topped with sautéed almonds on a bed of bread dumplings. I delivered a humble assembly of photographs of Mazen's stay in the United States and a collection of condolences from people in New York City, especially those at CPJ. The photographs in front of the White House took on a devastating new set of meanings now that Mazen had died at the hand of an American soldier. Mazen's eldest son, who was about ten and had inherited his father's penchant for photography, snapped pictures of me. Mazen's youngest daughter, not yet two, toddled cheerfully. His widow showed me snapshots of her charismatic, handsome husband playing volleyball in college and laughing with his children. His nephew took me for a walk in Hebron's old city, its narrow passages knitted together with archways. I remembered Mazen describing the acrobatics of rooftop commutes during Israeli curfews. It had seemed unlikely, but now I understood.

The family wanted me to stay a few days and come back soon. I was riven by their grief, grateful for their kindness. I was also confounded by aspects of my visit. Tens of posters and postcards of Mazen plastered his street, his relatives' homes, and his own home. I saw in a long video of his funeral that thousands of people had accompanied his body from the mosque to the graveyard before his widow and children bade him a wrenching farewell. As a newcomer, it somehow took a while for me to understand that these were the mediated forms of martyrdom in the second Intifada.

These many years later, I am no longer surprised when Mazen Dana is identified as "al-shahid" (the martyr) rather than "al-sahafi" (the journalist). But the visit was one of my first indications that a third major aim of my research would need to be understanding the effects U.S. and other Western news institutions had on Palestinian politics and society. What was the importance of journalism in Palestinian society during the second Intifada that qualified Mazen, a journalist slain in Iraq, to be regarded as a martyr for the Palestinian national cause? How are journalists, especially those who work for foreign news organizations, regarded in Palestinian society? Are they professionals or political activists, both or neither? Why did Mazen's brothers and wife and nieces and nephews do so much for a young American documentary maker they had never met before? What are Palestinians' assumptions about what foreign journalists and anthropologists can do for them on both personal and national levels?

On the way from Hebron back to Jerusalem, carrying a bundle of Hebron grapes from the Dana family's patio vines, I traversed the checkpoints and piles of dirt that were part of Israel's system of closure. As I traveled a route that had been illegal for Mazen and was still out of reach for his children, I knew that I had to understand the many ways that living in Palestinian society under military occupation affected journalists. I had to examine how geographical and political isolation framed Palestinians' views of foreign journalists and the field of politics in general. I could not study journalists without accounting for the surrounding society. Far beyond the image of the solitary journalist with his notebook, I soon discovered, was the brawny cameraperson working with his best friend, who held the boom; the producer whose birthday party was her celebration of a vast collection of acquaintances from government, non-governmental organizations (NGOs), and media organizations throughout Palestinian society in the West Bank and Israel; the reporter who wept more than once in a hard day of interviewing. And they all had families and homes that were integral to their work.

The news I was accustomed to reading and seeing in the United States looked quite different from the dirt mounds outside Hebron than it had from my New York apartment. The overarching objective of this book, then, is to analyze how our understandings of journalism as a form of knowledge production change when viewed from Palestinian society in the occupied territories.[24] What is the place of journalism in Palestinian society, and what can this tell us about journalism as a whole? How can we characterize the multifaceted and understudied relationship between mainstream news media and state institutions? The occupied Palestinian territories are an especially rich place for a study of journalism—especially international journalism read and viewed in the United States—because of presumptions in the United States about Arabs, recent U.S. wars in the Middle East, and Palestinians' statelessness.

For decades, academic consideration of journalism in the United States primarily investigated how domestic news institutions functioned. Outside of the academy, writing on journalism—sometimes authored by journalists, especially foreign correspondents—has emphasized the heroic individual reporter. Recent ethnographic work on journalism has expanded beyond U.S. borders to examine how foreign correspondents work abroad,[25] the effects of globalization, media conglomeration, and technological changes on news-making practices,[26] and how various national and regional journalisms manage relationships with state authorities.[27] As a complement to these fruitful approaches, viewing major U.S. and European institutions from the occupied territories—and focusing on the neglected topic of local journalists who work with foreign correspondents[28]—underscores how many more contributors there are to international news texts than foreign correspondents and their editors, even if these other contributors do not necessarily have the power to set the narrative for news coverage. Palestinian journalists might be regarded as frontline workers in our public sphere, even though they are geographically marginal to the United States. The skills and values of these journalists expand our understandings of practices and ideals that go into the news we read and view every day. Palestinian journalists also have different relationships to the news events they cover than do foreign correspondents and editors. The vantage point of the occupied territories also reveals that the news Americans read and watch is not only the product of economic considerations[29] or narrative frames.[30] It is also the product of deeply material processes and things. Some of them, like flying bullets or all too immobile piles of dirt, impede the flow of information. Others, like the embodied skills journalists have developed to manage restrictions, enable the production of knowledge. Still others shape processes of news production in more subtle ways. A rich tradition of studying journalism has analyzed how political movements are influenced by how they are covered in the news media.[31] Examining journalism from the occupied Palestinian territories illuminates the ways international journalism has profound cultural and political effects for the communities in which it is produced, even if community members rarely read the *New York Times*.

Finally, looking at journalism from this vantage point sheds new light on knowledge production in general. In recent years, science studies scholars have argued against the reification of scientific knowledge. They have used ethnography, among other methods, to confirm that knowledge is cultural and political, a result of institutional processes as well as broader social contexts. They have argued that these qualities do not in themselves undermine the reliability of knowledge because all knowledge is situated; that is, it comes from a location or perspective.[32] If, as science studies scholars have found, processes of scientific production are influenced by society's norms and national politics,[33] this is even more blatantly the case for journalism. Journalism is what Bruno Latour might consider one of the ultimate hybrids between science and society.[34] Not only do journalists cover topics like climate change as hybrids—science on the politics pages, and politics on the science pages—but also, as I show here, producing journalism involves methods and ideas about how to properly produce knowledge taken from the sciences and applied to that ultimate non-laboratory, the street. A science studies approach to journalism informs investigation of the minute processes of journalism—where to place a tripod to cover an event—as well as the values of journalism, especially because these values have been modeled off of ethics in the sciences. Examining journalism, particularly from the perspective of media workers who usually go unrecognized, contributes to a broader understanding of processes of knowledge production, too: of the implications of geopolitical and institutional hierarchies among producers, and the relationships among knowledge, violence, and the body.

WORLDS OF MEDIA PRODUCTION:
A METHODOLOGY FOR STUDYING KNOWLEDGE IN CONTEXT

Examining the place of U.S. journalism in Palestinian society demands an approach that accounts for journalists' practices but also situates these practices in broad cultural context. Faye Ginsburg, Lila Abu-Lughod, and Brian Larkin's concept of "media worlds" recognizes "the necessity of linking media production, circulation, and reception in broad and intersecting social and cultural fields: local, regional, national, transnational."[35] The concept of media worlds establishes the ways in which media can cultivate, renew, challenge, or sever social relations. Building on this multifaceted approach but focusing on production, I look at how news-making creates social and political worlds. That is, a foundational argument in media theory holds that media texts can shape cultural processes and beliefs; these then later influence the production of media, yielding a feedback loop.[36] I argue that even before texts are published, media production itself can be transformative, drawing people together, shaping discourses and silences, producing forms of security and danger, molding subjectivities. This is partly because media production itself entails circulation and consumption of other, preceding media texts.[37] Journalists are constantly recontextualizing existing texts, removing them from one framework or environment and placing them in another,[38] such that feedback loops can exist *within* processes of media production, too. Another reason that media production has social and political effects is that, far from occurring only in isolated environments like a studio, soundstage, or newsroom, media production happens in society.[39] Journalism draws in government officials, victims, and activists; farmers, mothers, factory owners, and children. All of them bring their own goals and perspectives to this enterprise. Many Palestinians are deeply concerned about how they and their struggle are represented in U.S. and other Western media. They have a kind of double consciousness.[40] Palestinians see themselves both through the lens of their own social and political values *and also* through what they know of the values and narratives of the United States and Europe. In a place as thick with journalists as the West Bank was during the second Intifada, those working with Western journalistic institutions have deep political and social influence.

Thus, in studying media production, I trace the social and political world fashioned by processes of news production, broadly defined: by cell phone exchanges between a journalist safe in Jerusalem and her colleague watching red tracer bullets speed through the night in Nablus; by coffee poured into small cups by a mourning mother and placed in a journalist's hand; by the tracks a journalist's car makes in a dirt road that had been unused until Israeli authorities closed down the main thoroughfares. This world of media production is also shaped by what happens in a journalist's wake: the chests filled briefly with the hope that news coverage will bring vindication or relief; the cheeks dampened from retelling the story of wounds, whether fresh or old; the conversations about how to plan the next protest so it will generate even better coverage. Thus, fieldwork with journalists was essential, but so was fieldwork before and after journalists arrived, or when journalists did not arrive at all.

I conducted the fieldwork for this book in the West Bank and Israel between September 2003 and May 2005 and in the summers of 2007 and 2009. The Gaza Strip was, unfortunately, inaccessible for much of this time due to strict Israeli control over those entering and leaving Gaza. A key component of my fieldwork consisted of interviews with U.S. foreign correspondents and Palestinian reporters, fixers, producers, camerapeople, and photojournalists. I also interviewed Israeli editors and photojournalists who worked with U.S. media organizations. I focused on Palestinian journalists because they, more than anyone, knit together U.S. news institutions and Palestinian society. I was fortunate to interview a few journalists working in Gaza, when they traveled. Though some Palestinian journalists were wary of speaking to me because they were expected to obtain permission from their employers before giving interviews "on the record," many others were happy to have the opportunity to communicate their perspective on the work they did with U.S. journalists, especially since foreign correspondents usually had the last (published) word. I sought to understand why they became journalists, what being a good journalist meant to them, and how they managed their relationships with foreign correspondents.

Due to disciplinary norms and to concerns about journalists' relationships with their employers and reactions of the Palestinian Authority (PA) or Israeli authorities, I have changed the names of all journalists, except when they are commenting "on the record" on published articles or on images that they have produced, or when I write about documented incidents of violence or quote journalists' published statements on such incidents. This epistemic practice of changing names, common in anthropology, is quite different from that of the journalists I was writing alongside of, and this difference sometimes raised eyebrows. For them, using names was a means of providing a path for verification of one's work. Many journalists insist that anonymous "background" or "off-the-record" material, obtained without permission to attribute it to a specific actor or to use it at all, should be used sparingly.[41] Still, in other cases, journalists recognized that confidentiality protected them. It is one mark of my disciplinary location that I followed anthropological rather than journalistic norms. As an ethnographer, I am after all less interested in journalists' individual stories and more interested in analyzing institutions and practices. Thus, in general, when on first mention I give only a first name, the name has been changed, while when I use a full name, this is a journalist's real name.[42]

I also conducted participant-observation[43] with journalists as they worked, especially as they covered the separation barrier[44] and Palestinian protests against it, Arafat's funeral in 2004, PA press conferences, and the presidential elections of 2005. I spent time in journalists' offices as they edited photographs or managed the ebb and flow of visitors, phone calls, and footage that made up their daily routines. I shadowed American and Palestinian journalists as they reported stories together. This helped me to understand the manifold ways in which the relationship between a U.S. journalist and a Palestinian producer or fixer can play out.

Territory, in the literal sense, was essential. Place orients embodied experiences of security and insecurity; identity and relations with others; knowledge, stories, and values. The physical characteristics of land as experienced sensually and culturally can ground expression,[45] or impede it. Thus, I needed to attend to where American and Palestinian journalists lived and how they moved. How did they commute to work? How did they circulate within the territory they regarded as their "beat," or the territory they were responsible for covering? How were beats defined, and how did they differ for Palestinian and American journalists? I examined how places—cities, villages, and refugee camps, certainly, but also construction sites, roads, government offices, and sacred spaces—were related to each other in local political and social cosmologies, and I paid close attention to how these places were represented in U.S. media as well.

Focusing on place in this manner heightens an attention to embodiment, the ways in which bodily experience is important to understanding social phenomena. One major difference between consuming news and experiencing Palestinian society under Israeli military occupation is in the ways that the body is called upon in acts of comprehension and interpretation. Reading, watching, or listening to the news is an embodied experience, whether one's lips and hands tense with anger or anxiety, one's eyelids droop with exhaustion at the lack of anything novel happening, or one's hands flutter with grateful distraction over a pile of dirty dishes as a broadcaster intones in the background. In contrast, producing the news in Palestinian society can involve balancing a tripod in the rubble, sweating or weeping through an interview, developing a sense of safety and danger that builds on awareness of one's specific location, and dodging fists, stones, or bullets. I did not master journalism's embodied skills; nor did I try to. However, my body was an instrument in this research. Like Palestinians and others, I learned about the politics of military occupation through my own fluctuating, embodied sense of danger and restriction. I explicate journalistic skills in part by reference to my own experiences, especially to skills that I myself lacked, in order to uncover, in contrast, the highly embodied form of expertise that journalists have.[46] In attending to my own gaps in embodied skills, I was able to identify historical and social conditions that incline Palestinians to have this expertise.

It was important for me to contextualize what journalists did on the job in terms of other parts of their lives. To this end, I spent time with journalists outside of work: in coffee shops and restaurants, with their families, as they did NGO work after hours, and as they zipped around town in that interstitial time between a work meeting and a family lunch that would bring them to the vegetable market or the repair shop to pick up a son's bike. I taught an English class to journalists that sometimes unraveled fortuitously into conversations about U.S. news articles. This downtime helped me frame journalists' work.[47] To understand how other Palestinians viewed journalists, I spoke to activists about their evaluations of journalists' work. I kept my eye out for representations of journalists in Palestinian popular culture, including plays, television shows, and art work, and my ears perked up every time I heard a clever teenager declare intentions to become a journalist, which was often. They, too, were part of the world that media production made.

Additionally, I aimed to view "news" in relief by examining the things that news texts excluded. By my own choices of where to live and with whom to spend my spare time, I experienced Palestinian life in the West Bank in ways distinct from those of most U.S. journalists, who tended to live in Israel and commute only when necessary to Palestinian areas. I first lived in east Jerusalem, which in many ways is the heart of Palestinian society in the occupied Palestinian territories and Israel, though it has suffered from its increasing isolation from the rest of the West Bank and Gaza due to Israeli closure policies. Eventually, I moved to Ramallah, the de facto capital of the PA and a center of Palestinians' journalistic activity. But both of these cities were fairly usual places for North Americans and Europeans working in NGOs to spend time. I benefited tremendously from moving outside of what many have called the "Ramallah bubble." From 2003 through 2005, I spent a few days a week in 'Aida Refugee Camp, Bethlehem, and made semiregular trips to Nablus; in my summer research trips of 2007 and 2009, I lived in or near 'Aida. Since most Palestinian journalists were or had become part of the middle class, and many rubbed shoulders with the PA's political elite, spending time in more marginal and differently politicized places was integral to my grasp of the limits of journalism's definition of the political. While most Palestinian journalists had access to this wider perspective on Palestinian politics and society through their own familial, social, and political networks, had I not made an effort to forge my own such connections, my own understanding of Palestinian politics would have been severely limited.

Experiencing how local Palestinians who did not know me well interacted with me shed light on a key set of social relations during the second Intifada and in its aftermath. I attended to how eagerly people struck up conversations with me in taxicabs and how they frequently invited me home to meet their families. When I did a bit of work as a journalist, reporting in an area of the West Bank where I knew few people allowed me to experience how Palestinians interacted with Western journalists. As in other sites where an international presence is pivotal to the workings of local and national politics,[48] the "international" (in Arabic, *ajnabi*, plural *ajanib*, literally "foreigner") has a high public profile. In the West Bank, internationals include foreign correspondents, NGO workers, students, researchers, and solidarity activists; they are most often Americans or Europeans, and sometimes individuals of Palestinian or Arab descent. Some are long-term residents and others short-term visitors; most live in Jerusalem or Ramallah while some live in outlying areas. Their numbers increased after 2005 as the second Intifada and Israeli operations cooled in the West Bank. Palestinians are sensitive to the internal diversity within the category of "internationals," but it is often assumed that those who have decided to live in the West Bank for an extended period of time have positive intentions, in part because they are submitting themselves to living under military occupation. Nevertheless, some Palestinian resentment can gather around internationals' class and geopolitical privileges. Disappointment mounts over the apparent ineffectiveness of the very visible presence of so many internationals, and tensions can arise over clashing values and goals.[49]

Just as living in the West Bank gave me a feel for the social location of the "international" as a Palestinian category, it also gave me a feel for the Palestinian category of the "Israeli." Palestinians more often imagined the international than the Israeli as a key interlocutor. In part, this was because in practice they had much more opportunity to speak to internationals than Israelis, because of the stark politics of separation during the second Intifada. As I elaborate later, Palestinians living under military occupation had a strong sense that they were being ruled by force, and thus that what they had to say was not important to Israeli officials. On a more ideological level, many Palestinians felt that the failure of negotiations and the ongoing military occupation should preclude a "normalization" of relations with Israelis. These were also barriers to imagining Israelis as interlocutors, or even an audience.[50]

As I had been doing for years, I followed the news, especially feature articles and photojournalism, carefully. But I also created new ways of reading the news through Palestinians' eyes. In the summer of 2009, I asked Palestinian students, activists, and journalists to analyze feature stories from U.S. news. In some cases, the readers were college students interested in journalism and accustomed to "assignments" like these. In other cases, readers were people I had known for years, who I anticipated would offer me insightful and impassioned interpretations. I selected some of what I considered to be the richest texts, as well as some texts that reiterated U.S. and European stereotypes about Arabs and Palestinians. I had these articles translated into Arabic and gave them to my readers well ahead of our conversations about them. Sometimes readers asked to have both the English and the Arabic versions, either so they could practice their English or because they thought they could better respond to the original. They would often arrive with marginalia and highlights to prompt their analysis. They found these articles to be in turns thought provoking, infuriating, and nostalgia producing. These interviews became the basis for this book's interludes, short essays between the chapters. Because I spoke with between three and seven people about each article and almost always interviewed people individually, in writing up the interludes I am remixing a number of different conversations, bringing Palestinians into a kind of dialogue with each other as well as with the journalist. These essays draw upon dialogical ethnographic research methods used in anthropological approaches to media, in which film or other representations of a community are brought back to that community for scrutiny and interpretation.[51] They have been inspired by anthropological work on the politics of representation that uses innovative methods of writing to describe how individuals interpret the world in ways that can be creative, contradictory, or strategic,[52] as well as by work that catalogues how indigenous people have commented on media old and new to create important counter-discourses on settler colonialism and reconstitute community history.[53]

These interludes are important because although Palestinians assume Western media coverage of the Israeli-Palestinian conflict is important, they seldom have an opportunity to read the articles that U.S. journalists write about them. Most of this book traces the ways in which knowledge and power are routed by journalistic norms, government officials, and journalists themselves. These essays expose other kinds of knowledge. I found expertise about protests dormant in unemployed young Palestinian men as they quietly drank minted tea; skills in kite-flying long unexpressed in a lawyer, seemingly melted into his chair; cultural critique readily available from a social worker after I asked her my opening question; as well as perspectives on what democracy, peace, and prosperity meant for these Palestinians. These interludes also redirect knowledge, encouraging Palestinians to appraise articles that are usually inaccessible to them and asking you, the reader, to listen to the political and social critiques of Palestinians who are rarely given the stage for commentary.

One methodological challenge of my work has been delimiting my primary object of study: U.S. journalism, English-language journalism, Western journalism, or international journalism. Obviously, just as there is tremendous diversity to trouble the categories of "West," "East," and "orient," immense differences exist between U.S. and Chinese journalism, and indeed between U.S. and British journalism. Both because of U.S. geopolitical power and because I live and teach in the United States, I am most concerned with the production of news that circulates in the United States. Thus, I examine here the norms and structures of U.S. media institutions, with some attention to Reuters news agency and Agence France-Presse, British and French companies whose news is consumed internationally, including in the United States.

However, from the on-the-ground perspective of news production in the West Bank, U.S. journalism is both practically inextricable from and conceptually linked to other journalistic enterprises, especially European ones. While differences crop up in style guides and editing rooms, Palestinian photojournalists working in the field for the French news service Agence France-Presse and the American news service the Associated Press do not have radically different practices; likewise it would be difficult to generalize about how Palestinian fixers arrange or translate interviews differently for American as opposed to British journalists. Another reason the Western media institutions' Jerusalem bureaus resemble one another is that they necessarily assume norms from Palestinian journalists' practices, and this is as true for U.S. media organizations as for Italian or Swedish ones. Moreover, a single Palestinian journalist might work for a variety of Western news organizations, sometimes alongside a Palestinian news organization. Therefore, it would have been difficult for me to speak to journalists only about their experiences with U.S. institutions. Instead, in my writing, I try to specify what makes an institution distinct so that differences among these national presses become clearer. Along the same lines, some Palestinian producers and fixers worked for a combination of newspapers and television stations, and their contributions across those platforms were similar. Thus, I have not limited myself to examining one form of media.

If "U.S. media" as a unit is difficult to isolate in terms of practices, it also has blurred boundaries on Palestinians' intuitive map of global media. Nonexpert Palestinians speak of the "international press" (*al-sahafa al-duwaliyya*) or the "Western media" (*al-'ilam al-gharbi*), though they are aware of differences among national presses, media institutions, and even individual correspondents. The "international media" of local parlance consists mainly of large, wealthy media organizations from Europe and North America. These are the most visible media institutions on the ground in the West Bank; among the most prominent are U.S. news organizations. Rarely do Palestinians in the West Bank encounter journalists from the global South, other than Arab satellite news stations. Moreover, when a Palestinian is being interviewed or photographed, it is not always clear to the subject where the journalist's work will be published or broadcast. Many non-Anglo European journalists conduct their work in English. The "front person" for many foreign correspondents or international news organizations—often a fixer, producer, translator, reporter, or photojournalist with whom a story's subject would interact—is, generally, Palestinian, except in the rare instances when a journalist speaks Arabic or an interviewee is speaking English or another language. Protesters who see a group of photojournalists covering a demonstration likely assume that they work for a variety of Western, Arab, and Palestinian news organizations.

This Palestinian view of "international media" or "Western media" as a somewhat indistinct category is justified by the dynamics of contemporary corporate media. Media conglomeration and the extension of certain media companies into new markets render it more difficult to draw strict lines between different national media.[54] For example, CNN International, BBC America, *Newsweek International*, and Al-Jazeera English all extend a media organization associated with a particular state or region far beyond that place of origin, and these extended entities have different characteristics from their parent organizations. They are meant to appeal to audiences different from those of the original channels or magazines, but they may draw on reporting by the same journalists. News agencies and other similar enterprises, like Euronews, are designed to produce news that can be quickly translated into multiple languages for broad consumption across national boundaries.[55] Thus while definitional conundrums about the boundaries of U.S. news raise many important questions, in practice they were not so difficult to manage. While I focused my energies on interviewing and accompanying journalists who worked for U.S. media organizations, I benefited from speaking to Palestinian journalists and foreign correspondents of all stripes.

THE SECOND INTIFADA AS A LOCATION FOR STUDYING JOURNALISM, AND VICE VERSA

If Palestinians have their reasons for being concerned about U.S. media and *al-sahafa al-duwaliyya* more generally, Americans have other reasons for being interested in the Israeli-Palestinian conflict, and a different approach to news about it. While Palestinians are concerned with this media because they recognize its power rather than its overriding quality, most Americans regard U.S. news as a transparent reflection of the conflict. This ethnography springs forth from a space of confluence, of overlapping (but asymmetrical) Palestinian and American curiosities regarding journalism about the Israeli-Palestinian conflict. Following Israel's trajectory has been a domestic pursuit in the United States and Europe. This is not only because the United States and Europe have been pivotal in creating and sustaining Israel and the PA. It is also because Israeli and Palestinian territories overlap so much with sacred geographies of the Judeo-Christian imaginary. U.S. and European concern with Israel is cultivated by and reinforces the very idea of Judeo-Christianity as a religious, cultural, and political unit. Israel's conflicts have at times seemed emblematic of U.S. and European concerns over such themes as terrorism and democracy.[56] In Israel and the occupied Palestinian territories, the footprint of U.S. and European curiosity is traceable in part in hotels, bars, and cafés in places like Jerusalem and Ramallah where journalists can be spotted by their cameras, notebooks, and many-pocketed vests. During the second Intifada, one could physically sense the U.S. and European interest in the Palestinian-Israeli conflict in these places.

Jerusalem has for many years had one of the largest contingents of foreign correspondents of any place in the world. But journalists have not always spent time in the Israeli-occupied West Bank and Gaza. For decades, the centers of Palestinian politics were elsewhere. Coverage of the occupied Palestinian territories intensified in 1987 at the start of the first Intifada (literally, *uprising*, an extended popular revolt against the Israeli military occupation, which itself had commenced in 1967).[57] As Israeli-Palestinian negotiations commenced with the Madrid Conference in 1991, a new narrative of the U.S.-mediated "peace process" took root, one that has continued until this writing. The signing of the Oslo Accords in 1993 and the establishment of the PA in 1994 led to a scaling back of the Israeli military's presence in Palestinian cities and towns of the West Bank and Gaza, and the beginning of limited Palestinian self-rule over matters such as education, media infrastructure, and some economic issues. U.S. journalists began to write about state-building processes: about the return of formerly vilified Palestine Liberation Organization (PLO) chairman Yasir Arafat to Palestinian territory and the new commercial and cultural opportunities offered by the PA's existence. And journalists continued to track the vicissitudes of the interminable "peace process" that was supposed to culminate in a full Palestinian state.

This all changed dramatically in 2000 when a new uprising broke out in the West Bank and Gaza Strip. It was a different kind of uprising from the first Intifada, in part because Israeli and Palestinian societies were more physically divided than they had been in 1987. The previous Intifada had involved large segments of the Palestinian population in demonstrations, tax protests, and other popular resistance. In 2000, the presence of the PA impeded some of these means of protesting the now more geographically distant occupation. The existence of the PA also meant that the Palestinian side had more small arms than they had in the 1980s. Israel's response to the second Intifada was immediately fierce.[58] All of these dynamics resulted in a much more heavily armed uprising than had occurred a generation earlier. Israel invaded Palestinian territories it had left years before. Palestinian activists staged demonstrations at checkpoints, and militants carried out shootings and bombings in settlements within the occupied territories and inside Israel. Foreign correspondents were no longer covering high-level negotiations; they found themselves chronicling a dangerous conflict.

One way to obtain a general picture of the kinds of news events journalists were responsible for covering in Israeli and Palestinian societies is to examine basic statistics about the second Intifada. In its first five years, from 2000 to 2005, the Israeli human rights organization B'Tselem counted 3,941 Palestinian and 973 Israeli deaths.[59] The vast majority of Israeli deaths resulted from either militants' bombings inside Israel and in the occupied territories or shootings directed at Israeli civilians or members of the security forces, mostly in the occupied territories. Bombings transformed Israeli social life in cities like Jerusalem, Tel Aviv, and Netanya during intense periods of attacks, causing people to avoid restaurants, coffeehouses, buses, and bus stops, and resulting in a nationwide decline in tourism. As serious as this situation was, the effects of the second Intifada and Israeli counterinsurgency on Palestinian life were doubtlessly more far-reaching. Palestinians incurred casualties in more ways and in more places: during frequent protests and Israeli military incursions, and as a result of extrajudicial killings, which often killed untargeted people as well. In addition to higher casualty numbers, Palestinians faced Israeli invasions into their neighborhoods and homes, intensified Israeli control of movement, widespread home demolitions, and the confiscation of land for the construction of the separation barrier.

Covering these events demanded new proficiencies on behalf of journalists and, especially, more work from Palestinian journalists. Palestinian journalists had begun working with foreign correspondents during the first Intifada, and during the Oslo years (generally defined as 1993–2000, even though Oslo is officially still in effect), they had become akin to national correspondents from Ramallah, the quasi-capital of the semiautonomous PA. During the second Intifada, they became integral to foreign correspondents' ability to discern what was happening in the occupied territories. This was in part because Israeli closure policies—a system of bureaucratic and physical restraints on movement within the West Bank and Gaza and between the West Bank, Gaza, and Israel[60]—limited mobility for everyone during the second Intifada. Also, violence was so commonplace in the occupied territories that foreign correspondents did not venture to the site of every extrajudicial killing or incursion.

Palestinian journalists had manifold responsibilities. They almost always arrived on the scene before foreign journalists, in part because they lived in the same cities they covered. Palestinian reporters called in eyewitness descriptions of what was happening, accounts that might later be published alongside those of the Israeli military spokesperson. Camerapeople and photojournalists captured the imagery of the conflict. Fixers and producers set up interviews for foreign correspondents based on the latter's priorities. Translators not only did linguistic work but, like fixers and producers, also accompanied foreign correspondents so they could travel safely and work effectively in the occupied territories. Foreign correspondents working on a budget might forgo fixers or producers and opt for drivers, but these drivers inevitably did more cultural work than a GPS would have. Palestinian journalists also continued to cover political developments in the PA. In essence, Palestinians were employed in almost the full range of positions in U.S. and European media institutions, but they were rarely, if ever, called upon to be bureau chiefs, foreign correspondents, or editors. Tellingly, journalists in these elite positions had the most influence in setting the agenda and the narratives for reporting.

A year after the Palestinian uprising began, Al-Qaeda launched attacks on New York City and Washington, D.C., and U.S. president George Bush declared a war on "terror." In the years that followed, Arab Americans, once "invisible citizens," became "visible subjects,"[61] increasingly targeted by racial profiling and hate crimes.[62] Arabs and Muslims have frequently been positioned as the ultimate outsiders and enemies. Conflicts around the world that had little to do with Al-Qaeda's attacks on the United States have been drawn into the framework of the U.S. War on Terror. Israeli leaders—and Osama bin Laden, too—did their best to equate Palestinians' struggle against occupation with Al-Qaeda's militarized and global take on jihad. Still, Palestinians were behind the news that Americans read every day, even at a time when distrust of Arabs was heightening, and though this news itself did not regularly portray Palestinians in a sympathetic light.

The intensity of the second Intifada has waned, as has coverage of the occupied Palestinian territories. Still, these basic dynamics—including both Arab and Muslim Americans' location as a new internal enemy *and* the collaborative relationship between U.S. foreign correspondents and Palestinian journalists— remain effective. U.S. audiences have a seemingly endless appetite for news about the Palestinian-Israeli conflict, but they do not recognize that Palestinians help to produce this media. This hidden cooperation is one reason why the West Bank is such a compelling site for the study of journalism and for knowledge production more generally. While objectivity and distance are predominant values of U.S. journalism, I demonstrate in Chapter 1 that objectivity obscures much more complex processes of authorship that in fact produce our news. In Chapter 3, I examine how Palestinian journalistic values are distinct from but not necessarily contradictory to American ones. I examine the limits of the journalistic value of disinterest for journalists working under occupation, and in Chapter 4, I consider its alternatives. Studying the production of news at this site is a way of examining a kind of precursor to U.S. popular political culture, one peripheral place where this culture is made. It offers a way of seeing in new light the knowledge on which we depend if we are to be informed people.

An ethnography of media production also makes clear that news is not the product of a narrow, unified ideology. Instead, it is shaped by journalism's on-the-ground and collaborative—though by no means egalitarian—exchanges. Studying journalism as a way of understanding the Intifada is critical because Palestinians are in so many cases concerned with their representation. Thus, at these sites of production, narratives are up for grabs. Foreign correspondents, Palestinian journalists, and other Palestinians each have their interpretations of events, and the locations of media production can be the sites of much jousting over these interpretations. Yet, in published media texts, this riotous free-for-all of interpretation is narrowed into long-standing narratives and priorities of U.S. news. Doing an ethnography of journalistic production has been rewarding for me because it has allowed me to experience and learn from the multiplicity that precedes a more single-voiced perspective. Chapter 5 attends to the process of covering popular politics surrounding the separation barrier and refugees, while Chapter 6 addresses how Palestinian officials and members of the public concerned themselves with how Western media might represent them as they took part in Arafat's funeral and the subsequent PA presidential elections of 2005. These chapters provide glimpses of the representational struggles among journalists, activists, and officials that are often obfuscated by the time news texts on these topics are published.

SPEECH, VIOLENCE, AND AN EMBODIED RESPONSE

As Mazen Dana's experience demonstrates, journalism during the second Intifada was a deeply embodied enterprise. Understanding the multifaceted ways in which this is the case hones our understanding of the entanglement of speech and violence. Dominant Euro-American notions of how language or meaning is and should be produced—the prevailing semiotic ideologies[63] of our time—presume language's separation from action, that language's primary purpose is to refer to existing things in the world, rather than to act on the world.[64] From this perspective, the ideal language for scientific or political progress is transparent and direct, unencumbered by poetics.[65] It is no coincidence that the standard news report fits these norms: straightforward and serious third-person prose, devoid of passion or play in its language. Some liberal incarnations of press freedom hinge on this separation between speech and action, because in this framework expression is assumed to be occurring among autonomous actors.[66] According to this view, speech should be free because it cannot hurt anyone. Furthermore, in these modern liberal semiotic ideologies, when meaning making is conspicuously bound to material practices, this is regarded as problematic because it calls attention to the larger ways in which the material world constrains or enables what we can say.[67] In contrast, in other semiotic environments, material qualities—the postures of bodies reciting a text, the shapes of calligraphic scripts, the sound of words[68]—are appreciated as factors that can heighten or clarify meaning.

I explore the implications of this dominant liberal semiotic ideology for the production side of the news. Drawing on linguistic anthropological work and on research on the materiality of media,[69] I urge a deeper recognition of how speech that we might consider to be "free" or unconstrained by context is in fact the product of material circumstances. This is another dimension of what Webb Keane calls "the intertwining of words and things, of meaning and economy, and of agents, powers, and representations."[70] When can speech function as action that constrains others' speech? When are actions dismissed as having no symbolic meaning, as mere accidents? When, on the other hand, can actions that are not necessarily aimed at constricting speech in fact do just this? And what do intrepid and smart media makers do in the face of these restrictions?

The answers to many of these questions hinge on speakers' relationships to a state. Citizenship, the normative relationship between an individual and the state,[71] does not always enable a right to speak, obviously, even in states that purport to provide freedom of expression to their citizenry. However, to be stateless is to speak from outside of the usual framework for political discourse. Stateless people can rarely be considered part of a constituency or a traditional public sphere, for both of these concepts are generally based on belonging in a polity like a state.[72] So stateless people—especially those who assert themselves through speech—can more easily be insinuated as part of political collectivities less sanctioned in our world of states: potential mobs or terrorists. The international community has often preferred refugees as silent masses.[73] It is no coincidence that statelessness, a lack of political representation, often begets something akin to voicelessness, a lack of media representation. While states constrain speech in manifold ways, some coercive and others less so, to speak politically without citizenship poses distinct risks. To petition for the ordinary rights of citizenship as a stateless person is often to call for a disruption of the order of established nation-states. Conversely, when state officials speak from within a working bureaucracy, they presume the efficacy of many institutions to carry out their imperatives and ultimately to provide them protection from any material consequences stemming from their speech. Of course, not all states are equal, and not all citizens have equal kinds of authority. In the field of journalistic production, foreign correspondents who hail from the United States enjoy subtle privileges. Their citizenship affords them not just mobility but also some basic assurance of protection in emergencies. Relative to other journalists, they have easier access to many officials. Palestinian journalists, in contrast, may have special access to Palestinian officials, but this is less dear in an economy of interviewees than access to U.S. officials, anyway. And they lack the comfort of assuming they have other kinds of clout or protection. Still, the success of both Palestinian and American journalists depends on collaboration.

In 1994, the establishment of the PA signaled the end of formal Israeli censorship of the Palestinian press that had been in effect in various forms for decades.[74] It seemed as though Israel was no longer restricting Palestinian speech. But because the constraints of Israeli occupation endured in other realms, Palestinians' ability to speak has still been compromised. As I discuss in Chapter 2, Israeli officials have taken different kinds of actions to limit Palestinian journalists' ability to work. They have stripped virtually all Palestinian journalists from the West Bank and Gaza Strip of Israeli government-issued press cards, which certify professional status and function as movement permits throughout the occupied territories and into Israel. In the process of denying Palestinians these cards, officials also made statements intimating that Palestinian journalists constituted threats to Israeli security, both because of what they said and what they could conceivably do. Israeli soldiers also shot several Palestinian journalists. These shootings happened in an array of circumstances such that it is impossible to ascribe motivation to each of the shootings. Yet, the shootings unquestionably affected journalists' abilities to work, and human rights organizations have decried Israel's lack of a response to the shootings. Constraints on expression took other forms, too. In the Conclusion, I discuss graffiti written on the separation wall. This space that seemed to have no restrictions regarding what could be written on it was fundamentally constricted by Israeli authorities. The wall also operated within the same system of Western media that valorized the words and ideas of Europeans and Americans and marginalized those of Palestinians. A key theme of this book, then, is the *differential capacity to speak* that is rooted in disparate material and institutional circumstances of statehood and statelessness. Limitations on movement and Israel's control of the physical environment in which these Palestinians live have impeded journalists' ability to work and other Palestinians' abilities to express themselves. When speech and action are conceived as being divorced from one another, these restrictions can be overlooked as having no relation to freedom of speech. Though press freedoms and a revitalized national media scene are often presumed to be one of the prizes of the Oslo Agreement of 1993, my research makes clear that press freedoms cannot be fully realized when military occupation remains in place and self-determination is lacking.

Palestinian journalists are attuned to these many kinds of restriction that affect their ability to communicate. As I explain in Chapter 4, Palestinian journalists have special methods to produce knowledge in these circumstances. They know how to locate themselves in positions of relative safety during demonstrations, and how to distinguish among the array of different weapons by the sounds they make. These methods are not effective all of the time, but they are better than nothing. Theories of the intellectual—here understood as "actors who have a special relationship to some mode of knowing"[75]—have often neglected the role the body has played in the production of knowledge. Palestinians' ways of understanding politics and producing knowledge suggest that embodiment is inseparable from intellectual perspective in processes of apprehending power. Palestinian journalists' forms of professional expertise result from being close to the society in which journalists work. They are an underrecognized complement to the better-known skills of foreign correspondents, who are often valued for having a fresh perspective or critical distance from their material. Palestinians' *skills of proximity* are a concealed condition of possibility for U.S. news.

Being a part of Palestinian society yields other, more subtle capabilities, too. Long-held stereotypes of Palestinians and other Arabs still circulating in policy and military circles hold that "all they understand is force."[76] Statements like these evince Palestinians' status as epistemic others. If taken seriously, this misconception raises a question: How is it that people who only understand force can be involved in making news that is central to a democratic society that thrives because of reason and the free flow of information? One obvious and important way to answer this question is to critique the premise. This might be a multiculturalist's approach. Arabs do not only understand force; they also, as historians of science and advocates for Arab Americans alike could remind us, understand astronomy, algebra, and poetry. They understand satellite television, cell phones, Facebook, and blogging, as chroniclers of the Arab revolts of 2011 might enthuse. This approach emphasizes similarity: that Arabs have contributed to "world knowledge," and that today we are all adept at using the same technologies.

But there is another approach that acknowledges difference—and politics, too. Alternatively, then, we might point out that while the idea that Arabs only understand force is presumed to be a cultural trait, it is no coincidence that the Palestinians and other Arabs about whom these characterizations have been made have largely been ruled by force. In this characterization, a reductive, essentialized notion of culture ("they are different in their orientation to knowledge because they only understand force") not only misstates and oversimplifies the situation but also erases power and history. That is, another way to approach this quandary is to consider the possibility that a special understanding of force—and about the relationship between speech and violence— might be a particularly enlightened position from which to write about military occupation, colonialism, or authoritarian regimes. It is because of their experiences that, as John Comaroff has observed, "colonial subjects . . . were not easily hoodwinked."[77] Under Israeli military occupation, politics—a politics in which force is never absent—permeates nearly every aspect of life, as I argue in Chapter 3. Palestinians have different relationships to political knowledge than most outside experts do, and this often cultivates a special understanding of force. Taking expertise as "not something one has but something one does"[78] opens the door to an ethnographic examination of the practices through which Palestinian journalists exhibit their political expertise. Studying journalistic production from the perspective of Palestinian journalists challenges preconceptions about Palestinians as epistemic others even as it also opens up our conception of what expertise is, tests our assumptions about objectivity, distance, and disinterest as central journalistic values, and challenges our ideas about the relationship between speech and violence. It is my hope that this perspective on knowledge production can encourage a closer attention to the kinds of epistemic skills—at once cultural, embodied, and intellectual—that enable a wide range of intellectual senses and sensibilities on the peripheries of the recognized boundaries of U.S. public spheres.

DOES A CHECKPOINT HAVE TWO SIDES?

"Checkpoints Take Toll on Palestinians, Israeli Army," published by Molly Moore in the Washington Post *on November 29, 2004,[1] bore an unusual dateline: not Jerusalem or Tel Aviv, but Hawara. The name of a hillside village, "Hawara" had become notorious for the eponymous Israeli checkpoint located just outside of Nablus, with its dreaded heavy traffic. "Hawara" no longer evoked images of the silvery leaves of the village's olive trees or its abundant spring wildflowers. The checkpoint was, as the first line of the article stated, "a sandbagged military checkpoint on a bleak patch of asphalt in the West Bank." And it was known for its harsh restrictions. As the article noted, "All males under the age of 30 were turned away. So were all students, male and female." Several anecdotes in the article gave a sense of the grim atmosphere at Hawara. An Israeli soldier told a twenty-nine-year-old Palestinian man who had been extracted from an ambulance, "I wouldn't let you in even if you brought God here with you." In the article, Moore, a two-time Pulitzer Prize-winning journalist who has served as the* Washington Post's *bureau chief in Mexico City, Paris, Istanbul, and Islamabad as well as Jerusalem, also recounted the story of a checkpoint scandal covered widely in Israel in which a soldier had forced a Palestinian carrying a violin to play it before he was allowed to pass.*

The Palestinians who read and interpreted this article at my request included a social worker, feminist leader, and mother, whom I call Aseel. I spoke with her in her book-filled salon, in what was for her a rare bit of downtime. I also spoke to an employee of a community-based organization, Samia, whom I lured away from her computer at work. I interviewed Marwa, a journalism student, at Al-Najah University in Nablus, where virtually every student would have had a stressful experience at the Hawara checkpoint. Aseel and Samia, who both lived in Beth-

lehem, may not have had extensive experiences at Hawara, but they regularly encountered other checkpoints in their own daily itineraries. All three appreciated the fine-grained description Moore presented about checkpoints, but they thought the article might nonetheless promote stereotypes of Palestinians and understate the power imbalance between Palestinians and Israelis.

A central story in the article involved an Israeli soldier beating a Palestinian father in front of his wife and children. As Moore described, it was a cold day and patience was thin on both sides of the checkpoint as a camera crew from the army's Education Corps collected video footage for a training tape. The crew caught an angry interaction on tape, as Moore narrated:

> "Go home! What's your problem?" shouted the checkpoint commander, a gaunt staff sergeant whose face was partially hidden beneath his helmet. The camera focused on the sergeant—a Bedouin, rare in the Israeli military—as he continued yelling in Arabic at an agitated Palestinian man grasping the hand of a small child. "Shut up! Shut up! Go back, go back, everyone go back. No one through—everyone go back."
>
> The video did not capture the next exchange, but other soldiers at the checkpoint said in interviews that the Palestinian man began screaming at the 23-year-old sergeant. The sergeant handcuffed the man with disposable plastic cuffs and ordered him to sit on the ground.
>
> Suddenly, the camera jerked toward the sergeant. He bashed the Palestinian man in the face with his fist. The man's hysterical wife and two weeping children tried to squeeze between him and the sergeant. The soldier shoved the Palestinian into a hut as the army cameraman followed close behind.

Aseel thought this passage rang true. "It shows how Palestinians are being humiliated at the Israeli checkpoints. It talks about how a Palestinian man was beaten in front of his children and wife, and how the Palestinian was humiliated. This is a positive element of the article, that it shows how Palestinians are suffering at checkpoints."

In her estimation, the article accurately portrayed Palestinians' outraged reaction to checkpoints. According to another passage in the article, a "chorus of angry [Palestinian] men" demanded passage. "As a thin man with a swath of black stubble across his face squeezed through the turnstile," Moore continued, "his 18-month-old toddler became wedged between the bars. 'Open it! Open it!' he screamed, cursing at the soldiers and gripping the whimpering child by one arm." Aseel appreciated this passage, commenting, "I like how the article describes the people at the checkpoint.

The article conveys the frustration and anger in people's faces." A passionate woman who had been active in politics for more than twenty years, Aseel was never afraid to have emotion enter politics.

But Samia, who had studied conflict resolution in the United Kingdom, thought that this description might stigmatize Palestinians as inclined to anger, especially if American audiences did not understand how checkpoints work. Although most of my interviews were conducted in Arabic, she commented in her British-accented English, "If I hadn't seen [Israeli] checkpoints or heard about them every day, . . . I might imagine them as just a normal checkpoint somewhere, and that these are aggressive people waiting to cross, and they can't wait . . . but since I live here, I know about how people wait for hours and how the situation at the checkpoints is really miserable, and hundreds of people can be stuck in one place. . . . If you present the context, then it is sort of clear why there would be aggression." Perhaps her time abroad had sensitized her to how audiences might misunderstand Palestinian politics.

Readers had two other hefty critiques of the article. First, they pointed out that it relied much more on quotes from Israelis than from Palestinians. Moore quoted Palestinians in statements she had apparently overheard at checkpoints, whereas she conducted interviews with a number of Israelis, primarily soldiers. As Marwa, the media student, summed up, the correspondent had "missed the point, that is to talk with the Palestinian civilians that are suffering at checkpoints."

Even more important, Palestinian readers found that the article created a false sense of balance between Israeli and Palestinian experiences at checkpoints. Though the article described abuses faced by Palestinians, Moore quoted an Israeli soldier lamenting, "Most soldiers prefer to be under fire than at those roadblocks[. . . .] [my ellipsis of Moore's description] The mission is dreadful. . . . [Moore's ellipsis] It tears you apart." Another soldier explained to Moore, "We're all told we shouldn't behave badly to civilians—never hit them, never yell. But after eight hours in the sun, you're not so strong." With intensity in her voice that seemed to recall her hours of waiting at Hawara, Marwa, the student from Nablus, critiqued these passages. "The idea the writer is sending is that the Israeli is suffering like the Palestinian. As much as the soldier is suffering, as he says, it cannot equal the suffering of the five thousand people who wait every day at the checkpoint starting before dawn." She concluded, "The Israeli soldier standing in the sun is not going to suffer like the Palestinians who are waiting in lines."

Aseel noted that these quotes from soldiers might elicit unwarranted sympathy: "The problem with this article is that it shows the victim and the occupier in the same basket. Both the soldier and the Palestinian are tired. But, who asked you as a soldier to come and serve in an occupied land?" Speaking in her living room, within a few hundred meters of a military installation and another major West Bank checkpoint, she thought the article lacked a critical bit of political context: "The article doesn't say the word occupation. It doesn't say that those soldiers are doing illegal work on an occupied land." For Aseel, the occupation was never far from home.

Along the same lines, readers puzzled over a pair of statistics presented in the article: "At least 83 Palestinians seeking medical care have died during delays at checkpoints, according to the Palestinian Human Rights Monitoring Group. At the same time, 39 Israeli soldiers and police officers have been killed at checkpoints and roadblocks, according to the Israeli military." Marwa wondered if these comparative statistics were the best way to gauge the justice of the checkpoints. "Is this a fair way of measuring who suffered more?" These numbers reflected that more Palestinians died at checkpoints than Israelis, but they did not emphasize a difference that could not be enumerated: that the Palestinians died as civilians, while the soldiers died on a military mission. For her, the losses were incomparable. But she also lamented, "Palestinians have poor statistics." She considered the possibility that Palestinians should do more to reach out to journalists: "Maybe the Israeli side managed to send their message to this journalist more effectively than the Palestinian side. Do you know what I mean? We shout a lot, but it seems like we are doing it in an empty room. No one is hearing us."

Finally, the readers considered what it meant that the soldier who beat the Palestinian father in the incident caught on videotape was an Arab Bedouin and that he had been punished and demoted.[2] This was, the article stated, "one of only a handful of checkpoint abuse cases ever brought to court." The readers saw this as evidence of racist politics within Israel. Marwa commented, "If this was a Jewish soldier, do you think he would be punished in the same manner as the Bedouin soldier? . . . Imagine if the journalist had addressed the Israeli justice system." Samia criticized the journalist for not elucidating the hierarchies within Israel. "Somebody who is in America will not know what a difference being a Bedouin makes in Israel. It won't be significant to them. But for us, we all know that Bedouins are not equal to Jews in Israel." Palestinians read this and other articles from two perspectives, voicing their own evaluation of a passage but also anticipating how an American might react to it and responding to this imagined response. They also contemplated how the journalist might have addressed her American audience more clearly. Though this article addressed checkpoints—a top political pri-

ority for Palestinians—and though it was largely reported "on location," readers regarded it as a deeply problematic article because it imposed a framework of balance on what was for them an essentially imbalanced political arrangement of military occupation.

1 BALANCED OBJECTIVITY AND ACCUMULATED AUTHORSHIP

I'm responsible for the complete picture outfit for this ongoing Israeli-Palestinian conflict. Basically I have to follow the news, I have to make sure that we cover breaking stories, that we present a complete picture of the conflict from both sides, from both viewpoints. Before I came here, I thought it might be a problem to be a foreigner. In fact I've never found it an issue at all. As a foreigner, you stand above the story. To be in charge of the picture operation, it would not be good if you would either be Israeli or Palestinian, nor [would it] be good to be Jewish or Muslim.

Reinhard Krause, Jerusalem Chief of Reuters' photojournalism department, in *Shooting Under Fire*[1]

In the documentary *Shooting Under Fire*, a staff of Palestinian and Israeli photographers reflect on perspective and national identity:

Nir Elias, Israeli photojournalist, in a room adorned with photographs: It's obvious that I have a point of view of an Israeli, and they have a point of view of Palestinians. It's different.

Suhaib Salem, Palestinian photojournalist, wearing a helmet and flak jacket, with displaced people in Gaza: I feel bad, because these people seem like us. We are, all of us ... Palestinians. OK, I am a journalist, but in the end I am Palestinian.

Gil Cohen-Magen, Israeli photojournalist, in front of the Western Wall: OK, you [on the Palestinian side] believe this, I [as an Israeli] believe this. . . . But we don't need to fight, we don't need to kill each other.

Ahmed Jadallah, Palestinian photojournalist, in a living room: Because I am Palestinian, [I am] looking at things in one direction. And the Israeli photographer also. But Reinhard [is] looking at the story from two directions.

Reinhard Krause, editing room: I'm trapped in the middle. I know exactly how
it looks like when a bus is torn apart from a suicide bomber, because that
happened just a few hundred meters away from our house. And I also have
been in Gaza when Gaza was shelled, and I saw [what] it looks like when
a missile hits a group of people. . . . And for me, both [are] exactly the
same—horrible.[2]

In these passages the Israeli and Palestinian photojournalists each resign themselves to the provincial perspective of their own nationalities, but Krause is presumed able to "[look] at the story from two directions." It is from this vantage
point that he can conclude that the experience of violence each side suffers is
"exactly the same."

Notably, in this documentary sequence the Israeli, Palestinian, and German
photojournalists are not sitting in the same room. Documentarian Mirzoeff has
edited together several interviews conducted in different places. Rather than
letting the audience hear longer quotes from any of the photographers, he as-
sembles a passage that creates a sense of balance, alternating between a Palestinian and an Israeli. The passage positions Krause, the foreigner, above the fray,
giving him the last word at the end of the scene. In this regard, the content subtly mirrors the relationships that made production of the documentary itself
possible. Mirzoeff's assembling of quotes from "both sides" so that they seem to
form a mirror image of each other constructs a logic of balance out of material
that could be organized in other ways. Both Mirzoeff and Krause are placed in
the position of the reasoned outsider between two opposing sides.

This is the logic of what I call *balanced objectivity*, an incarnation of objectivity characteristic of Western journalism in Jerusalem that at once describes
how journalists talk about their work, how their texts are written, and how
news bureaus are structured. Balanced objectivity also characterizes an ethic of
reporting and writing at this site. Objectivity is what Lorraine Daston and Peter
Galison have called an "epistemic virtue," in that it is a norm "internalized and
enforced by appeal to ethical values, as well as to pragmatic efficacy in securing
knowledge."[3] Though journalists do not use the term *balanced objectivity* and
instead tend to talk about the related terms of fairness, lack of bias, balance, or
objectivity, being objective and creating balanced journalism is regarded as an
ethical endeavor, as well as a practical one.

In fact, the Israeli and Palestinian photojournalists in the passage above
share more than is suggested by the logic of balanced objectivity, which can

tend to polarize and flatten out Israeli and Palestinian viewpoints. In an earlier sequence of the documentary, the Israeli Nir Rosen and the Palestinian Suhaib Salem each independently investigate a new Israeli military fence around a Gaza settlement. They have different visual perspectives on this fence because they see the physical structure from two opposing sides. Since the early 1990s, the Israeli system of closure—made up of checkpoints and other physical means, as well as bureaucratic measures[4]—has isolated Palestinians from Israelis. The Palestinian photojournalist cannot reach the Israeli side, and the Israeli photojournalist would have to take an uncomfortable and circuitous route to reach the Palestinian side, unless he was with soldiers. This system of closure plays no small role in reinforcing balanced objectivity.

But their political analyses of the significance of the fence do not point to dichotomous nationalist narratives. Instead, both see the fence as a means of Israeli expansion of territorial control. Their analyses contrast with the official Israeli logic behind such fences, that they are built for security reasons. Salem explains, "Every day they come at night, they demolish seven, ten houses, then after this they put wire in this area so no one should get in. After a month, they come to take another area and after another month, another area, like this." Surely drawing on the experience of living in Gaza and having watched similar processes unfold in other parts of the territory, like the southern border between Gaza and Egypt, he concludes, "Anyone who comes to this area after one month, where we are staying here . . . they will shoot him immediately because it's going to be close to the army post."[5] The Israeli journalist Rosen confirms this argument. "Maybe [the Israeli authorities] want to push a little, to push the crossing . . . a little inside and then stop it, and then say, 'Gaza finishes there, not there.'"[6] Israeli and Palestinian perspectives—and here I mean embodied points of views on the world—are divergent, because geographic separation between them has been so stringently executed, but that does not mean that their political analyses are always dichotomous. Perhaps because Mirzoeff's documentary allows us to hear at length from Israeli and Palestinian photojournalists, it permits this brief disruption of the norm of balanced objectivity.

"BALANCED OBJECTIVITY" AS VALUE AND STRATEGY

What does it mean to qualify the term *objectivity* as "balanced"? Objectivity might be considered one of what Timothy Mitchell has called the "principles true in every country," a bedrock of modern science and government, even though in fact it has a particular history, like other such ideas.[7] He aims to question the universality of such principles as the economy and development. Similarly, objectivity has authority because of its apparent unity as a concept. In this way, objectivity is like other seemingly universal categories that have seemed to originate in abstract Western thought, but that in fact have taken shape by way of the execution of real world projects in colonial and postcolonial contexts.[8] Indeed, there has been great variation in how those in different fields have defined objectivity. Historian Lorraine Daston has demonstrated that the concept of objectivity hardly refers to a clear standard or a single coherent idea. Its meanings over different historical periods have included aperspectivity, multiperspectivity, suppression of judgment, rejection of aestheticization, and reference to an ontological bedrock.[9] As Charles Briggs has found, these disparate meanings are linked by a deeply engrained "folk epistemology [that conceives] of 'the truth' as being singular, unequivocal, and semantically transparent."[10]

Likewise, the methods of producing objective knowledge vary across fields like the social sciences, biology, and journalism. Max Weber argued that objectivity in the social sciences is not value-free, writing that "an *attitude of moral indifference* has no connection with *scientific* 'objectivity,'"[11] but, he proposed, objective knowledge should be universal, unconnected to culture or nationality: "A systematically correct scientific proof . . . must be acknowledged as correct even by a Chinese."[12] In visual anthropology, Margaret Mead asserted that using a tripod and taking long shots produced suitably "scientific" footage that would serve anthropologists for generations to come.[13] In their study of visual representation in scientific atlases, Daston and Galison demonstrated that objectivity in the late nineteenth and early twentieth centuries entailed, for some scientists, the use of instruments like cameras to forge a "mechanical objectivity" that met "the insistent drive to repress the willful intervention of the artist-author" with procedures and protocols;[14] while mathematicians of the same period found objectivity in drawing abstract charts and illustrations whose meanings could be "conveyed to all minds across time and space."[15]

Journalism adopted objectivity as an epistemic virtue on the coattails of other fields of knowledge production. Objectivity started to become a central value of American journalism in the mid–nineteenth century, around a time when much of American public culture was orienting itself around science as opposed to faith. Emulating scientific values was a means by which journalists acquired public respect.[16] Objectivity also became dominant because of commercial developments in journalism. In the late nineteenth and early twentieth centuries, media consolidation left cities and towns with one or possibly two major newspapers rather than the previous era's multiple papers, which each had a distinct point of view. Publishers thus preferred to attract larger audiences with "objective" news that would sell to people of a variety of political viewpoints.[17] Yet objectivity, often parsed as a belief in a single, knowable, and representable truth, was never an ironclad standard. According to historian Michael Schudson, it "seemed to disintegrate as soon as it was formulated," perhaps because it became the prevailing approach to U.S. journalism in the wake of controversies about World War I propaganda and postwar publicity.[18] Even discoveries in the physical sciences—like the Heisenberg uncertainty principle—undermined people's faith in the human ability to find one complete truth. Objectivity was the accepted value that gave journalism public credibility, even as many practitioners and scholars recognized that objectivity in journalism was hard to define.

Critiques of objectivity in journalism have endured until today,[19] even as objectivity remains central to the public face of journalism in the United States. Foreign correspondents' professed dedication to objectivity may be surprising in a contemporary American news landscape that increasingly seems to thrive on subjectivity, as on cable news. In fact, my interviews revealed that even foreign correspondents working for media companies known for their partisanship were confident that the reporting they did was distinct from the opinionated talk shows on those same networks.

Still, I argue that objectivity varies across different locations even within the same field of American journalism.[20] According to journalism scholar David Mindich, American objectivity has been characterized by five traits that emerged sequentially in relation to political events, technological developments, and changes in newspapers' economic structures: (1) journalists' detachment from direct involvement in news events, (2) nonpartisanship, (3) the use of an inverted pyramid writing structure that places the most important information at the beginning of a report and that contrasts with a narrative writing style, (4) a stress on empiricism, and (5) balance.[21] Yet, in Jerusalem bureaus, balance clearly trumps the other characteristics of objectivity. Elite foreign correspondents are occasionally reflexive about their work in a way that is uncharacteristic of an attitude of detachment. They may write articles that refer to the effects of their own reporting or to their experiences as foreign correspondents, as when a journalist found himself "up close. Too close" to a suicide bombing.[22] On returning to the United States, one reporter reflected that her son encountered the toll booth at the Triborough bridge and "asked if we were at the American border"; in response her daughter "chided him, 'No, silly, it's just a checkpoint.'"[23]

Likewise, in relatively frequent feature stories, journalists cast aside the inverted pyramid model in favor of a narrative approach, or use the opening of an article to heighten suspense or the curiosity or sympathy of the reader. We find lyrical articles about a Palestinian militant whose "skin is the color of roasted pecans" from a bomb-making mishap,[24] Jewish activists who monitor checkpoints "armed with . . . notebook, mobile phone, and compassion,"[25] and the "ghost town" of Bethlehem that houses "abandoned restaurants" with names like Memories, where people are left to "celebrate Christmas behind a wall."[26] Description and interpretation have long been welcome in foreign correspondence because it is assumed that readers need more background and explanation to understand distant places.[27] In terms of internal Palestinian and Israeli politics, U.S. journalists are hardly nonpartisan either. Instead, they often exhibit favor for the Israeli and Palestinian parties seen as promoting the U.S.-sponsored negotiations process.[28]

This leaves balance as an organizing value, and the apparent contours of the Israeli-Palestinian conflict—with one group on each side of the hyphen—seem to justify it as a mode of objectivity at this site. Practitioners of balanced objectivity, who may or may not be true believers, do not have to claim to have found the single truth, as long as they have represented "both sides." To a certain extent, this is a matter of the structure of the "beat," or the journalistic assignment and its geographic boundaries. As *New York Times* bureau chief Ethan Bronner said in a February 2010 lecture at Brandeis University, "In the job I do in Jerusalem, the problem is that I have two completely contradictory narratives: the Israeli Jewish narrative and the Palestinian narrative. It's not like my colleague in, say, Rome, who covers Spain, Portugal, and Italy. She has a bunch of different stories; she has to get used to them. I have black, white, black, white."[29]

Talking about balance is a tactic of allaying criticism in this fraught field. The *New York Times*' first public editor Daniel Okrent commented, "It's this simple: An article about the Israeli-Palestinian conflict cannot appear in The Times without eliciting instant and intense response."[30] Foreign correspondents may point to criticism from both sides as the indicator of good journalism. For example, following criticism of an article he wrote about the separation barrier,[31] *New York Times* correspondent Steven Erlanger responded to activist letter writers who argued he had failed to be sufficiently critical of the separation barrier by addressing some of their specific concerns. Then he stated in his defense that the very same piece had generated a vitriolic accusation that he was anti-Israel.[32] Despite what Okrent called the paper's "effort to stick to the noninflammatory middle and to keep things civil," the polarized atmosphere regarding the Israeli-Palestinian conflict means that journalists cannot escape negative responses: "No one who tries to walk down the middle of a road during a firefight could possibly emerge unscathed."[33] Balance is a strategy by which journalists attempt to satisfy these audiences.[34] As we will see, though, addressing a mobilized and dichotomized audience is not the only practical reason for balanced objectivity to have emerged in this field.

Balanced objectivity leaves its mark on news articles. One common technique for balanced writing is to use terms that seem less loaded than those preferred by Israeli or Palestinian advocates. Bronner offered an example in his 2010 talk: "There is, for example, that thing slicing its way down the West Bank and into the West Bank, to some extent, called the, well, 'fence' to the Israelis because that sounds kind of neighborly, 'wall' by the Palestinians because that sounds kind of aggressive, and 'barrier' by the *New York Times* because we didn't think it sounded like anything more than what it was."[35] "Barrier" was politically safe. Moreover, given that the barrier is made up of both fences and walls, a strict adherence to either of the latter terms could obfuscate the matter, even as the word "barrier" could underemphasize the structure's formidable physical qualities (Figure 2). Even when a journalist does not produce balanced objectivity

Figure 2   "The Evil Fence." A sign at a demonstration against the separation barrier in Abu Dis refers to the structure as a fence, even though this site's concrete wall is visible in the background. *Source*: Amahl Bishara.

within a single text, he may aim to produce a balanced picture over a series of articles, for example by reporting at the funeral of an Israeli killed in the conflict and then at that of a Palestinian killed in the conflict. Another textual technique of balanced objectivity is to gather quotes from officials on "both sides" or to interview both Palestinians and Israelis about the effects of a major policy even if that policy may directly affect one side more than the other.

There are several drawbacks to the ways balanced objectivity shapes texts. First, the notion of two sides itself can lead observers to overlook the extraordinary diversity within Palestinian and Israeli societies. Israeli society comprises religious and secular Jews; Jews from Russia, the Arab world, and Europe; non-Jewish migrants; and a large population of indigenous Palestinians, many of whom have disparate ideas about Israeli identity and Israel's relationship with Palestinians. Similarly, Palestinian society in the occupied territories is made up of Christians and Muslims; religious and secular people; villagers, refugees, Bedouins, and city residents; and people who identify with their specific city or governorate. These distinctions, among others like class difference, are all politically significant. Within each society, fierce debates continue about how to solve the Israeli-Palestinian conflict.

Second, while the technique of creating a series of quotes from alternating Palestinian and Israeli sources seems an intuitive way of bringing in different perspectives, in fact it can fundamentally misrepresent the communicative space of the Israeli-Palestinian conflict. Most Palestinians rarely if ever have a chance to hear an Israeli speak in person—about the threat of bombings, his views on Palestinian rights, or almost anything else—because Israeli closure so thoroughly cuts them off from Israeli society. Nor do Israelis hear from Palestinians about the indignity of checkpoints or the terror of Israeli military incursions. People on each side may be familiar with the others' claims in general terms, and Palestinians may hear an Israeli talk about her fears of bombings or opposition to the checkpoints in translations of Israeli media that are broadcast on Palestinian television. But this is not the same as having a direct exchange with an Israeli, which is what is concocted when journalists string together quotes from Palestinians and Israelis. American news readers can "listen in" on constructed exchanges between the "two sides," even though Israelis and Palestinians generally cannot participate in such exchanges. These articles constitute a communicative space that has its own norms, norms that contradict those of the places they represent.

Finally, any balance drawn between Israeli and Palestinian violence in journalistic texts obscures differences in the scale and type of violence each side experienced during the second Intifada. As noted in the Introduction, the period of the second Intifada was far more deadly for Palestinians than for Israelis. From 2000 to 2005, more than three times as many Palestinians were killed as Israelis.[36] In addition to higher casualty numbers, Palestinians faced intensifying Israeli control of movement, widespread home demolitions, and the confiscation of land for the construction of the separation barrier. In their book-length investigation of *New York Times* coverage of the Israeli-Palestinian conflict between 2000 and 2006, journalism critic Howard Friel and international legal scholar Richard Falk argue that the *Times* did not cover all of these forms of violence to the extent that they should have:

> The unevenness of the *Times'* coverage is substantial enough that it veils a major fact about the conflict: Israeli violence against Palestinians far exceeds Palestinian violence against Israelis. This is true even for the period September 2000 to December 2006, which saw a sustained series of Palestinian suicide bombings inside Israel. While the *Times* provided comprehensive and mostly accurate coverage of the vast majority of Palestinian suicide bombings in Israel, as the predominant representation of the conflict, these reports, featured as such, were misleading given that many more Palestinians were killed by Israelis within this period.[37]

When writing up reports of the second Intifada that seem balanced in that they cover each side's deaths and each government's statements as though they parallel each other, journalists occlude the structural asymmetries between these two sides. While objectivity as a guiding approach to journalism may seem to have no rival, in practice objectivity as it takes shape in coverage of the Israeli-Palestinian conflict—as balanced objectivity—has severe shortcomings that may undermine readers' understanding of fundamental aspects of the conflict.[38]

Others have made a similar critique about balance in different kinds of American journalism. In science journalism, for example, journalists have presented evolutionist and creationist arguments about Earth's history and arguments that global warming is or is not occurring as two different perspectives, thus validating creationist and anti–global warming positions considerably more than the evidence does.[39] Those analyzing coverage of presidential elections have made a similar point. Criticizing both candidates may produce a kind of balance, but it does not necessarily illuminate the field for readers. If both candidates are said to have made a misstatement, for example, but one candidate's misstatement is an outright factual error and the other's is not, to draw an equivalency between them is misleading.[40] The distinction I wish to make in the Israeli-Palestinian case is that representing the two sides through the logic of balance obscures the difference in power between the two sides and erases the relationship between them as occupier and occupied. Also, beyond the textual criticisms presented regarding these other cases, here, geopolitical and institutional circumstances lent themselves to creating news under the rubric of balanced objectivity.

THE NEUTRAL AMERICAN:
OVERLAPPING FIELDS OF POLITICS AND JOURNALISM

The epistemic virtue of balanced objectivity is intricately related to geopolitics. Since the 1970s, the United States has been the prime negotiator of peace between Israel and its neighbors. Iconic photographs of a U.S. president standing between an Israeli and an Arab leader have made history for two U.S. presidents, Jimmy Carter in 1978 and Bill Clinton in 1993. The image of Clinton towering over Israeli prime minister Yitzhak Rabin and PLO chairman Yasir Arafat, nudging them together as though with the righteousness of the moment that he, apparently, created, illustrates some of the dynamics of this relationship.[41] Both in journalism and in politics, the model of "two sides" is actually a model of three parties, one of which attempts to make invisible its interests. The American is purportedly neutral, in the middle, idealized as rational, even-handed, and interested in the common good relative to the immoderate, self-interested Palestinians and Israelis. Of course, one reason the neutral American is able to project these values is because he or she is the one who tends to define what is considered rational and even-handed, what is on the table for negotiation or open for debate. Since policies are not only a mode of political action but also a form of cultural production that influences society at large,[42] the cultural work of foreign policy helps to naturalize journalists' and news consumers' conceptions of balanced objectivity as a proper structure for journalism in the West Bank and Gaza. The figure of the neutral American makes possible balanced objectivity as an epistemic value.

That is, *what* journalists represent serves as a model for *how* they do the work of representation. There is a mimetic relationship between the content of journalists' representations of the conflict and how they do this representational work.[43] While we tend to think of the press as independent of the state in democratic countries like the United States, in this case it helps to regard journalism and international politics as two fields, in Bourdieu's sense of the term *field* as a semiautonomous sphere of action that is socially, politically, and economically located in relation to other spheres of action.[44] Not only do journalists cover the actions of politicians, but the field of official political actions—of diplomacy and leaders' statements—also exerts great influence over the field of journalism, largely because journalists depend on officials for quotes and access to information.[45] For example, coverage of debates about foreign policy in the U.S. media tend to index bipartisan debates in Congress, but do not go beyond or outside of these debates.[46] Moreover, journalists have been penalized inside the field of journalism for questioning the assumptions of U.S. politicians, even when they are working abroad.[47]

Not only do U.S. foreign correspondents echo what U.S. officials say; they also position themselves as parallel figures. As U.S. negotiators mediate between Israelis and Palestinians, U.S. journalists do something similar, taking quotes from and aiming to represent each side. Journalists have occasionally explicitly taken on the role of mediator between Israelis and Arabs.[48] For example, at the beginning of both the first and second Intifadas, Ted Koppel, the former anchor of ABC's premier nightly news program *Nightline*, hosted roundtables in Jerusalem with Israeli and Palestinian luminaries. The primary reason Koppel could assemble these important figures was that he was a prominent *American* journalist. The broadcast of the second roundtable in 2000 blurred the line between a news program and political negotiations. The two sides could not agree on the conditions in which the roundtable would be conducted. The broadcast program included several self-referential scenes that emphasized the active role Koppel played as a mediator. It even included file footage of the 1988 roundtable, saying of that event that it "is certainly memorable in *Nightline*'s history and even occupies a small footnote in the history of this region,"[49] because it prefigured the negotiations that began years later. Critically, U.S. power underlies Americans' ability to project neutrality in efforts to bring Israelis and Palestinians to a television studio as much as to the negotiating table.

In the field as well, U.S. journalists served as de facto mediators. I once watched as a U.S. journalist hovered meaningfully when an Israeli soldier refused a Palestinian passage through a temporary army barrier set up near his home at a construction site of the separation wall. The journalist later told me that he had lingered knowing that his presence would facilitate passage, as indeed it had. Sometimes such informal mediations made their way into published texts. A Palestinian facing immediate expulsion from Israel despite the fact that his son was in the Israeli army evidently called upon journalists who had covered his story in the past in hopes that they would assist him.[50] Even journalists from lesser-known European publications who only looked and sounded like they might be American were asked to do this kind of mediating work. Americans, it was presumed, produced important representations, and they assumed authority on this basis.

The strength of the neutral American model was evident in a recent controversy regarding a U.S. foreign correspondent in Jerusalem. In 2010, the website Electronic Intifada broke the story that the son of *New York Times'* bureau chief Ethan Bronner had joined the Israeli Defense Forces (IDF).[51] Many, including the *Times'* own public editor, Clark Hoyt, called for Bronner to leave his Jerusalem post, arguing that there was at the very least the appearance of a conflict of interest.[52] However, Bronner maintained that his reporting would not be affected. His objectivity, he said, was an essential part of his professional identity that could not be undermined by external factors. When asked about it at the public lecture at Brandeis University, he responded:

> I think that the answer is that reporters are a subspecies of humanity. We don't feel the same way that other people feel. I'm not joking. I'm not very emotionally involved in this conflict. If I were, I don't think I should be reporting on it. I feel that people who are natural advocates shouldn't go into doing what I do. . . . [Regarding] my son who decided to join the army for a year and a half, my kids make a lot of choices that I don't approve of or endorse. I'm not actually telling you what I think of this particular choice, but it doesn't affect my sense of what I do. It really doesn't. If I thought it did, I'd leave.[53]

The *Times'* executive editor, Bill Keller, decided Ethan Bronner could stay on in his position, agreeing that Bronner could accomplish critical detachment. "My point is not that Ethan's family connections to Israel are irrelevant,"[54] he wrote on the *Times'* website in a reply to his own public editor. He continued:

> They are significant, and both he and his editors should be alert for the possibility that they would compromise his work. How those connections affect his innermost feelings about the country and its conflicts, I don't know. I suspect they supply a measure of sophistication about Israel and its adversaries that someone with no connections would lack. I suspect they make him even more tuned-in to the sensitivities of readers on both sides, and more careful to go the extra mile in the interest of fairness.[55]

All of this may indeed be true. Still, as M. J. Rosenberg, a progressive blogger, pointed out, it is difficult to imagine the same argument being made about journalists in other places. "Imagine if Bronner was covering Latin America and his son joined the Colombian defense forces!"[56] Or what, we might ask, if a journalist had a relative in a Palestinian militia, or in an Israeli jail? Rosenberg went on to stress, "And, no, this is not comparable to a reporter's son or daughter joining the American military. Americans who want to serve, can and do serve in their own army. . . . Serving in a foreign army is extraordinary."[57] This suggests that being overtly supportive of the United States' interests as officially defined is within the bounds of American journalistic ethics. Perhaps one reason that connections to Israeli officialdom are more acceptable than connections to other states is that there is a presumed alignment between official U.S. interests and official Israeli interests. Once again, this mirrors the U.S. position in negotiations: while the United States poses as an even-handed negotiator, in fact it has long deemed that its interests align with Israel's, for example in prioritizing a fight against militant organizations.

There are many complex cultural and political reasons that alignment with Israel would be read as political neutrality in a way that alignment with Palestinians certainly would not. But there is also a practical reason that journalists might be allowed to align themselves with Israel even as they continue to work under the banner of the neutral American. Some commentators have pointed out that Bronner's effectiveness as a journalist stemmed not from his neutrality but from his very connections to Israeli society. Jonathan Cook, an accomplished freelance journalist, asserted that being Jewish and projecting a close identification with Israel is important to many journalists' success in Jerusalem bureaus:

> Editors who prefer to appoint Jews and Israelis to cover the Israeli-Palestinian conflict are probably making a rational choice in news terms—even if they would never dare admit their reasoning. The media assign someone to the Jerusalem bureau because they want as much access as possible to the inner sanctums of power in a self-declared Jewish state. They believe—and they are right—that doors open if their reporter is a Jew, or better still an Israeli Jew, who has proved his or her commitment to Israel by marrying an Israeli, by serving in the army or having a child in the army, and by speaking fluent Hebrew.[58]

Cook was not the only one to voice this perspective. During the controversy about Bronner's son joining the IDF, the Israeli novelist and commentator David Shipler also suggested to the *Times* that having a son in the Israeli army might open doors for a journalist.[59] Paradoxically, a stance of neutrality goes hand in hand with a close relationship with Israeli officials.

Mainstream political journalists thrive on an alignment with powerful states because they rely on officials for a supply of news. In some contexts, this can simply mean that many political journalists become close to the governments they cover.[60] However, in the context of the Israeli-Palestinian conflict, journalists working for U.S. media are covering a site made up of a state (Israel) and a nonstate party (the PA) for the media of a superpower (the United States), and that superpower largely sets the political agenda in the conflict. By drawing close to the powerful parties, they create their own power. They repeat what influential officials say, whether they do so with direct quotes, by using government sources "on background" without using their names, or more generally by following the priorities of officials. In doing so, they are able to claim neutrality because the United States, and to a lesser extent Israel, largely establish the terms for debate—for example, what the "core issues" for negotiations are. This does not happen because individual journalists intend to mimic U.S. officials in either what they write or how they position themselves in the field. Instead, this mimetic relationship is the result of (1) the general relationship between political journalists and the state, (2) the global position of the United States in relation to Israel and the Palestinians, and (3) the fact that this position is recognized by everyone involved, from Israeli soldiers to Palestinian interlocutors to journalists themselves.[61]

By no means is Bronner the only journalist who might have a vested interest in Israel and the occupied Palestinian territories. Even if a journalist has no particular concern with the long-term outcome of the conflict, while there she must concern herself with her surroundings. Foreign correspondents live in the territory of a conflict where no neutral locations exist. Virtually all of the foreign correspondents for major U.S. news institutions reside and have offices in Israeli society, most often West Jerusalem or Tel Aviv, and only travel to Palestinian areas for a story. By many (but not all) measures, Israel is an easier place for most journalists to live, and this was especially the case during the hotter parts of the second Intifada. It offers a first world lifestyle, job opportunities for spouses, numerous good English-language schools for children, and a plethora of restaurants, cinemas, shopping malls, and museums—all of which the West Bank has to a lesser degree. In most conflict situations, journalists live in a more stable place and travel to conflict zones as needed,[62] and this conflict was no exception. But real estate is especially political in Israel and the occupied Palestinian territories. Even the Jerusalem apartment the *New York Times* bought in 1984 was built on top of the home of a Palestinian refugee family that was never allowed to return or compensated for their loss.[63] Foreign correspondents are inevitably locating themselves in the political conflict as they work, whether or not they are aware of the extent to which this is true.

Indeed, domestic life is inextricable from politics for many journalists. During the second Intifada, foreign correspondents living in Israeli West Jerusalem may have feared or experienced suicide bombings. In the wake of a bombing near his Jerusalem home, Reinhard Krause of Reuters acknowledged, "It's a quite small city. You are always within a short distance from places where bombs detonated. So it really determines your life."[64] They did not experience in their domestic lives the more frequent, pervasive, and varied forms of Israeli violence imposed upon Palestinians living under military occupation. Where and how one lives affects one's view of the world, and living in Israel likely had effects on the outlook of the journalists who shared their basic sense of security with Israelis around them.[65] As *New York Times* public editor Daniel Okrent acknowledged, living in Israeli society gives journalists a particular "angle of vision" that "determines what they see." Okrent even suggested, "a reporter with a home in Ramallah would most likely find an entirely different world. The *Times* ought to give it a try."[66] In terms of both comforts and dangers, foreign correspondents' experiences living in Israel gave them a specific lived perspective on the conflict.

The tools Israeli and Palestinian authorities employed to promote their views of the world to the foreign press also confound the logic of balanced objectivity. The Israeli Defense Forces' actions in the occupied territories are generally accompanied by political announcements from the Israeli government, including names for operations and statements of what the IDF has done in a particular operation, and why. These press releases include quotes from the military spokesperson, which facilitate a journalist's job. They frame each event as part of a war against terrorism. Whenever an Israeli is killed by Palestinians, the Israeli Government Press Office is quick to distribute personal information about the victim. The Ministry of Foreign Affairs maintains a comprehensive website listing victims of Palestinian violence.[67]

Palestinians' militant operations lacked such authoritative framing. Although Palestinians viewed these operations as resistance to occupation, leaders did not communicate this frame effectively to the foreign press. During the second Intifada, suicide bombers famously recorded videotapes before their operations, but these were neither made nor received as press releases. One might argue that it would be impossible to set forth organized, positive publicity about nonstate actors' violence, given the presumption that states alone monopolize legitimate violence, and given that many of these operations killed civilians. In any case, it is notable that the leadership did not even try to do such framing. Military and political wings of organizations acted at some remove from each other, in part to avoid becoming targets of Israeli counterinsurgency and in part to avoid losing their Western funding. PA leaders had an ambiguous relationship to the uprising: they did not speak for militants, but nor did they consistently disavow their relationship with militants. This undermined communications efforts. Moreover, for reasons that are harder to understand, they did not even systematically distribute information about victims of IDF violence. Indeed, the most comprehensive list in English of Palestinian deaths from political violence during the second Intifada, a list which comprises full names, ages, locations and causes of death, and whether a person was killed while participating in hostilities, is from the Israeli human rights organization B'Tselem.[68] On the one hand, some would argue that the PA should have had a better public relations infrastructure in place. On the other, perhaps it is not surprising that a quasi-state institution that was, at various points during the second Intifada, barely functioning and even incapable of paying salaries to its employees was unable to have such a public relations infrastructure. This is one material factor that contributes to the production of knowledge.

Israel also has a well-developed infrastructure for the production of international news. West Jerusalem houses a consolidated location for major international broadcast companies—Jerusalem Capital Studios (JCS)—with satellite uplinks and offices for many news organizations, including major U.S. television networks. Ramattan Studios, a newer institution in Ramallah, carries out some of the functions of JCS, but JCS remains the preeminent press headquarters. One prominent Palestinian spokesperson who lived in Ramallah felt that this difference in media infrastructure sometimes put her and her colleagues at a disadvantage. Often when she was asked to speak on television, she was first told that a photograph of her would appear as her voice was streamed over a phone line, while an Israeli spokesperson for the segment would be appearing in person at JCS. She would insist that a satellite link be procured for her image as well. Journalists benefited tremendously from Israel's more developed media infrastructure; many used Israeli newspapers as the basis for their own reporting. They did not find the same resources to draw upon on the Palestinian side. Ulf Hannerz identified this imbalance in existing media resources as one of the key reasons that "it is very difficult to avoid attending more closely to Israeli than to Palestinian conditions and perspectives."[69] This is a disparity that has narrowed somewhat in recent years, in part due to a proliferation of English-language Palestinian news sources on the internet, but no Palestinian source has assumed a place parallel to the highly respected Israeli papers *Ha'aretz* and the *Jerusalem Post*, both of which are available in English.

Asymmetries in how one must work in Israel as opposed to the occupied Palestinian territories have made the work of reporting in Israel quite different from working in Palestinian society and have heightened the importance of Palestinian media workers. Effective public relations is, in this case, one reflection of state power that affects how journalists work but that hides itself in coverage. News gathering in Palestinian areas requires more field reporting of more different kinds than covering the conflict in Israel. Due to the weaker PA press organization, tracking down quotes and facts from the Palestinian side is often more difficult. Much of this work has demanded the local skills and social networks of Palestinian fixers and reporters.

COLLABORATION AND ITS LIMITS:
PALESTINIANS AS EPISTEMIC OTHERS

During Israel's invasion of Gaza in 2008–2009, Israel prohibited foreign correspondents from entering the territory,[70] forcing U.S. media institutions to rely almost entirely on Palestinian fixers, producers, news agency reporters, and Arab satellite news stations for eyewitness reporting. Before the invasion, longtime *New York Times* fixer Taghreed El-Khodary rarely had received a byline—the line at the top of an article that states who wrote it—but she had instead supported the work of foreign correspondents. Suddenly, she received several in the space of a few weeks because she was the only person from the *Times* who could report from inside Gaza. During an online Q&A, she and her editor fielded questions, some of which addressed her objectivity: "Does Ms. El-Khodary consider herself objective about what she was writing about? I don't know her background, and if she is Gazan I can certainly understand if she is not," asked one participant. Her editor, Ian Fisher, responded by vouching for her personal professionalism and confirming that there were processes in place for creating "the most readable, complete and balanced report possible" from El-Khodary as from any reporter.[71] But when the war ended, the number of El-Khodary's single-person bylines again declined.

Palestinians are often seen as unable to be objective due to their political and geographic location. Their potential bias is, as the above inquiry suggested, "understandable" to many, because of the lives they have lived, but it does not help their claim to professionalism.[72] There are also other reasons that it is hard for many to conceive of Palestinians as objective. As I suggested in the Introduction, there are three dimensions to Palestinians' status as epistemic others, people presumed to have a different and lesser relationship to knowledge than Euro-Americans. First, Arabs are presumed by many who align or identify themselves with Western civilization to have radically different and lesser ways of knowing and representing the world. Many presume that the Arabic language and the ways in which Arabs communicate make Arabs prone to indoctrination.[73] Figures in academia and politics have both suggested that Arabs have a tendency to lie, as I discuss in more depth in Chapter 6.[74] Formal U.S. military training on cultural sensitivity for soldiers stationed in Iraq assumed that Iraqis could not apprehend new circumstances or cultural difference.[75] These are orientalist assumptions that rely on a belief that the East is essentially different from the West. They also reflect widespread presumptions that, as Arjun Appadurai has noted, non-Western, noncosmopolitan people are especially "immobilized by their belonging to a place," while Europeans are assumed to be able to have critical perspectives on their relationship to the places to which they are attached.[76] This was just the lenience afforded to *Times* correspondent Ethan Bronner.

Second, the Manichean discourses of the War on Terror have exacerbated these stereotypes. During the War on Terror, Arabs became enemies and threats, and Arab media were regularly construed as part of this threat. The United States bombed the Baghdad and Kabul bureaus of the Arab satellite news station Al-Jazeera, claiming in the case of the Baghdad bombing that the location was a "known al-Qaeda facility." Investigative reporting later revealed that the bombing of the Kabul bureau was intentional.[77] Was the assertion that the Baghdad location was an Al-Qaeda facility a misstatement or a sly intimation that Al-Jazeera and Al-Qaeda are indistinguishable? In an era in which people were either "with us or . . . with the terrorists," in the words of then U.S. president George W. Bush,[78] taking ideas or information from the enemy was both implicitly and explicitly proscribed. As of this writing, Al-Jazeera English still lacks a national U.S. distributor.[79]

Third, if Arabs as a whole have been deemed epistemic others, Palestinians inhabit a distinct space of alterity because of their statelessness. Citizenship undergirds claims to political expertise in many regards. Public spheres have traditionally been presumed to have national boundaries. Conversations in the public sphere address issues of national concern, under the assumption that a responsible state should address these concerns.[80] In an era when political personhood is often parsed as citizenship, to lack connection to a recognized state is to be on the margins of authoritative media institutions. One Israeli editor I interviewed argued that one reason some Palestinians cannot be trusted fully to participate in producing international news is that they are still vested in a national struggle, and their information thus is less likely to be objective. He agreed when I pointed out that Zionist Jews had been in the same position before the establishment of the state of Israel—but, he said, having achieved statehood opened the possibility for better journalism. Moreover, as we have seen, success in producing mainstream political news depends on maintaining a working relationship with a state's institutions and officials. So tightly affiliated with the state are mainstream journalistic institutions that calling them statist media might be at least as descriptive as calling them mainstream or corporate. Palestinians are epistemic others because they are not citizens, not members of any one of these normative national public spheres.

Assumptions about objectivity and authority affect how collaborations between U.S. and Palestinian journalists work and are acknowledged. Contemporary journalism can be seen as part of a modernist textual tradition in which the processes of textual production tend to be erased.[81] Norms of attribution that favor a single author obscure collaboration, especially with those whose knowledge might be regarded as suspect. At best, fixers are listed as "contributors" at the end of an article only when a fixer has done reporting independently.[82] A single foreign correspondent appears on television even though reporting television news abroad requires a team of journalists. Journalists' very avoidance of first-person narration assimilates multiple contributors into one impersonal, expert voice.

There are differences in norms of authorship among various kinds of media organizations. News agencies—large organizations like the Associated Press that provide reports to newspapers, magazines, radio stations, and television broadcasters—place less stock in an individual authorial voice than newspaper journalism does, maintaining instead a stricter just-the-facts sensibility. It makes sense then that Palestinian reporters more often receive bylines for this kind of work,[83] for they are accepted as fact gatherers if not as full authors who must use judgment and knowledge of the audience to write more nuanced stories. These reporters have better and more reliable salaries than most fixers, and they work more independently, but generally they have much less of a mandate to select and complete a story than a newspaper foreign correspondent. Since the Oslo period, the most coveted news agency positions for reporters have been in Ramallah, where journalists work and are paid steadily, and primarily cover the PA. As would a reporter in another capital city, they cultivate relationships with sources within government, and they have strong connections in Ramallah's NGO networks. In this sense, their connections may parallel the kinds of connections foreign correspondents have in Israeli government and society. Occasionally, these Palestinian journalists write a feature story that requires them to travel to another West Bank city. These journalists often write their own articles rather than simply calling their offices with facts, as news agency reporters in other Palestinian cities generally do. They tend to have good (but not necessarily fluent) English skills, and in a few cases French skills as well.

Sometimes a Palestinian reporter receives a byline for a news agency story that required a lot of on-the-ground reporting even if he is not necessarily the person who wrote the story. The person who wrote it might have been posted at a desk in Jerusalem all day, compiling reports from multiple locations. Bylines of this sort can cause problems of misattribution. For Palestinians negotiating long-term relationships with sources, questions of attribution can affect important relationships. One Palestinian journalist felt that he had been branded as an opposition figure to the PA due to how his agency had assigned him stories and given him bylines. This made his work with both international and local press more difficult. As he commented in frustration, "I don't want to be the bad guy, I want to be *the* guy!" On other occasions, Palestinian journalists received credit for articles that had a political slant with which they disagreed. One journalist had reported a routine story about Israeli soldiers' use of gunfire against stone-throwing Palestinians. He had been given a byline, but he had not been given the opportunity to approve the final text. In his estimation, the language of the article, which used terms like "crossfire," "clashes," and "melee," suggested that Palestinians had been hurt in a vague but relatively equal exchange of force.[84] When he protested this terminology and then asked his editors at least to remove his name from the story, they refused. He presumed that this was because he had been the only one on the scene and they wanted to use the dateline indicating that the story had been reported on location. He saw his agency's ability to foist authorship upon him in this manner as stemming partly from his own economic pressures: his employer knew he could not leave his job. The author, in this case, lacked authority, and in this sense was an author in name only.

The most successful Palestinian news agency reporters are still located within a geopolitical hierarchy in which they are occasionally tapped for their "local knowledge" or connections when a foreign correspondent with more clout is writing an article; in these moments they act more as a fixer or producer. This is a strong indicator of how labor hierarchies are not just professional but also ethnic or national. Most U.S. reporters would not be called upon to do work as fixers, and being asked to do this work has caused consternation among these Palestinian reporters, especially since they may not control how texts take shape following these joint ventures. I heard stories from two different Palestinian journalists who had set up and at least partly conducted interviews with top Palestinian leaders, only to have these interviews be attributed to a foreign correspondent. In one of the cases, the Palestinian journalist had to intervene when the official became upset with the foreign correspondent's line of questioning. The journalist felt she deserved more credit than she had received.

A third reporter described an instance in which she had worked as a fixer at the behest of a superior from abroad. She set up a visit to a hard-to-access site, a small victory in itself and one that relied on her local connections. At the time, international concern focused on whether the PA had a hold on power, and initial interviews at this facility indicated that it did. But the story took a new twist when, due to a chance meeting there, they gathered a colorful quote that undercut the message of the day. In the end, the only quote the foreign correspondent took was this one. It promoted exactly the opposite view of the rule of law and order in the PA from the one the Palestinian journalist had had in mind. Rather than highlighting successful governance, the resulting article pointed to vigilantism and the fraught subject of Palestinian collaboration with Israeli authorities. On this and other occasions, Palestinian journalists were valued by foreign colleagues for what they had to offer in local connections, but they were not always seen as equal authors, able to shape narratives and receive credit for doing so.

Indeed, despite the relative prestige of their jobs, even top reporters for the news agencies frequently felt their news organizations exploited them. Economics, and not only national identity, was a key variable. A news agency reporter recounted what happened when he suggested the name of a Palestinian American for a job opening. "The bureau chief told me, 'No, I don't want an Arab American working with me.' I asked him why. He told me, 'I want people who are starving. They need a job. The Arab Americans will work for me six months and get another job.'" Palestinian journalists at the very least felt they were much more constricted than foreign employees would be. In the harsh economy of the second Intifada, many of those who enjoyed employment with international institutions supported a large familial network with their income.

Some Palestinian journalists hold their peers responsible for their collective lack of influence. While some are vigilant about how their names are used, others do not have the time and English skills to write their own articles or to carefully read and understand a news story to which they have contributed. One journalist who spoke excellent English noted that she is always encouraging her colleagues to write their own articles, or at least to read what is written from their reporting. "Those who don't write their own stuff and can—they do not respect their own work," she said definitively. Still, as she was at the top of her field, her perspective on the leeway other journalists had might have been skewed.

In individual interviews and in Palestinian media conferences, Palestinian journalists and intellectuals seemed to take for granted the lack of influence Palestinian reporters have over how the international media covered their issue, for the simple reason that they must keep their jobs. One Palestinian reporter told me with a weary smile, "The Palestinian journalist becomes a tool, just an instrument in the hands of the editor. I think at this stage, everybody is obedient. They get scared of Israel, they get scared of their editors. You know. That's it." Some journalists remained in dialogue with editors about contested terminology and historical background, but another reporter concluded that media institutions were not set up for them to have editorial input. "I don't think that we have that much influence on the foreign media," he said. "What we have actually is access to information. We offer the information the way it is to the foreign press. And the editors are the ones to decide how to write the story. So unfortunately, with this large number of Palestinian reporters working with the foreign press, we don't have influence on the foreign press. Because we have editors and we have people who actually take only what they are interested in." Journalistic ideals about professionalism and objectivity, geopolitical power, and economic concerns—none of which can be isolated from the others—all contribute to fostering norms in which Palestinian reporters have limited authority as authors in the international organizations where they work.

None of this means that Palestinian journalists do not value objectivity in their own terms, even if they define objectivity somewhat differently, as I discuss more in Chapter 3. A year after the Gaza War, when Ethan Bronner's son was found to have joined the Israeli army and the *New York Times* decided to keep Bronner senior in his position, Taghreed El-Khodary had already been working under difficult circumstances. The *Times'* decision about Bronner led to El-Khodary's departure from the institution, as she had felt threatened by groups that might seek revenge.[85] As she told an audience in Washington, D.C.:

> I have succeeded to be considered a very critical journalist on the ground [in Gaza], and I don't want to lose that. If Ethan's son joined the Israeli army, OK, it's his issue. If the *New York Times* decided to keep him there, OK, they took a decision. But I took a decision too. . . . And I decided, because I don't want to lose my sources, and I don't want to lose my life, and I don't want him to lose his life, so it's as simple as that. . . . I don't want to be tainted like 'the one who writes for someone that has a son in the army.'[86]

In El-Khodary's case, professional imperatives and material circumstances—a desire to protect not just her access to sources but also her own safety—informed a more stringent definition of objectivity than that adhered to by the *New York Times* itself.

THE ROUTES OF MEANING AND ACCUMULATED AUTHORSHIP

If Palestinian reporters face constant struggles to have their work published in the manner of their choosing and under their names, Palestinian fixers' roles are even more circumscribed. Fixers arrange interviews based on the requests of foreign correspondents. They might be asked to find a farmer affected by the separation barrier or the parent of a suicide bomber. They also conduct cultural and linguistic translation for foreign correspondents as they work. They generally have only very limited influence on how the reporting they contribute to is written up or edited. As a professionally successful Palestinian fixer, who eventually decided to leave the field because he found it unfulfilling, put it, "[American journalists] rely on me for collection of data, for the raw material. But how to mold it, they consider to be their work."

Yet, fixers' work is interpretive too, whether or not this dimension of their work is recognized. Gathering and selecting information is itself an analytic act, because gathering and selecting involves understanding a fact in the context of a particular framework. As Mary Poovey has observed, the modern fact is distinguished by this peculiar paradox. On the one hand, it seems to exist independently, and on the other, it depends on an argument to give it significance.[87] Frames of interpretation often shift once facts move into foreign correspondents' or editors' hands. In interactions among fixers, sources, and foreign correspondents, authorship and meaning accumulate as knowledge moves through different geographic, social, and political spaces. While the value of balanced objectivity privileges the role of the neutral American, the concept of *accumulated authorship* offers a more complex formulation of how news is produced. This model is especially important for news that goes beyond the realm of high politics and addresses politics as it is experienced in occupied territory. The routes knowledge takes even before arriving on an editor's desk sketch out an infrastructure of knowledge production in Israel and the occupied Palestinian territories.[88] This infrastructure can consist of a chain of contributors, including (1) Palestinians closest to events, like activists, victims, and militants, (2) other Palestinian fixers or reporters based near those events, (3) Palestinian fixers or producers working for a major foreign correspondent with social and professional links all around the West Bank and Gaza Strip, and (4) U.S. foreign correspondents.

As this chain suggests, Palestinian fixers can occupy a variety of social locations and professional roles. The term *fixer* itself connotes low status, but sometimes long-term fixers for top foreign correspondents, generally well educated and highly trained, preferred to be called, and were called, "producers." As one of these newspaper fixers explained:

> I differentiate between those who work as guides and reporters or producers. These guides will be able to go to a certain field and interview people, to help journalists to have access, and to translate. But when they go home, they are paid, and that's it; the relationship ends. These people don't have the power to tell the reporters, 'You are wrong, you are right.' Even I didn't have that power in the beginning. 'Who are you,' the foreign reporter would say, 'to judge me on my work?'

After years of work with a single institution, this fixer had a long-standing relationship with foreign correspondents with whom he worked, and he even had a longer local institutional memory than the foreign correspondents themselves, because the foreign correspondents rotate out of Jerusalem every three to five years. He also had a network of other fixers and reporters around the occupied Palestinian territories with whom he was in contact.

Critically, the chain of contributors and the hierarchy between different kinds of fixers is maintained in part by legal restrictions on movement of Palestinians from the West Bank and Gaza Strip. A Palestinian journalist from Jerusalem who carries an Israeli identification card that grants movement privileges might, if talented, become the sort of fixer who has long-term professional relationships with foreign correspondents and works all around the occupied Palestinian territories. A West Bank journalist must work in narrower geographic boundaries. Thus, if one key element that circumscribes Palestinian journalists' roles is the tacit assumption that Palestinians are not capable of being objective, another is the legal categorization of most Palestinians as people with restricted rights of movement. These legal restrictions not only divide Palestinians from Israelis and foreign correspondents but also divide Palestinians into different categories that attenuated many Palestinians' professional horizons.

The work of top fixers and producers arguably involves more creativity and interpretive work than that of news agency reporters. While the latter generally collect political statements and statistics, a fixer or producer for a foreign correspondent gathers a wider variety of information. Fixers might talk to victims, activists, and small-business people for feature stories. They assist foreign correspondents in doing work that is ethnographic in its detail and analysis. They might note the irony of "Arafat Street"—a street honoring the national leader—being in a state of decay, or point out that "Nadim," the name of the owner of a beer company, means a drinking companion. As one U.S. television journalist who was based in Europe but frequently visited Jerusalem said, his producer made sense of things for him because things were "so cultural." Just as foreign correspondents must do additional interpretive work for their home audiences, they rely on local journalists to do some of this interpretive work for them.

Fixers and foreign correspondents who work together over a long period can also develop close and mutually respectful working relationships. Foreign correspondents and their fixers might exchange political interpretations over months and years as stories unfold. Fixers might also guide a foreign correspondent through dangerous situations. In interviews with foreign correspondents and fixers, I once heard the same story of being under fire told by both the fixer and the foreign correspondent. It was clear from both versions that they had grown close over the experience. Foreign correspondents and their fixers or producers often have intellectually engaged relationships built on multiple kinds of trust, even if these relationships are sometimes strained by the conditions of their work and the hierarchies built into the system of producing such reporting. These are the relationships that disappear when the words appear in print.

The idea of accumulated authorship came into focus for me as I analyzed a minor news story from the middle of the Intifada. The Israeli army had shot and killed a man in his thirties, whom I call Jamal, in the West Bank city of Nablus. According to reports, some of which drew upon a statement by an Israeli mili-

tary spokesperson, he had been killed as he fled from the army, ignoring soldiers' orders for him to stop. On that day, North American papers reported that
more than ten Palestinians had been killed as the Israeli army moved into multiple areas of the occupied Palestinian territories. But one journalist happened
to include in his article a quote from Jamal's elderly father, Abu Karam. Abu
Karam was quoted saying that his son's blood lay in a pool on the street like the
blood of slaughtered sheep.[89] It was sad and cryptic. It stayed with me for a long
time, so I tried to puzzle out how the quote had made it into a major U.S. outlet.

Why, out of the many people who had been killed that day, did we read
about this one? How had the journalist selected this quote? Signifying by way
of abstraction and decontextualization, rather than by a more literal significance rooted in the material world, the quote was powerful on multiple levels.
It was what Barthes might call mythical speech, sparse, "with poor, incomplete
images."[90] Whatever his motivations for the selection, by including the quote
without further explication the journalist was adhering to certain professional
norms. Journalists could not usually make such evocative or metaphorical
statements themselves. The journalist could never have described a death in the
way that Abu Karam had in his own voice. But in a quote, the words could take
their place in the article. The quote could be interpreted in a few different ways.
The image of blood on the ground, recalled by a grieving father, is viscerally
shocking, unquestionably a color quote. According to orientalist preconceptions, Arab language tends towards the imprecise, the florid, and the gory; the
selection of such a quote can certainly be seen in this tradition. For U.S. audiences, the quote might resonate with religious texts. I speculated that a U.S.
journalist hearing this quote had selected it because of the significance of the
lamb as a Christian or Jewish symbol. This was the angle that initially intrigued
me most. After all, the article had been published just as Easter and Passover
were coming to the minds of observant Christians and Jews.

Some foreign correspondents I spoke to were hesitant to say that religious
texts guided their work, perhaps because they were justifiably wary of assuming the conflict was essentially religious, as opposed to, for example, national or
colonial. Others felt that because religion was important both to the people they
were covering and also to their readers, they needed to learn more about the three
Abrahamic faiths. Serge Schmemann, a former *New York Times* correspondent
in Jerusalem, had prepared for his beat by reading the Bible.[91] Charles Sennott
wrote in a book he researched while he was the *Boston Globe*'s correspondent
that although he did not read the Bible as a text very often as a Catholic, on the

job he read the Gospels "as a reporter."[92] He explained, "For a correspondent here in Jerusalem, the holy books—the Hebrew Bible, the New Testament, and the Koran—cannot just sit on the shelves but have to be pored through in order for one to understand what the people on the streets of Jerusalem and Gaza are talking about."[93] Perhaps, I mused, the journalist writing of Jamal's death had also been thinking about Jesus as the Lamb of God, or about God's edict to Jewish families to mark their doorways with the blood of a lamb as a sign for God to pass over their houses during the plagues in Egypt. It was not clear.

Many months later, I arrived in the field. As I was still haunted by the phrase, one of my first tasks was to investigate how the quote had arrived in print and what it might have originally meant. I soon found that although the foreign correspondent had been in the proximity of Jamal's shooting when it happened, the quote came from his fixer, an experienced and well-respected journalist I call Elias, who, with a Jerusalem identity card, had the legal status to work in all of Israel as well as the West Bank. Elias was a "producer," and his professional skills and legal status allowed him to carry the responsibility for moving facts and quotes across multiple boundaries. When I asked him about the story, showing him the text of the article, he did not remember it well. In fact, though Elias had translated the quote from Arabic to English for the U.S. reporter, he said he had not obtained the quote directly from the father. He had received it from an important contact, a Palestinian reporter based in Nablus.

Still, Elias offered me his interpretation. He suggested that the metaphor emerged from the widely held belief that Israel treated Palestinians "like animals." This animal metaphor had a long history and a life of its own during the second Intifada.[94] Palestinian interactions with the IDF were often governed by the latter's arbitrary, physical control. This mode of domination was everyday proof to many Palestinians that Israelis treat Palestinians like animals. Even with my few months of field experience, Elias' explanation resonated with me. I had been at a crowded Nablus checkpoint that Israeli soldiers had closed for a while for no apparent reason and then reopened from the middle of the line. This had led to a certain amount of jostling. The soldiers complained to a foreign activist that the Palestinians were acting like animals, to which the activist replied, "Well, look how you are treating them." The metaphor of Palestinians acting like or being treated like animals illustrated at once the polarization of Israeli and Palestinian perspectives and a peculiar convergence.

However, Elias' interpretation was not the last word. I met the Palestinian reporter, Nur, from whom Elias had obtained the quote. Although he was not paid for the work, he was in effect the fixer's fixer. I wanted to hear his version of the story, and I wanted to try to meet Abu Karam. When I traveled to Nablus, Nur acted as my fixer, too. But as we wandered through Nablus' *qasaba* (Old City) looking for Abu Karam's house, Nur himself was not exactly sure where we were going. Winding through the alleyways, Nur would stop people for directions to the house of "Abu Karam, *al-maskin*" (Abu Karam, the poor man). Even for a professional and a local resident, small-scale geographic knowledge was dispersed; Nur assisted me not by knowing everything I needed to know, but by having culturally appropriate ways of figuring things out. Finally we arrived at Abu Karam's modest home, but he was at the mosque. Nur explained to his wife why we were there, and his wife replied, "What, an interrogation?" Nur laughed, putting her at ease: "But by a journalist, not by the police!" As we waited for Abu Karam to arrive, I was grateful that I had not tried to do this myself.

Abu Karam soon returned. Though he was in his nineties, he walked and spoke strongly. He wore a brown *abaya*, or robe, over his thin frame, and a white kaffiyeh, the simple headdress of many old men. Around his neck was a pendant with a black and white picture of his deceased son. Jamal had wide eyes and a drawn face. As so often happens in such journalistic interviews, our conversation was hardly set apart from the rest of social life. Abu Karam's wife, son, and neighbor, as well as a friend of Nur's that we had met on the way, were all present, listening. If Abu Karam was the natural center of the room because of my inquiries and because of his advanced age, his recent encounter with occupation violence did not distinguish him. Two other people in the room had lost close relatives during the second Intifada. Abu Karam's neighbor's nephew had been killed just after Jamal, and Nur's friend's mother had been killed earlier in the uprising.

Abu Karam began his account calmly. Jamal used to accompany him everywhere, he said, because Jamal had the mind of a child. Nur clarified for me that Jamal had been mentally disabled. Abu Karam continued that Jamal always said he did not want to marry; he just wanted to stay with his father, and so this is what he did. On that day, they were returning from the mosque together when Israeli soldiers detained them. Jamal gripped his father's arm. As he described this, Abu Karam began to weep. He reached out to grasp my arm, too. He remembered that Jamal had told him, "I will not leave you, even if this means I die." The soldiers told Abu Karam to sit on the ground and wait. They ordered Jamal to take off his clothes, supposedly so he could be checked for weapons. Jamal took off his clothes. Suddenly, Jamal was seized with fear.

"*Kan yu'ayyit*" recalled Abu Karam. I looked at Nur, confused; I did not understand this phrase. "*Kan yibki* [he was crying]," Nur clarified for me, using a more
formal term for crying that he correctly guessed I would know. Abu Karam recounted that his son began to run away, carrying his clothes under his arm. The
soldiers told him to stop, and he did not. They shot him. Then, they prevented
an ambulance from reaching him, and he bled there in the street.

That afternoon, Abu Karam did not repeat the metaphor about the sheep,
and I did not find myself able to ask him exactly what he had meant. However,
when I asked Nur about the Jerusalem journalist's interpretation of the quote,
he replied that he was sure that Abu Karam had not meant that Israelis kill Palestinians like animals. Jamal had bled copiously as they waited for the ambulance.
Abu Karam was simply describing what he saw. In a sense, the metaphor did
have religious resonance, though. Abu Karam, in his long life, had almost surely
slaughtered sheep or seen them slaughtered on occasions like *'Eid al-Adha*, an
important Muslim holiday commemorating Ibrahim's (Abraham's) willingness
to sacrifice his son as an act of obedience to God. Rather than abstract religious
symbolism from a shared Abrahamic tradition that might travel easily to U.S.
audiences, it was concrete religious experience in an old Palestinian city that
anchored the metaphor. This was not mythic speech. Rather, the metaphor of
blood flowing like that of a sheep was a concrete visual description.

Knowing the context of the quote also presents the possibility of narrating
this incident as a blatant human rights violation, since it indicates that after a
man was shot, ambulances were not allowed to come to his aid. This gives a
different sense of the event than did the sparse statements of the Israeli military
spokesperson, who indicated that Jamal had been shot because he ran away,
flouting soldiers' orders. It lends gravity to the B'Tselem entry that would later
be posted online, which declares, as do at least ten entries listed before his, that
he "did not participate in hostilities when killed."[95] The father's quote evokes
the slowness of so many similar Intifada deaths, a painful pace erased by succinct statistics.[96] Because the published facts of the story were so sparse—they
did not include the information about the ambulance or Jamal's lack of participation in hostilities—these meanings were inaccessible to readers.[97]

Rather than viewing Palestinian fixers as providing raw information to
foreign correspondents, this example demonstrates that Palestinians had their
own interpretations of statements and events that led to the production of
quotes and facts for publication, even if these interpretations were later obscured. And it was not that Palestinians all had "their" version, distinct from a

separate Israeli or American one—but that Palestinians interpreted statements and events in relation to their own distinct political and cultural backgrounds, as well as their own particular sensed experiences of news events, when they had direct experience. Moreover, this example demonstrates the complexity of the process of producing journalistic knowledge. Foreign correspondents work through an infrastructure of people organized by professional norms, social relations, and the political and geographic barriers erected by Israeli occupation. As the story of Jamal's death moved through this infrastructure, it was reduced to a vivid quote and the briefest narrative. Still, in the published account, Abu Karam's quote jolted the reader to attention, at least for a moment.

Authorship is a complex and historically shifting concept. While we tend to think of authorship as giving credit, in journalism, bylines carry a double significance of credit and responsibility.[98] On the one hand, bylines are sought after as the basis on which journalists receive recognition, but on the other, they verify that a journalist has been at the place from which the article is reported. As we have seen, when foreign correspondents work with fixers, bylines tend to go to journalists from the places where the articles are consumed rather than from the places where the events have occurred, because the former are entrusted with providing an account of events at hand with the interests of the audience in mind. Indeed, in the early twentieth century, Joseph Pulitzer wrote that a journalist is "a lookout on the bridge of the ship of state . . . there to watch over the safety and the welfare of the people who trust him."[99] This is still how trust functions in journalism today. Yet, as we've seen, foreign correspondents do not work alone. When "our" foreign correspondents are producing reliable knowledge, it is often because they have entrusted fixers and other journalists from the places where they are working.

Fixers and reporters—and here I am thinking of the reporters who work for news agencies, covering events but not necessarily writing articles—gather information that foreign correspondents and others who write articles incorporate into texts. When fixers and reporters pass on information, they often do so because they recognize a special significance to it. They pull a quote or an observation out of a complex event that offers dozens of possibilities of facts for extraction because they see it as part of a salient narrative.[100] In these collaborative enterprises, we see facts in motion, potentially pivoting between different people's narratives or arguments. A quote—which we might see as one kind of fact—can be repeatedly decontextualized and recontextualized as it is plucked from the flow of speech, inserted into a series of conversations journalists have, and then finally placed into the context of an article. In these circumstances, the argument for which a fact stands can change. Abu Karam made an utterance based on a particular sociotemporal experience, while Nur selected this utterance as a quote because it was evidence of a human rights crime, and Elias passed it on because he saw it as a statement about Palestinians' general status under occupation. The foreign correspondent incorporated it in a text perhaps because of its religious significance or its floridity. Once the foreign correspondent writes something down, it becomes related to an argument in a stable fashion. At this point, a byline is attached to it. It has gone through several contextualizations, yet the contextualization that occurs when a quote or another kind of fact is set in print is unique. From here, the text travels: it circulates, is cited, becomes part of a published record, and is even perhaps "the first draft of history," as journalism is often called. It is not only put in a new context, it is, as Michael Silverstein and Greg Urban would say, "entextualized," with all of the extra authority that this entails.[101] This is inevitably a matter of power, for "politics," as they write, "can be seen . . . as the struggle to entextualize authoritatively."[102]

This helps us to understand one reason that it has been difficult to recognize the intellectual contributions of fixers. According to standard notions of authorship and intellectual property, extracting information about the world is not in itself considered worthy of authorship or copyright. Instead, it is creative expression, putting this information to use for an idea or process, that can be recognized.[103] Thus it is difficult to recognize fixing or reporting in the absence of writing as demanding authorial credit because the fixer's reasoning behind selecting an element of an event as a fact is almost never made public. Even though fixers may have their own arguments for why a fact is significant, it is the foreign correspondent alone who objectifies the argument in a text.

When we study only texts, we miss the processes that precede them, and risk losing sight of the fact that "texts . . . represent one, 'thing-y' phase in a broader conceptualization of cultural process."[104] The concept of accumulated authorship recognizes that people along the way contribute their intellectual labor at each stage of the journalistic process. They add not just their hours of work or their physical exertion—though, as we will see in Chapter 4, these are not small or simple matters—but also their ideas. Each of the participants has in mind an argument that makes facts and quotes relevant, a spark of authorship that goes unattributed. When facts are fit into articles that flow in the conventional linear way, these other ideas are often erased. Authorship is accumulated even as each layer can supersede those that come before it. The epistemic virtue of balanced objectivity relies on the existence of a single authoritative author, producing knowledge that acknowledges "two sides" of the story. Accumulated authorship, in contrast, recognizes that before editors see a text, it is often already the product of many hands and minds, that the one or two perspectives represented in a final news text necessarily flatten out much more complex stories and positions.

CONCLUSIONS: WORK-LIFE IMBALANCES

The assumption that objectivity is a universal value—within journalism and beyond—enhances its authority in specific circumstances. But like other ideas presumed to be universal, objectivity is shaped by local conditions of practice. In Israel and the occupied Palestinian territories, the ideal of objectivity is made specific by the value of balance, for both ideological and material reasons that are inextricable from each other. These reasons include the widespread framing of the Israeli-Palestinian conflict as a national one with two symmetrical sides, pressures from interest groups that accuse journalists of bias, and political models of the neutral American. Also, balanced objectivity seems natural and practical when it is the American who can most easily move between Israel and the occupied Palestinian territories—but of course these restrictions on movement are the result of Israeli policies. There is a mimetic, iterative quality to balanced objectivity. Foreign correspondents cover negotiations in which the United States is purportedly the neutral, outside party relative to two parties with competing national claims, and these journalists position themselves in the same vein. The model of the neutral American enables both political and journalistic action. In truth, journalists are necessarily involved and invested, to different degrees, in the places they cover. Epistemic values are bound up with geopolitics as well as the practical elements of knowledge production. Nevertheless, balanced objectivity structures journalistic texts and organizations, as well as the ways that many journalists talk about their work.

The model of balanced objectivity and the neutral American is also a model for other kinds of intellectual and cultural production about the Israeli-Palestinian conflict because news—as opposed to art or film or novels or cookbooks—is the predominant mode of representing the Israeli-Palestinian conflict in the United States and indeed of representing the Palestinians as a people. Art exhibitions—hardly the locus for claims of balance—often exhibit Palestinian and Israeli art side by side, or in pairs of exhibitions. Plays about Palestinians in the United States often thematize dialogue between the Israelis and

Palestinians, creating a forum for balancing two different perspectives. Those that do not manage some kind of balance are often judged to be controversial. Because academic writing on the Middle East is also influenced by the sphere of politics,[105] the idea of objectivity as balance has also become a standard of writing about the Israeli-Palestinian conflict in many parts of academia. As political economist and Gaza expert Sara Roy observes, "Given the politically sensitive nature of my research, I have consistently been accused by those who disagree with my analysis of being nonobjective and lacking balance. . . . According to some, the relationship between humanistic scholarship and politics in writing about the Middle East must be based on some immutable (and to my knowledge, yet to be agreed upon) standard of objectivity, which mandates deference to balance, neutrality, dispassion, even indifference."[106] This is true even as critiques of objectivity abound among social scientists.

The stark asymmetries and practical challenges that characterize the processes of news-making in Israel and the West Bank complicate the value of balanced objectivity. U.S. journalists are generally more at home in Israeli society than in Palestinian society. The ideal of balanced objectivity erases traditions of collaboration among Palestinian and Israeli journalists.[107] As a textual strategy, balanced objectivity can hide the structural imbalance between Israelis and Palestinians, that Israel is an occupying power. Perhaps most important for this book, the value of balanced objectivity makes it difficult to acknowledge the contributions of Palestinian journalists, because as epistemic others they are not perceived as potentially objective authors. Indeed, as Chapters 2 and 4 detail, most Palestinians' perspectives are geographically bound to one side, largely because of restrictions on movement that confine Palestinians in the West Bank and Gaza Strip. Ethnographic analysis of journalistic production suggests that rather than imagining the U.S. journalist to be the singular objective author of news reports, we might properly see authorship—the full production of the text—as accumulated, and meaning itself as accrued and shifting through the complex hierarchies within which journalists work. In Jerusalem bureaus, balanced objectivity is at once a value and a normative description of a method of collaboration among professionals of different nationalities. Accumulated authorship describes this same process from a different vantage point. We can imagine accumulated authorship as an epistemic value, too, one that endorses collaboration and multivocality.

Accumulated authorship has relevance beyond journalism, in any field where data collection entails collaboration or even dialogue, ranging from ethnography to archaeology to field biology or other "big sciences" that involve many knowledge producers. It is of special importance in contexts in which collaboration occurs among people who have different sociotemporal experiences of knowledge production, cultural and political backgrounds, and kinds of power. Power differences among authors may stem from their positions in colonial, gendered, racial, class, or other hierarchies and from their positions in institutions of knowledge production.

Some have proposed "two-tiered" systems of authorship that distinguish between those who do data collection and those responsible for analysis, or those who make research possible and those responsible for its truth claims. We can find something similar to this hierarchy in some journalistic institutions' pairing of a byline at the top of an article with a list of contributors—usually reporters—at the bottom. But this only reifies the dichotomy I have tried to trouble here, a dichotomy that so often is underwritten by ethnic or national difference.[108] We can imagine another way of writing articles (or ethnographies) in which phrases could have hyperlinks to other arguments they support or suggest, and to other authors too, but this is not how news (or anthropology) is done today. Instead, we are left with an even more daunting responsibility as readers to imagine the perspectives embedded but invisible in the texts we read.

WORDS THAT FLY IN THE AIR

"It is a gentle piece of orchestration, a harmony of season and need. Every year, the summer sun heats the inland desert to the east, the hot air climbs, the sea breeze builds and the kites rise over Gaza." The first lines of the article "Rising Above, With Sticks, Paper and String," published in the New York Times *on July 18, 2003,[1] always elicit an exhalation from me, as though to emulate that sea breeze. James Bennet, then Jerusalem bureau chief who later became editor in chief of the* Atlantic, *wrote this article about the summer pastime of flying kites in Gaza. In a reverse of the usual journalistic norms, it features quotes from impoverished children rather than high-level officials. And these sources reflect on their inner states as much as on politics, as when a seven-year-old boy named Mahmoud announces, "I'm not angry when I fly kites. I'm happy. It's the nicest thing I do." The vivid descriptions Bennet offers are not of high politics but of smaller stranded dreams: "The wires of Gaza have claimed many trophies," he tells us. "Each lost kite—they hang above almost every street—is a compact story of foot-stamping disappointment, a haiku of chagrin."*

My own fondness for this article aside, I was unsure what my Palestinian readers would make of it. I worried it could have lost something in the translation, especially because it was such a lyrical article. Indeed, one reader strained to find a point, and so we went on to discuss a more straightforward article about militants in Nablus. But others sailed with it across the gulfs of age and geography that divided them from the article's young subjects to reflect on childhood under occupation. Perhaps it is not surprising that two of the closest readers of this article—Khaled, a refugee rights lawyer from Bethlehem, and Makram, a blogger from Nablus—wrote poems in their spare time. Naji, a student of political science, also seemed to have a contemplative manner. I was also fortunate to talk about this article with the fixer who worked on it, Taghreed El-Khodary. It was she who had identified these children as clever interlocutors long before Bennet reported and wrote the article. She had filed them away in a mental database of sources until the possibility of a story arose.

As West Bankers speaking in the relatively calm summer of 2009, Khaled and Makram could only imagine life in the besieged and impoverished Gaza Strip. Though the article offered little in the way of specific political background, it was clearly evocative for Makram, a blogger and a college student in his early twenties. As we spoke in a bare classroom at Al-Najah University in Nablus, it seemed he was transported:

> *Gaza, you know, it is misery and suffering; the children have nothing to do. But still, they are flying kites. Even if they are not wearing shoes, they can fly kites. If it flies away, then there is time to make another one. There is nothing but time in Gaza, and you have to make use of every second, because you never know what is going to happen, like an air strike or something.*

The article inspired Makram to recall his own childhood earlier in the second Intifada when Nablus had been besieged on multiple occasions:

> *I remember when I used to make kites. Things were really hard, and at the time I was really religious. I used to pray to God, and pray to God, and nothing happened, nothing changed. So I remember once, I wrote a prayer on a piece of paper, and made the kite out of it, and I flew it. [I thought,] hopefully from above he can read it. Maybe an angel would get a glimpse of it and deliver [my wishes].*

All of the readers expressed hope that this article on Palestinian childhood would bring Palestinians into the fold of a universalist vision of humanity for American readers. Khaled imagined the article would encourage U.S. readers to "reflect on another facet of Palestinians' lives. There was not fighting, shooting, or blood at that moment. These were children who wanted to play and live." Khaled could empathize with these desires. He had children himself. As much as he wanted to prepare them intellectually and emotionally for political struggle, which was an inevitable part of life in the refugee camp where he lived, he also sought to cultivate in them an appreciation for fun and creativity. This side of Palestinian life was, he felt, too often neglected. Similarly, in Makram's view, writing about Palestinian children was a way of challenging preconceptions about Palestinians as a whole, because "Western media in general dehumanizes

Palestinians, even children. [It is] like a Palestinian child is not considered to be a child." Taghreed El-Khodary put it most plainly when she commented on a central message of the article:

> Childhood is childhood, everywhere in the world. Children will always seek happiness. They want to feel like they are flying. . . . There are children [in Palestine] like everywhere in the world. But [American readers] have this stereotype; they always come with pictures of [Palestinian] children playing with toys that are guns or whatever. They don't see that these children are buying these [guns] because they are seeing the Israeli soldiers and are attracted to that image.

In this context, an article about kite flying was a profound intervention.

At the same time as it suggested some universally recognizable elements in Palestinian childhood, Bennet's article suggested that these Palestinian childhoods are not wholly like other childhoods. The article detailed how the children manufactured kites out of wild bamboo, ribbons of old cassette tapes, used paper, and string from the burlap bags of flour and rice distributed by UNRWA, the United Nations agency that aids Palestinian refugees. Bennet described how, in making a kite, one child "bent over a page of last year's religion homework, drastically revising the responses to questions about the Prophet's views on matters like cultivating land." These particulars communicated to Khaled something essential about how these children "fend for themselves. They make the toy with their own hands." He had done the same when he was a child in his refugee camp. He appreciated that from this article "an American may understand that life is not easy, even for children, who have to rely on themselves to fashion a simple toy. . . . There is poverty, these are simple people. It was very good that he talked about this." Makram noted, "It is not easy to make a kite. It takes a lot of time. Making it balanced to not fly into the ground. . . . The tail has to be a specific length. Going through all of this to build it because a child doesn't have the three dollars to buy a toy, this shows how deprived these children are." He had grown up in relative material comfort, and this was likely hard to imagine for him. In contrast, Naji, the political science student, resented a representation of Palestinians as impoverished.

The article described the children's kite flying in Al-Shati Refugee Camp during an Israeli incursion into nearby Beit Hanun, Gaza, as a mischievous means of crossing enemy lines. During the operation, the children "flew kites the colors of the Palestinian flag from their houses, trying to land them on the tanks." For West Bank readers, this inspired stories of how they had tried to overcome their own immobility through play. Makram recollected, "I remember once we were flying kites from the rooftop of one of my friends' houses, and the line snapped and the kite flew all the way behind the checkpoint. So, he said, 'See, my kite can go places that I cannot even reach.'" Naji also commented on the passage about kites trapped in wires overhead: "It shows that there are pressures that compress children's dreams. My house is in a high area in Tulkaram. Sometimes we see the sea shining in the evening. Why am I not allowed to go there? I have nothing to do with this conflict." They saw kite flying as an apt metaphor for Palestinian dreams of expanded horizons.

One of the aspects of the article I found especially alluring was that, as in life itself, the significance of a statement was not always clear. Readers debated the meaning of a boy's assertion that his favorite kite was one with the colors of the Israeli and Egyptian flags. Khaled thought this indicated his support for Israeli-Egyptian peace, while Makram thought the boy's comment was just an aesthetic evaluation. The article concluded with a similarly cryptic bit of political commentary from a fourteen-year-old kite flier, Muhammad. Bennet wrote, "Some say there may be peace here now, that the historic moment and the needs of both peoples have at last coincided. But Muhammad doubts it. 'Peace,' he said with scorn, 'is a word that flies in the air.'" Khaled initially thought the quote was a harsh indictment of the possibility of peace, as did another reader. Khaled even wondered at the statement's authenticity. "Maybe the reporter or the person who translated from the boy to the journalist made a mistake. Even the extremists don't say we are against peace, though they disagree on the definition of peace." Then he amended his interpretation of Muhammad's quote: "I can imagine a fourteen-year-old boy talking, especially since the whole thing is about kites, and saying 'peace is just talk in the air' [Al-salam kalam fi al-hawa]. . . . It means it is not tangible. All of them talk about peace, but for him, for the boy, it is all in the air. He's not saying he is with or against peace." Khaled also pondered how a U.S. audience would read the passage. "For me, this is understandable, and, yes, this quote may come from a child. . . . In the United States, though, children of this age are not involved with politics." He continued with a question for me: "I want to ask you about children in the U.S. Could U.S. readers imagine a fourteen-year-old boy speaking like that?"

Naji read Muhammad's statement as a child's wish for peace. "I think a U.S. audience will read it as, 'Children are dreaming of peace.' For them, peace is flying in the air like their kites. Their dreams are flying in the air, and they want someone to bring them down to earth." For Makram, the tone of the comment reflected on the idea of childhood in Gaza. "They are children. They say something, and they mean it. They don't try to lie; they don't try to make things sound better. They are not politicians. So, when a kid says, 'Peace is a word that flies in the air,' *he means it. People talk about peace, but he hasn't seen a day of peace in his whole life." For Palestinians—even for Palestinian children—the terms of diplomacy and high politics had deep resonance in everyday life. Even forms of recreation reflected on politics and economics. I still wonder what Muhammad, the kite flier himself, would have told me about "peace" all of these years later.*

2 ARMING STATE SPEECH, CONSTRAINING JOURNALISTS' WORK

*Everyone has the right to freedom of opinion and expression; this
right includes freedom to hold opinions without interference and to
seek, receive and impart information and ideas through any media
and regardless of frontiers.*

Article 19, the Universal Declaration of Human Rights

*I'm not worried about . . . freedom of the press. If there's any
limitations to it, it'll be restored. Any freedom can be restored. The
lives of Israelis cannot be restored.*

Daniel Seaman, Director of the Israeli Government Press Office[1]

The Committee to Protect Journalists (CPJ) named the West Bank and Gaza
Strip one of the worst places to be a journalist for three years running, from
2002 to 2004.[2] According to CPJ, the Israeli Defense Forces (IDF) "used threats,
intimidation, and, in some cases, potentially lethal force to prevent journalists
from covering its military operations."[3] Palestinian journalists bore the brunt of
this violence. Of the nine journalists CPJ determined were killed by Israeli weapons in the occupied Palestinian territories between 2000 and 2009, seven were
Palestinians (see box).[4] Dozens of others were shot or detained. The journalists
who were killed or wounded may have been targets of a soldier's ill will toward
media makers, shot in disregard for Palestinian life, or simply caught in one
of the innumerable dangerous situations of armed conflict. In any case, these
perils directly affect how journalists work. This violence is also aggravated by
bureaucratic actions and media statements. During the second Intifada, Israeli
authorities rescinded Palestinian journalists' press passes, challenging their professional status. This contributed to their physical vulnerability and exacerbated
their status as epistemic others, people presumed to have a problematic relationship to knowledge. Thus Palestinian journalists were at risk not only physically
but symbolically, too. With speech and actions, Israeli authorities not only chal-

lenged Palestinian journalists' credentials as objective authors and curtailed the ability of those journalists to do their jobs, but threatened their safety as well.

In response to these attacks on journalists, human rights organizations and other advocates have asserted that Palestinian journalists are exemplary professionals who risk their lives for their jobs. But in Israeli and American public debates, questions of Palestinian journalists' professionalism, safety, and freedom of speech are always entangled with concerns about Israeli security. During the War on Terror, as much a set of discursive operations as it has been a set of military ones, this tension between free speech and security has grown more widespread as democracies have attenuated protections for journalists and freedom of speech in the name of security. Discourses of both the War on Terror and human rights claim a universal scope, but in fact they have a variegated distribution around the world, and these two discourses can meet in contradictory ways. Discussions about Palestinian journalists' rights can be traced through multiple forums that extend from the occupied Palestinian territories and Israel to the United States.

Patricia Naylor's documentary *In the Line of Fire* reveals for audiences of PBS's *Frontline* the working conditions of Palestinian journalists in the West Bank city of Hebron. It analyzes one night in which eight journalists were injured by IDF soldiers, one seriously. The documentary spurred the following two remarks on *Frontline*'s website. First, from a commenter who identified herself as "Washington, D.C.":

> I think it most important to remember that this story is not about Palestinians, nor is it about Israelis. This story is about journalists—the people that we rely on to inform our conscience. The fact that ANY branch of ANY state knowingly and willingly endangers the lives of journalists is intolerable.[5]

Second, from "Ocky Milkman—Plainfield, New Jersey":

> So, let me get this straight, Ms. Naylor, please correct me if I'm wrong, but I'm supposed to get all concerned about rubber bullets bouncing off Palestinian cameramen while Palestinian gunmen are breaking into Israeli homes to kill whomever they find, including five year-old girls hiding under their beds and couples asleep in theirs, while Palestinian terrorists are blowing Israeli women and children to bits?[6]

The first commenter draws on the language of human rights and freedom of the press; the second draws on the language of the security state. With these two discourses in mind one can trace the routes by which different lines of reasoning become arguable and effective on the ground, if not universally or securely accepted as fact.

The image offered of rubber bullets "bouncing off Palestinian" journalists leads us back to the material dimensions of journalism, the relationship between speech and violence. This image suggests that rubber bullets are inconsequential to journalists' safety and their ability to do their jobs. Yet, Israel's "rubber bullets" are not as malleable as their name implies. The bullets that hit these journalists are made of a metal core surrounded by a hard rubber casing. When shot from a short distance, they can wreak havoc on flesh and bones. The fact that in many contexts these bullets are referred to as rubber might be regarded as a public relations victory for Israel. In addition to recognizing the physical effects of such bullets, we need to consider their effects on processes of knowledge production, for the former is surely entangled with the latter. The territorial logics of military occupation are another key material element of press freedom. Israeli military occupation fragments people and territory into different legal categories and geographic spaces. Achille Mbembe, building on work by the Israeli architect Eyal Weizman, identifies territorial fragmentation as a critical element of Israeli military occupation, a way of dividing territory that is not as stark as in older colonial forms but instead more intricate because of the way "two separate geographies . . . inhabit the same landscape."[7] This too affects who can speak, and how. For those on the front lines of journalism, the simple physics of free press matter as much as its symbolic dimensions. But it is a challenge to disentangle the relationships among discursive, bureaucratic, and military impediments to journalists' work.

DEEMED A THREAT:
THE WITHDRAWAL OF ACCREDITATION FOR PALESTINIAN JOURNALISTS

In November 2000, less than two months after the second Intifada began, the Israeli Ministry of Defense ordered that Palestinians working for Western news organizations should not have Government Press Office (GPO) cards, on the basis that they were biased.[8] From that time on, Palestinian journalists gradually began to lose their credentials. At the beginning of 2002, just months before Israel began its large-scale invasion of Palestinian cities, Israeli authorities began systematically refusing to renew the GPO cards of Palestinian journalists from the occupied territories, including those working for international organizations. The new restrictions affected individual journalists, the international media institutions that relied on their work, and ultimately the substantive coverage of an ongoing international conflict.

Journalists killed as a result of Israeli operations in the occupied Palestinian territories, 2000–2009

Muhammad al-Bishawi, Palestinian, Najah Press Office and IslamOnline
Nablus, July 31, 2001
An Israeli missile attack that targeted Hamas leader Jamal Mansour also killed Al-Bishawi, who was to interview Mansour for an article he was writing.

Raffaele Ciriello, Italian, freelance
Ramallah, March 13, 2002
Ciriello, a photographer, was covering fighting between the Israeli army and Palestinian gunmen. He was following Palestinian militants and positioned about a half kilometer or more from the location of the fighting when an Israeli tank suddenly appeared closer by. After he turned to photograph it, he was hit by tank fire. An IDF statement said that Ramallah had been declared a closed military area and journalists who entered the area were endangering themselves. Months later, the IDF said they had investigated and found "no evidence and no knowledge of an [army] force that fired in the direction of the photographer."

Imad Abu Zahra, Palestinian, freelance
Jenin, July 12, 2002
On July 11, Abu Zahra was photographing a disabled Israeli armored personnel carrier when he was struck by shots fired from an Israeli tank. Circumstances indicated that he should have been identifiable as a journalist, since he and his partner were both holding cameras, and his partner was wearing a flak jacket marked "press." Abu Zahra wore a multipocketed vest of the style that journalists typically wear. His partner indicated that they were standing alone in the street when Abu Zahra was shot, while the IDF said that a group of Palestinians had gathered and attacked the armored personnel carrier with stones and Molotov cocktails, and that soldiers fired back at the source of the attacks. However, photographic evidence supports eyewitness accounts that the attack on the vehicle started after the shooting. Abu Zahra was prevented from receiving care quickly enough to prevent serious blood loss, and he died the next day in Jenin Hospital.

Issam Tillawi, Palestinian, Voice of Palestine
Ramallah, September 22, 2002
Tillawi was, according to Palestinian sources, covering and participating in evening demonstrations in solidarity with PA president Yasir Arafat in Ramallah when he was struck in the head by Israeli gunfire. He was visibly marked as a journalist, wearing a jacket emblazoned with the word "press." An IDF spokesperson said that Tillawi could not be differentiated from the protesters or identified as a journalist.

Nazeh Darwazeh, Palestinian, Associated Press Television News (APTN)
Nablus, April 19, 2003
Darwazeh, wearing a bright vest labeled "press," was filming an isolated Israeli tank as youth attacked it with stones and Molotov cocktails. He was located at an angle from the youth. Journalists working with Darwazeh said that an Israeli soldier fired one shot toward the journalists, hitting Darwazeh in the head. The IDF said that Israeli troops trying to retrieve the tank were being hit with rocks, gunfire, and

explosive devices, while journalists said that at the time of the incident the area was free of gunfire. The IDF also claimed that it was unclear who killed Darwazeh, although video evidence and eyewitness accounts make clear that he was killed by Israeli fire.

James Miller, British, freelance
Rafah, Gaza, May 2, 2003

Miller and his crew, wearing jackets and helmets that marked them as journalists, had been filming for an HBO documentary the Israeli army's evening demolition of Palestinian houses. As they prepared to leave around eleven at night, they encountered IDF troops in an armored personnel carrier. As they called out and verbally identified themselves as journalists, the Israeli soldiers began firing, and one shot hit Miller. The IDF said that troops had been fired on by rocket-propelled grenades and returned fire. After the incident, the IDF said that Miller had been killed by a bullet from another direction, suggesting he had been felled by Palestinian militants, but a detailed investigation sponsored by Miller's colleagues, friends, and family refuted this claim.

Mohamed Abu Halima, Palestinian,
Al-Najah University radio station
Nablus, March 22, 2004

Abu Halima, a journalism student at Al-Najah University and a reporter for the university radio station, was shot near Balata Refugee Camp as he was covering an Israeli operation in the area. Israeli authorities commented, "As far as we know, [Abu Halima] was not a journalist." They asserted that he "was armed and he opened fire on IDF forces." According to B'Tselem, though, he was not participating in hostilities at the time of his death.[1]

Fadel Shana, Palestinian, Reuters
Gaza, April 16, 2008

Shana, a cameraperson, was filming hundreds of meters from Israeli military forces when he was hit by Israeli tank fire. Eight others, the majority of them children, were also killed in the attack. He was wearing a flak jacket marked "Press" at the time he was killed, and his nearby vehicle was marked "TV." Ehud Olmert's office said Israeli operations "make every effort" not to endanger innocent people. A subsequent military investigation exonerated the soldiers, finding that they had been "unable to determine the nature of the object mounted on the tripod and positively identify it as an antitank missile, a mortar, or a television camera."

Basil Ibrahim Faraj, Palestinian, Palestinian
Media and Communication Company
Gaza, January 7, 2009

Faraj was in a car with four other journalists returning from an interview on December 27, 2008, during Israel's Operation Cast Lead attack on Gaza, when shrapnel from an Israeli airstrike hit their car, injuring all of the passengers. The car had not been the target of the strike. Faraj died of his injuries several days later in a hospital in Egypt.

Sources: Unless otherwise noted, all data and quotes are from the Committee to Protect Journalists, "10 Journalists Killed in Israel and the Occupied Palestinian Territory Since 1992/Motive Confirmed," http://cpj.org/killed/mideast/israel -and-the-occupied-palestinian-territory/, accessed Nov. 7, 2011. Note that I have included Israeli responses to the incidents when available.

1. Palestinians Killed by Israeli Security Forces in the West Bank, 29.9.2000-26.12.2008," B'Tselem, http://old.btselem.org/statistics/english/Casualties_ Data.asp?Category=1&region=WB&sD=29&sM= 09&sY=2000&eD=26&eM=12&eY=2008&filterby= event&oferet_stat=before, accessed Nov. 11, 2011.

The rescinding of Palestinian press credentials was the last step in a long series of policies limiting Palestinian's access to GPO cards. Policies and practices around GPO cards, like other bureaucratic elements of the occupation, change over time and have different implications across space and for various groups of people, making generalization complicated, but perhaps this knottiness is part of the effectiveness of the policies. Even before 2002, Palestinian journalists had never enjoyed equality of access to GPO cards. According to CPJ, Israel generally granted press cards to Palestinian journalists "sparingly"[9] and "arbitrarily."[10] Palestinians carrying press cards tended to be those who either were from Israeli-annexed east Jerusalem or Israel itself or who had long been employed by international news agencies. The act of applying for cards was also different. Foreign correspondents generally apply for and obtain a press card in a single afternoon. The GPO's nondescript office is located on a quiet block just a few minutes' walk from bustling Jaffa Street in downtown West Jerusalem. Foreign correspondents fill out a form and provide passport-style pictures and a letter from their employers specifying the nature of their assignment in Israel. As procedures for obtaining press cards became more stringent later in the second Intifada, the GPO began asking journalists from smaller or lesser-known media outlets to show evidence of publications, and the office has denied some journalists because of the scope of their journalistic work.[11] When I unsuccessfully applied for a GPO card, I brought my passport pictures and a letter from a magazine editor I was working with to the GPO. Part of the standard process was for me to sign a form acknowledging the existence and jurisdiction of Israel's military censor, and that when I left the country my materials would be submitted to the censor. In practice, foreign journalists rarely submitted themselves to this.[12] Generally, for foreign correspondents, applying for a GPO card was and is a simple bureaucratic task.

For Palestinians from the West Bank and Gaza Strip, even gaining access to the GPO has long been difficult. When Palestinian journalists do not already have the permits required to enter Jerusalem, they might have their employers apply for a pass. They wait longer for a response from the GPO, because it investigates the applicant's history of political involvement. Palestinian journalists' appeals for credentials meld into the category of military permits, including medical permits and work permits that also allow Palestinians entrance into Israel. They all hinge on what Israel deems security concerns. Palestinians are incontrovertibly militarized subjects for Israeli authorities.

Just as obtaining the GPO card has entailed different procedures for Palestinians, the cards themselves function differently within Israel than in the occupied Palestinian territories. Within Israel, press cards serve as government-authorized passes that certify journalists' identities and grant them expeditious access to semipublic events like press conferences. In the West Bank, GPO cards facilitate movement, allowing journalists to enter certain restricted regions and to negotiate passage through the vast web of checkpoints that regulates Palestinian movement.[13] The United Nations Office for the Coordination of Humanitarian Affairs (OCHA) mapped fifty-nine checkpoints and ten partial, or nonpermanent, checkpoints in the West Bank in January 2004.[14] Journalists with GPO cards can afford to regard most checkpoints as inconveniences rather than outright barriers.

Complicating matters further, checkpoints are almost always more restrictive for Palestinians than for others. Not only are Palestinians forbidden to enter Israel and east Jerusalem, but they also face tighter regulations when they encounter checkpoints within the West Bank than do non-Palestinians. Palestinians are much more likely to face harassment at checkpoints than non-Palestinians. During my fieldwork, regulations regarding entry to Nablus, one of the largest cities in the West Bank, were variable and convoluted. For a long while, neither Palestinians who lacked GPO cards and were from places other than Nablus nor internationals with tourist visas and no GPO cards could enter the city, but accredited journalists generally could. When the situation eased somewhat, Israeli authorities permitted nonjournalist internationals to enter Nablus, but they still forbade entry to Palestinians who were not from Nablus. Such regulations render having a GPO card more pivotal to Palestinian journalists than foreign correspondents. In short, Palestinians in the West Bank are multiply constrained by their nationality and their location. They have never been able to obtain GPO cards easily because of their nationality, and they are always in the heavily restricted occupied territories. Even in this territory they face tighter restrictions than others. Full denial of GPO cards made these disparities starker.

In addition to impeding reporting, denial of GPO cards also severely obstructed Palestinian journalists' visits to their own bureaus in Jerusalem, which in turn limited their professional advancement. They could not attend meetings or go to Jerusalem-based trainings. In an interview in English in New York City before he received the press freedom award from the Committee to Protect Journalists, Reuters cameraperson Mazen Dana of Hebron described the movement restrictions related to never having had a GPO card: "For nine years, I am asking permission to go to my office in Jerusalem. I am not allowed. Really, I am going in an illegal way, smuggling [myself] and going. Two times, they [Israeli authorities] caught me in Jerusalem and they arrested me. And eighteen days I spent in jail, just because I entered Jerusalem illegally, without permission."[15] Similarly, before the outright ban, a Palestinian field-producer who lived in Bethlehem and had been offered a higher-level position as a producer in Jerusalem applied repeatedly for a press card and was denied each time. Eventually, the press organization hired a Palestinian who had a Jerusalem identification card that carried with it the same movement privileges within Israel as Israeli citizens have. Such hiring patterns contribute to a professional ceiling for Palestinians from the West Bank and Gaza.

The lack of press cards also constrains perspective. A journalist from Gaza who managed to receive a permit to go to Jerusalem and the West Bank for a few days after years of attempting to get such a pass remarked on all of the developments on the ground that she had missed out on because she could not travel. Though she was an expert on Palestinian politics and knew Gaza intimately, in talking to me she marveled at how eye-opening a few days in places like Jerusalem and Hebron could be.

Indeed, restrictions on movement can reinforce a sense of Palestinians as epistemic others. Palestinian journalists' confinement seems to condition their relationship to knowledge. "Natives," Arjun Appadurai has noted, "are not only persons who are from certain places, and belong to those places, but they are also those who are somehow *incarcerated*, or confined in those places."[16] In this case, there is a professional term that can be used to characterize this incarceration: a *beat*, which is the geographic or topical territory a journalist generally covers. In this world of journalism, wider beats—or the lack of a defined beat at all—can signify greater authority. News anchors or senior foreign correspondents, for example, might parachute from one continent to another for a major event because they are respected as generalists able to cover the whole world. While a foreign correspondent covers all of Israel and the occupied Palestinian territories (and sometimes even the entire Middle East), a Palestinian photographer from the West Bank might cover only the provincial northern West Bank city of Jenin and its surrounding villages, or the southern city of Hebron and its villages. Palestinian journalists, unable to journey to their bureau offices inside Israel or travel expeditiously through the hundreds of Israeli checkpoints in the West Bank and Gaza, are rendered irrevocably local rather than being seen as universally accredited professionals. While previously some Palestinians could escape this condition with the GPO card, the revoking of all Palestinian GPO cards made for a more categorical positioning of Palestinian journalists from the West Bank and Gaza. Indeed, it made restraints on Palestinian journalists even more categorical than movement restrictions on other Palestinians. Other Palestinians seeking to enter Israel in order to work, pray, visit, or seek medical treatment in Israel are at least allowed to apply for permits. With the 2002 policy of revoking press cards, Palestinian journalists did not even have this chance.

It was not only the actual denial of GPO cards that could lead Palestinian journalists to be seen as lesser professionals. It was also how Israeli officials *talked about* the denial of GPO cards. Defending the revocation of GPO cards to the press and in an Israeli Supreme Court case through which Reuters and Al-Jazeera challenged the policy, GPO director Daniel Seaman offered a series of ever-expanding justifications that illuminate the logic of a security state regarding free press. One argument Seaman made against the right of Palestinian journalists to be recognized as professionals was that Palestinians did not need Israeli accreditation, because the occupied territories under the governance of the PA were akin to another country:

> To date, the Palestinians have enjoyed a right that is granted only to Israeli citizens—the almost automatic right to receive an Israeli press badge. . . . Since until the establishment of Palestinian autonomy, its residents were under the auspices of the State of Israel, it was incumbent upon Israel to treat them along the same lines as residents of the State of Israel. Now the Press Office has decided to make the status of residents of the Palestinian Authority comparable to that of all foreign journalists.[17]

I will set aside Seaman's use of the word "auspices" as a euphemism for military occupation, as well as his misstatements that Palestinians had in the past an "almost automatic right" to the press card, and that the new policy regarded Palestinians as the same as foreign correspondents. Seaman's argument hinges upon the idea that the PA is a separate and sovereign state, and that Israel thus does not have the responsibility to secure rights for Palestinians. In fact the PA has never been a sovereign state, in part because it has never controlled its borders or had the right to constitute an army. Nor has it ever been territorially contiguous. The PA has never been able to effectively issue press cards to replace Israeli ones because it could never guarantee journalists freedom of movement. This is precisely why Palestinian journalists so desired Israeli press cards. The Foreign Press Association (FPA), an organization of foreign correspondents based in Jerusalem and working for non-Israeli media organizations, acknowledged this point and called Seaman's logic "bizarre" on the basis that during the second Intifada "the IDF has taken over most West Bank towns, its soldiers are everywhere, and they continue in all seriousness to demand of the Palestinians the same GPO cards that are no longer being issued."[18] Seaman's argument was essentially that rights are situated in the nation-state. Since Palestinians do not belong in the Israeli state, the argument went, they should secure their rights through other means. As commentators have increasingly been observing, for decades Palestinians in the occupied territories have effectively lived within the Israeli state, though they have not enjoyed the privileges of citizenship.[19] The logics of military occupation and Palestinian limited administration may obfuscate this fact, but as a practical matter Palestinians live under Israeli rule. Beyond this argument about the reaches of Israeli sovereignty, a human rights perspective would hold that all people have the right to freedom of expression no matter their geographic location or citizenship status.

Still, Seaman assumed that freedom of speech exists only within the frame of an empowered national community. This argument has worked against Palestinians in other ways in the past. One early example of how Israeli authorities set the legal parameters for Palestinian speech occurred in 1987, well before the PA was established. A Palestinian professor of political science at Al-Najah University, Saeb Erekat, had published in a university newsletter the statement "Palestinians must learn how to endure and reject and resist [all forms of occupation] until we regain our freedom."[20] For this, Erekat had been ordered to pay a fine equivalent to $6,000, was given an eight-month prison sentence, and was suspended from his university position for five years. Erekat's appeal of this decision landed in the Israeli Supreme Court, where the Israeli state attorney argued:

> The attempt of the petitioner to deduct by way of analogy from the law prevailing in Israel, to an equal case for the existence of fundamental rights of expression to prevail likewise in Judea and Samaria is without foundation. The right to freedom of expression was recognized as derived from, and integral to, the very democratic system of the State of Israel. . . .
>
> [In an] area under military control due to occupation from war, within which there does not exist either a democratic regime or a democratic procedure

of rule, no political institutions nor general elections, there obviously cannot be a derivation of the right of freedom of expression.[21]

The Israeli Supreme Court ruled in favor of the Israeli state.

Being stateless has also posed a challenge to Palestinians' ability to express themselves because having citizenship and belonging to a state normalize certain kinds of expression that are often criminalized or stigmatized for stateless people. Palestinian journalists have been presumed inadequate as journalists essentially because they have been associated with a liberation project in much the same ways that journalists from other places might have been affiliated with a state. For example, a 2005 *Jerusalem Post* article that became the subject of much discussion among Palestinian journalists asserted that Palestinian journalists were not credible because they mixed politics and journalism.[22] Tellingly, the article itself, published in the premier English-language daily newspaper in Israel, exemplified the double standards behind Palestinian and Israeli expression. A key source for this article impugning Palestinian journalists as unprofessional was an unnamed "veteran foreign correspondent," and the article itself had no byline. Both of these factors violate basic journalistic standards for accountability. The author of the article implicitly addressed an English-speaking audience with an assumption that his or her credibility and accuracy could not be questioned, even as he or she made the categorical argument that Palestinian journalists could not be trusted as objective authors.

The unnamed veteran foreign correspondent declared, "I . . . know of cases where former security prisoners have been hired as journalists and fixers for major news organizations, including American networks. Can you imagine what the reactions would be if they hired an Israeli who had been in jail for one reason or another?"[23] Many Palestinian journalists have indeed been in prison. Yet, Palestinian journalists are generally not former criminals but former political activists. From 1967 through 1993, membership in the parties that made up the Palestine Liberation Organization (PLO) was itself a crime under Israeli military law. During this time, many forms of expression—displaying a Palestinian flag, voicing support for the PLO, writing nationalist graffiti—were criminalized. Over 600,000 Palestinians have been in Israeli prisons since 1967.[24] Israel has imprisoned Palestinians for a variety of forms of unarmed resistance, and still regularly imprisons people with no charges at all, placing them in what is called "administrative detention." In January 2005, when the *Jerusalem Post* article was published, 848 Palestinians were being held without charge in administrative detention.[25] For the unnamed veteran foreign correspondent to suggest that having been in prison undermines an individual's credibility overlooks the fact that Israel has imprisoned people for doing the kinds of activities that would be considered part of normal civic life in other polities.

This inconsistency was not lost on Palestinian readers. One Palestinian journalist who had spent time in prison in the 1980s commented in response to the *Jerusalem Post* article, "You know, someone told me once that you never meet an Israeli journalist who hasn't served in the IDF, and you never meet a Palestinian journalist who hasn't been in Israeli jail. Israeli journalists, all of them, have served in the IDF, and we, all of us, have served in the PLO." In Israel, enlisting in the military is mandatory for most Jewish citizens, so the vast majority of Israeli Jews have served in the army. This is an important rite of passage for many Israelis. One might argue that Israeli journalists' service in the army similarly marks them as biased. Certainly, experience in an army during conflict can change one's outlook and attitudes toward others, though not always in predictable ways.[26] However, my point is not that Israeli journalists must necessarily be biased because of their experiences in the army. The political orientation of an article or a newspaper is the product of much more than an individual journalist's attitudes about the world. The point instead is that Israelis are presumed to be able to rise above this experience, while Palestinians are presumed unable to do so. There is an ethnic logic to this, as I describe below, but the issue is also that Israelis occupy the normative position of citizens of a state, while Palestinians are subjects of an occupation. While serving in a state army is naturalized as a normal means of expressing or defending a people's right to sovereignty, stateless peoples' imprisonment for nationalist reasons is delegitimizing to most outsiders. In fact, as suggested in the previous chapter, connections within a military or liberation organization might serve a journalist as he seeks access to high-level Israeli or Palestinian officials. But this argument is not only one about journalists' experiences; it is also about their fundamental assumptions. When Israeli journalists work from the assumption that there should be an Israeli or Jewish state, this is considered within the realm of objectivity; while if Palestinians presume that there should be a Palestinian state, this is regarded as an assertion of a disruptive opinion. This is another way in which statelessness is an impediment to Palestinians achieving their right to freedom of expression. In his talk about why Palestinians should not have GPO cards, Seaman mobilized Palestinians' outsider status in relation to the Israeli state—and the related tinge of criminality attached to them—to deny them accreditation.

The second and most noteworthy argument against Palestinians holding GPO cards echoed this history of delegitimation. Seaman's oft-repeated claim—inevitably made without supporting evidence—was that Palestinian journalists posed a complex twofold threat to Israeli security: generating bad press about Israel *and* promoting militant activity. For example, in a *New York Times* article, Seaman contended that this bad press was a threat to Israel:

> Appearing on [an Israeli] call-in radio show late tonight, Mr. Seaman charged that Palestinians employed by foreign [media] networks were "no doubt employed by the Palestinian Authority."
>
> "There is a war today between the Jewish people, the Israeli people, and the Palestinians," he said. "They will use every method to hurt us, including exploiting the media and Israeli democracy. We have to put a stop to this matter."[27]

Sometimes, metaphorical language erased the line between physical and discursive threats. As he told Canadian journalist Patricia Naylor, "When we're in a fight for our lives, sometimes we're going to have to limit some of these freedoms they were given, only for a period of time."[28] Similarly, Seaman referred to a "battlefield of international public opinion."[29] This language of fights and battles reinforced the insinuation that physical threats are inseparable from the discursive ones. When Seaman intimated that both bias and militancy were security threats, he asserted an equivalence between Palestinian speech and militant action.

Seaman's statements can be considered speech acts, verbal performances that, as J. L. Austin famously set forth, "do things with words."[30] More specifically, they might be regarded as what Judith Butler terms "state speech," extralegal speech from within a bureaucracy. Through this state speech, the power of the sovereign—and of the bureaucrat as sovereign—extends beyond the law.[31] Beyond merely denying Palestinian journalists GPO cards, Seaman's statements undermined Palestinians' claims to being full professionals. His statements benefited from and reinforced an atmosphere in which Palestinians' rights and abilities to speak freely have been called into question on the basis that Palestinian speech is dangerous. Seaman's arguments fit into a pattern of restrictions on speech deemed dangerous during wartime, especially during counterinsurgent wars. They also fortified the idea that Palestinian militants and civilians are indistinguishable from one another.

In her essay "Indefinite Detention," Judith Butler suggests a path for analyzing the kind of politics at work in the GPO's decision to rescind Palestinian journalists' press cards, and specifically Seaman's talk about that decision. In her analysis of U.S. detention policies during the War on Terror, she highlights how U.S. secretary of defense Donald Rumsfeld and other U.S. officials repeatedly made public statements about Guantánamo Bay detainees that intimated their guilt without the legality of a trial. Her argument is relevant first because of her incisive analysis of state speech that assailed another group of Arabs or Muslims stranded, in their own way, outside of the system of nation-states, since Guantánamo Bay detention camp is a military base where U.S. law does not apply. It is also relevant because of the political ties between the U.S. War on Terror and Israel's counterinsurgent efforts against the second Palestinian Intifada. In the wake of the September 11 attacks, many people in Israel and the United States elided the categorical difference between Al-Qaeda's religiously and politically motivated attacks against the global reach of U.S. power and Palestinians' militarized campaigns and popular struggle for self-determination. Israeli counterinsurgency arguments gained strength by drawing on antiterrorism rhetoric from the United States.

Similar bureaucratic processes were also underway in the two cases. Just as with the decision to indefinitely hold detainees at the Guantánamo Bay military base, the denial of GPO cards to Palestinians stemmed from an executive decision made outside of a legislative or judicial framework. As Butler writes, in these counterinsurgent wars fought by democracies, "Petty sovereigns abound, reigning in the midst of bureaucratic army institutions mobilized by aims and tactics of power they do not inaugurate or fully control. And yet such figures are delegated with the power to render unilateral decisions, accountable to no law and without any legitimate authority."[32] These petty sovereigns erode democratic institutions. Figures like Rumsfeld or Seaman mobilize the power of state speech. In fact, Daniel Seaman asserted in public accounts that from the beginning, the decision to change the policy had been mostly his own.[33]

In his work on speech acts, J. L. Austin established that the efficacy of any speech act—a speaker's ability to accomplish something by saying something—depends on contextual circumstances, or felicity conditions.[34] These may be institutional or social. For a racist statement to encourage or constitute harm, as Butler argues, building on Austin, the speaker must draw upon a history and social context of racism.[35] I argue that state speech is effective for at least three reasons. Most fundamentally, an executive branch official's statements often become effective by virtue of the fact that the official has a bureaucracy or military to execute them. Seaman stated that Palestinian journalists would no longer receive GPO cards, so—because of his place at the head of this office, located within the office of the prime minister—they no longer did. Second, state speech is effective because it is reported and repeated in the press, as Butler suggests: "These official statements are also media performances, a form of state speech that establishes a domain of official utterance distinct from legal discourse."[36] As we will see here, press sources and court cases quote each other. Finally, state speech takes place in broader cultural contexts and can be empowered by those contexts.

In short, Israeli officials' abilities to limit Palestinian journalists' professional capabilities by making declarations about them hinged on (1) bureaucratic and military institutions, (2) conventions of news production, and (3) social and political contexts in which Palestinians were already regarded as threatening. Building on this, we can identify two kinds of effects of Seaman's state speech, both of which define Palestinian journalists as illegitimate. First, the GPO's declaration that no Palestinian would receive a press pass is immediately effective because the utterance itself executes the policy to be carried out by a bureaucracy and an army.[37] Second, because Seaman's statements in defense of the policy are repeated in news media and because they enter into an already prejudiced context, his statements about Palestinian journalists have the *indirect* effect of reinforcing assumptions that Palestinian journalists are not credible.[38] This second level requires more explication.

In the immediate aftermath of the decision to rescind the press cards in late 2001, Seaman promoted the idea that Palestinian journalists were indistinguishable from militants in an article that appeared on a popular English-language Israeli news website, YNet, and that was later quoted in the decision of the Israeli Supreme Court regarding the GPO cards. There he asserted that Palestinian journalists were

> staging and directing filming in accordance with the instructions of the Palestinian Authority . . . [producing] false reports that stir up a desire for revenge; praise for, and glorification of, acts of suicide and murder; incitement to murder Israeli citizens and the destruction of the State of Israel. We do not delude ourselves; it is clear that these actions will continue. But the Government Press Office has decided that they will be done by people who do not carry a press badge of the State of Israel.[39]

In other words, Seaman was alleging that Palestinian journalists were engaged in dangerous speech acts like incitement. He did not support his claims about press card–holding Palestinian journalists with examples, and it would have been hard to do so. For one thing, most Palestinian journalists who held press cards worked within large international media institutions that rarely allowed Palestinian journalists to editorialize.

In other instances, Seaman suggested Palestinian journalists were a direct security threat. In his affidavit to the Supreme Court for Reuters' and Al-Jazeera's challenge to the new policy, Seaman acknowledged the public relations issue, but asserted this was of secondary importance. A *Jerusalem Post* article covering the court case quoted Seaman's testimony:

> "In the estimation of the security services, for the time being the mere entry into Israel of territories residents may endanger the well-being and security of the citizens and residents of the state in a most substantive manner," wrote Seaman.
>
> In the case of Palestinian journalists, the danger is even greater, he argued. "Granting a permit to a resident of the territories to enter Israel and work therein as a journalist—that is, granting a permit whose entire purpose is to permit free movement within Israel—is liable to endanger the public even more than a case when a regular [work or medical] permit is granted."
>
> Seaman warned that a journalist could "assist terror organizations in realizing their plans, for example, by collecting intelligence relating to activities within Israel or by assisting in the transportation of weapons into Israel and from place to place therein."[40]

Again, the question of actual cases of journalists engaging in military actions never arose. By comingling an argument about Palestinian journalists as military threats and an argument about biased journalism, Seaman's words served to delegitimize Palestinian journalists.

The logic of naming Arabs and Muslims dangers to national security is racially tinged, and yet it was also a logic through which Israel paradoxically staked its claims to liberal values. Representations of Palestinians as a violent group cast the entire Israeli-Palestinian conflict as a conflict of values between, as Wendy Brown has written, "thinking and tolerance, on the one hand, and . . . ignorance, bigotry, and fundamentalism on the other."[41] For Brown, writing a critique of the liberal value of tolerance, when Israel claims for itself the mantle of the thoughtful, the tolerant, the democratic, and the legal, the Palestinians are made to represent "bigotry and fundamentalism." Such oppositions between tolerance and fundamentalism seem to negate the possibility of Palestinian participation in liberal public spheres, because, as Brown confirms, "[t]he tolerant and the civilized think (for themselves); the bigoted and the barbaric merely follow instincts, leaders, crowds, or customs."[42] In other words, protecting liberal values comes to be used as a rationale for refusing to deal with a purportedly disruptive other, as in Seaman's comment to the *New York Times*, when he rejects Palestinians as a menace to democratic values, saying that they will exploit Israeli democracy to hurt Israelis. As these debates were covered in mainstream U.S. media and English-language Israeli outlets like the *Jerusalem Post*, Seaman aimed to fortify Israel's image as a liberal democracy, an image essential to its global standing and power. Surely these efforts were convincing for many. Seaman's contention that Palestinian journalists are a threat to Israeli democracy echoes George W. Bush's famous post-9/11 characterization of terrorism as not just a military attack but also an attack on the liberal democratic way of life, on freedom itself.[43]

Arguments that refusing to tolerate Palestinian extremism might be necessary in order to strengthen Israeli democracy have had an enduring presence in scholarship about Israeli press freedom. In legal scholar Pnina Lahav's edited volume entitled *Press Law in Modern Democracies*, published in the mid-1980s, Israel is placed in the company of countries like the United States, Sweden, and the United Kingdom. Israel is the only non-European country discussed other than the United States and Japan. Lahav's chapter on Israel mentions Israeli restrictions on interviews with figures affiliated with the PLO. Lahav wrestles with the conundrums this presents: "The prohibition was symptomatic of the increasing intolerance of the Israeli government toward opinions which are disagreeable to it. At the same time, one cannot deny that the Palestinian struggle for national liberation lacks a liberal spirit."[44] She concedes that Zionism was similarly illiberal before Israeli statehood, but she takes Palestinian illiberalism as a matter of essence. She concludes, "Given historical Jewish consciousness, the immediate colonial legacy, and the ever-present threat to national existence, Israeli democracy, and with it the Israeli press, have shown remarkable resilience."[45] Palestinian values are judged as a matter of unchanging culture, while Israeli values are evaluated in historical and political context. She determines that Zionism and liberal values are ultimately compatible, while the Palestinian struggle is irreconcilable with such values.

While Israeli rhetoric was bolstered by the U.S. War on Terror, the suggestion of an existential threat to Israel—that is, the threat to Israel's existence—has a long history of its own. Sometimes this threat is described as a material one, sometimes as discursive, sometimes both. To give just a few examples from the second Intifada, in early 2002, Israeli prime minister Ariel Sharon explained that suicide bombings had necessitated Israeli invasions of Palestinian cities in the West Bank because the bombings posed an existential threat to Israel. As he declared, "This is a battle for survival of the Jewish people, for survival of the state of Israel."[46] Similarly, in an article entitled "The Core of Muslim Rage," *New York Times* columnist Thomas Friedman argued that—beyond any actual bombings—this Muslim "rage poses an existential threat to Israel."[47] Discourses about an existential threat to Israel build on the strong moral consensus against genocide and the Holocaust, but they do so by making questionable analogies. In a sympathetic portrait of Seaman's work during the second Intifada, author Stephanie Gutmann paraphrased Seaman's own evaluation in the wake of a suicide bombing: "'[I]t is happening again,' he thought. 'Just as in the Holocaust or the Six Day War, we are fighting for our survival. This is not some PR campaign we are in; it's a war being conducted, and one of the battlefields is the media because they believe they can create doubt among Israelis, among supporters, and eventually affect us on the ground.'"[48] Yet, the logics of how scattered suicide bombings, the emotion of rage, or negative media coverage would lead to the destruction of the state of Israel—let alone a genocide against the Jewish people—are never spelled out.

Similarly, Israel's supporters often describe critiques of Israeli policies as both anti-Semitic and posing a threat to Israel's existence. They argue that these discursive threats to Israel warrant limits on free speech. In 2002, then Harvard president Lawrence Summers described divestment initiatives and academic boycotts geared toward criticizing the Israeli occupation of the West Bank and Gaza as a threat to the Jewish people: "Serious and thoughtful people are advocating and taking actions that are anti-Semitic in their effect if not their intent."[49] Summers's argument suggests a relationship between speech and action in this field, promoting an argument that certain forms of speech directed at a state should be proscribed because of potential violence against a group of people.[50]

I am not contending that we should dismiss the possibility that speech or symbolic action can incite or in some cases constitute violence, as in the case of hate speech. Instead, I want to argue that the ability to successfully reason that speech constitutes violence relies on the wielding of social or political power, and that ultimately this power is connected to material conditions. It is the more powerful party—in this case, supporters of Israel—that is able to assert that speech against Israel amounts to violence even as Israeli officials make statements that limit Palestinians' freedom of speech. Since the second Intifada began, supporters of Israel's hard-line policies have been able to argue that a wide range of speech constitutes violence against a state, in part by using arguments that resemble those of the U.S. authorities during the War on Terror. Using a logic that resonates in the United States buttresses Israel's claims because the United States is Israel's most important ally and is presumed to be a global bastion of freedom, just as Israel is presumed to be a bastion of freedom in the Middle East.

Another reason Seaman's statements might have been difficult to counter in public debate is their multiplicity. In addition to the arguments against Palestinians having GPO cards, presented in depth above, Seaman also made an economic protectionist argument, claiming that Palestinian journalists were taking Israeli journalists' jobs. As he told the *Daily Telegraph*, "The fact is that many of these jobs could be done by Israelis."[51] He additionally made the circular argument that Palestinian journalists' inability to renew their cards was a simple consequence of the intensification of the closure policy at the beginning of the second Intifada: "In order to be issued with a press card," Seaman explained, "you have to come to Israel and the closure doesn't allow this."[52] Such multiplicity and lack of cohesion of arguments—what Carol Greenhouse calls "discursive fracture"—can itself be a tactic by which authorities avert criticism.[53]

The aftermath of controversies surrounding Palestinians' GPO cards reminds us again that a fundamental reason Seaman's statements were effective was that they were enforced by a bureaucracy and an army. His speech acts relied on these very material conditions from the beginning to enforce his revocation of the GPO cards. These conditions remained important in the wake of legal challenges. In the spring of 2004, Reuters won its challenge to the GPO policy in the Israeli Supreme Court. The court declared that if Palestinian journalists had security clearance, they could not be denied press cards. It ruled the categorical refusal of passes for Palestinian journalists illegal. This should have set an important precedent for Palestinian journalists, but in the following year, only a few Palestinian journalists succeeded in reacquiring press cards. Under revised regulations, Palestinian journalists first needed to attain a work permit to enter Israel, a time-consuming and opaque process overseen by military authorities and involving extensive security checks, before they could be issued a three-month GPO card. Since security checks cannot easily be appealed, this meant that the granting of a press card remained at the whim of Israeli authorities. In a meeting with Joel Campagna of CPJ after the court decision, Daniel Seaman "made it clear that the process of obtaining cards would be difficult for Palestinian staff."[54] Bureaucratic offices within the executive branch issued the order to rescind the GPO cards, and their decisions proved difficult to challenge in a legal framework. They were the actions of what Butler calls a petty sovereign. Today, Seaman has departed from his post, but the restrictions on Palestinians holding GPO cards are even more explicit. As stated in the government-issued criteria for press cards:

> E. Cards and Certificates will not be given under these rules to any person convicted of an offense against state security. . . .

> F. Cards and Certificates will not be given under these rules to any applicant if the Director is of the opinion, after consultation with security authorities, that providing the Cards and Certificates may endanger the state security.

> G. Cards and Certificates will not be given to residents or citizens of enemy states, or to a resident of an area which is in an armed conflict with the State of Israel, unless the GPO Director is of the opinion, after consultation with security authorities, that the possibility of the existence of danger from such a resident or citizen to the welfare of the public and security of Israel, may be ruled out.[55]

The security qualification allows Israeli authorities to deny almost any Palestinian application, because designations of who constitutes a security risk are unilateral and cannot practically be appealed. Moreover, the statement that no resident of an area in armed conflict with Israel shall receive cards is another way of categorically denying Palestinians from the Gaza Strip, at the very least, from obtaining GPO cards. For Palestinians, GPO cards have become even more like—and dependent on—military permits. Though the right to free speech is meant to be universal, in fact, it must be secured in a political context, and for Palestinians, there is little way for them to escape the category of military subject.

If, because of the power of the military and the GPO, Seaman did not need to do all of this talking for the policy to be effective, why did he do it? On one level, Seaman was responsible for responding to press and legal inquiries. But it also seems plausible that the talk itself was politically advantageous. Just as not having GPO cards impeded both Palestinian journalists' practical work and also their claims to being unbiased professionals who could do their jobs anywhere rather than merely reporters with a small local beat, Seaman's talk about denial of the press cards not only effected a policy change but also undermined Palestinian journalists' claims to objectivity and professionalism. His talk threatened the fragile category of the Palestinian journalist and suggested that all Palestinians are not only epistemic others but also security threats. State speech did cultural as well as governmental work.

THE DANGERS OF BEING A THREAT

Being a security threat was hardly a discursive matter alone, as Palestinians knew too well. It was also an embodied status. During the Israeli incursions of 2002, many Palestinian men were rounded up and detained on the basis of their nationality, age, and residence alone. Journalists were caught up in these detentions. When GPO director Seaman spoke of the detention of Associated Press reporter Muhammad Daraghmeh from the early morning until the evening of April 16, 2002,[56] it was not that Daraghmeh was a reporter but that he was Palestinian which explained it all: "He was arrested just like dozens of other Palestinians were arrested."[57] Approximately fifty men had been detained in the same raid.

We have seen that Seaman's arguments defending the denial of press cards to Palestinians both drew upon and reaffirmed preconceptions of Palestinians as dangerous. Because these arguments worked in concert with other racialized discourses and practices within Israel,[58] they promoted an atmosphere in which soldiers could detain or shoot Palestinian journalists with impunity. The circumstances surrounding the deaths of the nine journalists killed by the IDF between 2000 and 2009 varied. Some observers contended that attacks on journalists exhibited a racialized logic in which Palestinians were regarded as being categorically different and of lesser importance than Jewish Israelis and foreigners. In a radio interview about Associated Press Television News cameraperson Nazeh Darwazeh's death during a confrontation between Palestinian youth and the Israeli military, Abed Qusini, a Reuters photographer from Nablus, explained:

> In the last two years we have had bad experiences with the Israeli army. They are dealing with us as Palestinians. In the curfew and in the bad situations, they stop us and they don't stop the foreigners. They say: "You are Palestinians before you are journalists." ... [A soldier] asked me for a Palestinian ID, he said: "You are a Nablus guy, you are under curfew. You are Palestinian before [you are a] journalist." They say always: "No immunity for Palestinian journalists."[59]

The use of the word "immunity" is telling. It suggests that all Palestinians are criminalized, and journalists are no exception. Qusini's description also underscores how Palestinians from "hot" areas of the occupied territories are especially stigmatized. Israeli photojournalist Avichai Nitzan made a similar argument. He was shot in the shoulder while he stood with several Palestinian journalists; the soldier apparently shot him believing he was Palestinian. Nitzan clarified in an interview with Canadian journalist Patricia Naylor,

> I was standing with another five or six Palestinian photographers, and the soldiers hate Palestinian photographers. For the soldier, I know from later he told people when they spoke to him that he thought it was a Palestinian photographer. And then he saw me being dragged over to his side and then he understood that I was of his own religion and served in the same army as he did and had a girlfriend and stuff. So I think that's when it hit him, because as long as it was an Arab, he didn't really care.[60]

Others felt that a disregard for press freedom put journalists at risk regardless of their nationality. In the documentary *In the Line of Fire*, Tim Heritage, a Reuters bureau chief during the second Intifada, suggested that the Israeli military was not eager to have journalists in the field of conflict, whether or not they were Palestinian:

> We have an incident a week probably where someone gets shot at. We routinely protest. We don't really hear anything back from the army. We demand investigations. We don't really get very much. . . . Why are we being shot at? Because they don't want us going places that everyone's doing things. They don't like us, they don't want—there's obviously a lot of things they don't want happening. They don't want us getting into the war zone or whatever. I'm not sure it's a deliberate policy or anything, I don't know if other people have suggested this to you, but I think it's just more haphazard, and there's a lack of control. There's a lack of sense of being punished if you do it, and we regard it at Reuters as a gross violation of media freedoms. I mean these are journalists going about their job, and being prevented [from] doing so.[61]

Definitively determining motivation or intent in such circumstances is almost impossible, especially without hearing from soldiers and their officers. Still, CPJ held Israel accountable for the pattern of shootings: "CPJ is concerned that in at least some of these cases, IDF soldiers may have targeted journalists deliberately (the IDF denies this). Based on the available evidence, we are convinced that the IDF has at the very least been guilty of gross recklessness."[62]

The West Bank and Gaza Strip are zones in which civilians' lives are valued less. Gideon Levy, a prominent Jewish Israeli journalist for *Ha'aretz* newspaper, gave his take on the shootings of journalists and the failure of the government to investigate them. He advised, "Don't separate shooting journalists from shooting all the others, because it's the same rules of the game today. There is no difference between journalists and others. That's the policy of the army, not to investigate. There are very few restraints. Your life is in danger. They [the IDF] don't take it seriously, and it will happen again."[63] The circumstances surrounding some of the deaths of Palestinian journalists evince this. In 2001, Muhammad al-Bishawi, a reporter for the Egypt-based Islamonline. net, was killed in an Israeli missile attack on a Hamas leader. He had been interviewing the Hamas leader when the missile strike occurred. Al-Bishawi's death was an unexceptional consequence of Israel's policy of extrajudicial killings. During the first five years of the second Intifada, the *Journal of Palestine Studies* counted at least 176 bystanders killed in extrajudicial killings, along with 322 targeted people, and 64 people killed in ninety-six other failed assassination attempts.[64] In December 2009, Basil Ibrahim Faraj, a cameraperson for the Palestinian Media and Communication Company, was injured along with three other media workers when his car was hit by shrapnel and debris from an Israeli attack on a Hamas-affiliated charitable organization. Faraj, who later died from his injuries, was just one of more than 1,300 people killed in Israel's three-week attack on Gaza, more than half of whom were civilians.[65]

In other instances, circumstances seem to indicate that soldiers could or should have known of journalists' professional identities. While working in Nablus and covering daytime clashes between Palestinian youths and Israeli troops in April 2003, Associated Press Television News cameraperson Nazeh Darwazeh was shot in the head by a single shot from a distance of ten to twenty meters. Darwazeh was wearing a fluorescent jacket marked "press," and the two other Palestinian journalists he was with were also wearing gear that marked them as journalists. Moments before the shooting, they had called out in English and Hebrew that they were journalists.[66] As with the GPO cards, identity and geography overlapped to especially endanger Palestinian journalists in the occupied territories: Palestinian journalists were doubly imperiled because they were Palestinians and they were in the occupied territories.

One of the most notorious and well-documented attacks on Palestinian journalists occurred in 1998, well before the second Intifada began. It illuminates Israeli tactics in dealing with shootings. On the evening of March 13, 1998, in the West Bank city of Hebron, IDF soldiers shot eight Palestinian journalists from news organizations including Reuters, AP, and ABC News with rubber-coated metal bullets. Hebron is one of the largest Palestinian cities, but it has a small population of Israeli settlers living in its downtown.[67] In the last decades of the conflict, it has been the site of some of the worst acts of settler violence against Palestinians as settlers motivated by religious nationalism wrest more and more territory from Palestinians within the city, and Israeli soldiers stationed there protect the settlers, even when settlers are the aggressors. That day, the journalists had been covering a settler march and Palestinian counterdemonstration in the city, but by the time of the shooting, demonstrators had begun to disperse. The journalists were readying to go home and were at least 200 meters from the Palestinian protesters when they heard gunshots. They shouted out that they were journalists, but the soldiers continued to shoot. The most seriously injured that night was a Palestinian soundperson who worked for Reuters, Nael Shiyoukhi, mentioned in the Introduction as a colleague and friend of Mazen Dana.[68]

The journalists managed to record what followed. The video begins after a rubber-coated metal bullet hit Shiyoukhi in his forehead and he has fallen to the ground. The camera's onboard light illuminates Shiyoukhi's prone figure. His colleagues call out to the soldiers to stop shooting and shout for an ambulance. As they attempt to rescue him, we hear more gunshots and the rescuers themselves are injured. The footage shows Shiyoukhi bleeding from his head as he is shot a second time. He pulls himself up on his elbows, and blood drips from his forehead. He is shot a third time, and he falls again. Finally, one of the journalists succeeds in pulling him away.

The video catalyzed wide coverage of the incident. It appeared on Israeli television the next day, alongside interviews with the Israeli military commander of Hebron and Nael Shiyoukhi himself. The Israeli military commander defended the IDF's actions: "The journalists were working within the mob. The soldiers acted in a reasonable way. You need to remember that Hebron at night is dark. It's difficult to see everything. The situation is very complex."[69] Yet, the footage reveals that the journalists were standing alone on that section of the street—indeed, no crowds are visible anywhere nearby—and that the scene was in fact well lit, in part because of the journalists' camera lights. After all, remarked Shiyoukhi himself in a later interview, if they could not see, how is it that soldiers managed to hit him three times?[70] Israeli spokespeople have frequently deployed the logic that Palestinian journalists were shot because they could not be distinguished from a Palestinian crowd, as after the death of Imad Abu Zahra (see box earlier). The commander's assertion echoes Seaman's comments about journalists being threats indistinguishable from the broader dangers posed by all Palestinians.

In the Israeli news report, Shiyoukhi, his head wrapped in bandages, spoke from his hospital bed. The Israeli journalist asked what he had to say to the soldiers, and he replied in clear, if accented, Hebrew: "I want to tell the soldiers not to shoot at us. We are not terrorists. I am a human being . . . and the soldier is also a human being. One doesn't shoot another for no reason. We are working together, all the time we work together. His job and my job . . . everywhere we work together and we should be friends. Why shoot at us?"[71] Here, Shiyoukhi not only draws on a humanist language but also takes professionalism to an unlikely extreme, purporting an equivalence between a soldier and a journalist as two people doing their jobs in the same place. He elides the obvious imbalance that the soldier holds a gun and acts from a position of political authority. Perhaps, speaking to an Israeli audience, the strongest assertion he feels able to make is one of balance, even as he is, visibly, the victim.

The commander's response to Shiyoukhi's shooting also exhibits a willful disregard for evidence, suggesting that Israeli authorities imagine their statements will be effective at quelling criticism even if they are implausible.[72] Israeli officials' refutation of eyewitness accounts and video footage indicates the presumptive power of state speech in the context of military occupation. They assume that what they say will be authoritative—or at least authoritative enough—perhaps because they do not have to be convincing to a Palestinian public, as this public is excluded from their polity, and perhaps because, in this case, no other official account would dispute their own. After all, the PA had its own history of repressing Palestinian journalists, and it lacked an effective public relations system for responding to such incidents. It was the Israeli officials' word against that of the Palestinian journalists.

In mainstream press coverage, the Israeli position was also shielded from serious criticism by textual norms of "balanced objectivity," discussed in depth in Chapter 1, wherein contrasting claims are often presented without conclusive evidence that would indicate which evidence is valid. For example, when the *Washington Post* reported about Nazeh Darwazeh's shooting, it presented it this way: "The soldiers would not discuss the matter [of the shootings of journalists] today. Their officers said the soldiers could not distinguish the reporters from the others at night. But Connie Mus, president of the Foreign Press Association, said the reporters were clearly distinguishable on videotapes."[73] Neither the *Post* nor the *New York Times*[74] quoted Shiyoukhi or any other Palestinian journalist who had been on the scene, and neither drew a strong conclusion about the truth of the events under consideration. Whether a reader deduces from such news coverage that the IDF's statements are reliable likely depends on one's preexisting opinion of the IDF.

One major challenge for human rights organizations working in such circumstances is holding governments accountable by demonstrating intent or willful neglect. The Committee to Protect Journalists generally categorizes journalists who die in the occupied Palestinian territories at the hands of Israeli soldiers as killed "in crossfire/combat," and not murdered, a term that is less ambiguous with regard to intent. For the Hebron incident, CPJ's analysis presented clearer evidence than that in the newspapers that the IDF was at fault, but such reports circulate much less widely than news articles. CPJ's report presented more details about the attack. Annual and special reports on violence against journalists during the second Intifada made clear that such events were not onetime incidents but rather that they "follow a long-standing pattern" in which "in some cases . . . the IDF fired only a few rounds, hitting journalists in the legs or camera-holding hand with what seemed like pinpoint accuracy."[75]

The difficulty of incontrovertibly attributing blame returns us to the theme of the line between speech and action, because some actions are dismissed as inconsequential, as saying nothing in political terms. A onetime random shooting would be unfortunate but not significant in the way that a pattern of violence is. Officials might convince the public that the former lacks political meaning, while when violence is represented as a pattern, it obviously signifies something. By putting actions in context and examining them in detail, CPJ's reports claim that Israel's actions are significant. Still, official Israeli responses to such violent events do their best to dismiss such significance. In such cases, a government representative often issues a statement for media and human rights organizations, but officials are aware that there will generally be few implications to what they say. Just as the intellectual or factual rigor of Seaman's arguments about the press cards was not integral to the execution of GPO policy, neither was the content of statements about shootings always of great consequence. Israeli officials performed a participation in transnational and Israeli public spheres by commenting about shootings, even if the content of what they said shed little light on the incidents.[76]

Noting that "the IDF's record of investigating cases in which journalists have been wounded or killed by IDF fire or physically abused by soldiers is dismal," Ann Cooper, executive director of CPJ, concluded in a letter to the Israeli military dated February 4, 2004, that the Israeli failure to investigate these cases "suggests official indifference that could be interpreted by field commanders and soldiers that the IDF tolerates improper or even criminal behavior."[77] Far from speech acts being effective in motivating an active policy, as they were when Seaman rescinded press passes, here official statements and the silence that followed colluded to promote an atmosphere in which there was, to return to the words of Tim Heritage of Reuters, a perilous "lack of control."[78]

In other cases, officials' responses to journalists' deaths adhered unapologetically to the overarching narrative of national security. After Israeli tank fire killed Italian journalist Raffaele Ciriello, Seaman was clear: "I am more afraid that an Israeli soldier will not shoot in such a situation and get killed than I am that the journalist will get killed."[79] Similarly, the IDF commented that journalists in the area had endangered themselves, because the area had been declared a closed military area. After British journalist James Miller was killed in Gaza, Seaman was again straightforward: "It's a split-second judgment, whether or not to shoot. I prefer that in situations like that, they shoot, because I prefer that there will not be a dead soldier."[80] The IDF deemed the unidentified officer believed to be responsible for the shooting blameless, and declined to bring criminal charges against him. According to the IDF, the officer had "allegedly fired his weapon in breach of IDF rules of engagement,"[81] but firmly connecting this to Miller's fatal neck wound was not possible. Official reactions to the shootings of journalists may thus enable violence against journalists by validating Israeli soldiers' sense that they are only defending themselves or fulfilling a mandate for national security, or that they will be protected no matter what they do. This is especially true when these official statements are echoed by other public discourse diminishing the importance of Palestinian civilian deaths at the hands of the IDF. Israeli responses to the shootings of journalists were one of many different ways in which states can, as anthropologist Winifred Tate has argued, "contribute to the production of impunity."[82]

There was, then, a paradox regarding what kinds of words and actions are regarded by various audiences as meaningful at this site. While officials defending the rescinding of Palestinian journalists' GPO cards asserted that Palestinian journalists' speech constituted a threat to Israel's security, Israeli authorities effectively maintained that their detentions and shootings of Palestinian journalists were accidental, that they had nothing to do with journalism at all, or that they were justified by security imperatives. The rhetorical multiplicity that Israeli officials presented in response to shootings resembles the same kind of "discursive fracture" seen in discussions about the GPO card.[83] By offering these multiple resignifications and denials, they attempted to limit the significance of the shootings in the global public sphere.

CONCLUSIONS:
A MOVEABLE BOUNDARY BETWEEN SPEECH AND ACTION

The combination of Israeli state speech and Israeli military actions has contributed to closing down possibilities for Palestinian journalists to work, and by extension, it has limited journalistic output for international media. Actions like stripping Palestinian journalists of their GPO cards have overlapping symbolic and material consequences. Many Palestinian journalists have been rendered incapable of covering events outside of a very narrow radius. The smallness of their beats has diminished their claims to expertise and cosmopolitan knowledge, and it has in some ways constrained their actual perspectives on the world. Shootings of journalists also made news production more difficult during the second Intifada, creating an atmosphere in which journalists knew that being on the scene could be dangerous. Talk about shootings of journalists by Israeli officials only entrenched these effects.

State speech like that of Daniel Seaman's about Palestinian journalists is made effective by three main factors. First, there are the material conditions of state sovereignty, most notably, in this case, the control of territory but also the materiality of bullets, handcuffs, and prisons that constrain Palestinian bodies and speech. Second, state speech is made effective by the established patterns and roles entailed in the mainstream news media representations of the state. Media amplify officials' speech, and the norms of balanced objectivity make it difficult to directly challenge what officials say in everyday reporting. Third, state speech is made effective through political and cultural formations. During the War on Terror, these formations have been transnational and have seemed to align U.S and Israeli concerns in opposition to Arabs and Muslims.

Just as Seaman's speech was fortified by his place from within a bureaucracy, Palestinians' abilities to participate in international institutions of media production are undermined by their statelessness. They do not have the proper accreditation to deal expeditiously with the very militarized circumstances they cover. They do not have freedom of movement to attain training, meet with their colleagues, or gain perspective by experiencing other social and political contexts firsthand. They cannot feel safe and secure while doing their work. Statelessness is an impediment both to free expression of the individual and also to the vitality of our interconnected world of news production.

Finally, this material helps us to think about the shifting line between innocent speech and dangerous action. It is not only state actions that enable state speech; it is also state speech that influences the abilities of journalists to work.

Israeli state speech contributed to erecting different borders between speech and action for various parties: Israeli speech was just speech, while Palestinian speech was sometimes regarded as threatening action. That is, Israeli officials and supporters of Israel blurred the categories of discursive and physical attacks on Israel to make discursive ones seem more dangerous, and argued that limitations on Palestinian journalists' speech were essential for Israel's physical security. Yet, this speech itself functioned as a kind of speech act. It maligned Palestinian journalists as biased and threatening, which in turn impeded their work. At the same time, when the Israeli army injured or killed Palestinian journalists, Israeli officials had discursive tactics for producing impunity for individual soldiers and the state as a whole. These actions, they claimed, were not politically significant. Israeli officials asserted that Israeli violence was merely the by-product of a larger conflict in which protecting Israeli security was of paramount concern. In short, the boundary between what is recognized as innocent speech and what qualifies as dangerous action is itself the product of political struggles. While speaking may seem to be an act unbound from physical constraints, the case of Palestinian journalists highlights the many ways in which material conditions, especially those concerned with a relationship to a state, produce a difference in the capacity of Palestinians and Israelis to speak.

AN INNOCENT EVENING OUT?
REPRESENTING CULTURAL LIFE AND RESISTANCE

"Palestinians Take Back the Night in Ramallah," published on August 31, 2004, in the Christian Science Monitor,[1] *is about the opening of Darna, a swank Ramallah restaurant. When I first read this article by Joshua Mitnick, a Tel Aviv-based journalist who has written for the* Wall Street Journal, *the* Washington Times, *and the* Jewish Week *in addition to the* Christian Science Monitor, *I was tickled to find a Palestinian restaurant making headlines thousands of miles away. The article even recounted Ramallah's history as a breezy summer getaway: "Pleasant weather and pastoral surroundings earned the tiny city the nickname 'the Bride of Palestine.'" It all seemed as innocent and agreeable as a good meal out.*

But a closer read of the article's opening started me thinking. Mitnick contrasted the restaurant with then PA president Yasir Arafat's besieged compound:

> *Just a few minutes drive from Yasir Arafat's half-destroyed headquarters, Usama Khalaf's version of upscale Ramallah dining is taking off.*
>
> *His restaurant called Darna occupies a grand renovated stone villa with high-ceilinged archways and a second-floor patio that draws scores of young Palestinians. It serves large dishes of innovative Middle Eastern fare, but, more importantly, offers fragments of normalcy, which has become so elusive during the past four years.*

This was the central premise, that the restaurant offered a return to normalcy for war-weary Palestinians. "I had an obligation to my hometown," the restaurant's owner explained in the article. "When they saw someone investing despite the closures and incursions, it gave people the willingness to stay."

The Palestinian readers I consulted recognized the news narrative of a return to normalcy (in Arabic, journalists might use the phrase al-raja' 'ala al-wada' al-tabi'i, *literally a return to a natural situation), but they harshly criticized this version of the narrative. As Khaled, a refugee rights lawyer accustomed to close textual analysis, responded, "Of course the question is, 'fragments of normalcy' for whom?" From his refugee camp home, he continued: "This place is for a particular type of people, people in Ramallah, politicians: the type of politicians who work with the PA and international organizations. It's people who have money who can go there."*

Indeed, the chasm between what some have taken to calling the "Ramallah bubble" and the rest of the West Bank—a divide which had only widened between 2004, when this article was published, and 2009, when I conducted these interviews—colored how readers saw the article. Makram, a Nablus-based student and blogger commented, "This happens only in Ramallah. If you had been in Nablus in 2002, you would know what I am talking about. Nablus was cut into three sections. There was no electricity or water. It was curfew all the time." One part of the article described how even under curfew another popular restaurant, Sangrias, stayed open, primarily for journalists:

> *Patrons desperate to break the monotony of the citywide lockdown surreptitiously found their way to the bar. "I used to open up when people would go home and the tanks would come out," [owner Danny] Jafar says. "Lights would be off and curtains would be drawn, but there were people inside. It was a hangout."*

Makram found this dissonant with his experience of having lived in Nablus during the second Intifada. "I don't think people would dare to go to dinner and then find their way back home, walking between tanks, saying 'Good evening' to the Israeli solders." In his estimation, it would be neither pragmatic nor appropriate. In sum, he said, "Ramallah is totally different. This does not represent the West Bank and the Palestinians. It represents Ramallah. . . . There is nothing like that in cities like Nablus and Jenin, and the journalist should have acknowledged this in the article." Perhaps Mitnick had not traveled far enough into the West Bank for this story.

By the time I conducted these interviews, a new sense of normalcy had in fact arrived in the West Bank. There were fewer Israeli military incursions, but the economy was still stagnant. I asked my readers how they would portray the economic situation in the years after the second Intifada waned. Lamia, a student of English in Nablus, suggested writing about small-store owners, "who suffer more, because they are poorer than the restaurant owner who could afford to pay $800,000" to open his restaurant, as the article noted the owner of Darna had

*done. Khaled suggested going to the vegetable market in his city. "For example,
an old woman who leaves her village of Battir at 5:00 A.M. carrying a bundle of
mint and parsley just to have a spot in the market—she wants to make do under
the occupation. Or the man who carries peaches from the village of Beit Ommar.
Yes, these are small projects, but each person has a story, and these stories reflect
on Palestinians' real lives, not Darna." He noted that the return to normalcy after
the Intifada had been woefully insufficient. After all, village women selling their
produce would prefer to go to Jerusalem, where they could get a better price, but
this was illegal and extremely difficult because of Israel's closure policies. Telling
their stories, he suggested, would present a richer portrait of economic life in the
stale aftermath of the Intifada.*

*Mitnick described how at Sangrias, "On a recent Saturday night, recordings
by American rapper 50 Cent played from a stereo in the courtyard and smoke
from nargilla water pipes floated among diners under illuminated walnut trees,"
and one evening at Darna saw an assembly of "20-somethings wearing American
athletic jerseys [who] had gathered to lounge in the patio." Readers recognized that
this article might lessen American fear of Palestinians by making them seem more
"Westernized," but they suggested other elements of Palestinian cultural life that
could have been covered in an article to show that ordinary Palestinians also know
how to have fun. Makram told of his poetry circle. Lamia, who was religiously
observant, said she resented the article's privileging of a Western ideal of fun re-
volving around consumption and evenings out. She spoke in a fluid mixture of
English and Arabic, using the former to emphasize a few key sentences and terms.
"I don't care about nightlife. . . . I care more about 'day life,'" she said, emphasizing
the last two words in English. What did this "day life" mean to her? She continued
mostly in Arabic: "If I wanted to talk [to an international audience] about this
'day life' in Nablus, I would clarify all the misconceptions that come from outside.
. . . I work with two British girls, and they think of themselves as 'the model, the
perfect model,' and that we are the odd ones." She said she enjoyed socializing in
a favorite café with her friends after class. "I've realized that it is not about how
many places you have to go to; it is about knowing how to have fun" wherever you
are. Similarly, Khaled took issue with the article's positing of the restaurant as a
"revival of a cultural scene." "This is not part of our culture, this Darna . . . I see
it as an effort to create a new culture, and not as a 'revival of the cultural scene.'"*

*Readers also analyzed what this article implied about the relationship between
military occupation and Palestinian culture. From one perspective, Khaled maintained that Palestinian culture had survived under Israeli occupation even when*

there were no wealthy institutions like Darna or the then newly built Ramallah Cultural Palace, also described in the article (and discussed here in Chapter 6), to support it. "Yes, society has been under occupation, but there have always been cultural activities . . . even inside much smaller organizations. Because Palestinian culture is part of our resistance, a proof of our identity. Even when there is a curfew, checkpoints, or whatever, Palestinians will always be singing, dancing, listening to music—because they consider it part of their resistance."

Voicing a different view, Makram said that if he were trying to send a message about the resilience of Palestinian culture, "I would convey in a way that we do have a social and cultural life, but it is not unaffected by the Israeli occupation. It is severely affected. Here it suggests that we don't have a problem with the Israeli occupation." Returning to the story about the bar and restaurant staying open during an incursion, he argued that when Israeli tanks are in the street, "it would be unrealistic for someone to put on a tuxedo and go to dinner."

Finally, the end of the article spurred commentary about the conundrums of generating American sympathy for Palestinians from Khaled, who was never at a loss for words when there was a pot of coffee and a pack of cigarettes nearby. The article read, "When the restaurant [Darna] was featured on Israeli television news magazine, Ariel Sharon is said to have been 'amazed' at the site of such an establishment, owner Khalaf recalled with satisfaction." In the article, Khalaf was given the last word: "We're not just suicide bombers. We don't love just blood. We have another face. Ultimately, we have a desire to live." Khaled presumed that Khalaf would be an appealing figure to most American audiences. "Khalaf is a successful person, as a businessman who invested his money well. . . . Americans will like him, because he is a success." But Khaled did not like what Khalaf's message insinuated about resistance. It suggests, he said, "There is a group of 'terrorists' among Palestinians" who force Israel to interfere in their lives, "but the majority of Palestinians just want to live." It is "as if the 'good' people among Palestinians, like Khalaf, are against resistance." Like many Palestinians, Khaled saw resistance against the occupation as an important element of being a good Palestinian, though he and other Palestinians debated what kinds of resistance were appropriate. Khaled feared that fostering sympathy for Palestinians in the way this article did was to promote a fundamental misunderstanding of Palestinian politics and society.

3 WORKING FROM HOME
Disinterest and the Scope of the Political

The limestone walls must have been a half-meter thick, cool in the summer, warm in the winter, smooth and solid all year long. Arches marked the passageways between rooms, and a dome lifted attention skyward. A journalist I call Rana had furnished the apartment to match its traditional architecture. The bright wool carpets were from the Hebron district in the south. Side tables featured Jerusalem's traditional blue and green tiles, painted with verdant leaves and succulent fruits. Political posters with the sleek graphic designs of decades past adorned doorways. Here, Rana regaled visitors with stories from her work. In ways one rarely read in published news texts, she recounted wrenching moments from interviews that illuminated how Palestinians perceived Israeli violence and Palestinian steadfastness. She described the most atrocious Israeli military operations she had covered and narrated the incidents that had most traumatized the foreign correspondents with whom she worked. As she told such stories, it was easy to interpret the wool carpets and stone arches as symbols of what was at stake for her in her work: the survival and vitality of Palestinian culture.

Rana had doubtlessly bought many of her furnishings from places she knew from her work throughout the West Bank, Gaza, and Israel. Only a handful of journalists, NGO workers, and activists routinely traversed the multitude of political and physical barriers that isolated the Palestinian communities in these places from each other. For the vast majority of people from the occupied territories, such travel was impossible due to Israeli closure policies; for those from east Jerusalem or inside Israel, it was still daunting. Perhaps this is why those like Rana so relished their travels. Being connected—being able to listen to so many different Palestinians' stories—was itself a political accomplishment in this time of widespread closure. By her own assessment, some of the articles she had produced for foreign correspondents had turned out well, and others poorly. Still, her relationships with Palestinians in so many places, and all of her own stories, were the unambiguous fruits of her labor, something from which she could not be alienated. Her home represented all of this in a material fashion.

Hassan's vision of making a home as a journalist was probably more common. Hassan, a reporter for a Western news organization, had moved from his family's village to one of the outlying cities of the West Bank to work as a journalist and then had relocated again to the PA's de facto capital, Ramallah, when he received a promotion. When I asked Hassan to describe his career trajectory, he told me briefly about his politically oriented student journalism. Then he described in detail how each of his subsequent professional choices had been rewarded by a growing salary. When I met him, he and his family were renting a comfortable apartment as they waited to move into a condominium they had purchased in one of Ramallah's new buildings. On a visit to the construction site, Hassan's teenage children staked out their rooms, and his wife, a civil servant, extolled the views. Buying the Ramallah apartment signaled his family's hard-earned financial success and would, he hoped, ensure them comfort in the years to come.

On another afternoon, I ran into Hassan as he was covering a springtime demonstration against the separation barrier on the edge of a nearby village. It was Land Day, an annual remembrance of Palestinian protests against Israeli land expropriations in the Galilee in 1976.[1] This year, Land Day had special urgency in this Ramallah area village. When completed, the separation barrier would isolate the village from its agricultural land and restrict farmers' abilities to work. Hassan and I stood on a hill overlooking the area of the demonstration. Photographers disappeared behind curtains of tear gas below while we looked out on geese on the adjacent farms, new spring leaves on the fig branches, an older man resting in the shade of a tree. Hassan, who was working on a feature story about Land Day for a Palestinian paper in addition to doing basic reporting about the demonstration for a Western news organization, relished these bucolic details. Someone was riding a horse nearby. I inquired as to what purpose the horse might serve for its owner. "Perhaps it's just for fun," Hassan replied. "It's nice to have a horse." Hassan, for all of his reporter's pragmatism, was not lacking in whimsy.

He told me that he had wanted to build a house in a village like this one, but practicalities prohibited him from doing so. His wife preferred being in the city for the sake of their children's schools and her own commute. Hassan, too, recognized that Israel could install a checkpoint at any time, rendering it difficult for him to cover breaking news from an out-of-the-way village. Looking out at the green countryside, he said that in his retirement he would like to have a small farm, and so we talked about the different trees that would make up his orchard and whether he should tend goats or sheep or chickens. As we watched the white spirals of tear gas spin through the air and fog the valley below, he assured me there would always be space for me to visit. Like Rana, he was hoping his work as a journalist might lead to his own version of a good Palestinian life. Certainly Hassan sought to create a middle-class lifestyle for his family, but part of his dream was also to be a farmer connected to the land as his family had been for generations before and to someday feel secure in that land as no Palestinians did during the second Intifada.

When I arranged an interview with Adnan, another reporter for a Western news organization, we met close to his house and walked to where he lived. As we wound through narrow streets, he told me that his family had recently moved. They had once lived in Jerusalem, but then, in the relatively optimistic late 1990s, they had bought a more spacious home on the outskirts of the city, expecting that this area would be part of a future Palestinian state. When the second Intifada started, checkpoints cut him off from work, so they moved closer to Jerusalem. A few years later when the wall was built, it disrupted Adnan's commute and his children's routes to school, so they bought the apartment where they currently lived at prices inflated by the political changes. The neighborhood where he now resided was cramped, the kind of place where children competed with cars in narrow alleyways. Many of the walls in his neighborhood were painted white, but the streets were strewn with trash. Adnan finished telling me about these peripatetic years just before we began climbing the stairs to his penthouse. He apologized for the lack of an elevator. "So, do you want to see the house?" he asked with a smile as he opened the door. Inside, their furniture looked new and welcoming, but I could tell by his lingering shortness of breath that this was not his ideal home. During his interview, he chronicled the frustrations of working with foreign editors and Palestinian authorities. But, he said, he needed to continue working as a journalist until his children made it through college. Adnan hoped to send at least one child to the United States or to Israel's Hebrew University to study.

Rana's, Hassan's, and Adnan's relationships to work and home life indicate how career, domicile, and national politics can be interrelated in the West

Bank. Like virtually all professionals anywhere, journalists are laboring to support their domestic lives. The building of a home in the West Bank or Gaza Strip can hardly be isolated from national politics, neither for journalists nor for any other Palestinians. Being comfortable at home requires political stability and, many Palestinians would say, self-determination, since Israeli zoning regulations, checkpoints, walls, and land expropriations constrict normal domestic life. Politics shape domestic aspirations in another way as well. For many Palestinians, a good home is one that is palpably Palestinian, whether that Palestinian-ness manifests itself in the building materials, the décor, the backyard garden, or more simply, the habits of home.[2]

American journalistic ethics center on disinterest, a concept that hinges on a separation between the politics journalists cover and the lives they live. Disinterest is related to objectivity, but it more explicitly addresses the identities of producers and what they do outside of work. To ensure disinterest, ethical standards of U.S. media organizations may ask that American journalists avoid campaigning for candidates, participating in protests, financially benefiting from information gathered or connections made during their work, and having cozy relationships with powerful sources. These ethical standards assume that in eschewing these kinds of activities, journalists can prevent the appearance of a conflict of interest. The ethical stance of disinterest is related to the project of professionalizing journalism, a mode of authorizing journalism as a pursuit of properly educated, independent actors.[3] In this sense, journalism echoes older and more explicit norms in the sciences in which knowledge production was charged to wealthy men whose judgment could be trusted because it was not colored by want.[4] We might say, the ethical stance of disinterest builds on assumptions that knowledge production is an undertaking for individuals who are already comfortable at home. Such people require neither political change nor extra income. This vision of journalistic disinterest presumes that some people are not vulnerable to the vicissitudes of politics, or that politics is isolated in a public sphere quite distinct from the private sphere of one's life.

It is hard to conjure what disinterest might mean for those living under occupation, where few people are untouched by political struggles over sovereignty. It is often assumed that the politics of sovereignty exist in a separate realm from the domestic sphere. I argue here that in defining values such as disinterest we must analyze the place of the politics of sovereignty in a particular context.[5] Theories that regard politics as either neatly fitted into a particular sphere or always utterly pervasive can miss the ways in which the location, shape, or energy of politics is itself an ethnographic and historical question. In certain moments, politics can have momentum and seep into domains usually isolated from them, or state politics can feel as though they are in retreat. To put this in terms of the field theory referenced in Chapter 1, we must ask how autonomous other spheres of cultural production are from the field of state politics—if they are autonomous at all—for disinterest is only conceivable if there is space outside of the political realm. I draw here on similar arguments made about other categories of social analysis. Talal Asad has critiqued the idea that the modern European category of religion is a transhistorical and trans-cultural sphere marked off from politics and society.[6] These assumptions about religion have led to negative judgments that Arab societies are unable to be truly modern because they cannot properly separate the private and the public. In a similar way, assumptions about what spaces of life the political should oc-cupy and where the private life of the individual should begin can stigmatize Palestinians as unable to stand apart from politics. On some occasions, these ways of stigmatizing Palestinians as unable to separate themselves from politics may seem like disingenuous tactics to disqualify Palestinians' voices. But the plausibility of these arguments also relies on a basic misunderstanding of how politics are located in different systems of rule and for people variously posi-tioned within these systems. Military occupation is one of the most obvious cases in which the politics of sovereignty intrudes, in an everyday and pervasive way, in arenas of life often presumed to be free of state politics.

Yet even here what counts as political depends on perspective, and the ability to authoritatively define something as political or apolitical is a mat-ter of power.[7] The specific contours of the politics of sovereignty and how they interact with other parts of society in this and other contexts is a crucial ethnographic question precisely because ethnography can be a good way of investigating social phenomena from subaltern positions. Headline news can be regarded as a proxy for the dominant definition of the political. In study-ing how Palestinian journalists inhabit and negotiate the porous boundary be-tween "news" and "life," we can illuminate the configuration of the political for those living under military occupation. American feminists of the late 1960s and early 1970s made a similar argument in asserting that the personal is politi-cal and that a false division between the public and the private obscures how power operates to produce that division; these assertions widened the scope of their struggle for justice.[8] Likewise, locating the political here delineates how power operates, and how it closes down certain possibilities for depoliticized, or disinterested, subjectivities. As we will see, understanding the contours of the political is also an important point of departure for a more nuanced understanding of Palestinian journalists' own professional ethics.

BECOMING JOURNALISTS

The professional trajectories of Palestinian journalists demonstrate the changing significance of the professional stance of disinterest, and illuminate how the political realm is not delimited from the rest of society in the Palestinian context. While the West Bank and Gaza Strip were under direct Israeli occupation from 1967 to 1994, Palestinian journalism was intensely politicized for both ideological and practical reasons. Journalism was a nationalist pursuit. Journalists were entrusted with the task of "consolidat[ing] and translat[ing] national activity which has flourished and grown up against the occupation," as one Palestinian newspaper editor, Ma'amun as-Sayyid, put it in a roundtable with Palestinian journalists published in the Jordanian newspaper *Al-Dustur* in 1980.[9] Another Palestinian journalist, Abed al-Latif Ghit, confirmed, "The press here is an attempt at national expression, and every person with national sentiments also has ambitions in that area. For us the press is not a profession, nor is it a hobby, but a need and a means of expressing national problems."[10]

But it was not only that journalists tended to be committed to the national project because they saw the press as a tool in the liberation struggle; being nationally committed also gave them tools integral to being a journalist. At that time, being a member of the PLO was illegal under Israeli military law, and therefore the identities of the PLO leadership in the occupied Palestinian territories were not public information. The political leadership was available for comments and interviews only to those with the necessary connections. The realm of formal politics at this time was not public. All of this—so different from norms of politics in liberal theory—made disinterest an impractical motivating ethic for journalists.[11]

It might also be said that statelessness reorganized career goals, pushing more people into journalism because of limited career options. Some had been politically active or wanted to be politically active, but they could not find a way to make money to live out of these aspirations. When, in 2005, I asked one journalist, Shafiq, why he had become a journalist in the 1980s, he answered: "I studied Middle East studies and political science. I had a dream of being an ambassador or whatever in the future, but we didn't have the state that I imagined. In 1986, after I graduated, I was unemployed for a few months, and we had some contacts with [a major West Bank newspaper]. So the editor invited me to join the team." Shafiq confirmed that Palestinian journalism before the establishment of the PA was overtly nationalist: "When I started working as a journalist, . . . I used to look at journalism's role as [a way] to mobilize the people. . . . Later I started working as a professional journalist and learned from my contacts with the foreign and the Israeli press that this is not the role of a journalist."

As in other locations around the world,[12] these local journalists became sources for foreign correspondents. This was especially the case during the first Intifada, from 1987 to 1993, when Palestinian political action refocused in the occupied Palestinian territories after having been centered in PLO bases in the Arab world in the previous decades. As the Western press grew more interested in stories from the occupied territories, many Palestinian journalists for Western news organizations obtained their jobs indirectly *because of* their involvement with Palestinian politics. This, after all, was what gave them access and expertise, given that political figures were not public figures in the ordinary sense. Some reporters who had worked in Palestinian journalistic organizations initially conceived of assisting international news organizations as doing nationalist work by communicating Palestinian perspectives to an international audience. They saw this as a complement to their primary careers in local journalism. Shafiq recalled how he began working with international journalists while employed at a prominent Palestinian newspaper in the 1980s: "I remember the first time a foreign journalist asked to pay me. I kept resisting for fifteen minutes, saying, 'No, I'm doing it for free as a volunteer.' You know, I thought, 'We [Palestinian journalists] can help foreign journalists. I'm being paid by my newspaper.' So I felt as a Palestinian I can help and convey the message." Now he expresses reservations when he evaluates the effects of his work with the Western media organizations. Even his valuation of the economics of different kinds of journalistic work has shifted. Today he uses the income from working as a producer for foreign journalists to do NGO work developing Palestinian journalism.

Another writer, who had been a poet in his college years, followed a similar professional trajectory. His entrée into Western journalism came after he published a series of articles in a Palestinian newspaper about the burgeoning Islamic movement during the first Intifada. Though he himself had been affiliated with Fatah, the largest and centrist party that dominated Palestinian politics for decades, the Islamic activists were happy to talk to him because they did not have their own media outlets at the time. Western journalists followed up on his reporting, and soon one offered him a job. He too has become disillusioned with working for international media organizations, and though he did not leave his job with the foreign press, he returned to poetry as a way of expressing himself more freely.

If politics was the path many took to journalism, others entered the field from other neighboring professions, including photography. These were pragmatic career decisions for journalists seeking to make a living. They signal a different dimension of the location of politics under occupation. Several Palestinian photojournalists started working for news organizations only after working in community photography: studio, wedding, and tourist photography. Those who worked with low-paying media outlets and who had family businesses continued to work in conventional commercial photography even as they established careers as journalists. That people should move between these two fields indicates the extent to which financial pressures or an interest in the craft of photography—rather than ideological interest—may have motivated their photojournalism.

One Armenian family shared the responsibilities of multiple kinds of work in photography.[13] Together, mother, father, and son staffed a studio in Jerusalem, the walls of which displayed poster-size images of beautiful places in the occupied Palestinian territories and beyond. At the studio, they documented the milestones of Palestinian life, both sentimental and bureaucratic: early childhood portraits, passport-style photos required to obtain Israeli-issued identity cards at age sixteen, graduation pictures, and wedding portraits. Their photography of the region circulated in tourist publications.

The father, Atom, had been working in photography since he was a child. He started working in a photography shop in order to help support his family just a few years after they became refugees in 1948. By the late 1950s, he was an expert in the latest camera equipment. His foray into journalism began when he was a teenager:

> One day, the owner of *Filasteen* newspaper came [to the photography shop] and said that they wanted a photographer to accompany a reporter. The boss said that he had no qualified person available, but I told him in Armenian that I wanted to go. When the journalists heard that, they were surprised. . . . The boss gave me the camera and I knew how to use it. I went to the Jerusalem airport at Qalandia, and a UN plane landed. A person came out of the plane, but I could not tell who it was. The guest suddenly stopped and approached me. He said that this was the first time he had seen a young boy as a photojournalist. He asked me

who I worked for, and I told him that I worked for a newspaper. I was wearing sandals and the simplest clothes. He asked me how the pictures would turn out, and I replied to him in English that the next day he'd be able to see the pictures in the newspaper. That person was [U.N. secretary general] Dag Hammarskjöld.

Atom had been captivated by his first brush with history as a journalist.

He would continue to mix community photography and photojournalism in his early years. After the start of the Israeli occupation in 1967, he was repeatedly detained for questioning by the Israelis, because he was presumed to have been in so many different homes for his work, and thus to have information about social and political networks. But, as he said, "One thing I am good at, and why everyone wanted me to be their photographer, is that they know I don't talk." In those days, Palestinian families trusted only wedding photographers who demonstrated great discretion to photograph their daughters. It was not only the technical skills of camerawork that carried over when he began working in journalism; it was also his ability to maintain professional connections by using a combination of restraint and publicity. He continued his work with international news agencies, often doing video recordings. By 2005, he had mainly retired from journalism, but a lucrative short-term contract convinced him to go to Iraq for a U.S. network just after the Iraq War started.

A younger photojournalist from another city in the West Bank, newly employed with an international agency, had also been an experienced photographer from a young age because his father had a photography studio. However, as an adult, he had chosen to become a musician. He belonged to a band, and he DJ-ed programs on one of the many local radio stations that prospered in the late 1990s. When the second Intifada began and casualties began to mount, the light popular music programs he had been hosting were regarded as inappropriate. One day he happened to be at a demonstration, and he thought to call into his radio station with news of what was happening. With that he launched his new career in journalism. From his work as a reporter in local radio he started to work as a backup for other photographers, and finally secured a job with a Western photography agency. A drum remains in his office, a reminder of what he would have preferred to be doing.

A few photojournalists had experience in artistic photography. A Palestinian citizen of Israel spoke of how he had practiced photography as a hobby before working for alternative Israeli news outlets, mainstream Israeli newspapers, and finally international news agencies. Another photojournalist had studied fine art and film production in Europe, but upon his return to the Arab world he encountered not only a dearth of jobs but also disapproval from his family concerning his career in fine arts. He began to work in weddings and advertising. After working for a low-paying Palestinian newspaper, he found a job with an international news organization. When he spoke to me of his work, he often explained the aesthetic dimensions of decisions he made.

Some people, especially drivers, translators, guides, and those involved with the business end of journalism, happened upon work in the field of journalism by way of careers in tourism. These individuals may not actually identify as journalists (*sahafiyin*), but instead may say that they "work with journalists" (*bashtghil ma' sahafiyin*). One man had operated a successful alternative tourism business, wherein he would give visitors bus tours of Jerusalem that highlighted inequities between Palestinian neighborhoods and Israeli settlements in east Jerusalem. When the second Intifada started, few tourists were venturing into the area, but journalists were plentiful. He began working as a fixer. His deep knowledge of the lived geographies of local politics and his ease with hosting international guests rendered him as effective in working with journalists as he had been in working with tourists. Both kinds of work were politically gratifying for him.

For another man, both tourism and media were good business. He had been employed in the management of a renowned Jerusalem hotel for fifteen years, but, he told me, he left in frustration when he found no remaining opportunities for advancement, suggesting that Palestinians could go only so far in the organizational hierarchy. He took a job at a luxury hotel in Bethlehem a short while before this hotel closed down at the start of the second Intifada. After about six months of unemployment, he took a job at a new Palestinian journalism production company that provided studio space, satellite uplinks, and other technical services for journalists. He remarked that he had the same responsibilities at his new post as he had in his previous post: "public relations," as he termed it. When I asked what his company had over the well-established Israeli production company with which it competed, he remarked enthusiastically, "They have me! I know everyone, and I can take care of them." Having worked at a hotel in Jerusalem for so many years, he said, he had excellent relationships with many journalists. These crossovers highlight a telling conjuncture. Tourism and journalism are two cultural practices central to Palestinian society through which Palestinians interact with Europeans and Americans. Each has its commercial and political dimensions, especially with the flourish-

ing of alternative tourism in the latter half of the second Intifada and in its aftermath. Moreover, they generally have an inverse relationship with each other:
when there is less breaking news, tourism thrives, and when breaking news is
bountiful, tourists tend to stay away.

Some Palestinians became journalists after training in a different field entirely, when demand was high for journalists but low in many other fields. In describing how he came to work as a fixer for Western news organizations in 1994,
a U.S.-trained engineer explained in perfect English:

> I started by sheer coincidence. I had studied biomedical engineering in the United
> States, and I had lived there about five years. When I came back, the economy
> was really slow. It was a bad situation in the Palestinian territories for selling
> biomedical equipment, which is what I wanted to do. The first Friday after the
> massacre at the Ibrahimi mosque in Hebron, protests were expected in various
> places, including at Al-Aqsa mosque. My in-laws were living 100 meters from
> the mosque, and their roof overlooks al-Haram al-Sharif. So [a major European
> news network] wanted to film from there to have a clear view. My mother-in-law
> asked me to go upstairs with them, just to watch over. I got to talking with the
> journalists. One asset all Palestinians have is that they are politically educated.
> They know what is going on. I explained briefly what had happened the week
> before, and they liked my attitude and how I spoke and presented myself, so after
> the prayer finished, they asked me to go down and do some street interviews
> with them. And the end of the day, they offered me a job.

He took the position, he said, because of the difficulty he was having finding
a job in his field, and because "it was exciting to hang around with these international TV correspondents." He said that in his experience, his bilingual
communication skills and his political knowledge were more integral to his
success than any formal training in journalism would have been. As for the "art
of reporting," he learned that, he said, "on the job."[14]

As the second Intifada wound down, journalists once again made plans
for alternate careers. One experienced photojournalist predicted that talented
photojournalists would continue working for international media while others
would have to shift to less lucrative work. Another photojournalist published
a book of Intifada photos and then established a website that sells pictures of
nature, holy sites, food, and Palestinian traditional dress. A few others made
their way to Iraq for short-term contracts. Some of the most successful photojournalists who experienced the most violence during the Intifada accepted

transfers outside the West Bank, where they could continue in their career with less fear of being injured or killed. It was another way of adapting to changing political circumstances while striving to support their families in the most effective way possible. They knew they were lucky if they stumbled upon fulfillment along the way.

In examining the shifting relationships between journalism and the related fields of political activism, photography, and tourism, we can see how the politics of sovereignty seep into seemingly unrelated fields like wedding photography. These pragmatic interconnections map the sweeping reach of the political in the occupied territories. Palestinian journalists are not disinterested in the events they have covered; indeed, these events condition their lives at home as well as their career choices. But it is difficult to generalize about the specific ways in which political circumstances condition their lives and career choices. The fact that before and during the first Intifada a political activist had connections and skills that facilitated becoming a journalist may seem to signify that Palestinian journalists are blatant nationalists, while the fact that wedding photographers became photojournalists seems to suggest that journalists are only opportunists. Yet, both of these career trajectories are more complex than they seem: Political activists became journalists to make a living, while wedding photographers-turned-photojournalists found that the skill of discretion needed for each kind of photography overlapped in surprising ways.

AN ERA OF PROFESSIONALISM AND UPRISING

After the Oslo Agreement established the PA and granted it administrative control over parts of the occupied Palestinian territories, the political realm that had been utterly illicit became public and institutionalized in a parliament, a judiciary, and most prominently, a presidential office. Broad shifts occurred in the relationship between Palestinian journalists and the political figures they represented. Universities established or strengthened programs in journalism, and international organizations conducted journalism trainings that were meant to foster democratic institutions of the anticipated Palestinian state. This formal journalistic training emphasized the values of Western-style objective journalism at the same time journalists were adapting to a new political atmosphere. A new ethos emerged as journalists developed the investigative skills required to cover, as independent journalists rather than allies, the new government entity. In general, however, major Palestinian media outlets were restrained from being critical of the PA. Before and during the second Intifada, the three major daily newspapers had financial ties to the Fatah-controlled PA, and the PA committed serious breaches of press freedom, shutting down media outlets temporarily and coordinating physical attacks on Palestinian journalists who had reported material adverse to the PA.[15]

Just as important, the establishing of the PA changed the orientation of the Western media toward Palestinians and the idea of Palestine. Western media organizations came to regard Ramallah as an incipient national capital, and they consolidated their journalistic resources there by hiring more Palestinians. As discussed in Chapter 1, these Palestinian journalists, especially those working with news agencies, were required to maintain a clear distinction between work and politics. They were forbidden from participating in demonstrations or other political activities; they had to obtain permission from their superiors before speaking to other journalists or researchers about their work as journalists. For journalists working in Ramallah especially, the realm of the political assumed a somewhat different, more delimited shape. They covered official events and needed to cultivate a combination of distance and familiarity with officials that might be familiar to journalists working for news agencies in other national capitals.

Here again, economic considerations were key to how journalists regarded their jobs. The growth of positions in international journalism in the West Bank and Gaza Strip during the Oslo period and the second Intifada was part of concurrent cultural and economic trends toward professionalization in international organizations, particularly internationally funded NGOs.[16] By the middle of the Intifada, the private sector was in a state of collapse, and positions with the PA were low-paid. Working for an international organization was considered one of the few paths to economic stability. Many positions in both NGOs and journalism required college degrees and stressed Western notions of professionalization. Like NGO workers, many journalists could feel that they were simultaneously contributing to their society and building a better future for their families—even as they often felt torn between local and international agendas.

While the Oslo period had made for an enduring shift in how journalists regarded their professional identities, such that they clearly could not occupy roles of political actors, at the height of the second Intifada politics could not be cordoned off from the rest of society. News played out nightmares and organized dreams. Smart girls often expressed their desire to be news broadcasters, just as tough boys were eager to get their hands on a video camera to become photojournalists. Journalists were everywhere because news—events obviously marked as political—was everywhere.

The pervasiveness of politics sometimes made it easier for journalists to produce news. They covered events at checkpoints simply by way of going about other business. One journalist told me that when the second Intifada began he had been living in Jerusalem but working primarily in Ramallah. At that point, the checkpoints were newer and more erratic, and they demanded more coverage, so he would take pictures of the checkpoint each day on his way to work. On several occasions, I ran into photographers from the West Bank who were picking up papers or equipment from Qalandia checkpoint, because they could not enter Jerusalem. They always brought their cameras along, and they would stop for a few pictures of the latest developments: a new set of turnstiles expanding the effective size of the checkpoint, bulldozers working on the separation barrier nearby, or a new coil of barbed wire. There is a paradox, of course, in journalists making the most of their enclosure to do their work, but this space of constraint-made-opportunity is where these journalists live and work.

Likewise, one could run into news while going about one's personal business. One day a journalist exclaimed to me happily, "You know it really pays off to be in touch with people!" He described how he had contacted a cousin living in another city. While asking her about her own life and activities, he was led to an interesting story, which he consequently researched and wrote. The boundary between work and social life is permeable for journalists and many others in Palestinian society because familial, social, professional, and political networks are dense and valuable, and the politics of sovereignty reaches so far into everyday life.

Beyond being about the everyday, journalism entails domestic labor, too. Homes are not an uncommon location of news production. I accompanied Palestinian journalists to the homes of farmers whose land had been confiscated for the separation barrier and families who had lost children and parents. We drank tea and coffee and orange soda; we sat on the fanciest couch in the house, or we sat on plastic chairs that were replacements for furniture destroyed in an army incursion. Sometimes interviewees' tears punctured the restraint of an interview; on other occasions, journalists themselves wept. Sometimes children listened in on the worst part of a story, and sometimes they served cold drinks carefully presented on shiny trays. Often, satellite news was on mute in the background. These scenes indicate how the domestic and the political seep into one another in ways both routine and painful.

Palestinians are famous for splendid spectacles of hospitality, and journalists—whether foreign or Palestinian—are special kinds of guests. On the occasions when I was swept into these performances of Palestinian culture, I recognized the multiple purposes they can serve, quite aside from gustatory pleasures. I was treated to some of the most elaborate meals of my stay when I inhabited the role of foreign journalist. In Nablus, I received a lunch invitation from a man I had interviewed whose brother, a midlevel militant leader, had been killed in an Israeli operation. First he showed me around his family's overcrowded and underfurnished refugee camp apartment. It was a succinct and sad education in the lived socioeconomics of the second Intifada. Then we sat down in a room very nearly plastered with pictures of his slain brother. We shared a deliciously spiced meal of rice with lamb and vegetables topped with cashews, alongside roasted chicken and *mulukhiyya*, a spinach-like soup that could have been a meal on its own. (On such occasions it did not escape me that it was often the men who did the inviting and the women who did the cooking.) Hosting internationals gives Palestinians the chance to tell their stories on their own terms and schedules and to probe guests for their perspectives.[17] Hosting also presents the opportunity for a display of an element of Palestinian culture about which Palestinians are proud.[18]

Like nonjournalists, Palestinian journalists also host foreign correspondents as a way of showing guests a different side of Palestinian life, deepening relationships, and perhaps taking matters onto their own turf. Palestinian producers and fixers may invite foreign correspondents out to their favorite *sha'bi* (literally, "popular," or "of the people") restaurant, or to a fancier establishment. One journalist told me that she always tried to invite journalists with whom she worked to dine in Palestinian cities, like Jenin, that would be off the beaten path for most foreign correspondents so that they could experience a novel vantage of Palestinian society. Palestinian journalists might also invite the foreign correspondents with whom they work to dine with them in their homes. In his book *A Season in Bethlehem, Newsweek* correspondent Joshua Hammer describes how Samir Zedan, a businessman-turned-fixer, initiated contact with him to offer his services. Then, perhaps recognizing that Hammer was intrigued by his life in the historically Christian town of Beit Jala, Zedan invited him to several "Sunday afternoon feasts" with the family.[19] Once again, such occasions serve multiple purposes. For one thing, they secured Hammer and Zedan's relationship. But they were also substantively important for Hammer's understanding of Palestinian politics and society. As he expanded his reporting into a book, he drew upon descriptions of his fixer's taste for Palestinian-made Taybeh beer and his host's loquacious wife to paint a portrait of Palestinian Christian society and contrast it with the rest of Palestinian society. "It was through Zedan," he writes, "that I began to look at the world through Palestinian Christian eyes."[20] As always, one must recognize that a key informant offers a partial vision of a society.

In many ways, then, the second Intifada was an especially complicated period for Palestinian journalists. On the one hand, top journalists had "professionalized" and adopted some of the values associated with Western journalism. On the other, politics reached deep into peoples' lives in the most conspicuous ways, and the number of journalists working in outlying areas increased. Recognizing the personal stakes of the events journalists were covering was unavoidable. Their very homes were often at stake. The sense of a common purpose of ending military occupation shared by virtually all Palestinians sometimes brought professionalized journalists into conflict with militants and political activists, in part because some of the latter assumed that all Palestinians should support their movements. One news agency cameraperson told me of a time when he was summoned by an armed group to record an unspecified event. This event turned out to be the shooting of a Palestinian collaborating with Israeli security officials. He found himself filming an execution. "I had seen lots of bodies, and I had seen lots of shootings," he said, "but I had never seen such an intentional killing happen right before my eyes." Then, one of the militants thought better of the public relations image they had created, and forced the journalist to destroy the tape, threatening him in the process. The journalist had been appalled by what he had seen—but he felt that once they had invited him to film, the tape was his. On another occasion, a militant group charged an Al-Jazeera cameraperson with not covering their events enough. They threatened him and prohibited him from coming to a rally as punishment. The journalists in this city called a meeting and discussed the situation with the militants. They contacted neither their bosses nor outside free press organizations. They were confident that they could resolve the conflict by their local connections, because they were, as he said, "*abna' al-balad*," or sons of the city.[21] As I detail below, such social and political skills are a hallmark of Palestinian journalism.

Militants and activists occasionally asked journalists to undertake political acts that would compromise their work: for example, to avoid photographing a stone-throwing youth because it could lead to his arrest, or to transport weapons across a checkpoint using their press credentials. Concerning the stone-throwers, journalists generally continued with their work, concluding, reasonably, that Israeli intelligence has many sources of information other than their pictures, including collaborators. On occasion, youth were pleased by these pictures anyway, a dynamic I explore in Chapter 5. Had protesters wished to hide their identities, they could have done so, for example, by wearing kaffi-yehs as masks, as first Intifada activists often did. As for arms transport, journalists were adamant that they never became involved in such forms of resistance. One photojournalist who worked outside Ramallah expressed his opposition to doing such work by insisting that *all* of Palestinian society was involved in a struggle against Israeli occupation, but that within this struggle a division of labor was imperative: "In order to be effective in our society's struggle, each person must carry out a specialized duty. A journalist cannot do the work of a militant." Echoes of journalists' viewpoints from the 1980s can be heard in his statement. Palestinian society remains united against occupation, and many journalists still believe they have a role to play in this resistance. But—and this difference is critical—today they believe that in order to be successful they must adhere to the standards set forth by their profession and their employers. These journalists saw their work as relevant to political struggle, because this struggle is so all-encompassing in Palestinian society under occupation, even though they might disagree with militants on what their roles as journalists should be.

Journalists occasionally experienced tension with civic activists as well, especially as the latter developed their own independent media but remained frustrated by the lack of mainstream media coverage of their nonviolent, popular activism. For example, Yazan, an activist in Nablus, complained that a local reporter for an international news agency, Kareem, did not follow up enough on how the stories for which he gathered information were written. In 2008, Yazan had organized a memorial commemorating the fifth anniversary of the American solidarity activist Rachel Corrie's[22] killing by the Israeli army in Gaza in 2003. Yazan was pleased that at the last minute Corrie's parents decided to come. When they spoke to the press, Kareem was there, reporting the story. Photographs on the International Solidarity Movement's (ISM) website show Rachel Corrie's mother, Cindy, holding a picture of her daughter and smiling as a Palestinian flag waved in back of her. The photographs show that hundreds of Palestinians, many of them also cradling Rachel's smiling photograph, attended the event. The ISM article reported that Rachel's father, Craig, told the assembled group:

> There's nothing more we can do for Rachel, but we can all work so that these children, our children—for they are all our children—can have a life that we

would all want our children to have. And we will work so that bulldozers do not destroy the garden walls of a family's garden, but that they destroy the walls that imprison us here, and people everywhere.[23]

The event had been a success, but the next day, when Yazan scoured the internet for Kareem's and other news agency journalists' reports, he was disappointed. Absent such moving quotes, the stories merely suggested that Corrie's parents had come to the West Bank only because they were reluctant to go to Hamas-ruled Gaza. For example, the Associated Press reported, "The parents did not say why they placed the memorial in the West Bank instead of Gaza." The article continued, "But Gaza is mired in violence and ruled by the militant Islamic Hamas, while moderate President Mahmoud Abbas administers the West Bank, which is relatively calmer. In a 2006 visit to Gaza, the Corries were apparent targets of an unsuccessful kidnap attempt by Palestinian militants."[24] The story included only a ten-word quote from Rachel Corrie's parents. It is not clear what Kareem reported to whoever wrote the story. What is clear is that the story was cast in terms familiar to its Western audience. A nonviolent commemoration of an activist's death is more newsworthy for a Western audience when put in the context of the political split between the two major Palestinian parties, Hamas and Fatah, or a media-contrived fear of rampant violence in Gaza. While Yazan had every right to be frustrated by the coverage, it was not unusual. It was Yazan who was extraordinary, in that he read the English-language press. This kind of coverage illustrates the consequences of structural arrangements of journalism in the West Bank and Gaza discussed in Chapter 1. Kareem's English was not good enough for him to write his own articles, and he was not expected to do so. He was only the reporter, and it was someone else's responsibility to write up the report on the day's events. Thus, he forfeited editorial input over articles for which he reported.

Journalists with close connections to the communities they cover have ways of forging connections with civil society activists, even if this does not mean producing coverage the world can see. A photojournalist who lived in an outlying city where most of his work was not of officials but of demonstrations and incursions told me of his efforts at maintaining strong connections within the city and nearby villages. He had an archive of photos of youth and activists at demonstrations, and he would sometimes give them to families after their subject had died. Still, a local professional ethics was in play. He never gave families gory pictures, of which he had many, and he did not give youth pictures of themselves throwing stones, because he was worried that Israeli authorities would consider that to be incitement. Another prominent journalist for a top news agency conducted video workshops for children and often videotaped civic events in which his agency would not be interested. This helped him to maintain his good name around town. This pro bono work indicates the complex relationship between political, social, and professional practice. Journalists could shore up a reservoir of good political will with what amounted to social courtesies. One cameraperson told me he filmed martyrs' funerals for much longer into the second Intifada than his editor considered them to be newsworthy. He did this out of respect for families he knew, who viewed his presence as an expression of social solidarity. He apparently knew the Jerusalem bureaus well. A Jerusalem-based Palestinian producer who was unaware of or unmoved by these social complexities complained to me that his camerapeople were sending him dull and repetitive footage of non-events like martyrs' funerals!

Journalists have experienced angst over their shifting position in the field of politics. Even as they reported on the scenes of the most deadly and turbulent moments of the second Intifada, journalists were sometimes torn between conflicting allegiances. One Palestinian producer told me more than once of a wrenching incident he experienced during the invasions of 2002. He and the foreign correspondents with whom he worked had gone to great lengths to enter the city of Nablus, where some of the most intense fighting was taking place. They slipped into the Old City, where Palestinian militants were making a bold stand against the Israeli army. As the foreign correspondents did their work, the militants asked him to help carry the bodies of the dead. He told them he could not. He was a journalist, he told them, not an activist or an emergency worker. His refusal would haunt him. Perhaps, he reflected years later, he could have carried injured people, because that might have saved a life; but carrying dead militants in front of the foreign correspondents he worked with—and potentially, he said, in front of Palestinian collaborators who would tell Israeli authorities what he had done—exceeded, he thought, the boundaries of professionalism and personal safety.

AN ETHICS OF "TRUTH"

Despite such dilemmas faced in the field, in the products of their work Palestinian journalists often told me that they did not usually see a conflict between quality journalism and journalism that elucidates what for them are basic truths of Israeli occupation. They see their job as complementing coverage that would otherwise be predominantly pro-Israeli. Being disinterested was not a prerequisite for this job, but they did use a language of balance, albeit balance as an ongoing corrective process. After all, their beat was to cover the occupied Palestinian territories, where events hewed closely to the narrative of Israeli violence. They never were asked to cover Palestinian suicide bombings in Tel Aviv. One Palestinian reporter who works in a large office in which many of the journalists are Israeli—some having served in the IDF or having children who have done so—concluded, "If you want to take it from a professional perspective, you have to deal with the devil in order to voice a Palestinian perspective." As one high-level producer told me:

> I cover the Palestinian side. I successfully manage to get [my news organization] the Palestinian narrative of the story. As you know, all articles must have the other narrative of the story. That is the Israeli side [covered by two people based in Jerusalem who this reporter had noted were Israeli or Jewish]. I cover the Palestinian side . . . I send it to them, sometimes by e-mail, sometimes on the phone. Then they combine it with the Israeli narrative of the story. That's the news. . . . I have pressure from the Palestinians; they have the pressure from the Israelis. It's always like that. . . . There are always challenges. But the important thing is to get the word out.

Some Palestinian journalists have faced criticism from other Palestinians who think they serve pro-Israeli ends by working in U.S. organizations. To this kind of critique the same producer replied:

> Should I stay home and work for an Arab paper? What's more important for the story, to work for [an important U.S. news outlet] or to work for a Gulf paper, where I will make more money or whatever, where it's going to be easier? What's more important? That's the question. And who are they going to replace me with? I feel a responsibility for the truth to come out. My main goal is the truth.

Journalists working for U.S. organizations note that while they do not have the fame that comes with being a journalist for an Arab news outlet, they believe they can make a political contribution by influencing the conversation that is happening in the United States on the Israeli-Palestinian conflict. Said one reporter, "Many journalists who started [working in journalism] ten or fifteen years after me have became famous on the Palestinian or on the Arab level, while I am still nobody for anyone. For me this is something satisfactory.

As long as I still have these five hundred or seven hundred words even in the sixteenth page of an American newspaper, or hiding somewhere in this book, or that website, I still feel that I can do something to promote my goals and the story of my people." Some Palestinian journalists have concluded that foreign correspondents come in with preconceptions and only look to reinforce these views. They see themselves working against the grain of most U.S. coverage of the conflict, and conceptualize their role as educating their colleagues. Voicing a sentiment I heard more than once, a reporter told me, "When I press editors to change something, I am not cheating. I am talking about the reality." Cheating, in his mind, meant advocating, abusing the position to promulgate untruths. This reporter, who seldom complained about the political strictures of his job, told me with some passion in a 2005 interview:

> We are involved in daily debates with editors and other journalists. Unfortunately foreign media in general have a negative perspective of Palestinians. They look at the Palestinian cause from a very narrow perspective. And sometimes when I accompany an American or European reporter here, I feel like he is looking for something that could prove something that he already brought in his mind. He wants to prove that Palestinians are terrorists, that Palestinians have no future, that there is chaos in the Palestinian territories, and so forth. I think that they have this prejudgment. Mostly when I look at their stories, I see that they handle the Palestinian problems without remarks on the source of the problems, the real source. . . . If I want to write about suicide bombers, even children suicide bombers, I can't do this story in [isolation from examining the role of] Israel. I can't do this. Who made [suicide bombers behave] like this? If I want to say that Palestinians are killing Israeli civilians, I should mention that Israel has made Palestinians' lives hell. Every city has become not more than a jail. People are losing hope, losing horizons, losing everything. And in desperation they are behaving like this. I have to mention that.

He sees his job as providing context and balance to U.S. journalists not equipped to do this, a truth-making that recognizes its limitations as only one part of a process. Notably, his and other journalists' notion of balance is pragmatic and corrective. It acknowledges his position as a Palestinian and thus is quite different from the ideal of balance that prevails among many American journalists, as I discuss in Chapter 1. But his critique of objectivity is more institutional than epistemological, and he does not see it as a limit to producing truth. Instead, it is the foundation for understanding what is going on around him.

Not everyone is comfortable being a corrective voice within the journalistic enterprise. As I discuss in Chapter 2, Palestinians are particularly vulnerable to accusations of bias. One high-level producer told me, "I try to separate myself from this situation of being a Palestinian under occupation, or someone who suffered under occupation, and try to be a professional journalist, because this is the way that I can develop myself [professionally] and gain credibility and respect. So when I say something, people trust me. Otherwise, if I am just a propaganda machine, nobody will trust me." Another journalist in a large media organization who clearly believed that Palestinian journalists have a political role to play within their organizations painted a grimmer picture: "Unfortunately many Palestinian journalists working in this field think it is good enough that they have these jobs, so they do not challenge editors." While the vast majority of journalists I spoke to were convinced that media will play a major role in the future of the Israeli-Palestinian conflict, one cameraperson casually dismissed this possibility. Instead, he told me once, the conflict would be won or lost militarily. Still, he sought to cover stories that he believed would expose the injustices of the military occupation.

CONCLUSIONS: PERVASIVE POLITICS, EVANESCENT DISINTEREST

One of the first people I met when I began my fieldwork was Tamir, a friend of a friend who I hoped might do some transcription for me. He struck me as the prototypical populist Palestinian intellectual, wiry and wily, subsisting on cigarettes and coffee. He was cynical, extremely funny, and up on the intricacies of every political development. Though his gait swayed with a strong limp and his right arm was almost paralyzed, he insisted on taking me for walks around Ramallah as a kind of moral and epistemic exercise—reading graffiti and the like. I presumed that he had been the victim of a childhood disease, or that he had multiple sclerosis, until the friend who had put us in touch told me that he had been a major political activist during the first Intifada. He had been the target of an Israeli shooting that left him in the hospital for months on the edge of death. These years later, his injury was permanent. Another time, I was in a Palestinian journalist's office in Jerusalem, helping him edit little bits of news about the PA in English. Like Tamir, he had a dry sense of humor and a quick, deep intelligence about Palestinian politics. Unlike Tamir, though, Mohammad had the salubrious heft that signaled (in this context) that he was well fed by someone. He drove a luxury car—albeit one made at least a decade earlier— and always wore a nice shirt. He seemed comfortable. So I was surprised when he told me his father had passed away when he was quite young. "Cancer?" I asked. He looked at me over his wire-rimmed glasses. "My father was the first Palestinian to die in Israeli custody." Over the next months, I would come across others: a journalist whose parents met while her mother was in prison and her father was her lawyer, a professor who had leapt from his window to avoid arrest the night before his final high school exams began, a social worker who had been imprisoned as a teenager while protesting with the man she later married, a nurse whose house had been destroyed by Israeli forces when she was in high school. In many of these cases, stories were not recounted as great tragedies or the pivotal moment of a life; instead, they were the painful but ordinary stuff of lives lived in a place where politics reached into childhoods, marriages, education, and everything else. The expectation that journalists inhabit a position of disinterest may be unrealistic in any context, but it is especially unimaginable in a place where almost everyone's lives have been intimately affected by national politics in ways they can clearly identify.

Even a simple story like that of the onetime DJ who called his radio station when he happened to be at a demonstration and thus began his career as a journalist speaks to the difference in political context between Palestinian and U.S. societies. During the 2011 Occupy Wall Street protests, at least two public radio journalists were removed from their positions because they were seen participating in the protests. Their employers could not afford for them to appear "interested" in this way, even though one of the journalists was the host of an opera show, and the other worked only part-time for a news show.[25] Being visibly involved with protests undermined these journalists' claims to disinterest, and apparently public radio leadership felt this threatened their claims to objectivity. In the Palestinian context, protests are hardly so cut off from everyday life as they are in the United States. While Palestinian journalists working for foreign news agencies would also avoid such visible participation in protests, demonstrations and other political gatherings were, and are, more integrated into Palestinian life.[26] From what he told me, it was unclear whether the DJ happened to be at a demonstration because he had encountered it while doing something else or because he had come in order to participate in it. In any case, it was doing something that signaled political involvement that was the immediate cause for him joining a career in which disinterestedness is valued. And he was not the only person for whom this was true. For the journalist who was offered a job after reporting on his parents-in-law's house's roof, too, it was proximity, not distance, that led to his work in journalism.

International journalism is a domestic affair in the West Bank. Understanding the multiple dimensions of this domesticity complicates the enshrined epistemic virtues[27] of disinterest, distance, and neutrality. Many Palestinian journalists are laboring for their homes, with all of the complications and forms of ambivalence this can entail. They report on politics to make a living and provide a home for themselves and their families, to build toward their version of the Palestinian good life, whether that means an apartment in the city with a decent commute, a recognizably Palestinian home, or an abundant garden. But the political developments they cover in turn affect their abilities to make their homes. Journalism brings them into their compatriots' homes, as well.

Palestinian journalists are a part of Palestinian society, and so they are situated within the high-stakes political contests they cover, and in ways that foreign correspondents generally are not. But the implications of Palestinians' situatedness are not monolithic. While some foreign critics insist that Palestinian journalists who work for U.S. media are politically motivated and therefore biased in their reporting, some Palestinian activists criticize Palestinian journalists for being insufficiently committed politically and merely interested in making money. Many Palestinian journalists enjoy what they do because it feels like politically relevant work, and yet they are also obligated to make compromises with foreign correspondents in order to keep their jobs. They may have strong professional identities and deeply value objectivity and eyewitness reporting as important epistemic values. Still, their commitment to these values may be colored by the distinct circumstances of Palestinians' struggle for liberation, which can impose its own set of ethical commitments. Whatever their personal beliefs about journalism, they work within complex institutions that tend to especially limit Palestinian journalists' ability to express themselves.

Palestinian journalists who work with Western media have to constantly assess multiple layers of personal, professional, and political commitment, and they find few simple solutions or safe positions. Critics who deem Palestinian journalists to be biased because of their attachment to Palestinian nationalism build their arguments on the fact that some journalists have indeed had a relationship to the political world in which they live. Certainly, like virtually all Palestinians in the West Bank and Gaza Strip, these journalists desire an end to Israeli occupation. The more complicated question of *how* a political location affects their work is better answered when one also understands how political location has been an essential condition to reporting within the West Bank, and why Palestinian journalists see good reporting as consistent with spreading the word about the injustices of Israeli occupation.

The prominence of the politics of sovereignty at this location is revealing. Many Americans, including many journalists, may perceive participation in national politics as a choice: to don a campaign button, to hold a sign at a rally. Disinterest, too, appears to be a choice. From this perspective, the mundane ways in which the politics of sovereignty shapes Americans' lives—filing returns on tax day, driving down a well-paved highway or a bumpy one, drinking clean water, visiting a government-funded museum exhibition, speaking publicly without fear of repercussions, or taking off shoes at an airport—do not figure as major biographical events. Yet they do underscore how few lives today are untouched by the politics of sovereignty, whether because a state is working or lacking, oppressive or enabling. Ethnographically analyzing whether and how politics are recognized to be a part of other domains of social, economic, or familial activity—or whether people delimit the domain of politics as something separate at all—is a crucial anthropological starting point for analyzing interest and disinterest as well as a wide range of other social and political phenomena.

A RELIABLE SOURCE?
PRISON BARS AS SOUND BARRIER

The article "Palestinian Moms Becoming Martyrs"[1] tackled one of the most poisonous topics of the second Intifada: women who have carried out or attempted to carry out bombings inside Israel. But this was probably one of the easier articles Tim McGirk had reported in the last decade. He had covered Afghanistan, Pakistan, and Iraq, and in 2006 he did groundbreaking reporting on a massacre of twenty-four Iraqis in Haditha. He wrote this article, published in Time *magazine on May 3, 2007, while relatively new in his position as* Time's *bureau chief in Jerusalem. The article opened with a description of a Hamas video:*

> In late March, a macabre music video appeared on a television show for Palestinian children. "Duha," 4, as pale as a porcelain doll, is sitting on a bed, watching her mom dress before leaving home. "Mommy, what are you carrying in your arms instead of me?" the girl sings. The next day, Duha gets the answer from the evening news. It turns out her mother was carrying explosives and had blown herself up, killing four Israelis. The final scene shows the girl wistfully rummaging through her dead mother's bedside table. She finds a hidden stick of dynamite and picks it up. The implicit message is that someday Duha will follow her mother into blazing martyrdom.

The foregrounding of such polarizing material was not the only controversial element of the article. It also suggested that political organizations and families coerced Palestinian women into carrying out operations, and even hinted that Palestinian women saw death as preferable to life in Palestinian society. According to McGirk, "Behind the motives of religion and rage at Israeli occupation, Palestinian women, far more than men, tend to choose self-sacrifice as an exit from personal

despair, while others are pushed into it for having broken taboos in strict Palestin-
ian society." The main thrust of the article is, in the words of a key source, Anat
Berko, "These women are both victimizers and victims," victimizers of Israelis and
victims of their own purportedly toxic culture.

To say that Palestinians were frustrated by how stories like this represented
them—and readers did presume that this article would reflect on all Palestinians
for American readers—would be an understatement. Tareq, a journalism student
whom I interviewed at his university in Nablus, came into the classroom where we
were meeting itching to talk about this article, as though to get it out of the way
and move on to ones he found more palatable. On the Hamas video, Tareq commented that "I am angry that we make shows like that, but this is not the whole
truth." Aseel, an experienced feminist leader and social worker, also dove right into
a critique of this article. It did not make for a warm conversation over the sweet tea
she had prepared for our interview in her home. She, too, lambasted the article's
portrayal of Palestinians: "It is as if the article is saying, 'Their women have no
mercy, and they don't even love their own children. They send their own children
to death.' This is how they are showing us." This was a reprehensible view to Aseel,
who had done overtime as an advocate for women's rights even as she cherished her
time with her own children. "This is unfair. That doesn't mean that there are no
individual cases in which people have made mistakes. . . . But they don't represent
all Palestinians."

While other articles earned nuanced evaluations, readers met this one with
serious doubts about its basic factual accuracy. These doubts likely stemmed partly
from the wrenching subject matter of suicide bombings. Perhaps for some it was
hard to reconcile all that had happened in the second Intifada. But readers also
questioned the cultural logics of some of the stories the article presented. One anecdote in the article described a Palestinian woman, now imprisoned, who had
been recruited to bomb the Israeli burn unit where she had once been treated. The
article reported that militants had convinced this woman to carry out an operation
because she would never get married. Tareq remarked, "This has no logic, the idea
that no one would marry her," and that this would push her to carry out a bombing. Something about this story seemed false to him. It might have been the assumption that an unmarried life is not worth living, or that militants would be so
callous in their recruitment efforts. He reiterated, "It just doesn't happen like that."

Palestinians' doubts also stemmed from the methodology of the article itself. As
Aseel observed, virtually all of the information in the article came from "an Israeli
woman who is studying the psychological side of the suicide bombers." Specifi-

cally, as the article says, Anat Berko is "an Israeli counterterrorism expert at the International Policy Institute for Counter-Terrorism in Herzliya, who spent thirteen years inside Israeli high-security prisons interviewing convicted terrorists." It was she who had interviewed women prisoners. The article quoted no Palestinian commentators by name, though one quote was attributed to an unidentified Palestinian professor. Zayd, a math teacher and father, commented that to report on such sensitive and complex stories—like one about a woman who was allegedly convinced to carry out a bombing to atone for having had an adulterous relationship—the reporter should have talked to many more people. "Even if these allegations are true, or even half true," he said, "the journalist should have supported them with more facts, with testimony from her husband, from her family. He should have given the names of the Israelis who supplied these accusations against her." Zayd suspected that the article primarily relied on Israeli security sources from the Shin-Bet, or Israel Security Agency, and thus asserted, "There is a big question mark over this information." For the same reason, Aseel concluded that this was "a biased article. It relies on this one researcher for information, and she maintains that the reasons behind these bombings are personal. She is trying to ignore the national struggle." In the end, she said, Berko "is a source from the occupation. This is not objective."

Indeed, several readers lamented that the article failed to mention the political framework of occupation. Saida, another journalism student whom I interviewed at her university in Nablus, commented on a strange sense that she had as she read the article: "For a second I thought we are the occupiers and the oppressors, and they are the oppressed, because the article didn't mention anything about what the other side is doing to the Palestinians." Aseel reiterated the same problem: "This is not about hatred, or some kind of a personal argument. This is a national struggle. There is occupation, and these are people who are struggling for their freedom. It is time for the world, especially the Americans, to understand this." She concluded, "If there were no occupation, there would be no bombing operations."

Readers had divergent views of the relationship between social problems and suicide bombings. Tareq, the young journalism student, reasoned, "I am against suicide bombings, but we should still try to understand bombers' motivations. What makes them do this? I think psychological pressures, social pressures, and bad economic and social situations that the occupation in part causes all contribute to people carrying out bombings." Aseel, who had dealt professionally with family problems in Palestinian society for nearly twenty years, had a slightly different take. "Many people [here] have social problems. Why don't they all go and *explode themselves? There must, then, be other reasons." With a wry smile, she continued, "If social problems inside Palestinian society were the reason for bombings, then half of the Palestinians would all go and bomb themselves!"*

For his part, Zayd rejected the idea that self-sacrifice for a cause was itself pathological. Gesturing toward his living room television, he turned to American popular culture to make his case. He cited the movie Armageddon, *in which Bruce Willis decides to sacrifice himself to save Earth from an asteroid:*

> *Anyone who saw the film would think . . . that this character is a hero, because he sacrificed himself to save America, or even the whole world. So I wonder why an American finds it so incomprehensible that someone should sacrifice himself or herself to save his people, or his home, or his family. . . . When I watch action films, I often get the message that it's OK for Americans to have this privilege of sacrificing one's self for the sake of others, but still, it's taboo and forbidden for Palestinians to do the same to save their families and combat occupation.*

Aseel offered a broader critique of the article's assumptions about the relationship between nationalist involvement and women's rights:

> *I believe that in all societies that live under occupation, women . . . suffer more than others. . . . The woman in Palestinian society is still subjected to social oppression, and you add to that the occupation. So she is facing double oppression. . . . At the same time, I see many women who have liberated themselves socially because of their involvement in politics. . . . The society respects women who struggle. This is a way for women to break many social barriers. When she works in politics, she can finish her education, work, choose her husband, and no one can force her to marry at an early age.*

Indeed, her own life experience reflected much of this. The idea that women were coerced into committing acts of resistance by men or because of their apparent deficiencies as women misrepresented the kinds of agency Palestinian women could garner by way of political activism.

Finally, readers offered their own ideas on how the issue of female suicide bombers should be covered. They took into account the fact that many bombers or would-be bombers would be dead or inaccessible in prison. "I would meet with families, examine their histories, and study their social circumstances," said Aseel, perhaps drawing on her own professional practices as a social worker. She suggested that a reporter ask, "How did these women live? How were they raised? What was their economic situation and their experience with the occupation? Any phenomenon you want to study, you need to look at many elements. You cannot rely on one source." Saida, the journalism student, proposed a portrait of one person, a typical model for a human-interest story:

> *If the story starts with the moment she went and bombed herself, it gives the very opposite sense than what I would want to communicate. I recently visited a woman who was just released from prison. She had tried to go to a settlement near Nablus with a knife after her brother was shot. She was looking for revenge. Someone who just hears about her going to the settlement would think that she is a terrorist. But if you start with when her father was arrested, her brother was killed three days before his birthday, and she was not allowed to go to school because it was too dangerous, you find a different story.*

Both were essentially describing a problem of sources. To whom do we listen to grasp the hardest-to-understand phenomena in our political worlds: someone close to our own experiences or someone far away?; someone with special expertise or not? Where do we turn when the subjects of our inquiries are dead or silenced, or if their words are almost certainly reframed by material constraints like imprisonment? Are there limits to how the conventions of news can handle these challenges?

4 THE EMBODIED AND UP-CLOSE WORK OF JOURNALISM

Doing participant-observation at a demonstration against the wall often left me wondering where to be. It was difficult to see a demonstration from the back, which was where I often ended up, but being at the front was not much better. Though the signs people were carrying could be seen, one really only glimpsed the first few rows of people. If one stood on the side, everyone passed by quickly and at too close a proximity. Crowded streets made for different challenges than hilltops, and tear gas called for different strategies than processions or prayer gatherings.

In Al-Ram, a neighborhood on the periphery of Jerusalem, the separation barrier took the form of a wall approximately five meters high. Israeli authorities were building it in a process that entailed a great deal of destruction. At one Friday demonstration, people were forming lines to pray on the dirt surface that had once been the main road through the neighborhood. Organizing a protest around Friday prayers guaranteed a good turnout and compelling images, and it could also dissuade army aggression. I was juggling a notebook, a camera, and a voice recorder—before the days when the tasks of taking notes and pictures and doing voice recordings might be consolidated in a single device. I wanted a few images to show for my fumbling. But as usual I found I was more successful in noting what journalists did to capture good images than in capturing those images myself. One journalist had drawn close. With his video camera on his shoulder, he had stayed right in front of the protest. This had invited an older man in a white robe to approach him to speechify at great length against the wall, waving his arms as though to make his small frame bigger (Figure 3). The decision to obtain the close-up had produced a gripping event within the

Figure 3   Covering a protest up close. Photojournalists both capture and encourage a protester's expression of outrage against the separation barrier being built through Al-Ram, a town between Jerusalem and Ramallah. *Source*: Amahl Bishara.

event, the old man's impromptu speech. Another journalist had taken a different approach. He had scaled a pile of rubble to position his video camera's heavy tripod on one of the larger slabs of asphalt that remained on the side of what used to be the main road (Figure 4). Elevated a few feet from the rest of the demonstration, he could, I imagine, capture the whole thing quite well. At another demonstration against the wall in the village of Al-Walaja, I saw a journalist do the same thing. He stood on a flat wedge of cement that had been the roof of a destroyed home on the side of the road as protesters filed by.

Positioning tripods in the rubble was part of an efficient local ecology of occupation, resistance, and representation. It has been noted that stones were a renewable resource for Palestinian protesters, always being generated anew by processes of destruction. Kicking back tear gas canisters lobbed at protesters was another way in which Palestinians made the most of their physical surroundings as they resisted occupation. I was familiar with these dynamics, but I was initially surprised that journalists, too, had a place in this ecology. Journalists used rubble—yesterday's news, really—to gain perspective. And this was

Figure 4 Positioning a tripod in the rubble. A photojournalist balances his tripod in the rubble of the destroyed main road at a demonstration against the barrier in Al-Ram. *Source*: Amahl Bishara.

not an abstract historical perspective; it was literally a way of obtaining a view on an event. This underscores for me the extent to which knowledge production has a specific local praxis, in which journalists creatively make the most of their material circumstances.

In describing this representational ecology, I underscore the way in which place, in its material qualities and its tendency to ground personal histories,[1] enables representational strategies, and the ways in which representation is linked to other kinds of practices that operate on the same terrain. In some ways, this representational ecology calls attention to an overlap between what protesters and journalists can readily do. Both can scale rubble, for example, and both see it as a part of the geography that offers the potential for perspective or protection. When the army tries to break up a protest, both figure out how to position themselves to stay safe and avoid tear gas by crouching behind barriers or dodging behind corners. In other ways, there is a complementarity between journalists and protesters. They stake out distinct positions in relation to the army. Journalists want to represent protesters, and protesters want to be represented. When journalists draw close, protesters may perform by delivering speeches or confronting soldiers. I consider here how journalists' skills are adapted to this political and geographic environment. Palestinian journalists have what Tim Ingold has called a "taskscape": an interrelated collection of social and materially grounded skills needed to thrive in a particular environment.[2] This professional taskscape is built upon the taskscape of Palestinian life under occupation. A kind of honed habitus, these skills are cultivated by political and cultural circumstances. Far from requiring distance and objectivity, Palestinian journalists in the West Bank benefit from long experiences living under occupation. These experiences, along with professional experience, refined a set of *skills of proximity*.

The idea of skills of proximity may seem intuitive in one regard and unorthodox in another. In journalism the idea of being close has always been important, because being on the scene as an eyewitness is a central professional value. However, the concept of skills of proximity developed over a lifetime challenges assumptions that emotional distance is necessary for journalism, and that political journalists draw on an interchangeable set of skills applicable around the world. Moreover, examining skills of proximity stresses the material dimensions of journalistic labor. Viewing journalism from the perspective of Palestinian journalists illuminates how intellectual and embodied skills are inextricable from one another, clarifying another dimension of the relationship between speech and the material world.

SKILLS OF PROXIMITY

Widespread understandings of objectivity suggest that disinterest and distance together ensure a properly impartial stance. Yet, as journalists labor to cover occupation, they are also submitting themselves to working within the constraints of occupation. Working under occupation today does not entail coping with direct censorship, but it does entail managing constraints on movement and make one vulnerable to exchanges with Israeli soldiers, who have a great deal of power at the checkpoint or protest at which they are stationed. Obviously, journalists are not the only ones trying to work under military occupation. So are entrepreneurs, teachers, doctors, farmers, and construction workers—Palestinians of every professional stripe. Apparently, routine tasks that many might attempt, such as working inside Israel, visiting a neighboring Palestinian city, and leaving the country, bring Palestinians into contact with Israeli authorities, as can importing goods for a small business or harvesting one's crops. To undertake any of these endeavors, it is not only factual knowledge or professional skills that are vital; equally essential are the active and embodied tactics of managing military constraints. In part because politics so thoroughly permeate lives, as discussed in Chapter 3, the skills of navigating the political realm are widely dispersed. Moreover, because covering the news brings journalists into so many intimate spaces, experience and ease in Palestinian society are also useful professional skills. Experience under occupation and in Palestinian society renders Palestinian journalists an important kind of expert in all of these local matters.

Somewhat paradoxically, living in a repressive situation can give some Palestinians skills to do productive activities well beyond merely coping.[3] If the Israeli army frequently bombards a community with tear gas, as was true of many communities during the Intifadas, young residents develop abilities to withstand tear gas while simply walking home from school or hanging around their own home. As a result of this learned steadfastness (*sumud*), they may find participating in demonstrations where there is a risk of encountering tear gas to be less daunting. And they might be ready to cover demonstrations as well. This speaks to the way in which skills, understood as "intelligent action," are the results of historical and political processes.[4] This insight cautions against seeing skills as intrinsic to an environment or as universal across a professional field.

Fixing, reporting, and field-producing especially require this kind of culturally constituted expertise. A thirty-year-old Palestinian with an interest in politics would have fairly deep knowledge of political figures and events of the last fifteen years, a precious resource for a U.S. foreign correspondent newly arrived to the scene. After a foreign correspondent asks a fixer for a fact over the phone, the fixer's word will be checked, but at least it provides a plausible starting point for investigation. In some cases, Palestinians' expertise is more difficult to codify. On the day of Arafat's funeral in 2004, I found that an experienced producer was asking her relatives, who had no experience in journalism, if they wanted to work as fixers for the day. The job required doing basic translation and looking out for the foreign correspondent amidst the surging crowds. The foreign correspondent would hire such a fixer in part to visibly have Palestinian accompaniment on a day that might become chaotic. This fixer-for-a-day could be anyone with the geographic knowledge, language skills, and aplomb to bring a foreign correspondent where she needed to be and ensure that she remained safe and comfortable as she worked. This fixer should also be someone a foreigner would trust, thus likely someone who could embody a certain professionalism and familiarity with foreigners as well. I came to know this from my own experiences on that same day. Amidst the armed forces, masked activists, and thick crowds, I realized that I would not have wanted to be attending the event alone. Local Palestinian friends staked out a position from which to watch the events, negotiating with the owners of a building whose roof we occupied, and they helped me make my way in the crowded streets. My friends' logistical competences—the ability, while on the move through what was to me an indecipherable scene, to identify flags, uniforms, and guns and to discern whether we were safe or not—made me feel more at ease and let me do my fieldwork. In more intense conflict zones, such skills took on special urgency, and many bonds were forged between foreign correspondents and fixers when they were under fire.

The ability to cover such public events drew upon Palestinian journalists' nonprofessional experiences. Most Palestinians have attended demonstrations as protesters and martyrs' funerals as mourners, and thus they have a sense of how to handle the events that are likely to ensue. Both men and women attend protests, but disproportionately more men consider themselves adept at handling the "frontline" action, and to do so is an esteemed element of Palestinian masculinity. Similarly, men make up almost all of the ranks of photojournalists, the journalists who must do the most "frontline" work.

I learned a great deal about what was needed to cover a demonstration during a major day of protest against the separation wall in Abu Dis. Processions of school children, solidarity activists, and others passed by the wall, some stopping to write graffiti or do stenciling. I was absorbed with following the rhythm of journalists' "standups," or first-person reports, set to a U.S. morning news schedule, when suddenly Israeli troops emerged from behind the wall to storm down the hill on which we were standing. Immediately, boys and young men began throwing stones at the soldiers and running down the street. It seemed like the journalists were stuck in the middle. I heard explosions that I could not identify, and soon I was enveloped in tear gas. Unlike the Israeli and Palestinian camerapeople, who kept filming, or the Palestinian emergency medical personnel on alert, I could not grasp what was going on around me. I could not distinguish the noise of the stun grenades—which cannot hurt but aim to startle and scare protesters with a big boom—from the bullets, nor could I identify what kinds of bullets were being fired. I reminded myself that tear gas was only a short-term nuisance, yet I was surprised at the visceral effects it was having on me, which later seemed comic (of course, tear gas is effective!). Unaccustomed to representational work in this environment, I found myself disoriented. With my eyes full of tears and surrounded in smoky gas, I could not figure out whether Israeli soldiers were still coming down the hill into the area that would position me in front of them, or whether Palestinian stones might in fact come down on me.

As usual, the tear gas, sound grenades, and bullets did their work rather quickly, and protesters dispersed. I soon felt better and was left only with how to regain my composure and return to the journalists I had been shadowing. This was one of the moments when I realized how important embodied experience, a refined sensory (in this case, auditory) palate, and local geographic knowledge are in handling such situations. Journalism involves embodied skills, and the skills of journalism in the occupied Palestinian territories include the skills of any active participant in society. At demonstrations protesters, journalists, and concerned onlookers—passersby, neighbors, and parents of protesters alike—must be able to identify the sounds and dangers of Israeli weapons. Distinguishing different kinds of weapons and having a sense of their capacities is even more important during incursions, when a journalist must be able to report on which weapons are being used, evaluate what these different weapons mean tactically and politically, and stay safe. They must be able to distinguish among the various explosions of Israeli tear gas, sound bombs, flares, and Palestinian pipe bombs, and contrast the raps of Israeli rubber bullets, live ammunition, and tank fire. They should be able to differentiate between the sound of Israeli M-16 fire and Palestinian AK-47 fire and to identify the sober boom of a home demolition. Using visual and auditory senses, they must be able to discern the different ranges and threats of Apache helicopters, F-16s, and an array of Israeli tanks and bulldozers.[5] This is not the kind of lesson one learns in books or even in journalists' safety manuals.

Palestinian journalists, like protesters, make fast decisions about where to position themselves in order to be safe. Photojournalists avoid crossfire and ensure that their location is distinguishable from that of protesters—even as they must also position themselves to take a good picture. In photojournalist Abed Qusini's account of his colleague Nazeh Darwazeh's death on April 19, 2003, during protests of an Israeli arrest raid in the city of Nablus, Qusini emphasizes journalists' attention to safety and also the inevitable risks of covering military actions:

> At the time, before 10 o'clock, we were on another road where there were tens of youths throwing stones at two Israeli tanks and a jeep standing at the end of the road. We tried to get closer to the scene to take closer pictures. We were four working with AP and Reuters trying to get closer. We were standing at the opposite side of the stone-throwers. . . . If you are talking about the Israeli army we were at their right, and the stone-throwers were at the left side of the soldiers. . . . We were standing at the gate of the house taking pictures, and the soldiers were aiming their weapons towards the stone-throwers. Suddenly one of the soldiers lifted his [rifle from the] Hummer armored jeep and went down the tank and shot one bullet toward the right, toward our side. One bullet hit Nazeh Darwazeh's head over his right eye, the eye [through] which he [was] looking inside his video camera.[6]

On this occasion, Darwazeh was gravely unfortunate, but Qusini's explanation nevertheless shows how journalists made an effort to stay safe by positioning themselves carefully. They tried to stay together, and they maintained a location distinct from that of both the soldiers and the protesters.

In managing other forms of violence, Palestinian journalists and others must know to use a combination of might and restraint. Photojournalists generally need to be strong in order to carry heavy cameras and other equipment. Sometimes, holding onto a camera is itself a challenge, as when journalists have come into contact with aggressive settlers in Hebron. As Patricia Naylor's documentary In the Line of Fire shows, when journalists have attempted to cover settler aggression against Palestinians, settlers have turned on the Palestinian journalists.[7] Footage taken by photojournalists in Hebron shows journalists struggling to control their equipment as Israeli settlers attempt to wrest it from them. One scene shows a teenage girl trying to grab the camera of a burly cameraperson as two teenage boys approach the journalist from the side to kick him. The journalists endeavor to stand their ground, but they know that the use of force on their part would be disastrous, because Israeli soldiers and police are primarily concerned with protecting the settlers.[8] A certain kind of Palestinian masculinity is on display here, which we might also see in other Palestinians' encounters with soldiers and settlers: an ability to be tough, to intimidate through shouts and looks, but to know when using one's physical strength could be perilous.[9]

Journalists, like other Palestinians, also deploy verbal skills to deal with soldiers, even when it might seem that the outcome of an interaction would be determined by the sheer force of the army's authority. This attuned copresence of intellectual and physical skills is at the crux of journalists' work under occupation and within a repressive regime. Journalists have developed assertive but measured ways of speaking to soldiers, which can keep them safe. For example, on one occasion, a Palestinian journalist told me to call him if I needed help getting through a checkpoint, because, he said, he knew how to speak to soldiers at that particular checkpoint. Similarly, journalists knew how to negotiate with soldiers during protests. In a June 2004 protest against the separation barrier, soldiers fired tear gas cannons directly at several Palestinian photographers covering the event, and two journalists were injured. Abed Qusini, the photojournalist from Nablus, was detained in an Israeli army jeep. According to Reporters Without Borders:

> Photographer Abed Qusini of the British Reuters news agency narrowly avoided arrest. . . . Qusini said he was with a group of Palestinian journalists and filming, when a soldier ordered his arrest on the grounds that the area had been declared a "closed military zone." Qusini, who reads Hebrew, asked to see the written order and to photograph it to show to Reuters that all journalists were banned from the area. One soldier and then a second grabbed his wrists and tried to seize his equipment. The journalist struggled and tried to use his mobile phone to call for help. An officer then ordered his arrest and soldiers attached his hand to their vehicle with plastic handcuffs. Fifteen minutes later, he was released, but threatened with further arrest unless he immediately left the scene.[10]

A picture of Qusini under detention shows the constraints he faced (Figure 5).

Being physically constrained would seem to undermine the disinterest and objectivity of journalists. When we read news, we rarely envision a journalist

Figure 5 Photojournalist Abed Qusini being detained by the Israeli army. The photographer, Alaa Badarna, gifted this photograph to Qusini. *Source*: Alaa Badarna, courtesy of Abed Qusini.

being tied to the object she or he is charged with covering. But under Israeli occupation, pervasive endangerment and knowing how to negotiate it is a condition of possibility for the production of eyewitness international news about the conflict. That day, Abed Qusini managed the threat of expulsion or arrest by speaking Hebrew and highlighting his connections to the British news agency Reuters. Asking to see the military order was not just a way of reporting to his superiors why he had not obtained coverage; it was also an attempt to hold the soldiers accountable. Had he not invoked Reuters, he may have faced harsher consequences, such as a longer detention or a full-fledged arrest. In negotiating with those who wanted to hold him captive, Qusini deployed powers that legally and physically it seemed he might not have had. After all, the IDF can declare "closed military zones" whenever it pleases, and soldiers can easily take people into detention on the basis of their presence in these areas. Qusini performed the role of a journalist with the right to free speech and freedom of movement, even though circumstances hardly supported his inhabitation of this category. These small performances are one way Palestinians may indirectly respond to verbal and physical attacks. Israeli officials have suggested that Palestinians should not be recognized as journalists because they can pose a danger to the state of Israel, and have even suggested that Palestinians have to be managed with force. With such performances, Palestinian journalists, for their part, assert that they operate with speech even in the face of force. Their cultivated calm is itself an embodied skill given the fear or rage these journalists may be experiencing. These performances are reflexive, embodied actions that "break with context"[11] by disrupting ongoing violence with talk. Emphasizing the embodied dimension of these performances is especially important here because using speech stops the momentum of other forms of embodied interaction between Palestinians and Israeli soldiers. Palestinians use speech as though to assert that they are not to be ruled only by force.

Successful Palestinian protesters and community leaders exhibit similar verbal skills in the face of Israeli military force. People I knew from 'Aida Refugee Camp, in Bethlehem, also defused potentially dangerous situations with speech. During a period when teenagers were regularly being arrested for their protests against the building of the separation barrier nearby, I watched with astonishment as a man retrieved a boy from Israeli soldiers about to arrest him, cajoling them with just the right touch of deference, pragmatism, and confidence. In another instance, an intervention did not prevent an arrest, but it gave a family marginally more control over a potentially dangerous and degrading situation.

At around one o'clock one winter morning, tens of soldiers and military police encircled the apartments and courtyard of an extended family and approached the door of twenty-seven-year-old Sa'eed. As he described the episode:

> [The soldiers] started yelling at me, at my house, "Come out, it's the army," and so forth. . . . My door is a little broken, and when you open it, it makes a loud sound, almost like some kind of weapon. So I thought, here they are coming, anxious and on edge at night, what should I do? I turned on another light, and I started talking to them. I told them, "OK, OK, I'm opening the door now, there's no problem." When I opened the door, there were four of them, kneeling on the ground, with their M-16s and their lasers raised, pointing at me.

Then, he negotiated with them about how he would be searched. His verbal performance to the soldiers (and later to me) was characterized by a deliberate demeanor. When the captain of the military police came to talk to him and asked him about where in the large family house each of his brothers lived, Sa'eed first insisted that his elderly parents be allowed to return inside. In the next few minutes, Sa'eed's teenage nephew, Jalal, was arrested, but Sa'eed asked to speak to his nephew before he was taken away:

> Jalal went down with the army, without a jacket, without shoes, so I had to get involved. . . . I asked if I could talk to Jalal. At first they refused. I told him, "No, I want to talk to him for a minute; I want to give him a jacket and shoes. It's cold." So they said, "OK, but don't be long." [As they left,] they wanted to give me his glasses, but I put them in his pocket, and I told him, after they tied his hands and blindfolded him, "Here are your glasses in the pocket of your jacket. Always ask for them. Tell them, 'I can't see without glasses,' and don't deal with them at all if they don't give you your glasses. Here they are in your jacket." And those were the last words we shared. "Here are your glasses, and God be with you. Hopefully we'll see you soon."

Though Sa'eed was not able to avert his nephew's arrest, he mitigated its violence and he advised his nephew on how to do the same in the ensuing hours or days. In doing so, Sa'eed was also perhaps sending a message to the soldiers that this young man had been prepped and would not be easily scared. Sa'eed's performance exemplifies how many Palestinians used to dealing with the Israeli occupying army have become accustomed to meeting force with words in an effort to accomplish basic goals. For both journalists and other politically engaged Palestinians, being an effective political actor entails disciplined embodied stances and measured performances. Palestinian journalists' effectiveness as journalists in occupied territory requires them to use skills they have developed living in close proximity with the Israeli army. They know how to cover a protest despite Israeli attempts to quell it. They know how to speak to soldiers with a combination of restraint and determination. These skills of proximity—skills of surviving at home—are the basis for journalists' professional skills.

DRAWING CLOSER

A subset of skills of proximity includes skills that involve physical proximity or social intimacy. Robert Capa's famous quip has become a photojournalist's truism: "If your pictures aren't good enough, you're not close enough." Drawing "close enough" to take pictures at public events requires physical and social acrobatics. When I tried to shadow journalists as they covered a martyr's funeral in Nablus, I again found myself sorely lacking. I more or less watched from the sidelines and struggled to keep up as the photojournalists made their way through crowds of grieving family members, friends, and compatriots. The photojournalists sidled up close to mourning parents, and then ran ahead to stand on a car, ledge, or hill to obtain wider shots, only to later wrangle their way back into the tightest spaces of bereavement to take a close-up as the body was buried. Photojournalists' passage through the crowds is aided by their cameras, professional tools that also signal why they are moving so decisively, and by the fact that people often recognize them. Drawing themselves into the action, especially during moments of heightened emotion for their subjects, is a skill of proximity that many Palestinian photojournalists have mastered.

At another funeral, in a rural setting, a Palestinian journalist took a striking picture of a corpse prepared for burial. Israeli soldiers had killed this young, unarmed man as they tried to arrest his brother.[12] The picture, taken from a rooftop above the funeral procession, belied the negligible interest his death would spur in international news. The body was wrapped in a traditional black and white kaffiyeh scarf and a Palestinian flag, and it was elaborately framed by kaffiyeh-wearing pallbearers and a spring grapevine growing on a trellis. The intricate patterns of the checkered kaffiyehs and the light green lacy grapevine hinted at the ways this man was ensconced in a culture—while so many representations of Palestinian victims of violence depict raw flesh. To capture the photograph, the journalist had to stand on a rooftop just over the funeral procession. The photographer told me that after so many funerals, he was looking for a new angle, and the grapevine had inspired him.

Experienced photographers know what to expect at a funeral, and they can maneuver through complex social and physical settings to attain the picture they have in mind.

Palestinian journalists' expressions, body postures, and habits also help them to establish rapport with the Palestinians they are interviewing. This is another integral way of drawing closer in a single moment. For example, during Ramadan, Leila, a fixer who had become an expert on the separation barrier, took several foreign journalists around an agricultural area in the city of Qalqilya, which is surrounded by the separation barrier. Ramadan was a difficult time to do such reporting, because interactions that would usually take place over a cup of coffee or tea were unbound by such pleasantries. People tended to be tired and, on this particular day, hot. But as Leila made her way from work shacks to residential mansions, she remembered names and always knew when to insert a political comment, a joke, or an empathetic expression, like *"Allah yufrajkum"* (literally, May God free you), for those whose land had been lost to the wall. Everywhere I saw this dynamic woman go, people knew her or were drawn to her, and thus were eager to talk to her.

For Walid, another Palestinian fixer on the job at a different section of the wall, it was not his gregariousness that made the difference but his embodied social position and his graciousness. Only one team of journalists witnessed the eight-meter section of wall being assembled at this particular location on a chilly winter night. Spotlights shone on the construction site as the workers labored. The team of journalists was interviewing a pair of women, one old and one young, whom they happened to have encountered. The older woman recounted her life story of multiple displacements due to political events. Now, it seemed, she would be displaced again, since her home was going to be on the other side of the wall from that of her daughter. The younger woman had brought her mother to the wall to prove to her that she should continue to live with her or risk being stranded. The older woman was frail and distraught. Her daughter was anxious to bring her home.

The journalists had happened upon an excellent story. But the daughter had also identified a resource in Walid. The street was dark and empty, and this journalist was a middle-aged, professionally dressed Palestinian man, a perfect outside authority figure to enlist in this small crisis. "Please," she implored Walid, "tell my mother that she must come home with me." The U.S. journalist stood back as Walid reasoned gently with the woman, with an empathy that might have emerged from the fact that his own family's home had also been compromised by the building of the separation wall nearby. But Walid did not mention this—he rarely did. I had always been impressed by this journalist's easy politeness, the way he could always ask a favor smoothly, his use of all the right expressions. It was this facility that allowed Walid to assuage the older woman—and at the same time do excellent reporting—that night. Such moments exemplify the skill and grace that are the products of emotional and cultural proximity. In this regard, too, Palestinian journalists obtained some of their most valuable professional skills in their everyday lives as socially capable people in the occupied Palestinian territories. Many Palestinians spend a significant amount of time in multigenerational gatherings, and everything from wedding celebrations to solving family problems entails dealing with extended networks of relatives and friends in a capable and respectful manner. Reporting involved these skills as well, and foreign correspondents relied on their Palestinian colleagues' having these skills.

During my fieldwork, I experimented with using more of the polite and often religiously inflected language that I heard people like Leila and Walid employ. I found that it did indeed place some people at ease. Yet, I also recognized that I needed to be careful to use it with the right people. More secular conversation partners may have thought I overused expressions like "*In sha Allah*" (God willing) and "*al-hamdu lillah*" (thank God). Part of these journalists' skills was their ability to use such expressions appropriately. Deciding when to use such terms was a skill that came naturally to socially adept native speakers who had experience conversing with people of different backgrounds, but this skill was relatively rare even among the internationals who spoke good Arabic.

A final, and pivotal, skill of proximity is emplacement: the ability of Palestinian journalists to expeditiously arrive on the scene. One of the pillars of the U.S. journalistic institutions within which Palestinians work is eyewitness reporting. Being on the scene is essential to thorough and ethical reporting.[13] Eyewitness journalism offers readers a direct link to the events being covered, and this is meant to guarantee credibility. During the second Intifada, arriving to the scene was often an ordeal due to Israeli closure policies. These can be dated to the early 1990s policies preventing Palestinians from the West Bank and Gaza Strip from entering Israel and east Jerusalem, and limiting Palestinian travel between Gaza and the West Bank.[14] These policies intensified dramatically during the second Intifada. In January 2004, the United Nations Office for the Coordination of Humanitarian Affairs (OCHA) counted 763 barriers to movement in the West Bank, an area slightly smaller than the state of Delaware.[15]

These barriers included fifty-nine checkpoints staffed by Israeli soldiers, ten partial checkpoints that operated sporadically, and forty road gates, long metal gates the Israeli army could open or close. Other obstacles restricted vehicle movement without Israeli soldiers being present: 479 earth mounds, including the piles of dirt, rubble, and rocks scattered around the Bethlehem district in areas that would later be closed off by the separation wall; seventy-five trenches like the one that surrounded Jericho on three sides; and one hundred road-blocks made of one-meter concrete blocks too massive to move without heavy machinery. The separation barrier, on which construction began in 2002 and which has still not been completed, is also part of the system of closure. Perhaps even direr for journalists wishing to arrive on the scene of an event quickly, Israeli authorities could erect checkpoints whenever they liked and could de-clare certain neighborhoods, villages, or cities closed military areas, prohibiting journalists and other civilians from entering. Given their imperative to be on the scene of events, Palestinian journalists have become experts in emplace-ment. In a telling conjuncture, emplacement is not only a journalistic value; it is an esteemed Palestinian skill, one that, like other journalistic practices, is also associated with challenging authorities and asserting one's freedom. Though emplacement—being on the scene so as to provide an eyewitness account—is important for journalists working around the world, the practical steps needed to enact emplacement are quite different at various sites. Usually it is not even recognized as a skill.

As I have suggested, closure policies affected movement on a variety of dif-ferent scales, and journalists utilized a range of different skills to overcome restrictions. When in New York before my fieldwork I interviewed the Hebron-based journalist Mazen Dana about movement restrictions that hindered his work, he told me that he sometimes traversed through the Old City by leaping from rooftop to rooftop. At the time, I thought this was an extravagant claim. But when I went to Hebron, I saw that the Old City's Ottoman-era buildings were densely packed. During a tour, a middle-aged Palestinian woman told my group of American visitors that during curfews she traveled by rooftop to bring her grandchildren home from a nearby youth center. Rooftop travel was not only plausible; it was a widespread strategy. As with other skills of proximity, Palestinian journalists draw upon some of the same skills as nonjournalist Pal-estinians to cope with closure.

If jumping from roof to roof had an adventurous dimension, Mazen's trip to work was tedious though unpredictable. He explained that his home in Hebron was in an area under full Israeli control, while most of his work was in down-town Hebron, parts of which were under Palestinian administration and parts under Israeli control. His commute involved passing through a checkpoint:

> Many, many times soldiers stop me when I am trying to go back to my home [from work in downtown Hebron] because it is in Area C, which means it is under Israeli authority. It [the detention] takes half an hour, one hour, and sometimes they ask me to go back. They do not let me, one way or another, to go home, to my home.[16]

Mazen had many opportunities to hone the skill of negotiating with soldiers. Again, these problems of closure were widespread in Palestinian society, es-pecially during the second Intifada. For example, a Palestinian teacher I knew commuted daily from Bethlehem to Abu Dis, but during the Intifada I would often find her home early because she simply had not been able to make it to work. When she did make it to school, it was a small victory. The challenges and rewards of being a Palestinian journalist paralleled those of being an active Palestinian in general.

Intercity travel during times of crisis often involved cunning and a reliance on local knowledge. A few journalists from Jerusalem told me of their experi-ences entering besieged cities during the major wave of Israeli invasions into Palestinian cities in 2002. Passage required that they deal with soldiers effec-tively and mobilize their extensive knowledge of checkpoints and alternative routes. For instance, during some of the worst parts of the fighting, a Pales-tinian from Jerusalem who was working with an international journalist and using an Israeli car marked with a yellow license plate entered a Palestinian city by driving through a friendly neighboring Jewish community and then over a back road. The foreign journalist's professional credentials and foreign pass-port would have offered them some protection had the Israeli army intercepted them, but this was still a daring itinerary. Knowing how to travel under condi-tions of closure is not only a matter of being familiar with the terrain and the latest checkpoint developments. It also entails understanding how people of different legal and social categories might be treated by the IDF.

Similarly, journalists know how to advise internationals on navigating the West Bank, taking advantage of internationals' generally enhanced movement privileges. When I tried to enter Nablus, I was often in rather intense touch with journalists there via cell phone. Being able to guide foreigners into the city was a critical professional skill, since they could not work as fixers if internationals could not enter their city. Moreover, journalists and others in Nablus were eager for visitors to witness the calamitous effects of Israel's counterinsurgency in their city. Each time I was stopped outside Nablus, my cell phone counsels produced an array of strategies for evading the checkpoints, many of which were tailored to someone with a U.S. passport. One journalist told me to just cut around the line of Palestinians at Huwara checkpoint and tell a soldier that I needed to enter urgently—a tactic that could not be used by most local Palestinians. Another time I was trying to enter Nablus, a journalist told me that if I had trouble I should call him and he would come talk to soldiers he knew and thus secure me passage. Still another time, two different journalists guided me by phone from the main Huwara checkpoint to another, lesser-used army installation at the District Coordination Office, about a ten-minute drive away. They suggested that the outpost could provide special entrance privileges to internationals. On another occasion, a journalist suggested that I travel to a nearby village where a friend of his might be able to guide me into Nablus through a back route that involved a donkey ride through the mountains. The very last visit I made to Nablus during my 2003–2005 fieldwork was exceptional. The only time the bus stopped was for passengers to buy ice cream along the way.

Palestinian journalists know that when they can, they must perform the empowered journalist. I watched from the back seat with some trepidation as a Palestinian journalist in a Palestinian and thus, green-license-plated SUV marked PRESS swung around the queue at a minor checkpoint between two Palestinian areas. The very fact that he had refused to wait in line could suggest that he had the authority to do so, even as it could also cause alarm. A journalist's professional status can also impede movement, however. A cameraperson working in Ramallah summed up, "they [Israeli soldiers] could allow you to pass or prevent you from passing just because you are a journalist," or, he continued, they could refuse to recognize the journalist's professional status at all. The unpredictability of closure made contingency plans essential.

I found this to be the case when traveling with Suhad, a top producer, and a group of international journalists in the winter of 2004. Suhad had organized a trip for a group of journalists to a press conference and protest in the village of Beit Sureik, located in the Jerusalem governorate in the West Bank. According to Israeli plans, the separation barrier would surround Beit Sureik on three sides. Palestinian advocates stressed that this would destroy homes and leave the village without adequate water resources. As part of the growing popular resistance against the separation barrier, village leaders were planning a protest that would bring residents of six nearby villages together to march to the site where the wall would be built.

Suhad was a fast-talking, trilingual field producer, as dynamic in English as she was in Arabic and Hebrew. She had been hard at work for two weeks, arranging for a group of journalists to attend this protest, and drumming up the interest of European and American journalists working for radio and newspaper outlets. She was taking some of the same journalists to Abu Dis later in the week, but there the wall was already built. She considered the trip to Beit Sureik to be an opportunity for journalists to see what Palestinians were losing because of the barrier, losses too often hidden at the sites where the wall had already done its work. She said that the group would meet a family who had been served confiscation orders for their land, a Palestinian member of the Israeli Knesset, a member of the Palestinian parliament, and a well-respected priest. We met at the American Colony, a hotel and restaurant that served as the elegant hub of many foreign correspondents' and wealthy Palestinians' social lives in east Jerusalem. As we embarked, I could not help but notice that Suhad had more energy than most of the journalists she was leading—and also that some of the foreign correspondents, pleased to have a prearranged day of reporting ahead of them, were not clear on where we were going and why.

Israeli soldiers stopped the first part of our four-car caravan at a roadblock outside of Beit Iksa, one village away from Beit Sureik. The soldiers asked to see our identity cards and our press passes. They tentatively let us pass, even though we did not all have press passes, but as we were waiting for the remainder of the cars to arrive, a police car swung around in front of us, and the soldiers announced that we could not pass, because we were heading into a closed military area. Soon, at least seven cars were being detained. Suhad started mobilizing, both to try to secure passage and also to illuminate closure for the foreign correspondents. Suhad summarized for us what was going on and why. She called Israeli military authorities and encouraged other journalists to do the same. The authorities replied noncommittally that they were working on the situation. In the meantime, Suhad asked a soldier to show her the military order that designated the area as a closed military area. She even took the order in her own hands to examine for a while. It mapped out a region around Beit Iksa, and said that the closure was in effect from nine in the morning until eight at night. The closures meant that Beit Sureik was inaccessible. Some of the foreign correspondents snapped pictures, realizing that this might be the only story they reported on that day (Figure 6). A BBC journalist asked Suhad if the

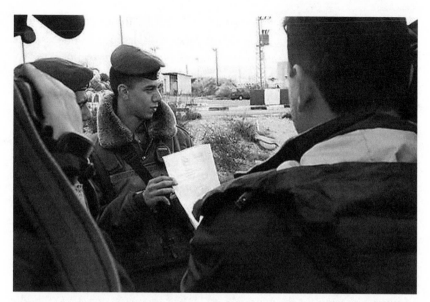

Figure 6   Photographing the paperwork of closure. Photojournalists record a soldier holding the military order denying access to the village where a demonstration is to take place after a Palestinian producer asked the soldier to provide it. *Source*: Amahl Bishara.

soldiers had given a reason for the closure, and she reported that they had not. The Orthodox priest who was also headed to the protest arrived and joined the blockade-turned-impromptu-event, giving a few small interviews about the injustice of the wall and the need to protect human rights.

The outcome of the trip was mixed. We heard that of the people who had planned to speak at the protest only the Palestinian parliamentarian had made it there from outside the village. Suhad said that the Palestinian radio reporter and a reporter from a major Palestinian newspaper had also been prohibited from entering. Still, while the army did effectively prohibit journalists from covering an important press conference and protest, Suhad had nevertheless managed to deliver an event. One journalist commented that Israeli authorities were "so stupid" for closing down the area. After all, he said, just a day earlier, Israel had organized its own tour of the wall for journalists, so to him shutting down this protest seemed heavy-handed. Were the authorities happy to trade a story about popular protest for a revealing moment about closure?

We waited around for a bit, hoping to get through eventually, and then someone gave word of another demonstration. We piled back into the cars. There is, it seems, always another event nearby to cover. And there is always someone else to tell a story. On the way, the taxi driver chronicled the area through which we were driving: a history of land expropriations, displacement, and loss. One of the foreign correspondents spotted potential for an article in his narrative. When we arrived at the next village, though, we were told the demonstration was a half-hour walk away through the mountains. Most of the journalists decided the walk was too far, and they did not want to risk leaving any heavy, expensive equipment in the car. We went home.

ETHICS ON THE SIDE OF THE ROAD

Perhaps a group of Palestinian journalists would have approached a half-hour walk through the mountains differently. When the process of reporting entails challenging Israeli restrictions—forging over this mountain or around that checkpoint—this itself can be rewarding for Palestinians. After all, movement itself can have a strong affective and ethical dimension.[17] Palestinians' explicit professional ethics, discussed in Chapter 3, center on objectivity as a means of expressing truth for the national cause. They are not inconsistent with liberal norms in which language refers to an external, preexisting truth. However, these professional ethics are echoed by a more subtle ethics of embodied practices and affective stances. Very often the everyday activities of being a good Palestinian journalist involve challenging the occupation, even if journalists working for U.S. or European organizations are not able to narrate stories in ways that disrupt mainstream narratives in the United States or Europe. Practicing journalism in itself is a way of creating a place for expression and mobility in the midst of a regime that to such a large degree rules by force. Everyday practices of journalism like challenging closure with one's own body, listening to victims of political violence, and prudently but directly defying soldiers resemble some of the things activists might do to confront the occupation. Enacting this *ethics of practice* is part of what makes journalists' jobs meaningful to them. The work involved with being a journalist produces what Kathleen Stewart calls "a haunting doubled epistemology of being in the midst of things and impacted by them and yet making something of things."[18] No matter what is published from journalists' work, this is significant.

One dimension of this ethics of practice reframes something as simple—and integral to basic journalistic practice—as conducting an interview or doing eyewitness reporting. An ethical practice of being present and listening has a healthy tradition in Palestinian civil society. Making visits to people who have suffered from Israeli policies or attacks, listening to their stories, and expressing sympathy with them is a common mode of witness and social solidarity. I once accompanied a group of teenagers as they visited the families of other teenagers in their community who had been imprisoned for political reasons. This long afternoon of tea and conversation was not a political act of the sort that could be covered in the news, but it fostered a vital ethic of caring political involvement. Drawing close to the suffering of others and thereby insisting that those who have suffered most under Israeli occupation do not suffer alone is a subtle but important way in which Palestinians shape the lived experience of a dire political situation. In this regard, the round of visits was akin to a political act, in Charles Hirschkind's sense of politics as "the activities of ordinary citizens who, through the exercise of their agency in contexts of public interaction, shape the conditions of their collective existence."[19]

Likewise, for many journalists, attending funerals, visiting families of martyrs or prisoners, and listening to elders' stories of past conflicts and traumas are not just ways to gather information; they are meaningful for their own sake. During one Ramadan, I accompanied a news agency reporter who was writing a story about families that had lost at least two people to Israeli violence. On this occasion, too, we were offered tea or coffee at each house, and the reporter was visibly moved by what he heard. He was the kind of reporter who would not be writing up his own article, as he did not write well in English. However, the act of conducting these interviews was obviously significant to him, as it moved him to tears. When journalists conduct interviews that double as political visits, they may find reporting itself to be meaningful, no matter what is finally published from their work. They ask their interviewees more questions than a nonreporter would, but they also have some of the same affective reactions to their subjects as they would were they visiting people in their community with no professional motive.

Similarly, the fundamental professional demand of eyewitness reporting, which necessitates being on the scene, often requires that journalists challenge military closure, an action that Palestinians recognize as politically valuable. This was especially true during the hot days of the second Intifada. The journalist who, out of concern for his safety and his professionalism, was hesitant to carry the wounded during an Israeli incursion could be proud of his ability to find a back way into a besieged city, for it made him not only a good producer, but also an exemplary Palestinian civic activist. The explicit goal of a journalist taking a dirt road to reach an isolated village to chart the path of the barrier is professional, but in this case, too, resisting closure has deep political resonance. Journalists scaled dirt mounds that served as roadblocks and then fastidiously wiped their dusty shoes, as though to reassert their professional status. There might be a moment of smoothing over the seam between the political act of defying closure and the professional act of arriving on the scene for eyewitness reporting, but generally there was no contradiction between the two. The mere act of staying in touch with Palestinians from many walks of life and in many places is politically significant when military closure is pervasive.

Sometimes this ethics of practice entails physical feats. Palestinian photojournalists who put themselves in the line of fire, or in the cloud of tear gas, are assuming embodied political stances that have undeniable moral significance in Palestinian society. After a demonstration in which I stayed well behind the frontline of conflict with Israeli soldiers, I was chatting with a reporter when a photojournalist who had been in the midst of the demonstration emerged. He blinked his eyes and shook his head vigorously with a grin as he told us, "Wow, it's been a while since I've had a taste of that tear gas!" Being in the thick of things was an ethically resonant enterprise, even if one was not participating in the demonstration directly. It signaled one's willingness to suffer for representation, and also tuned or retuned the body so that one could be ready to participate if one so desired.

It follows that when a journalist is killed on the job, this journalist dies a politically honored death. Journalists emphasize that they are not parties to the conflict, and yet they also express their willingness to die for their work in terms similar to the way an activist or militant might. Journalists who are killed on the job are considered martyrs to the national struggle, albeit ones who are killed for the "truth" rather than any particular party or faction. In his acceptance speech to the Committee to Protect Journalists (CPJ), Mazen Dana, the cameraperson from Hebron discussed in the Introduction, had declared his willingness to die for his work, to endure hardships to create the words and images that are a "public trust" "even if it costs me my life."[20] Palestinians might have interpreted his statement as continuous with a readiness for martyrdom, even as war correspondents might have recognized it as the kind of dedication necessary for the job. After he was killed in Iraq with his camera on his shoulder, his colleagues confirmed that Mazen had risked his life on a regular basis. A photographer, Hussam Abu Allan, remarked, "Mazen was always convinced that it is a thousand times better to be killed as a free man than to be killed as a captive or a coward. For him there was no question about it being a human right to live freely."[21]

In sum, Palestinian journalistss cultivate steadfast commitment to the community by drawing close to the action in a demonstration, crossing checkpoints in a fractured territory, or conducting interviews with ordinary people who have lost family members.[22] Moving and listening are political actions in these circumstances. The practices of journalism influence a political world even if freedom of expression and freedom of movement are not achieved, and even if the news stories Palestinian journalists help produce do not challenge mainstream narratives.

CONCLUSIONS: WHEN YOUR HANDS ARE TIED, USE YOUR MOUTH!

U.S. foreign correspondents are generally posted to new positions every three to five years with the understanding that a fresh perspective is important to successful journalism, and that the tools of journalism that apply in Moscow are applicable, with a few adjustments, in Jerusalem, too. Looking at journalism from the perspective of Palestinian journalists' practice suggests that foreign correspondents' global mobility requires that other journalists stay in place. Although the norms of Western journalism are rooted in policies set by Western media institutions, the specific practices of journalism in the West Bank and Gaza Strip are shaped to a large extent by the circumstances of life and work under military occupation. As they labor, Palestinian journalists draw upon reservoirs of social and political knowledge that they have developed throughout their lives. While some would argue that their location inside Palestinian society compromises their ability to be good journalists, examination of skills of proximity makes it evident that it is by virtue of being inside Palestinian society—physically, culturally, and emotionally—that they can effectively do the work they do and complement the work of foreign correspondents.

Examining the practices of Palestinian journalists reveals a complement to their stated professional ethics, which often revolve around familiar values of objectivity paired in a context-specific way with nationalism. Aside from the ethics relating to the published outcomes of journalism, we can see here that journalists have a set of values related to their own sense of themselves and how the practices of journalism subtly affect the world around them. Journalists find it rewarding to travel among many Palestinian communities, because doing so builds connections among these fragmented places. They may take pride in challenging Israeli soldiers, even though this is not the goal of their work. While journalists may have to compromise with foreign correspondents and editors with respect to the narratives they create, in the field they often can comport themselves according to a code of conduct that both benefits their work and also promotes their sense of themselves as active and positive participants in Palestinian civil society. An ethics of practice concerns the side effects of labor. It is distinct from the professional ethics that guide the outcomes of professional practice; that is, it focuses on practice for its own sake. It looks at the sometimes submerged ethical codes that inform how people make their work meaningful, how they are sensitive to the multiple effects their work can have on communities around them, and how they can fashion or maintain an ethical self as they work.

Studying journalism with an eye to the experiences of Palestinian journalists also highlights the extent to which journalism involves embodied skills: the ability to position oneself as safely as possible during a protest, knowing how to stand in a way that expresses respect and concern when conducting an interview on the street, being able to discern and cope with the various weapons used to disperse crowds at a protest. Sometimes the embodied skills of journalism demand staying still, restraining one's self against fury. Calling attention to the diverse and embodied dimensions of journalism is important not only because it challenges our understanding of the kinds of labor that journalism requires, but also because it suggests an ethical reason to recognize embodied journalism. Due to media conglomeration and convergence,[23] as well as cuts to the budgets of international desks, on-the-ground reporting in foreign countries is being done by fewer people, while more news outlets take reports from news agencies like the Associated Press and Reuters. One reporter might ferry information to journalists working for the same company on multiple platforms of television, print, and internet reporting. Journalists may also take information from officials' press releases rather than conducting their own investigations.[24] The results of this have been called "sedentary journalism,"[25] in which more journalists write news from office desks rather than from the scene of events. Still, some journalists, like the Palestinian reporters and photojournalists at the center of this book, remain in the field, gathering eyewitness accounts of events. They also help make it possible for foreign correspondents to venture into the field during moments of intense conflict. These journalists obviously endanger themselves more than those who stay at their desks, and for this reason recognition of their work is important. But we might also wonder about the effects of an increased proportion of "sedentary journalism" on news content. What are the implications of having those who experience events removed from narrating them?

Recognizing the embodied dimensions of journalistic labor also gives us insight into intellectual production in general. While anthropologists have challenged the Cartesian divide between mind and body for decades, an assumption persists that intellectual labor is disembodied, that we produce knowledge with our minds rather than our bodies.[26] Palestinian journalists would not be successful in their jobs if they did not know how to use their eyes, ears, and feet effectively to discern the events around them, to position themselves in places that grant perspective and allow them to stay safe. Indeed, journalists' work reveals that embodied skills cannot be separated from social and intellectual ones. Interpreting the world enlists all of our senses, even if our interpretations must be condensed into words. Embodied skills are entailed in an array of forms of discernment that Palestinians must practice. When we do not recognize the body's role in producing knowledge, or when we do not exert an embodied effort to investigate and comprehend power, we risk overlooking systemic violence that has been concretized into the environment, as in the case of checkpoints. We risk missing perspectives that require going somewhere inconvenient: scaling a pile of rubble, taking a path through the mountains to reach a protest, or drawing quite close to the people about whom one wants to learn.

Finally, the body is not only an instrument for perception. It is also a player in performances. The dynamics of military occupation often seem absolute: the weapons and legal authority are both on the side of Israel. Yet, Palestinians make something different of this imbalance when, from positions of constraint, they talk to soldiers as though they have rights. The rewards of these performances are small but substantial: securing an earlier release from detention, for example. These are some of the tricks Palestinians have up their sleeves even when their hands may be cuffed.

LOCATING THE FOREIGN CORRESPONDENT AT A DEMONSTRATION

The weekly protests against the wall had captured the passions of many Palestinians and solidarity activists by October 2005 when "At Israeli Barrier, More Sound Than Fury" was published.[1] But while protests were weekly, coverage, especially in major U.S. outlets, was rare. In this article, Steven Erlanger, a New York Times *correspondent who shared a Pulitzer for his work on Al-Qaeda and who has also edited cultural news and covered diplomacy in Washington for the* New York Times, *wrote about one of the centers of popular resistance against the wall. He suggests that a protest in the village of Bil'in was a skilled performance by protesters and the Israeli military alike. The opening of the article reads, "The Israeli Army and a crowd of protesters squared off almost joyfully on Friday for their weekly tactical battle here over the construction of Israel's separation barrier, one of the closest spectacles the region provides to Kabuki theater." I was certainly open to the idea of protesting as performative, but I was curious as to how interlocutors who had participated in such protests would respond to the characterization of these performances as joyful and theatrical.*

For my Palestinian readers this was the kind of article that invited long conversation, because it dealt with a topic many people cared about deeply and knew well. So when I conducted an interview with one young man, Ahmed, in his cramped home in 'Aida Refugee Camp, we finished cups of tea, and then soda, and then coffee, each balanced on a plastic stool that served as a table. And a friend who had stopped by could not help but chime in. Another resident of 'Aida Camp, Qusay, whom I interviewed alone, let on that his brother had contributed to the marginalia I saw scribbled on the printed-out article I had given him. I also traveled to Bil'in for an on-the-record response of a leader of the popular resistance movement there, Iyad Burnat. We met in his salon, furnished with an old and formal living room set. There, too, an activist photographer who happened to be visiting could not help but contribute his read.

The bulk of Erlanger's article described a single protest, and readers dissected it almost sentence by sentence, starting with the first line's description of the protest as a kind of theater. Burnat, the organizer from Bil'in, explained to me, "Because the army failed to repress these popular protests . . . they have tried to call them theater, a game, anything." But, he insisted, the stakes are high for the villagers: "Truly, what happens in Bil'in and other villages near the wall is certainly not a game. There is land that has been confiscated which we are trying to defend." Moreover, the demonstrations themselves had serious consequences. He explained that since demonstrations started years earlier,

> *Thirteen hundred people have been wounded, including Palestinians, Israelis, and internationals who have come in solidarity. There are people who have been injured tens of times. More than seventy people have been arrested, most of them children. This is the game the Israeli army is talking about? Excruciating beatings, use of great force to repress these demonstrations. Last night, more than seventy soldiers came into town. If this were a game, why would they come to the village to arrest people?*

Other passages in the article suggested that demonstrators had provoked Israeli violence. "The protesters," Erlanger wrote, "were eager to take their case against the barrier to the world through the news media and to try to provoke the army and the police into overreacting." The army, for its part, was "trying to deny these experienced protesters any scenes that could be construed as brutal behavior." Qu-say, a frequent participant in demonstrations in 'Aida Camp, rejected the idea that Palestinians tried to provoke the Israeli army when I interviewed him at his workplace, a local community-based organization.

> *He is portraying the Palestinians as though they are trying to take on the role of the victim . . . as though the army just responds to violence [as opposed to instigating it]. . . . But we are not faking this. These are our lives as people who were forced to leave our land. We are the victims of occupation. He wants to suggest that going to protests is our hobby as Palestinians, but this is not true. I don't like to go to demonstrations. I want to live in security. I want to have a good future, to go to school, to have a house and a family, to travel and have fun. Demonstrations are not a hobby. This situation has been imposed upon us.*

He continued, *"He describes Palestinians' demonstrations as a way to provoke the Israeli army to shoot at them, and to show the world that the army is shooting at them. . . . It's a silly idea, as if I want to die in order to show the world that I am dying."*

Yet, according to Erlanger, the protest was conducted *"with relative good nature on both sides despite the din."* Even one tumultuous arrest involved *"no visible use of truncheons or fists on either side, just a lot of heated shouting and scrambling about."* The protest came to an end *"with the requisite points made,"* and as the end of the daily Ramadan fast approached. As the article described, at this point, *"both sides settled into a set of relatively jovial debates, in a mixture of Hebrew and Arabic that might have been sponsored by a nongovernmental organization."* Ahmed suggested that one look at the soldiers that were usually deployed to such protests would contradict the article's description of the protest as a site for discussion:

> An Israeli soldier is wearing a bulletproofed vest and a helmet, is carrying weapons, is wearing a scary uniform. This guy wants to talk? I don't think so. Why would he be carrying weapons if he wants to talk? Why is he wearing a helmet if he wants to talk? There are circumstances that are clear all by themselves, without explanation. If you gave this article to a twelve-year-old, he wouldn't believe this scene.

A description of an exchange between a soldier and a protester caught Burnat's attention. According to the article, *"One officer said to a Palestinian boy, 'Go home, it's Ramadan.' The boy looked at the sun in the sky and answered, 'No, there's time left.'"* Burnat could not remember this specific protest out of the many he had attended, but to him the exchange sounded implausible:

> Such interactions with the army never happen. Sometimes the army will call out over the loudspeakers, "OK, it's time to go home." But face-to-face, there is never a dialogue with demonstrators, because soldiers are never that close to demonstrators. After they throw tear gas and so forth, the demonstrations break up. Soldiers and demonstrators are not close together. Regarding Ramadan, our demonstrations start at 1:00. Ramadan fasts end at 6:00 or so. Never would a demonstration last that long. . . . Maybe this kind of an exchange would occur between a soldier and a farmer [as a farmer waited to pass through a gate in the wall], but it wouldn't happen in a demonstration.

Readers also critiqued how the article described injuries at the demonstrations. Marwa, a media student in Nablus, disapproved of the journalist's attention to an injury suffered by a soldier even though injuries to Palestinians occurred more often.

"He shouldn't focus on the soldier who lost his eye" in a previous demonstration, she said. "Instead, he should focus on the children who were injured, and the internationals." After all, risk was part of a soldier's job. Burnat likewise commented, "The article should use the right terms for weapons. They should describe the type of gas and how, even though soldiers are supposed to shoot it from 500 meters away, up in the air, in fact they shoot it from 20 meters away, directly at people. So a gas canister is transformed into something like a bullet." In the months before my interview with Burnat, this use of tear gas canisters had caused serious injuries in Bil'in.

Despite their insistence that the demonstrations were not merely a game or a performance, these activist readers acknowledged that the media had a role to play in their struggle. According to Burnat, "The media is very important. The media eases the attitude of the Israeli army toward demonstrators. We have learned from experience that the Israeli soldier is very afraid of the camera, even more than of the M-16. More than once, we have seen them coming to beat someone, and then they see a camera filming and stop." Perhaps these dynamics had shaped the demonstration Erlanger had covered. Qusay made a more philosophical point. "It's important to have international media coverage because people outside must know about this struggle. We live on the same planet. We must have communication among us, so we can sympathize with each other, know each others' problems, and support each other." Still, according to Mohammad, a local photojournalist from Bil'in, most journalists missed some of the most serious violence that occurred in Bil'in, because they were only present during the day. Only he, a resident of Bil'in, had filmed the arrest raids that happened at night.

Perhaps the crux of the problem were the sources Erlanger had consulted. Marwa observed, "He basically talked to the officer and two of the [Israeli] peace activists." Indeed, the article comprised four quotes from an Israeli army major, two quotes from two different Israeli activists opposed to the wall, two quotes from soldiers, and the brief exchange between a soldier and a Palestinian child about when the demonstration should end, quoted above. Qusay rebuked the journalist on this account as well, surmising where Erlanger had located himself to cover the protest. "It seems he was at [Israeli major] Levi's side, and Levi is telling him everything." He continued, "In my opinion, the journalist is supposed to be neutral and honest. I am not a journalist, and I don't study journalism, but this is my understanding. He should be the world's tongue [lisan al-'alim], but he is taking a side here." Qusay had taken only a few college classes; in fact, he had taken his high school exams in prison. His commentary was a subtle assertion that perhaps his political experience was as valuable a background for truth-telling as any other.

Indeed, these issues of where Erlanger stood and the resulting sources quoted in the article were reflected in Erlanger's summation of the arguments in favor of and against the barrier. He paraphrased the basic case for the barrier: "The Israelis say there will be gates in the barrier so Bilin residents can farm their land. They also argue that the barrier is an effective measure against suicide bombers and that it is temporary, able to be moved or removed following a final peace settlement, or a court order." And he quoted an Israeli activist from B'Tselem to counter this logic. The activist stated that the wall aimed at the "annexation of new neighborhoods" to Israel and declared that "as much as 50 percent of the productive land [in the village of Bil'in] is on the Israeli side of the barrier." These were apt critiques that bore a substantive similarity to what one would hear from Palestinian activists. But Ahmed, drawing on his own experiences protesting the wall and living near it, offered a more fervent appraisal:

> I read in the article that the wall is there to prevent violence, but the wall itself is violence. It makes people increase their resolve to resist the wall, and even their violence. Sometimes, I go to my friend's house and I go out to the patio [overlooking the wall], and I think to myself, why is this area off-limits? The wall took people's land, the olive trees, the fields where the children used to play. All of this causes violence.

Said Muhammad, the photojournalist, "If you want to understand the situation, you need to live with people for a week to see what is happening." Maybe the problem was not only where Erlanger had stood during the protest, but that he had apparently gone home so soon after it concluded. He had come for the play but did not stay around the neighborhood after the curtain fell.

5 THE SEPARATION WALL AS STAGE FOR REFUGEE IDENTITIES

It was a hot afternoon in August 2004 when a Palestinian photographer for Agence France-Presse (AFP) captured a moment that threatened to slip out of hand. On the hard-edged periphery of a West Bank refugee camp near Bethlehem, a young soldier, packed into his helmet and his bulletproof vest, stood with his M-16's barrel inches away from the face of a T-shirted teenager (Figure 7). And yet the energy of the image suggests not that the soldier is about to shoot but that the teenager might throw a punch. Their backdrop is the latest icon of the Palestinian-Israeli conflict: slab after slab of the 8-meter concrete panels that make up parts of Israel's separation barrier. The photographer, Musa Al-Shaer, explained to me the significance of the picture: "It shows a confrontation between the isolated, unarmed Palestinian citizen and a soldier, who is carrying a rifle and a whole collection of weapons. And also, behind them there is the wall." The wall of which he speaks is part of a planned 709-kilometer (440 mile) structure that cuts through Palestinian territory with the purported objective of preventing Palestinians from entering Israel.[1] But it is not just a backdrop; in fact, it is more like a stage, a catalyst that brought protesters, soldiers, and the photographer together for this transitory tableau.

According to liberal democratic tradition, protests are meant to sway the public or the authorities about a specific policy in order to instigate change. As we saw during the Arab revolts of 2011, even the leadership of autocratic states can be influenced by protests, especially when they are mediated for the world to see. In Arab authoritarian nation-states, there remained some pretense that governments should rule on behalf of their people.[2] In contrast, Palestinians do not necessarily anticipate that protests will influence Israeli policies; on

Figure 7   A confrontation during a protest against the wall. Such confrontations are forged by a Palestinian habitus of protest that has a long history. *Source*: Musa Al-Shaer, Agence France-Presse/Getty Images.

the occasions when they do, even in small ways, this is exceptional. The Israeli authorities who decide how and where the barrier will be built do not see Palestinians as part of their constituency; the Israeli public that elects those authorities is not especially concerned with Palestinians' well-being. This is a central reason that protests against the separation wall do not only aim at holding the wall at bay. Instead, they are at least as much about various social dynamics internal to Palestinian society, as well as influencing amorphous—but crucial—audiences outside of the region about both the barrier and the Israeli occupation as a whole. It is in this sense that the wall is a stage for political assertions.

During a period when photojournalists had been covering protests against the wall in great depth, it was quite reasonable for Palestinians to imagine that the photographs taken of them by Palestinian journalists who worked for the Associated Press, AFP, or Reuters would be available to "the world." By the same token, Palestinians were also likely to see some of these images in their own newspapers, because these newspapers relied heavily on news agency reporting.[3] This photograph of confrontation is a case in point of how images reached both Palestinian domestic and international audiences. I found it on the Yahoo! slideshow of the

Middle East Conflict, a source for the latest photographs of the conflict. Each day tens of news agency photographs were uploaded to the slideshow for those who wanted to watch a parade of the day's official press conferences, activists at protests, military operations, and mourning families. The image was also published in a Palestinian newspaper. Both online and in print, news photographs of this sort can pass quickly into obscurity. Even if an individual treasures an image, he will not imagine it to be transformative on a national or global scale. Taking my cue from the fleeting place of these images in this economy of news and politics, I focus here less on an in-depth visual analysis and more on the production and circulation of the image.

Images like this help explain why Palestinians see themselves—and imagine how others see them—through news media. This circuitry of media gives Palestinians a double consciousness akin to what W.E.B. Du Bois described for African Americans as a practice of "always looking at [themselves] through the eyes of others, ... measuring [their] soul[s] by the tape of a world that looks on in amused contempt and pity."[4] Protesting for a global audience can make for disappointing politics. Many Palestinians have the sense that people in the West see them either as terrorists or as abject victims. Despite all of the media coverage, Palestinians see few positive actions taken by the international community. During protests, activists perform for audiences they do not know well and will likely never meet. This is an unusual configuration of a public. A public is often conceived of as a group made up of strangers but constituted as a collective through shared attention to a text, what Michael Warner calls a "social space created by the reflexive circulation of discourse."[5] Ariella Azoulay similarly conceives of a "civil contract of photography." She argues that photography creates a civil space made up of those in front of the camera, the photographer, and the audience, and that this space is somewhat autonomous from the state and from nationalist logics.[6] Here, I find that through an ethnography of photographs—in their production and circulation—we can gain a sense of the strengths and limitations of news photography as a tool for making connections among people with different kinds of power and cultural assumptions. From the perspective of Palestinian photographers and activists who angle for a photograph to be taken, news photography might constitute a transitory, transnational audience, but even with new media technologies that aid in distribution, the configuration of the audience—the way people look at images—is shaped by state politics. Palestinians sense only imperfect possibilities for exchange with audiences beyond Palestinian society.

Still, political involvement—including planning and attending protests and other public events—constitutes a vital and meaningful part of life for many Palestinians. This may be because Palestinians in the West Bank also view their world through the lens of their own nationalism. This preserves the possibility of Palestinians valuing their lives and perspectives on their own terms even as they sometimes evaluate media through the lens they imagine those in the West might have. Palestinian activists may feel proud of the stands they take, and yet simultaneously be convinced that their stories and experiences are politically insignificant, even when represented in the international media. Palestinians also perform for each other at public events: for the people assembled around them and also for those who might see their picture in a Palestinian newspaper the next day.[7] Through public political action, Palestinians make claims for other Palestinians about who they are as refugees, villagers, or city residents; as men, women, teenagers, and children; as Christians, Muslims, poor people, the educated, "peace-loving" people, those dedicated to resistance, or victims. These categories, too, have been shaped by media processes and texts and the double consciousness that they have engendered. Media are involved in "making up people," just as a wide variety of people are involved in making media.[8]

So attuned are activists and other Palestinians to the vicissitudes of representation that it is not only media *products* that can influence Palestinian politics and society but also the very processes of media *production*. That is, even the anticipation of a media presence and journalists' potential representations can influence how activists organize and protest. This chapter begins to explore this last key theme of the book. In a location like the West Bank, where news events and media production have been so much a part of the fabric of everyday life, the processes of media production themselves shape politics and society even independently of specific media texts. Complementarily, organizers and protesters can often be counted among the producers of news texts, because they make active decisions about how they would like to be represented.

A CHILDREN'S MARCH AGAINST THE WALL

The photograph of confrontation between a teenaged protester and a soldier holds but a few hints of context. The ground is the bare, packed dirt of a construction site. A distant gap in the wall in the upper left of the image as well as the lack of graffiti on the wall also indicate that work is still underway. Along with the two central figures in the photograph, another soldier looks as though he is about to intervene, and an older Palestinian with glasses and gray hair around his temples is restraining the younger man. A moment like this—a moment with momentum—passes by with the swift blink of a digital shutter, but it has a long prehistory, and the resulting image can go on to have a life of its own. In this section I explicate three overlapping media and political processes that led to the existence of this photograph: the planning of the protest, the journalist's taking and publication of this picture, and the cultural and personal factors that led to this confrontation. Then I discuss the photograph's circulation.

To understand how this image came to be, we must first examine how and why the protest occurred. If we were to pull the camera back to capture a wide shot of the protest around the confrontation, we would see tens of children and a handful of alarmed Europeans and Americans carrying posters in English, Arabic, French, and Italian; a crew of teens brandishing canisters of spray paint; several Palestinian adults holding the hands of the littler children and hurrying them away from the soldiers; a few journalists huddling behind a boulder. Across the street from the wall, we see concrete apartments piled on top of each other like haphazardly stacked blocks in three, four, and even five stories on an irregular grid of streets and alleyways. This is ʿAida Refugee Camp, one of three refugee camps adjacent to the city of Bethlehem. The unfinished wall, the raised gun, the fact that approximately 60 percent of camp residents are under the age of twenty-four[9]—all can be taken as reminders of a much larger truth, that social and political processes are in flux, here as elsewhere, and that much can be at stake in a single moment. In this case the stakes are raised not just by the gun at the center of the image but also by the camera behind it.

Coming to understand these stakes depends on historical perspective. Located just south of Jerusalem's municipal borders, ʿAida Refugee Camp is home to over 4,700 registered refugees.[10] It was established in 1950 in order to accommodate people dispossessed of their land when the state of Israel was established in 1948 in what Palestinians call *al-nakba*, or the catastrophe. Once consisting of tents, and then of concrete rooms surrounded by small gardens, ʿAida's 0.71 square kilometers (175 acres) have been almost entirely paved over, as growing families have built up and out. The camp is so crowded that goats and sheep reside on rooftops. During the early years of the second Intifada, the camp had been pummeled by Israeli incursions, as it was located on the northern border of Bethlehem and Jerusalem and just meters away from a major Israeli military encampment. Also, refugee camps tend to be sites of intense militarization because refugees have been on the forefront of resisting Israeli military occupation, and ʿAida Refugee Camp was no exception. Dozens of homes had been badly damaged. The girls' school was hit repeatedly; finally, it was reconstructed without windows on one side to prevent bullets from breaking them again. Tens of people had been injured, and among the dead were parents, a teacher, a shopkeeper, a painter.

By 2004, the building of the separation wall was many residents' most urgent political concern, both for its immediate effects and for its long-term consequences. Construction of the 8-meter wall less than 20 meters from residents' houses had brought a relentless presence of soldiers and armed guards along with earthmovers and cranes to this community. Teenagers staged their protests with stones, and Israeli soldiers quelled them with tear gas, sound bombs, and bullets. The Israeli army had arrested and imprisoned tens of teenagers for their roles in these protests. Such arrests had wide-ranging social effects.[11] But if construction was bad, the residents dreaded even more the long-term consequences of the wall. It would entrench the militarization of their community with the installation of watchtowers on the periphery of the wall and military roads on the perimeter, and it would cut residents off from the only open space to which they had access, an olive grove owned by the Armenian Church. For decades, the church had hired camp residents to harvest the olives, and residents also used this land to gather herbs and greens and to graze their goats and sheep. Children played soccer in a makeshift field amongst the olive trees. Although camp residents did not own the land, they would feel its loss dramatically. It would also further isolate the camp from the rest of Bethlehem and from Jerusalem.

This was why a local youth organization I am calling 'Awda Center had organized this protest.[12] 'Awda Center, a politically independent organization founded by former activists who had been disenchanted by politics under the PA, had organized this protest to coincide with its international summer work camp. The annual camp was a two-week program during which international volunteers—mostly Americans and Europeans—divided their time between meetings with community members and leaders, a service project undertaken with teens from the refugee camp, and recreational activities with children. Billed as a children's protest against the wall, this protest stood out from most of the demonstrations that occurred in the camp because rather than being spontaneous it was organized by an NGO. Also, it would feature the presence of internationals and children. This made it less likely, NGO leaders hoped, that the Israeli military would react violently. They also hoped it would encourage wider participation from people beyond the camp and be substantial enough to attract press coverage.

In addition to voicing opposition to the wall, the protest, like much of 'Awda Center's work, had a tacit goal of promoting constructive and safe ways for youth to participate in politics. The Oslo period of the middle and late 1990s and the second Intifada had seen shifts in youth and masculine identities. These shifts especially affected poor teenagers and young men like the one in the photograph. Palestinian nationalism, like other nationalisms, has had masculinist overtones.[13] During the first Intifada, beatings and imprisonments were akin to rites of passage, as they symbolically transformed boys into men and generated respect from the community.[14] By the new millennium, though, Palestinian nationalism had shifted in its styles from emphasizing the role of the "hero" to foregrounding that of the "martyr."[15] Human rights discourses contributed to shifting the social and political significance of being beaten and imprisoned. Instead of being seen as assertive political actors, children and young men were viewed as victims. Moreover, early in the second Intifada, the kinds and significance of resistance shifted.[16] Israel reacted to the first days of popular uprising with a more heavily militarized response than during the first Intifada, and Palestinians utilized more arms. Involvement in resistance movements posed extraordinary risks, and this limited participation of both men and women. As the second Intifada wore on, certain forms of civil disobedience and popular resistance—once signatures of Palestinian political activism—had been somewhat discredited because many Palestinians came to associate the concept of nonviolence with the NGO sector and its international donors.[17]

These transformations undermined boys' passages to manhood. Political participation no longer had the rewards of a generation earlier, and it could even more easily lead to death or a long prison sentence. While militants and martyrs were heroes for some, Palestinians' awareness of representations of Arab men during the War on Terror as irrational and violent made militarized resistance symbolically risky for others.[18] This crisis in masculinity had an economic dimension as well, as high unemployment and low wages meant that fewer men could support their families.[19] In 'Aida Refugee Camp, earlier generations of poor, uneducated men had earned the money needed to build houses and marry by working inside Israel or in the Gulf countries in construction jobs. The current younger generation was prohibited even from these difficult jobs by Israeli closure and a less welcoming stance by the Gulf states.

Perhaps because young Palestinian men were vulnerable political subjects, Palestinians looked to preserve the category of the child. Advocates often called attention to the injustice of the fact that Israel follows the standard international legal definition of the child as anyone under the age of eighteen for Israeli citizens but defines Palestinians as adults at age sixteen. This renders sixteen- and seventeen-year-olds vulnerable to higher sentences and harsher treatment. 'Awda Center, the organization which organized the protest pictured above, has held human rights courses and painted murals that emphasize "the rights of the child." While in earlier years, teenagers could become respected men as a result of their activism, today's older generations often look after teenagers as though to prolong their childhood. In the photograph, the older man restrain- ing the teenager is enacting a stance typical of this period.

The concept of the Palestinian refugee in Palestinian nationalism has also shifted over time. For decades, refugees were at the symbolic heart of Palestinian identity, both because of their suffering and struggles, and because the restora- tion of their rights seemed to be essential to fulfillment of Palestinian national rights. Yet the image of the refugee was also seen as somehow undercutting Palestinians' assertion that they were a national group, ready for modernization and progress.[20] Contemporarily, many Palestinians still believe refugees' right to return to the villages they lived in before 1948, now inside Israel, is at the core of the Palestinian national claim, and a growing refugee rights movement has mobilized around the issue of refugees' right to return. However, key PA officials and other leaders have hinted that Palestinians will have to relinquish that right. Despite renewed refugee advocacy, this political trend has weakened the centrality of the category of the Palestinian refugee to Palestinian national- ism on the world stage. It is telling, then, that the protest, billed as a children's march against the wall, had as its primary goal opposition to the separation wall but also aimed to foreground refugee issues for both Palestinian and inter- national audiences.

On the day of the protest, the children and international volunteers gathered to write signs with slogans like "As the Wall is raised, we are raising a new genera- tion" and "The Wall Must Fall" in four languages (Figure 8). I observed an atmo- sphere of rhetorical openness as both Palestinians and international volunteers tossed around ideas for signs and then wrote them out. The presence of posters in English and other European languages points to the fact that one audience for this kind of protest was the international public sphere, but still the posters had different meanings for Palestinian and most Western readers. Palestinians might be aware that one sign, "If the olive trees knew who planted them, then their oil would become tears," was one activist's translation of a line of poetry by the famous Palestinian poet Mahmoud Darwish (*Law yadhkur al-zaytun gharisahu,*

Figure 8   Protesting the wall in 'Aida Refugee Camp. Children and internationals gather for a protest against the separation wall. In 'Aida Refugee Camp, the wall is close to Palestinian homes. *Source*: Amahl Bishara.

lasar al-zayt dam'an). For internationals, the line might have inspired other lyrical posters, like "I will become a kite and fly over the wall."

After making their signs, people from 'Awda Center and others from Bethlehem gathered for the protest just outside the camp on a main road in Bethlehem. Marching from the main road, the procession entered the camp chanting slogans, as though the rhythm of the words would keep protesters moving forward and their posters would steel them against anything the army had to offer. The plan was to write graffiti on the separation wall, but as we neared it, we found not just the usual armed guards—private contractors who wore bulletproof vests on top of plain clothes—but also a cluster of Israeli soldiers. Children began to assemble several yards in front of the separation wall with their signs. Teenagers wrote graffiti on another wall nearby. In the midst of all of this, the teenager in the AFP photograph approached the soldiers and began shouting at them. One of the soldiers pulled out his sidearm pistol, demanding that the teenager back down. Soon after, the soldiers began throwing tear gas and stun grenades. Older siblings looked out for younger ones in the ensuing commotion. Adult volunteers from 'Awda Center scrambled to gather the smaller children. The internationals were hustled back towards the safety of the youth center around the corner. For their part, the Palestinian youth who were used to these kinds of confrontations returned with a volley of stones. The protest ended quickly. These fast and violent conclusions to protests were one barrier to a wider movement of popular protests, because they made people hesitant to participate.[21] In the end, organizers were disappointed by the protest because of low attendance by people from outside the refugee camp. Some had even peeled off from the demonstration when they saw the soldiers in front of the wall. "They were afraid to come to the camp!" complained some of the adults from 'Awda Center. This was not a model for protest that was to be repeated.

Still, the protest generated some press coverage. This brings us to the second level of investigation of how this photograph came to be: Why did a journalist come to this protest and take this picture? Small protests like this one garnered international news coverage as a result of the institutional structures and day-to-day practices of journalism in the West Bank. During the second Intifada international news agencies' demand for Palestinian photojournalists skyrocketed. For the first few years of the uprising, there was a constant stream of events that could generate compelling—and presumably profitable—images from the West Bank and Gaza. By 2004, some of the worst violence had ebbed in the West Bank, but this new popular movement against the wall guaranteed another steady flow of images. Most Intifada images were produced by Western news agencies and sold to newspapers and magazines around the world. Paradoxically, harsh Israeli closures in the occupied territories may have promoted the development of a large network of Palestinian photojournalists. Hundreds of physical restrictions to movement like checkpoints and roadblocks prevented journalists from expeditious travel between Palestinian cities. As a result, the news agencies hired Palestinian photographers in each city to cover breaking news. They were often stringers paid by the day or the image. In the West Bank, an area slightly smaller than the state of Delaware, a news agency might have relationships with photojournalists in six different cities. It would behoove them to go to these smaller protests on the off chance that they could catch a newsworthy image. Musa Al-Shaer, who took the photograph in 'Aida Refugee Camp, is paid by the day, and he said that he generally tried to go to all of the protests in the Bethlehem area. The political and geographical contexts of knowledge production have a profound effect on what media are created.

Moreover, the separation barrier was a hot topic for Western journalism. It had generated attention from journalists as soon as Israeli prime minister

Ariel Sharon announced the idea, in April 2002, of building a fence to prevent Palestinian suicide bombers from entering Israel. It was often the barrier as spectacle—hundreds of miles long, made of electrically monitored fences and high concrete walls—that attracted Western journalists' attention. The wall inspired comparisons to other famous walls in history, like the Berlin Wall, the Great Wall of China, and Hadrian's Wall.[22] It was an especially easy target for photojournalists. In the first few months of 2004, for example, journalists regularly went to the town of Abu Dis to snap pictures of the wall's progress. Abu Dis was perhaps a twenty-minute drive from downtown Jerusalem, and the barrier in this area took its most dramatic form of 8-meter-high concrete slabs. Metaphors were rife in wall photography by news agency photojournalists in Abu Dis and elsewhere, but it was not always clear what particular symbols meant. Did the bird perched atop the wall at sunset in a photo by an Associated Press photographer highlight how people, in contrast with birds, are trapped by the barrier? Did it suggest Palestinians' desire for freedom? Did the sunset make the wall less ugly? It was not clear. Other images from Abu Dis showcased elements of Palestinian daily life or tradition with the wall as a backdrop: shepherds with their sheep, children playing soccer, old men wearing kaffiyehs, a bride and groom being videotaped. Did these images suggest that Palestinians were surviving despite the wall? Or that they were oblivious to it? Another Associated Press image, which showed a Palestinian worker sleeping next to the wall, might signal the worker's weariness from the oppression of poverty and occupation, or it could suggest his apathy. Still other images from Abu Dis, when the wall there was relatively new, veered towards the absurd, depicting a man doing a somersault in front of the wall, or an Israeli fashion show in front of the wall apparently designed to contrast the models' beauty with the wall's ugliness. A few images seemed to call attention to the spectacle of representation itself. An audience watched a film called *Wall* projected on the flat gray structure. A woman holding her head in her hands immediately in front of the wall was surrounded by no fewer than six photographers pointing their lenses in her direction. The image was ambiguous enough that it was not clear whether the woman was upset by the wall or by the photojournalists, whether she was sincere or performing for the cameras. Polysemy—or the availability of multiple meanings—seemed to make for media that could move easily across geopolitical boundaries, as news agency images are certainly designed to do.[23] As with many other media spectacles, photographs sometimes obfuscated key issues as much as they elucidated them.[24] Such photographs of the barrier's physical qualities did not necessarily shed light on debates about security or the long-term consequences of the barrier.

Compared to these polysemic images of the wall, images of protest tended to have somewhat more definitive meanings. They generally contrasted unarmed Palestinian protesters on their land with armed Israeli soldiers. In this way, Palestinians' staging of demonstrations was successful in encouraging the portrayal of what they saw as the fundamental power asymmetry of occupation. Indeed, Musa Al-Shaer told me that at demonstrations he looks for "something that reflects the reality of daily life under occupation."[25] Notably, photographs covered the movement against the wall for an international audience much more frequently than news articles did. While writing a story about the barrier might require research and extensive interviewing, photographs of demonstrations are relatively easy to produce, as protests happen regularly and require just a few hours of work to cover.[26] These were the reasons why a relatively small protest like this one attracted the attention of a photojournalist working for an international news agency.

Thus far, I have explicated two kinds of processes that led to the production of this photograph: activists' planning of a protest, and photojournalists' interest in such protests. A third question about how this image came to be revolves around why Munjid, the teenager in the image, would have dared to approach the soldier at all. Munjid Hamdan was fifteen years old when the photograph was taken in 2004. Packed into his performance that afternoon were (at least) three years of fury and grief. On October 25, 2001, 'Aida Refugee Camp had been under curfew for days as the Israeli military conducted house-by-house searches. Munjid's younger siblings were playing just in front of their house in a narrow alley hidden from the military base and the Israeli army snipers. When it came time for lunch, Munjid's father, Salameh Hamdan, leaned out a second-floor window to call his children in, and in that moment a sniper's bullet hit him in the head.[27] About a year after their father was killed, Munjid's oldest brother, then fifteen, was arrested and imprisoned for about a year and a half for throwing stones and Molotov cocktails at Israeli jeeps during protests. A few months after his release, Munjid's second brother was arrested and imprisoned for about two years. Then, just two days before the demonstration, Munjid himself was arrested. He had been released on the morning of the protest with just enough time to pull on a clean T-shirt, comb his hair, and join the protest. An audacious posture was the result. "Since I was a child, I've been seeing the Israeli army in the camp," he told me years later. "I see what the army does to people, so my fear has been broken. . . . Their presence has become something ordinary."

His stance of barely restrained contempt fits an embodied cultural pattern. When Palestinians come into close proximity with soldiers during protests, women and children especially often shout at soldiers, as they are somewhat protected from the worst violence by their identities. They might point a finger in admonition or thrust olive branches toward a soldier as a reminder of what their community has lost. Such stances make up a honed habitus of protest that has deep ethical significance for Palestinians and these confrontations are often photographed. With these stances, Palestinian protesters perform their view of their relationship to Israeli soldiers. They assert that they are righteous, restrained, and strong in contrast to the soldiers, whose force relies on weapons alone.

These are visually compelling moments for photojournalists and other Palestinians alike. As photographer Musa Al-Shaer explained, the photograph of Munjid "shows the fear in Israeli society, especially in the Israeli soldier." One can imagine other readings of such images—that Palestinians are unruly or that they pose a threat to soldiers—but for Palestinians, such images recalled their heritage of popular resistance at a time when a militarized uprising was reaping grim results and the Palestinian political leadership was moribund. Rather than exhibiting Palestinians as indistinguishable and passive victims, as is all too common in photographs of human rights victims,[28] these photographs are tableaus of an assertive Palestinian brand of popular resistance.

The next morning at the summer camp, I awoke to find the teenagers abuzz. Munjid's photograph had been published in *Al-Quds* newspaper, they told me. They were thrilled. As Gregory Starrett has observed, photojournalism "engages the passions of a diffuse audience," serving as "the expressive art of the modern political order,"[29] and this is even more the case when a published photograph circulates among a tight group of friends and activists. Munjid was delighted, too. He recalled, "I must have sat for two hours looking at the picture, thinking, 'How did I do this?'" He explained the meaning of the image: "This picture means that we are against the wall and we are a people who wants resistance and freedom." Drawing on the salient—and shifting—local category of the child, he continued, "It says that the children will resist occupation sometimes even more than the adults."

The photograph was important beyond its semiotic significance. Its physical presence was also powerful. Elizabeth Edwards finds that photographs as material objects "extend time and space through sets of multiple relationships, their piled-up significances, an aggregate of relationships."[30] Munjid told me that many of his friends had put the clipping up in their houses. Weeks later, one of Munjid's friends was carrying it around in his wallet. He took it out and displayed it for me, holding it between his fingers, declaring with pride, "This photograph expresses Palestinian commitment to resistance." The photograph as a tactile object materialized the bravery and political commitment to which he aspired.

Not everyone was as praiseful as Munjid's friend. The photograph extended networks of both concern and retribution within and beyond the camp. "When my mom saw the picture, she said, 'Come on now, son, that's enough. Stop doing things like this,'" Munjid recalled. When, months later, Munjid was arrested again, the Israeli interrogator asked him about the picture. "I told them, 'I don't regret what I did. This was right, what I did.'" He conceded to me, "It did cause me some beatings in prison. The interrogator hit me, not just because of the picture, but yes, that was part of it." Still, in prison, he was welcomed by other Palestinian political prisoners who had clipped the image from an Israeli paper and posted it in their cell.

Four and a half years later, the picture still has a presence in Munjid's life. It is one of his Facebook profile pictures, and was for many months his actual profile picture. Munjid, like many of the youth associated with 'Awda Center, uses Facebook in part to keep in touch with international volunteers who have come to 'Aida Camp. This photograph is so valuable to Munjid because it represents him well both for his friends at home and for the solidarity activists he has met and stayed in touch with on Facebook. Palestinian youth knew that only some images would signify heroism to their Palestinian peers while not signifying terrorism to internationals. This was just that kind of image.

RELIGION AS A FRAME FOR NONVIOLENT PROTEST

A few days later, 'Awda Center and its international guests participated in another protest of about the same size. This one took place in Beit Jala, a town that neighbors 'Aida Refugee Camp within the Bethlehem metropolitan area. This time the same photographer published an image of a priest in black robes holding a poster that depicts children waving a Palestinian flag and breaking apart the wall (Figure 9). None of the youth from 'Awda Center are represented in this image, but the poster the priest is holding was produced by the youth center. In explicating the different factors that led to the production of this image, I again examine three processes: how this image was selected, how this protest was planned, and how the poster was created.

Once again, Musa Al-Shaer was attending a relatively small protest in hopes that something visually interesting would present itself for him to photograph. His presence at this protest is a result of the same professional and economic factors that led to his presence at the protest in 'Aida Refugee Camp. But this

Figure 9 Capturing the distinctiveness of a Bethlehem-area protest. A priest holds a poster made by 'Awda Center at a protest against the barrier in Beit Jala. *Source*: Musa Al-Shaer, Agence France-Presse/Getty Images.

time around, lacking a moment of potential violence, he chose a very different kind of image to send to his editors. He explained the multiple elements of the image as he described for me why he decided to do so:

> I selected it because it features a religious man, a Christian. It reflects the full participation of Palestinian society in confronting Israeli aggression. It suggests that Israeli aggression does not affect only one part of Palestinian society. . . . And the image contains important symbols: children are carrying flags and destroying the wall. It says that in the future, the Palestinian will be victorious over the isolation caused by the separation wall.

Al-Shaer's explanation delicately emphasizes Christian and Muslim unity in talking about "full participation" and the way in which Israeli policies do "not affect only one part of Palestinian society." This was a sensitive subject in Bethlehem, but the Christian community was what attracted the attention of Western audiences.

Indeed, this photograph's focus on the priest is consistent with the narrative proclivities of Western journalism about Bethlehem. Photojournalists around the world focus on the most visually distinctive aspect of an event and attempt to evoke the local color of a particular place.[31] They select this "color" to match long-standing conceptions of a place among their audiences.[32] Not only are the priest's robes more visually distinctive than the other protesters' T-shirts and button-downs, but also Israel and the occupied Palestinian territories are often covered by way of religion. The decision to photograph the priest and publish this image thus reflects long-standing Western interest in Israel and the occupied Palestinian territories as the "Holy Land." In Bethlehem, this always meant featuring Christian history and presence.

Foreign correspondents' frameworks had, in this case, the support of a Palestinian NGO, the Open Bethlehem project. It advocated for the tearing down of the separation barrier around Bethlehem using a cautious politics of religion. Founder Leila Sansour suggested that Bethlehem's Christian character made it a city which embraces universal liberal values and stated that Bethlehem "confounds the stereotype of Palestine seen in the news cycles. It is a modern and dynamic society—though one caught in the torpor of imprisonment. Bethlehem is a city of highly-educated, multi-lingual people."[33] She emphasized the importance of maintaining Bethlehem's Christian community: "Bethlehem is the anchor of Christian community in Palestine. Almost half of Palestinian Christians live in our city. . . . If Christianity cannot survive in the Holy

Land with its 2000 years of uninterrupted tradition, it has very little chance of surviving elsewhere in the Middle East."[34] Sansour was quoted in some of the Western media coverage that year.[35]

For several reasons, though, others were wary of such coverage. As the mayor of Bethlehem commented to the *Times* of London, "We are remembered one day a year. On Christmas Eve all the world speaks of Bethlehem, but they give nothing to us."[36] Many also thought religion was an improper frame for the conflict, which they perceived as a national and colonial one. Finally, some regarded coverage of Bethlehem for its place in Christian history to be a mixed blessing because of tensions within Bethlehem around religion. The Bethlehem metropolitan area comprises three towns, including Bethlehem and Beit Jala, all of which have historically been home predominantly to Christian residents, and three refugee camps whose residents are almost exclusively Muslim. The three towns have also become home to significant Muslim populations since 1948, as some refugees have moved out of the camps and others have come to Bethlehem from surrounding areas. The Bethlehem area's refugee population has been growing faster than that of the Christians because refugees tend to have larger families and because many Christians have emigrated to the Americas or Europe. Only about one third of the population of the metropolitan area is now Christian.[37] However, the Bethlehem area maintains its Christian quality in that churches support many important institutions in the area, such as schools and hospitals. Moreover, local political power remains largely in the hands of Christians. As stipulated by a PA law meant to provide representation for minorities, the mayors of the three towns in the Bethlehem area must be Christian. Also, there is the perception—borne out by statistics[38]—that the camps are places of poverty. While the refugees were dispossessed of their property in other parts of historic Palestine in 1948, Christians tend to be the landowners in the area, having had a historic presence. In conversations in which Christians and refugees are the marked categories and terms of discussion, religion stands in for class as well as for local political power and belonging.

Although Palestinian Muslims and Christians have long cherished their good relationships with each other in Bethlehem, over the past few decades there has increasingly been strain between the two groups in the Bethlehem area.[39] Visitors like myself occasionally heard admonitions from nonrefugees against going to the camps, lest one be exploited in some way. Some Christians felt refugees had changed social norms in the city for the worse. Refugees resented their marginality to local political and economic power, as well as others' negative characterizations of their communities. Existing low-level strains had intensified at the beginning of the second Intifada. Palestinian militants, who were disproportionately refugees, took advantage of the high mountains of Beit Jala to fire on the neighboring Israeli settlement of Gilo. This precipitated Israeli attacks that destroyed many houses, including several unfinished Christian emigrants' mansions. Christians saw this damage partly as a consequence of militants' disregard for them and of militants' lack of clear strategies. Refugees, for their part, sometimes asserted that Christians were less politically committed than they were. Tensions between refugees and long-term residents are hardly limited to Bethlehem,[40] but they may have been especially pernicious because political status was coded as religion.

The protest in Beit Jala, where the photograph of the priest was taken, was planned such that it would bridge these divides. It was organized by a multiparty coalition established to coordinate political activities like protests and martyrs' funerals. If religion, politics, and class sometimes divide Christian locals and Muslim refugees in Bethlehem, the separation barrier is just one aspect of Israeli occupation that has connected them, in this case quite literally. The path of the barrier leads from 'Aida Refugee Camp to Beit Jala along the northern edge of the Bethlehem metropolitan area.

The part of Beit Jala where the barrier was to be constructed had already been transformed by the architecture of occupation. In the late 1990s, Israel built a network of bypass roads so Israeli settlers could drive through the West Bank without going through Palestinian cities. One of these roads was built under Beit Jala, by way of a tunnel constructed through one of Beit Jala's mountains. The road emerged in the middle of a valley, on both sides of which were Beit Jala neighborhoods. Despite its going under the Palestinian town, Israel forbade Palestinian drivers from using this road.[41] Years later, the separation barrier was to be built in order to protect this bypass road. This valley—a place where residents had already felt the dangers and losses involved with Israeli land use in the West Bank—is where the protest was held.

The principal organizer of the protest was a refugee who lived with his extended family in a small but handsome house that overlooked the road. He had ties in both 'Aida Refugee Camp and Beit Jala and saw the benefits of bringing the communities together for this Sunday afternoon protest. He invited religious leaders, church groups, and also the youth center from 'Aida to attend this demonstration. Churchgoers came in dresses and dress pants, and about twenty-five people, teenagers and adults, arrived wearing white T-shirts emblazoned with the logo of 'Awda Center. Also mixed into the group were a number of Europeans and North Americans, many of whom were from the international summer camp, which was still in session.

So it was that this modest but motley assembly embarked together from the main road in Beit Jala through the narrow streets of the town and toward the construction site. Some of the teenagers from different parts of town inspected each other with wary curiosity. Others just socialized with their own friends as they casually held signs rejecting the wall. Many people held the same poster that the priest carried. Some of the teenagers from the camp who were regular participants in stone-throwing demonstrations against the barrier near their own homes were once again ready for action. But after the previous week's demonstration had ended in tear gas and confusion, the teens had been told to keep things calm.

The group walked across the backyards of people whose olive trees were being cut down to make room for the barrier, and international visitors stopped to take pictures of green branches strewn around trunks with severed limbs. We descended about two-thirds of the way into the valley, as far as we could go without breaching a chain-link fence that provisionally kept Palestinians from the bypass road. The leaders with their megaphones called out slogans against the barrier, and the crowd called back. People hung their signs on the fence, but because of our elevation there was no way that Israeli drivers below would actually see the signs (Figure 10). This physical separation between the protesters and the drivers to whom they were, in some sense, petitioning, is relevant to this book's theme of the material dimensions of expression. Palestinians' lack of control of space and their physical separation from decision makers made it more difficult for them to speak effectively.

The only way for protesters to make their ideas heard to anyone but each other was by way of the journalists who covered the event. The absence of an Israeli audience—despite the commuters' proximity—is an apt metaphor for Israel's lack of receptiveness to Palestinian concerns about Israel's unilateral actions. Many Palestinians had ascertained that they had no voice in Israeli policy decisions, and that their own government, the PA, was powerless on many matters of concern. The building of the wall was only the most recent evidence of this. For this reason, Western media that might reach audiences in the United States, Israel, France, and beyond, as well as other Palestinians, assumed central importance. Still, the procession up to an unguarded fence was anticlimactic. There would be no heroic performances on this day. Once they had gathered

Figure 10 Protesting invisibility? Protesters at this Beit Jala demonstration against the separation barrier are elevated too far above the bypass road for Israeli drivers to see them. *Source*: Nidal Al-Azraq.

and displayed their signs, protesters had little else to do. They milled about and soon departed.

Having examined the journalistic infrastructure that led to the taking of the photograph of the priest, and the political relations inside Bethlehem that led to the organization of the protest, we can now examine the production of the poster that the priest carried that day. 'Awda Center had created this poster for its annual international summer work camp. The posters were hanging all around Bethlehem. One of the directors of 'Awda Center, whom I call Rashid, owned billboards and worked in advertising, so he knew well the value of making a name for the youth center. Indeed, this was why he had instructed the protest delegation to wear their T-shirts.[42] And he was especially happy that so many people, even those with no association with the refugee camp or the youth center, were holding the poster.

The graphics of the poster expressed 'Awda Center's political values. The use of computer-generated imagery in the youth center's poster allowed designers to produce an ideal scene, replete with symbols that Palestinian viewers would understand. In the poster, a giant key is deployed as a lever for dislodging and breaking down the wall. The key represents Palestinian refugees' right to return, because in 1948 many Palestinians fleeing conflict left their homes and took their keys with them, expecting to come home soon. Denied that right, Palestinian refugees have held onto their keys, and today bring them out when they describe their home villages for their grandchildren or for visiting reporters and photographers. Rashid, who had commissioned the poster, explained to me that it was meant to make a connection between the right of return and opposition to the barrier. He said it suggested that despite the separation barrier, these Palestinian children were determined to build better lives for themselves and their community by carrying out the right of return. The fanciful use of a symbol—a larger-than-life key—to do physical work hints at the conundrum these Palestinians faced in representing resistance. A photograph of the popular protests youth staged against the wall—in which they sometimes threw stones at the wall and at army jeeps—would have appeared "too violent" for an NGO poster. This is the case even though stone-throwing against Israeli military positions had been a crucial part of the popular protests of the first Intifada that won Palestinians international approbation. Cartoon children working together to wield a key was a more digestible image of hope for the future.

In the poster, a village with the limestone and domes of Palestinian vernacular architecture can be seen behind the barrier, indexing an idyllic past that the children strive to revitalize. The skyline of this village includes both a mosque and a church. While there were mixed Muslim and Christian villages before 1948 and such villages still exist, this is not the norm. The inclusion of these two symbols asserts that both groups play an integral role in Palestinian society. This poster is evidence of these Palestinian refugees' conviction that Christian-Muslim harmony is an important political value, a part of Palestinian tradition, and, they suggested, a foundation for a better future.

On the surface, this news photograph seemed like a successful end result of the protest. Rashid was pleased to find it in a Palestinian newspaper the next day—though he was not nearly as elated as the teenagers had been the previous week upon finding Munjid's picture. For local readers who saw the photograph, it demonstrated Palestinian dedication to resisting the barrier in Bethlehem and steadfastness on the refugee issue, as the photographer had suggested the image would. It documented a moment of partnership between Christian leaders and refugees, which, while hardly unprecedented, would be seen as positive. For those who had seen ʿAwda Center's posters up all around town, the picture also implicitly promoted its work, even though the center's name and logo were cut off. Local activists involved with the event surmised that this news agency-produced image would travel to international audiences, as it did at the very least on the Yahoo! slideshow of the Middle East Conflict, where I found it.

Yet, this image would have a slightly different set of meanings as it circulated abroad. Another leader of the youth center, whom I call Jawad, perceived this as a generally positive image for global circulation. "For us, children signify the future, hope, human dignity, and real peace. In contrast, the wall means despair, cruelty, antipathy, inhumanity. In short, the poster carried by the priest was made to say: 'We the Palestinians, Muslims and Christians, believe that the wall does not destroy our lives only; it threatens our children's lives also.'" Jawad's explanation implicitly recognizes that the message about refugees' right to return drops out as the image circulates outside of Palestinian contexts, because an international audience is less likely to know about the meaning of the key—or even to see the key, as the image is reproduced in small formats. Jawad's interpretation takes for granted the fact that refugees' presence is erased in exchange for critical representations of the barrier, and that priests are good publicity for Palestinians.

On a practical level, too, it became clear to Bethlehem activists that it was easier to organize demonstrations on the model of the Beit Jala protest, with religious themes, than on the model of the camp protest—which after all had quickly been dispersed by violent means that scared many participants. On Palm Sunday, 2005, a Bethlehem Christian organization led a children's march against the barrier in coordination with an international Christian delegation that was visiting the region. The march was organized around the idea that the barrier cut off Bethlehem from Jerusalem and thus severed important biblical routes. The march incorporated a number of symbols that would recall biblical stories, including palm fronds, donkeys, and the child as the harbinger of peaceful redemption. It was meant to resonate more broadly than would the image of Palestinian children breaking down the wall and returning to their families' villages. It also suggested that a Christian ethic of passive nonviolence was the route to justice. The youth of 'Aida Refugee Camp were invited to this protest as well, since they could turn out good numbers and since the residents of 'Aida certainly agreed with the Christian organization about the barrier.

Palestinians' awareness of the political proclivities of audiences abroad authorized certain kinds of political action and marginalized others. This Palm Sunday procession became an annual ritual. Such protests have a subtle impact on the political subjectivities of the second Intifada, especially in Bethlehem. Children and Christian symbols had their place—but what of young refugees like Munjid, whose childlike innocence was far from clear? Palestinians' awareness of international media preferences have helped to structure a kind of politics in which a Christian organization could call up the refugee youth center and invite children to a Christian-themed protest, but no association from the refugee camp could as successfully do the reverse. The camp was a more risky place to protest—where one would almost surely encounter Israeli soldiers—and also a less appealing place at which to frame Palestinians' argument against the barrier. These dynamics shifted Palestinian refugees' views of their own local forms of political action. Perhaps one reason why the teenagers had greeted the image of Munjid with such elation was because it broke outside the boundaries of these expectations.

Since the completion of the wall immediately next to 'Aida Refugee Camp in the summer of 2005, more children and youth have been injured. Israeli soldiers posted in one of the watchtowers of the separation wall shot Jawad's twelve-year-old son in the stomach with live ammunition as he played with his cousins on the balcony of his house during an otherwise calm afternoon. Because of such incidents, the barrier is a constant source of anxiety. Walking through the streets of the camp or sitting on a patio, one is always aware of whether one is in view of the watchtowers. Even in these difficult circumstances, some young men seemed hesitant to talk to international visitors and journalists about the breadth of their own experiences, perhaps because they doubted their experiences would be moving to these audiences. In the summer of 2007 after Jawad's son was shot, a British journalist came to the camp to write a story about the barrier. Jawad brought two young men who had spent time in prison because of their protests against the barrier to talk to the journalist about their experiences. Among them was one of the teenagers who had treasured Munjid's picture in the newspaper. Before the journalist arrived, Jawad told them they should not shy away from discussing the active popular resistance they had engaged in by throwing stones during protests. Yet, when it came time for the youths to speak, I heard them tell only the stories of their terrifying arrests and of the deprivations they endured while they were in prison. That is, they told stories of being victims rather than activists.

Having spent a good amount of time with these youths, I knew there were other stories they could have told. They often spoke with pride about how they, fortified only with stones, had confronted armed soldiers and guards in armored jeeps who had come to their neighborhood to build a restrictive wall. Their pride sprang from their belief that an uprising based on popular resistance like

their own would be more beneficial to their cause than a series of suicide bombings, and from their knowledge of a long history of such popular resistance in
the refugee camps. While youths throwing stones were a key positive image of
Palestinians in Western news during the first Intifada, during the second Intifada and the War on Terror, images of youths throwing stones, even against
soldiers in armed and armored jeeps, have generated less sympathy. These acts
were not exactly regarded as militant or terrorist during the War on Terror, but
they did not quite qualify as "nonviolent," either. These youths also could have
told a historical narrative, which many in the camp shared amongst themselves,
that upon the establishment of Israel their grandparents had become refugees,
pushed out of their villages, and that now, with the building of the barrier, Israel
was cutting them off from the small bit of land they had known all their lives.
These young men could have told compelling stories of activism as refugees. Yet,
they did not consider it prudent to narrate that story for an international audience they perceived to be important, that of the U.S. and European mainstream
media. If Christians were associated with peaceful protests and nonviolence,
they knew that they, young male refugees, were associated with chaos and violence. These preconceptions were powerful both locally within Bethlehem and
internationally. Through their failure to find a way to communicate effectively
with outsiders except as victims of Israeli oppression, a stance connected to
human rights arguments that centered on the individual rather than one connected to collective political rights,[43] they were also in a sense contributing to
the *unmaking* of the Palestinian refugee as a political category, at least in those
moments.

DECIDING WHEN TO SAY NO

Over the next few years, 'Aida Refugee Camp received more and more visitors as
the ranks of tourists and solidarity activists grew and as word circulated about
the bleak wall around the camp. Palestinian youth centers, including 'Awda
Center, took groups of students, pilgrims, and others to some of the same
places that had made headlines in previous years: the house where a teacher
and mother had been killed when Israeli soldiers used an explosive to open
the door, the alley where Munjid's father had been shot by the Israeli sniper,
and of course the wall. International visitors became part of the fabric of the
camp, inviting discourse and exchange of many kinds. Children called out to
foreigners with friendly hellos or exhortations to photography; on other occasions they tried to steal cameras. Teenaged boys tried out their English on

the young women travelers. Hosting visitors gave people a sense of prestige, as when an august patriarch of the camp encountered a group of Korean tourists who had wandered over to the camp from the Church of the Nativity in order to see the wall. He invited them for lunch, even though they did not share a common language. With the guidance of leaders of 'Awda Center, some of the youth who had been hesitant to tell their story on their own terms to journalists grew adept at telling visitors about their time in prison and their commitment to returning to their home villages.

Still, it seemed that for some, publicity had become an end in itself. For the sixtieth anniversary of *al-nakba* in 2008, one youth center in the camp built a giant key as a gateway to the refugee camp near the separation wall. They approached the Guinness Book of World Records in hopes of certifying it as the largest key in the world. Ten meters long and weighing two tons, this symbol of the right of return was unveiled in a ceremony attended by local officials as well as many people in the camp. In the flow of everyday events in the camp, it had the appearance of a major event, but it won only a brief mention in international news.[44]

Not everyone greeted publicity consistently. In 2009, Pope Benedict XVI was planning a visit to Israel and the occupied Palestinian territories to support the dwindling Christian population in the Holy Land and encourage interfaith dialogue among Christians, Jews, and Muslims. Word arrived that the pope wanted to visit 'Aida Refugee Camp. Organizations in the camp, among them 'Awda Center, composed a committee to coordinate how to receive him, recognizing that this could be an important opportunity for the camp to narrate its story to a wide audience. Jawad and Rashid were on the committee. Jawad emphasized that from the beginning local leaders wanted to have a say in how the visit would take shape. "We decided that we would receive the pope, and that there should be a *political* meaning to the visit. It should not just be a visit to wretched poor people, refugees, devoid of a political meaning." Jawad wanted the event to emphasize two periods of dispossession and loss the refugees had experienced: *al-nakba* of 1948, and the contemporary building of the wall.

The committee began working on logistics. 'Awda Center's *dabka* popular dance troupe was to perform for the pope—an honor the children of the troupe treasured, as they had effectively triumphed over two other local troupes. The children regarded the pope as a highly esteemed guest. The committee also decided to build a small outdoor theater. It would be a handsome structure, made of white limestone, but it would also showcase the ugliness of the separation barrier, as it would be built on the sliver of land between the houses and the wall where Munjid had staged his confrontation with the soldier. The theater would in effect materialize what had been true for years, that this space in front of the wall was an important stage for political action. Following negotiations with the Armenian Patriarchate, the owner of the land, the committee began building the stage. However, Israeli troops stormed into the camp and threatened to demolish it on the basis that it was in Area C, land designated as being under Israeli security control in the Oslo Accords. People in the camp suspected that although Israel said the stage posed a security threat, in fact Israeli authorities did not welcome the potential public relations debacle of the pope photographed in front of the wall.

Work on the stage continued, but representatives of the Vatican and the PA urged the committee to move the ceremony into the yard of a United Nations Relief Works Agency (UNRWA) school, located across the street. Some on the welcoming committee assumed that Israeli authorities had pressed the PA and the Vatican to accept this alternative arrangement. Representatives of 'Awda Center decided they would not participate in the reception if it were to be held in the schoolyard. As Rashid said, "As far as we were concerned, since we were hosting the pope, we in the committee should be able to decide where the ceremony would be held. It was very important that it be held near the wall. And we wanted to challenge the Israeli decision to stop work on the stage." Jawad confirmed this sentiment, arguing that their position was "a protest to the pope and to Mahmoud Abbas himself because why shouldn't the celebration be on the stage, even if Israel doesn't want it to happen there? It's a political issue—it shouldn't be that everything Israel demands we agree to."[45] These refugee activists wanted to assert that they had some autonomy over what happened on their own turf.

Negotiations continued until the last hours before the visit. 'Awda Center leaders told the dance troupe to be ready to go on stage if the ceremony were to be held next to the wall. But other members of the committee were resigned to the compromise location. "We'll try to slow down [the pope's] convoy as he passes the wall so that the maximum of photos can be taken," Adnan Ajarmeh, a member of the welcoming committee, told Agence France-Presse.[46] He pointed out that the temporary stage erected within the school's courtyard was also positioned such that photographs would show the wall as a backdrop, albeit less prominently than from the stage they had built. He was reservedly hopeful that the pope's visit would raise the profile of refugee issues: "I'm not gullible enough to think that the pope will bring us back home, but his visit will remind the world of our suffering, which can be used as a political lever."[47]

On the day of the visit, as I was told, banners of miniature Palestinian and Vatican flags flickered above the street. Graffiti extended a greeting—"Welcome Pope in Aida Refugee Camp"—as armed PA security forces took their positions on rooftops. Just hours before the pope was to arrive, PA president Abbas attended an opening for the newly built stage, where 'Awda Center had installed an exhibition of photographs of early refugee life after 1948. As the popemobile neared the camp, its streets and alleyways were teeming with children waving Palestinian and Vatican flags, and adults with outstretched hands and extended cameras. Women held photographs of their imprisoned relatives. The popemobile passed under the giant key gate, in front of the wall, and into the schoolyard for the ceremony. Youth from another center danced for the pope, and families of martyrs and prisoners showered him with gifts. 'Awda Center declined to participate.

That day, the pope lamented the wall without explicitly assigning blame for its presence: "Towering over us . . . is a stark reminder of the stalemate that relations between Israelis and Palestinians seem to have reached—the wall," Pope Benedict said. "In a world where more and more borders are being opened up—to trade, to travel, to movement of peoples, to cultural exchanges—it is tragic to see walls still being erected."[48] He also expressed his sympathy for refugees. The separation barrier was featured prominently in many of the photographs of the day—indeed, in wide-angle shots it was hard to avoid.

But 'Awda Center's leaders were glad they had sat this one out. Jawad referred to a motto of 'Awda Center, that it taught children "to say yes when they should say yes, and no when they should say no."

> This message is a foundational part of the philosophy and upbringing at 'Awda Center. The children must learn freedom of choice. They must learn that when they have to say no, then they should say no—and in a loud voice, without being afraid. . . . What happened during the pope's visit . . . expresses this message very well. We faced a problem with the PA, because they said we were mobilizing against the pope and his visit, and that this might make security problems. [Our problem with the PA] went so far that the center faced a lot of "supervision" at that time. But our position was clear—no—and we said it in a loud voice.

Sometimes, taking a stand meant *not* being represented in the international media.

According to Jawad and Rashid, the people of the camp ultimately had not been impressed by the visit. The presence of PA soldiers had been overwhelming, and in order to enter the school people had to have a kind of permit from the PA. Jawad lamented, "We had envisioned a popular celebration, but little by little, they diminished this possibility." They said that some of the most consequential outcomes of the pope's visit had occurred before the pope himself had arrived. Rashid concluded, "People had expected that the pope's visit would yield something new for the camp, but this did not turn out to be true. As the expression goes, '*Zay ma aja, zay ma rah*' [As it was when he came, it was when he left]. The only outcome, really, was that some streets were repaved in advance of his visit, and of course the stage that was built." The stage is frequently used for community events like movie screenings and dance performances. As far as they were concerned, the positive effects of the visit were not a result of what the pope said, or how the media covered it, but rather how local leaders tried to stage it for the media.

CONCLUSIONS: LEAKY CIRCUITS OF MEDIA PRODUCTION

Media scholars have conceived of media production as a kind of loop in which producers make media in relation to the cultural context around them, and then these media become part of that media context and eventually influence future media producers.[49] This loopy quality bears a similarity to arguments about social construction that have established that media make categories on which the people they define can work.[50] Studying the sites of media production, however, reveals that the circuits of producing news are leakier than they may first appear to be. There are more inputs to journalistic work than are easily recognized when one stays within the bounds of media institutions. In a location where even small organizations have media strategies, it is important to consider organizers and protesters as active participants in media production. They plan public activities and even design their own media, like posters, with an awareness of news narratives.

Palestinian activists are especially sensitive to news media for a number of reasons. First, because Palestinian media publish material from Western news agencies, there is an overlap between the news that appears in Palestinian outlets and news that is published in Western sources. Palestinians obtain a feeling for what is being published about them by watching their own media, even if the latter are not a perfect index for the former. Second, this ambiguous doubling of Palestinian media and international media is amplified by the ambivalent, even bifurcated logic of protest at this site. It is not necessarily clear to whom and for whom protesters make their stands. The scene of Palestinian protesters in Beit Jala gathered above and out of sight of Israelis speeding by on a road that Palestinians are forbidden to use sums up the impasse that these demonstrators face. They rarely feel they have direct recourse to those who ultimately govern them. They instead have the sense that they are always either reaching Palestinians who already agree with them or performing for international audiences whom they will rarely engage in extended dialogue, and who are unlikely to take action on Palestinians' behalves. Global audiences are often inchoate and transitory, as they certainly are for photojournalism posted on the internet. Protesters send messages without the expectation of reply. This is an attenuated version of a transnational public sphere. Still, just because other Palestinians agree with protesters on basic political issues does not mean that they are not important audiences. Protest also is a means of reinvigorating popular politics at home, of inspiring one's friends, even if the content of what one is saying is not new.

For ethnographers of media, staying on after the journalists leave underscores a second way in which the cycle of news production is leakier than we might imagine: the extent to which news products include not just images, texts, and ideas but also attitudes, actions, and objects. Munjid's photograph generated pride at a time when young refugees saw little opportunity for positive political contributions. But it also apparently generated a few blows from Israeli security upon Munjid's arrest. The image of the priest promoted a positive image of resistance in Bethlehem for international consumption and publicized 'Awda Center's work. For international audiences, it may have reinforced the assumptions about Bethlehem as a Christian place, while those who knew of 'Awda Center and could recognize its poster might see the image as indexing the shared purpose among Muslim refugees and Christian long-term residents. Studying journalism in broad social context requires analyzing how media production relates to other kinds of social processes. Through ethnographies of journalistic production, social transformations—in this case, small shifts in identity politics and nationalist discourses—can be tracked as they are caught up in the processes of media production.

In a momentary performance like Munjid's, born of embodied cultural habits of protest as much as of personal grief and bravery, a person of the type usually pushed to the margins of the world stage can capture local attention and imagine a global audience, if only fleetingly. The impact of a photograph, like that of any media, is difficult to measure. This is especially true of worka-day images that are unlikely to win prizes or have wide circulation. Yet, for the people directly involved in the events they record, images like these can have a lasting impact. They may be pinned up on walls and bulletin boards so long that they curl around the corners, or they may be greeted with less passionate approval, or disapproval, and discarded, perhaps remembered for what they did not do. Even if they do not seem transformative, they flicker through a social world illuminating social and political pressures and personal tragedies.

Finally, focusing an ethnography of media on one little town over several years illuminates the extent to which national politics have important local iterations.[51] The presence of Christians in Palestinian society is of national importance as it indexes Palestinian diversity, but for those in Bethlehem it is also a pressing local issue with its own politics. Bethlehem, with its distinct communities of refugees and Christians, is by no means representative of Palestinian society, or even Palestinian society in the West Bank. Yet, here we see the fine-grain impact of news on individuals and communities. The presence of a journalist can push some to the front of a crowd and encourage others to lag behind. And when the demonstration or interview is over, journalism can leave people with a feeling for what their lives are worth, how their experiences are valued, whether to hold the next protest or just stay home. At a time when protests are frequent and journalists visible in large numbers, identities—never fully formed—are especially fluid. While making the case against the newer disaster of the separation barrier in Bethlehem, Palestinian refugees may have sometimes been unmaking the Palestinian refugee as a key concept and political issue in Palestinian nationalism. As they planned protests and spoke to journalists, they knew which way the winds were blowing, and they shaped their messages accordingly, even if this compromised their ability to express their own experiences and their political ideals. It is not always easy to reinvigorate one's neighborhood friends at the same time one reaches out to friends afar on Facebook. Bending one's message to fit that of dominant Western news narratives can be unsatisfying for activists who want to conduct political actions in their community according to their own values. As activists plan and carry out protests that they expect will attract media coverage, these are some of their considerations. In some cases, as during the pope's visit, the refusal to be represented at all can be an eloquent statement.

PARSING "CHAOS"

Yasir Arafat had been the leader of the Palestinians for four decades as chairman of the Palestine Liberation Organization (PLO) and president of the PA, but in his last years the man who had shaken Israeli prime minister Rabin's hand on the White House lawn in 1993 to establish what was supposed to be a historic peace had fallen into disrepute in the United States and Israel. When he died in November 2004 following two and a half years of being confined to his offices by Israeli threats, U.S. media pundits expressed optimism that a new day was dawning for Palestinians. However, the PA's plans to move forward by burying Arafat quietly went awry when thousands of Palestinian mourners insisted on participating in the funeral, streaming into the Ramallah compound where he was to be interred. The ensuing spectacle was covered by hundreds of journalists, including many who had flown in for the occasion. I asked five Palestinians to read two articles that typified U.S. coverage of the funeral. Each of these two articles, "Life After Arafat," published in Newsweek,[1] *and "Arafat Death Sparks Anger, Grief, and Relief," published in* USA Today,[2] *was penned by a pair of journalists with different professional backgrounds. Dan Ephron (*Newsweek*) and Michele Chabin (*USA Today*) were journalists based in Israel, while Michael Hirsch (*Newsweek*) and Andrea Stone (*USA Today*) were high-ranking journalists who had worked around the world and parachuted in for the occasion. Two of my interviewees, Wajd and Majdi, were also a pair, two students of political science from Nablus. Though I had only asked one to come, the second had given the articles a quick look and tagged along to our meeting at their university. It was sometimes difficult to dive into an analytical conversation with people I'd just met, but the chatty rapport these two men had with each other made up for any hesitance that might have otherwise* *colored our first conversation. I also interviewed another Nablus student, Anwar, on his own. Finally, I interviewed Qusay, an employee at a community-based organization in 'Aida Refugee Camp, and Ramzi, a Bethlehem-based civil society activist, both of whom I'd known for years.*

Coverage of the funeral in U.S. media portrayed the mood as angry and chaotic. Palestinian readers had various interpretations of this perspective, depending on their own experiences of the funeral and their evaluations of Arafat and Palestinian politics as a whole. A passage in Stone and Chabin's USA Today article about the rampant gunfire during and after the funeral particularly sparked discussion: "The sound of M-16 and Kalashnikov rifles boomed every few minutes. In an alley off the square, a man whose face was covered with a black-and-white keffiyeh—the headscarf worn by Arafat and that has come to symbolize the Palestinian cause—fired a pistol in the air before melting into the crowd." According to Wajd, one of the political science students from Nablus, "This is proof that there is disorder in terms of security. . . . There were many people who had unregistered weapons. There was not order; there was chaos." He anticipated that for American readers this passage would read like a "dramatic scene that would work for Hollywood." Majdi speculated that an American reader "will conclude that in happy times we shoot, and in sad times we shoot—we shoot in all events. We're a chaotic people, and we like to shoot for the sake of shooting. This is what happened, and when Americans read this, they'll get that message. . . . Shooting is a problem here."

Qusay, a Bethlehem refugee who was on an indefinite hiatus from college, disagreed. He had attended the funeral himself and had found it very moving. "Anyone who has known the Palestinian reality during the second Intifada would know that shooting during funerals or demonstrations is an honor for the martyrs, not an indication of chaos. In Israel, when a soldier dies, Israel fires twenty-one shots in the air. What is the difference—Israel fires twenty-one shots, and here we shoot more?"

Anwar, another college student in Nablus, wondered why the journalist included the detail about the man in the alley with a pistol at all. He too speculated it would carry an insidious meaning for Americans: "This guy is carrying a gun, he fired it, and then he disappeared among the civilians. It is like there is no line between civilians and the fighters." This was a major point of contention in the second Intifada, and it had serious implications. Israel often claimed that civilian deaths were unavoidable in its counterinsurgency efforts because militants hid among the civilians. This student imagined that U.S. readers would associate the keffiyeh with terrorism, but he asserted that there was a practical reason for the shooter to have been covering his face. "There are collaborators among Palestinians. . . . It is a protection for them as fighters, because their lives are in danger."

The Newsweek *article by Ephron and Hirsch asserted that the turmoil of the funeral reflected Arafat's legacy: "Even in death, he was stirring up the same questions and confusion, the rumors and the conspiracy theories (was he poisoned by Israel or the CIA?), the frenzied masses and the volleys of gunfire." Ephron and Hirsch quoted a Palestinian economist who commented, "Abu Ammar would have liked it this way," and they confirmed, "Indeed he would have. Sadly, Arafat's legacy of passion and purpose—and of bullets, bombs and blood—is almost certain to cast a shadow across the region for many years to come." Qusay did not appreciate this portrayal:*

> The writer said that Abu Ammar would have liked "the bullets, the bombs, and the blood." . . . [But] we have learned that Israel, America, and the international community are fickle. Arafat earned a Nobel Peace Prize. . . . After Oslo, Israel and the United States were declaring Arafat a partner in peace, saying that the best opportunity to make peace is with him. But when Arafat said no [in the 2000 Camp David negotiations] he became a bloody killer in their eyes.

Qusay defended Arafat's stance in these negotiations. "Arafat and the negotiators gave up a lot in Oslo . . . but at Camp David, Arafat said to them, 'If I give up on these essential national commitments, I am inviting you to my funeral.'" Qusay thought Arafat had had a mandate to stay firm. As Ramzi, a civic leader from Bethlehem, said, Arafat's actual funeral years later had gathered so many mourners because Arafat still had the confidence of his people. "They knew that Arafat died without giving up on Jerusalem or on refugees, so they went to support these principles." Qusay agreed with Ephron and Hirsch that Arafat would have liked the funeral, but he had different reasons. "Ninety percent of the people who were at the funeral cried. Hundreds of thousands of Palestinians came to Ramallah, even though there was a siege and cities were closed. If Arafat could have seen that, he would have liked it, because he would have felt how much people loved him."

Wajd of Nablus was more inclined to agree with the interpretation of the American journalists. He hinted that Arafat might have liked the funeral because he

> had a dictatorial side to his personality. He liked authority. He transformed the liberation project into an administrative authority to satisfy his personal wishes. He wanted to be the symbol, the father, the leader. When the article says that Arafat will be happy with the funeral, it means he liked disorder. It suggests that he built

the disorder. . . . I do share in criticism of Arafat on this point. He did encourage disorder in the security sector, and he catered to political gangs.

By doing this, suggested Wajd, he was able to maintain his own place at the top. Still, Wajd asserted that representations of Arafat in the U.S. media pointed to a "double standard in the West. *[Avigdor] Lieberman [Israel's right-wing foreign minister] is the most extremist person in the world. He is asking for Palestinians to be transferred [outside of Israeli-controlled territory], and what was the West's response?"*

I talked with several of my readers about the word "chaos" used to describe the funeral in the opening lines of the Newsweek article:

> *[Arafat's] successors wanted an orderly funeral. They brought in bulldozers to clean up Yasir Arafat's broken-down headquarters in Ramallah. They sealed off the compound to keep out the crowds. They even cleared a hall in which Arafat would lay [sic] in state while dignitaries passed by the coffin. What they got instead was the untidy drama of the old regime, the kind of chaos that Arafat thrived on.*

Wajd thought the term "chaos" (fawda, a key word in Palestinian politics and society) accurately described the funeral and indeed was indicative of Palestinian political culture. As he said,

> *One of our historical mistakes from the beginning of the modern revolution in 1964 was that the kind of political culture we had was not democratic and civilized. It was revolutionary: "Let's fight, and we're going to liberate our lands and return to them" . . . there wasn't a theoretical framing as there should have been, and there wasn't a democratic enculturation, either. So what I liked about [the Newsweek] article was the tie between the chaos that Arafat caused and its effects after he died. This chaos even affected his own funeral. . . . Democracy must not happen only in elections; it is also a mindset. It must be present in schools and in our other institutions. Democracy should happen everywhere.*

Wajd thought that this chaos had weakened Palestinians' political position in the long term: *"It is hard to be strong when there is chaos. . . . And to have peace with Israel you need power, because Israel doesn't care about peace. They are happy to have this conflict continue so that they can expand the settlements more and more. So if you want to put pressure on Israel, you need to be united rather than disorganized."* Still, Wajd added that the chaos was not all the fault of the PA: *"Let's not forget the role of the Israeli occupation in spreading the chaos, by bombing the*

PA's headquarters and destroying the PA's projects. For example, just as the PA is trying to impose security in Nablus, or to collect the stolen cars from the street, the Israelis invade and destroy the whole plan. The chaos makes them comfortable." His experience as a resident of Nablus gave him a particular perspective on the chaos and security problems of the second Intifada and its aftermath, because in Nablus, even more than in other cities, the PA had become impotent, with militias taking advantage of the breach in authority.

For Ramzi, the Bethlehem civic leader who had organized many an event, the chaos was a logistical issue. "There was chaos because there were lots of people and the place was small. If the place had been bigger, there would not have been chaos." Qusay had a third outlook on the topic of chaos. Having been at the funeral, he did not deny that it had been chaotic, but he contended, "There is something called 'organized chaos' [fawda munazzama], and this can be something beautiful. It is unreasonable to draw a line and expect people to always walk upon it." Organized chaos, he told me, drawing on some of the theories of civil disobedience he had learned during a stint in prison, involved "expressing your opinion in your own way," and sometimes this was a necessary step. He also emphasized that even if the funeral had been disorganized, it had not been dangerous. "As far as I am concerned, when there is real chaos, there is damage, like what can happen in England after a soccer game. They go into the streets and start fighting; sometimes they break into stores." Here, it was just that "people insisted on burying their leader. It was people's love for Arafat that made them enter [Arafat's compound] the Muqata'a to participate in his funeral."

There was hardly one Palestinian reading of these articles. Instead, interpretations hinged on individual assessments of Palestinian politics and of how media function to represent Palestinians abroad. Readers brought a deep awareness of international political debates to their interpretations, from concern about an appearance that militants hid amongst civilians to cognizance of arguments that Arafat was not a good "partner for peace." And they also harbored political knowledge and theories that few Americans would have: concern that militants should be able to hide from collaborators, and the concept of organized chaos. What if these people appeared as commentators on CNN?

6 WATCHING U.S. TELEVISION FROM THE PALESTINIAN STREET

To say that Palestinians have had a problem of representation is an understatement that opens up a history of failed negotiations and declarations, a tangle of stereotypes, a maze of accusations. Exemplifying some of these dynamics, former Israeli prime minister Ehud Barak once contended that PA president Yasir Arafat and his people were naturally inclined to lie. This explained Arafat's—and Barak's—inability to come to a peace agreement. Interviewer and prominent Israeli historian Benny Morris described how Ehud Barak recounted the events: "Barak shook his head—in bewilderment and sadness—at what he regards as Palestinian, and especially Arafat's, mendacity: 'They are products of a culture in which to tell a lie . . . creates no dissonance [Morris's ellipsis]. They don't suffer from the problem of telling lies that exists in Judeo-Christian culture."[1] This accusation drew on long-standing orientalist stereotypes of Arabs as liars[2] that have found renewed circulation.[3] Publication of this conversation in the *New York Review of Books* set this assertion in motion through many kinds of public discussion. A Google search of "Arafat's mendacity" illustrates the long path the allegation has traveled in the years since, including a 2010 *Jerusalem Post* article that refers to Arafat's "persistent mendacity"[4] and an article posted on the Foundation for Defense of Democracies' website that cites his "innate mendacity."[5]

An even more widespread Israeli argument used to explicate the breakdown in negotiations in July 2000 and in the following years suggested a different kind of representational failure on Palestinians' part. In late summer 2000, Barak suggested that Israel might have "no partner" on the Palestinian side with whom to make peace.[6] This phrase was picked up by U.S. columnists shortly after the second Intifada began, as in October 2000 when *New York Times* columnist Thomas Friedman asked, "What do you do when there is no partner for peace and there is no alternative to peace?"[7] In July 2001, Barak published an op-ed in the *New York Times* entitled "Israel Needs a True Partner for Peace,"[8] and his successor as prime minister, Ariel Sharon, adopted this claim as well.[9] The assertion that there was no partner with whom to negotiate was mobilized to legitimize Israel's attacks on Palestinian cities.[10] After Arafat's death and the election of the "more moderate" Mahmoud Abbas, the narrative shifted, but the "no partner" argument endured. While Arafat had been elusive and untrustworthy, Abbas was not an adequate partner for peace because he was weak.

Importantly, many debates about Palestinians' representational failings themselves have happened in and by way of elite U.S. news media outlets like the *New York Times*, the *New York Review of Books*, and the *Washington Post*. These are relevant forums because the United States exerts considerable power over both Israel and the PA, and because U.S. news discourse is an important extension of discussions carried out by U.S. policy makers in other venues. This network of official statements, news media publications, and political actions is difficult to trace, as are its consequences. Yet, these ongoing debates about Palestinian representation indicate the extent to which statelessness impedes authoritative speech. As though in recognition of the difference formal statehood might make, Palestinian leaders have declared statehood or asked for recognition of statehood on several occasions, most recently in September 2011, despite the fact that these declarations have little chance of changing Palestinians' lack of sovereignty on the ground. One reason behind these declarations has been the prospect of gaining a better position from which to speak during negotiations.

Examining media portrayals of Palestinian leaders calls attention in a dizzying way to the dual meaning of the word *representation*. As thinkers from Gayatri Spivak[11] to Bruno Latour[12] have explored, while speaking and doing are held apart in many spheres, two meanings of the word "representation" suggest how speaking and doing are in fact bound together. Representation can refer to those kinds of processes that media typically undertake, like speaking, writing, or photographing; or to acts of governing, like gathering people into a single polity. Following Latour's discussion of this topic, I call the kinds of representations that media are typically imagined to make *representations-as-depicting* and the kinds of representations that governments are typically imagined to specialize in *representations-as-gathering*.[13] Representations-as-gathering are obviously a kind of doing, while representations-as-depicting are often presumed to be transparently making copies of the world, just plain speaking.[14] These two kinds of representation are also judged and legitimized differently, as Latour points out. Representations-as-depicting are generally judged by whether they seem to represent the world accurately: has the quote been mangled or the image been doctored? Representations-as-gathering are generally judged by whether the processes used to gather people together are legitimate: were the elections conducted fairly? The term "representations-as-gathering" is also useful because it allows us to consider formal acts of constituting polities, like elections, alongside other kinds of gatherings through which people—especially those lacking adequate formal representation—assert their shared purpose, sentiment, or identity, like protests and funerals.

Of course, these two forms of representation regularly commingle with one another. Governments, for example, are entrusted with producing depictions, like census data. Any depiction, like a photograph or a painting, gathers its elements together in a single frame and thus suggests an affiliation—think family or class photos. Many kinds of speaking constitute a type of doing,[15] like hate speech, incitement, and, as I argued in Chapter 2, the kinds of state speech that deemed Palestinian journalists to be threats. Many gatherings, like protests, are performative in that depictions of them are anticipated by their participants, as I discussed in Chapter 5. The gatherings are intended to be future depictions. However, by distinguishing these two processes at the outset of the chapter, it becomes easier to track the ways in which depicting and gathering—speaking and doing—are interwoven in practice. For it is the case that both the press and the government may encounter criticism when they overstep their presumed representational boundaries. When a government becomes too involved in depicting the world for the sake of promoting itself, this is sometimes derisively called spin or propaganda. When a media institution is accused of not representing issues transparently, it is often said to be overstepping its bounds and producing events, rather than representing them, or to be practicing "advocacy journalism."[16]

The Palestinian case is especially useful as an example of how representations-as-gathering can depend on representations-as-depicting. For a long while, many Palestinian leaders and elites—with a telling exception in the contemporary Hamas leadership—have been highly responsive to how the United States and officials from other powerful Western states have viewed the Palestinians. Especially since the 1990s, the Palestinian leadership has accepted the idea that the United States, perhaps in concert with other members of the international community, will play a key role in resolving the Israeli-Palestinian conflict.[17] The approach of Palestinian leaders apparently springs from their belief that resolving the Israeli-Palestinian conflict is a U.S. or international priority. PA president Mahmoud Abbas's request for recognition of statehood at the United Nations in 2011 can be seen as a shift away from acknowledging U.S. centrality in this process,[18] but it continues to revolve around respect for an international perspective.

The PLO leadership's decision to sign the Oslo Accords in 1993 and establish the PA can likewise be seen as a prime moment in a pattern of seeking the backing of powerful foreign bodies in its struggle for liberation. After support from revolutionary movements and third world countries had waned, the PLO, which defined itself as a revolutionary liberation organization, largely ceded its space on the world stage to the PA, an administrative body merely responsible for domestic matters in parts of the West Bank and Gaza. The millions of Palestinians living outside of PA limits, as in Lebanon, Jordan, and Israel, were politically marginalized. This marked a portentous transition in terms of the Palestinians' representation-as-gathering. Before the establishment of the PA, the PLO had gathered virtually all Palestinians under the same umbrella, but as it was deemed a terrorist organization for most of its existence, it was generally unable to speak for Palestinians in the places that mattered. The PA won the Palestinian leadership the authority to continue to speak for Palestinians in multiple rounds of negotiations with Israel, but effective power and real statehood remained elusive.

PA leaders essentially decided to perform statehood, despite ongoing Israeli occupation evident in such factors as Israel's continued control of borders, movement of people and goods, and ultimate military authority. Under the PA, the "state-in-waiting" or "state-in-exile," as analysts had dubbed the PLO's decades-long enterprise of institution-building in Tunisia and Lebanon, came to resemble a kind of "theater state."[19] In this case, the theater was most effective for an outside audience. As internal critics pointed out in interviews with me, during the Oslo period PA officials had little use for the word "occupation," because PA leaders were gaining not only official titles but also, in many cases, company franchises and luxury cars from their positions in the PA. Performing statehood meant obscuring occupation, that Israel was still the sovereign power in the West Bank and Gaza Strip. Their failure to emphasize that Israeli occupation had not ended was one reason that the very word "occupation" made only rare appearances in U.S. journalism during this period.[20]

Indeed, in carrying out conventional journalistic practices, reporters for Western news agencies were complicit with this performance. For years, journalists attended press conferences in Ramallah that produced the same style of news as press conferences in any capital city. They wrote about Arafat as the "president" of the PA. Most journalists rely to a great extent on official sources because they offer readily available and, by definition, newsworthy material.[21] As a result, officials' statements and the governing institutions with which they are associated accumulate authority by way of news publications. The norms of news writing, which favor events like press conferences and explosions, did not generally permit inclusion of details and explication of long-term trends that would communicate to international readers how the PA was in fact much less than a state, and Arafat less than a president. It was easy to write about what PA officials did and said, but much harder to write about the limitations of their power, despite the fact that these limitations were eminently visible in everyday life in the occupied territories. While Western journalists were covering the high diplomacy of negotiations that were supposed to lead to full statehood, Palestinians could observe that Israel was continuing to build settlements and roads in the occupied Palestinian territories. These conventions exemplify the statist quality of mainstream media.[22] These journalists' labor is part of the work that produces the state, defining it in relation to the society[23] and the "community of nations,"[24] even, or especially, when the state's existence is so profoundly up for debate, as is the case for the PA. Importantly, these effects are not the result of individual journalists' actions or neglect but rather are a product of the institutional norms of journalism. As journalism scholar Timothy Cook writes, "By following standard routines of newsmaking, journalists end up hiding their influence not only from outside actors but also from themselves."[25]

But there is a third party involved in both representations-as-gatherings and representations-as-depicting: the Palestinian people, both as a concept and as actors in protests, funerals, and elections. This third party is integral to the success of the performance of statehood, or more specifically the nation-state. Studying these issues in the Palestinian context is fruitful because Palestinians are especially sensitive to what foreign media can do—to how representations-as-depicting have force in the world. U.S. and other Western media do not only represent what the PA does; they also affect PA actions and how Palestinians gather themselves for representation. Moreover, because processes of Palestinian political representation are unstable, it is especially obvious how both kinds of representation are involved with constituting "the Palestinian people" out of a diverse and dispersed collection of people with different interests and experiences. Palestinians are at once the objects of representations-as-gathering and representations-as-depicting and watchful overseers of both of these kinds of representation. Viewing elite debates about political authority alongside street politics elucidates how journalists and officials each rely on Palestinians to constitute "the Palestinian people," even as they later try to delimit and direct what this category means. Moments like the funeral of a national leader and national elections crystallize these processes.

"ARAFAT IS ALL OF THE PEOPLE, AND THE PEOPLE CANNOT DIE"

Yasir Arafat represented Palestinians in too many ways, as authoritarian leaders tend to do. He was known for arranging his iconic headdress, the black and white kaffiyeh, in the shape of historic Palestine, an act of representation-as-depicting that let him subtly personify his homeland. He had been chairman of the PLO since 1969, and he was elected as the first president of the PA in 1994, a position he continued to hold in 2004 because elections scheduled for 2000 had been suspended. If one person embodied the Palestinian liberation struggle, with all of its spectacular failures and also its uncanny ability to persist, it was surely Yasir Arafat. When he died during Ramadan in 2004, after years of living under a tight Israeli siege and in the wake of a damaging Israeli campaign against the Intifada, his successors saw an opportunity for remaking Palestinian politics. There would be reforms, new elections, new photographs to be hung in homes and offices. But first, there would be a funeral.

After all of the negative publicity of bombings and the ineffective Palestinian public relations efforts about Israeli incursions, the funeral was an event that the new generation of PA leaders likely imagined they could craft with care and precision. Perhaps they remembered the legendary millions who helped to lay Egyptian leader Gamal Abdel Nasser to rest, or King Hussein's funeral—smaller, but coinciding with an Emergency Special Session of the UN General Assembly in his honor. But coordinating a Palestinian public in mourning would not be easy. Surely they recognized that how Palestinians gathered on these days of mourning would produce depictions that either would or would not be appealing for influential outside audiences. Palestinians were being courted for representation by the PA, and it was clear that U.S. media representations would hinge on their performances.

The evening before Arafat's funeral, I was with a group of refugees I knew from Bethlehem in the home of one of their relatives in Ramallah, where the funeral would be. All had been politically active, and the older two, in their midthirties, had spent years in Israeli prisons for their participation in the first Intifada. Now, all volunteered in 'Awda Center, a politically independent youth center, and no one except the youngest, a teenager, took part directly in party politics. For teenagers from the refugee camp, involvement in party politics and active resistance was a primary mode of sociality. The others were reluctant to invest their energies in a political structure that seemed so empty. Indeed, by this time in the second Intifada, many Palestinians had grown cynical about PA politics. For all of them, work with the youth center was their way of promoting positive social and, they hoped, eventual political change outside the framework of existing parties. Jawad, who had been a leader of the first Intifada, was especially ardent in articulating that he had established the youth center because he found party politics to be so corrupt and hopeless.

These refugees' desire to attend the funeral might seem to be in conflict with their skepticism about contemporary Palestinian politics. In another way, though, their commitment to being there emerged from their convictions and their biographies. Having lived their entire lives with Arafat as a political leader, they saw his passing as a major event in their own lives. They wanted to pay him their respects, although they did not approve of all of his decisions as a leader. Perhaps most of all, it was obvious from their frequent attendance of martyrs' funerals, protests, and rallies, and even from their constant and committed gathering of information during the hottest of Israeli military incursions, that they enjoyed being in the thick of things. They valued participation for its own sake. This was both a personal proclivity and a political stance, given the shift in the second Intifada away from the popular forms of uprising prized during the first Intifada and toward forms of resistance that actively involved a smaller number of people.[26] Their zeal to be on the scene was, on this and other occasions, my good fortune.[27]

But before the funeral, we had a job to do. The family we were staying with in Ramallah owned a sign-making shop. They had a tall order that night for signs calling for democratic elections. The signs were to consist of plastic lettering rubbed onto coated corrugated cardboard. Making them was a laborious process. The sheets of lettering were printed, but the background to the words had to be peeled off, as when cookies have been cut out of a large sheet of dough. All of the letters' small dots had to stay on the sheet, but the insides of round letters, like the inside of an "o" in English, had to be removed. We would start to peel the backing off with razor blades, and then pull it off with our fingers. When only the text remained, we rubbed it onto the cardboard sign, and then hammered the sign to a wooden handle. With the youngest child having fallen asleep in the car, we worked well into the night. The physicality of this message-making work reminded me of so many other arduous tasks involved with communication and media in Palestinian society. We were not wrestling with heavy cameras or dodging bullets, but meaning making here was also an embodied process. The sociality, too, was resonant.

When we finally came home, we settled down to watch television and have *suhur*, the predawn meal eaten during Ramadan. But the broadcast from our hosts' satellite dish repeatedly cut out. "Don't worry," explained one of the teenaged daughters. "That's just because of the drone plane overhead." During the Israeli invasions of Ramallah, their satellite service had frequently been disrupted. Now, though, they surmised that the plane was just doing surveillance. It was another instance that underscored the materiality of media. The technologies of Israeli occupation disrupted media even when this was not the primary goal of those technologies. Despite the bad reception, we managed to catch the late broadcast of one of the most popular Ramadan serials of the year, *Taghriba Filastiniyya* (The Palestinian diaspora).[28] This Syrian-produced epic, broadcast on the premier Saudi satellite station, MBC, chronicled a Palestinian family's experiences as villagers near the coastal city of Haifa in the early 1920s, as refugees in the Jordanian-controlled West Bank from 1948 to 1967, and finally as subjects of Israeli occupation immediately after the 1967 war. By coincidence, the episode that night considered an argument about the proper attitude Palestinians should exhibit toward foreign journalists.

In the show, a Western photographer had come to take pictures in the family's refugee camp. One Palestinian man was giving him a tour, pointing out the crowded, substandard housing, the open gutter running through the middle of the camp, an inadequately clothed toddler playing in the street. A younger Palestinian man castigated the guide for showing off their misery. He mocked the photographer with exaggerated expressions of destitution, anger, and powerlessness that he thought epitomized what the journalist desired. I was captivated—especially because my hosts occasionally gave similar tours of their refugee camp to visiting internationals. Did they feel castigated? By the end of the episode, I was relieved to see that the younger man who had made fun of the journalist had reconciled with his friend the guide, and admitted that his behavior had been impulsive and foolish.

The episode seemed to reflect a contemporary dynamic in which Palestinians closely attended to how powerful outsiders saw them. Palestinians regarded the international community (often glossed in informal conversation as "the world," al-'alim) with interest in part because the international community, often in the form of what many Palestinians call the "international media" (al-sahafa al-duwaliyya), had so thoroughly persisted in showing them regard.[29] Palestinians living in Ramallah, Bethlehem, Nablus, or Gaza could expect to see journalists regularly. It was not unusual for Palestinians to be interviewed if they were prominent activists, if tragedy had struck their families, even if a child passing by a journalist's camera was particularly eager. Even though many Palestinians have ascertained that media coverage has not aided them in recent years, many continue to insist to the journalists they meet that they should cover the political situation in a sympathetic way. Palestinians' widespread accord with the argument that "the world" must be convinced of the justice of their cause enables an extraordinary role for the Western press.[30]

In Ramallah the night before Arafat's funeral, my hosts saw the episode of *Taghriba Filastiniyya* as a matter-of-fact reflection of the contemporary conundrums they faced as they hosted internationals. These problems in some ways echoed quandaries of news-making. My hosts gave tours regardless of the enduring and unfounded accusations from neighbors that they were receiving financial remuneration from their visitors. At the same time, as tour guides they also had to manage the combination of pity, suspicion, surprise, and judgment that clouded the air when Western visitors sized up the camp in relation to their expectations. During the tours, visitors encountered poverty but not, in the case of this Bethlehem camp, destitution; damage and decay, but not devastation. Not all political and economic troubles were visible on the surface of things. The lived realities of decades of Palestinian dispossession and occupation, and by this time even the aftermath of the major Israeli invasions of Bethlehem and other cities in 2002, lacked the sharp edges of new violence; things were worn down, less distinct. The television episode about the visiting journalist passed almost without comment, perhaps because media coverage itself was so routine. We talked and laughed about small things, went to sleep very late, and woke up tired, matching the mood of the West Bank during that fall of 2004.

Arafat's death—although by all means a major news story—had the rundown quality of a death for which people had been waiting, and not only because his health had been poor. Arafat had been a Palestinian leader for forty years and a major international figure for almost as long. After decades of U.S. isolation on the basis of charges that Arafat was a terrorist, U.S. president

Ronald Reagan authorized a dialogue with Arafat in 1988. Just six years after being invited into the circle of international legitimacy, he won the Nobel Peace Prize, along with Israeli leaders Shimon Peres and Yitzhak Rabin, for signing the Oslo Accords. However, by 2004, after accusations that he had directed suicide bombings during the second Intifada, his reputation in the United States and Europe had once again plummeted. Among Palestinians, his reputation was tattered because of the PA's record of bad governance and his inability to protect his own people during the brutal attacks of the second Intifada. For the last two years of his life, under Israeli threats of arrest or worse, he did not leave his walled Ramallah compound, the *Muqata'a*, except to be evacuated to a Paris hospital shortly before his death.

As Arafat's political and physical incapacity became more and more pronounced, Palestinians' disappointment in him was leavened by their sense that he at least suffered alongside them, abstemiously and under military siege, and that at least he appreciated their presence. In this sense—and only in this sense, given his cancellation of elections and his cronyism—Arafat could be considered a populist (*sha'bi*) leader. Some of the same attributes for which Arafat was ridiculed—for example, his generous bestowal of kisses on visitors—were at the same time part of his charisma. The frivolous kisses were damp mementos of his keenness for receiving guests, even when Palestinian visitors arrived by scaling the walls of his compound, against the wishes of his guards, as happened on a few occasions during the second Intifada. These were not sanctioned or official representations-as-gathering, but still Arafat welcomed his public. He allowed them the indulgence of constituting themselves as a people, his people, even when they did not properly subject themselves to the emerging norms of the Palestinian security nonstate.[31] People are not always so welcomed into the inner sanctums of power, even in more highly functioning democracies. As a native Northern Virginian, when I heard about people scaling the walls of Arafat's headquarters, I thought of how, around the same time, the U.S. Capitol was increasingly being cordoned off from visitors. Vote, the new regulations seemed to say, but do not get too close. In this regard, at least, Arafat offered a refreshing contrast. Arafat gathered and stood for his people in an intimate but not always effective fashion. In his death, Palestinians identified with the father of their nation more than they lionized him, in wide recognition of the fact that he had failed in such significant ways to represent them. After all, many Palestinians who had been involved in national struggle felt that they had fallen short, too.[32]

The PA leadership that would take Arafat's place was much less populist and even more pragmatic in its orientation than Arafat. For the funeral, these leaders had planned a private event in which Arafat's body was to be flown in from abroad, following small formal ceremonies in France and Egypt, and buried in the *Muqataʿa*. This plan did not fulfill Arafat's stated wish to be buried in Jerusalem, which Israeli officials had forbidden. So Palestinian officials declared the gravesite to be a temporary one, imported soil from Jerusalem, and proclaimed that Arafat's remains would be moved to Jerusalem once a Palestinian state had been established. Officials and dignitaries alone were invited to witness the burial. Only after Arafat had been interred was the Palestinian public to be allowed to form a line to pass by the grave.

This plan incorporated none of the rituals of a Palestinian martyr's funeral, which normally consists of a large public procession accompanying the body from a town center to its final resting place.[33] Many observers presumed that with this plan, PA officials sought an orderly event rather than a procession in which mourners might chant slogans unappealing to Western audiences. Officials might even have feared, as my hosts speculated, that were there to be a procession, the people might march not to the "temporary grave" in Ramallah but to the checkpoint on the way to Jerusalem—and perhaps beyond—in an attempt to carry out Arafat's last wishes. Leaders whose international stature depends on the maintenance of order would surely wish to avoid such risks.

My friends and I had arrived in Ramallah the night before the funeral because we were unsure whether the checkpoints would be open the next day. With my U.S. passport, navigating my way to Ramallah from Jerusalem through two checkpoints had been relatively simple. But for the four men who lived in a Bethlehem refugee camp, the trip had required considerably more exertion. They had been at a procession for Arafat in Bethlehem when they learned that the funeral would be held the next day in Ramallah. They heard that the roads were already beginning to close down as permanent checkpoints became more restrictive and as the Israeli army erected temporary or "flying" checkpoints in other locations. Without stopping home, they were on the road. What, without checkpoints and other forms of closure, would have been a forty-five-minute car ride took around six hours. They took several taxicabs short distances and walked large portions of the trip over parched autumn hills to avoid the checkpoints. In the more dangerous areas, one person from the party would go ahead and then call back to the others on his cell phone to tell them if the area was clear of Israeli soldiers. Under occupation, representation-as-gathering demanded stamina and commitment.

In contrast, the hundreds of journalists who arrived to cover the funeral had flown in from around the world on foreign passports that, like my own, facilitated mobility. This was "parachute journalism," in which top foreign correspondents fly into a location for a brief time to cover a major story. It is often identified as the least contextual kind of journalism, as compared to foreign correspondents' or stringers' reporting.[34] Parachute journalism allows senior correspondents to cover more of the most important stories, but it also reflects a preference in U.S. journalism for correspondents who are deeply aware of the orientations of their audiences, rather than correspondents who know with a similar depth the country where they are working.

The morning of the funeral on November 12, parachute journalism took on a new meaning. It looked in some places as though journalists had actually been air-dropped onto the prime elevated locations around the *Muqata'a*: rooftops of homes, street-side scaffolding erected for the occasion, the upper floors of an unfinished apartment building. Journalists working on the cheap were getting a boost from the detritus of yesterday's news as they stood on piles of rubble on the sides of the road. The visible presence of all of these foreign journalists—their tripods and telephoto lenses, their powerful camera lights shining like clusters of bright suns—only confirmed Palestinians' sense that influential foreigners were concerned with Palestinian politics (Figure 11).

Palestinians—of all ages and genders, but predominantly young men—were scrambling for a view, too, joining journalists on the rubble, climbing on rooftops that had not been rented by journalists, perching themselves on walls and atop electricity poles (Figure 12). Many, like the journalists, brought cameras to take pictures of each other and themselves on this occasion. Some brought signs made by political parties, village councils, or companies. A few brought children dressed for the occasion. One toddler was wearing a kaffiyeh and holding an olive branch and a toy gun, in reference to Arafat's famous 1979 speech at the United Nations in which he noted that both were symbolically at his disposal.[35] As the child's parents surely had anticipated, the child attracted the attention of international photojournalists and nonjournalist Palestinians with cameras. Processes of watching and performing, of depicting and gathering, overlapped with each other, and all involved both ingenuity and sharp elbows.

Perhaps because of their ambivalence about Arafat or about the effectiveness of performing for the U.S. and European media, the refugees from Bethlehem did not want to be in the news. They wanted to see for themselves what was going on, and they wanted to analyze how journalists were going to cover

Figure 11 Conspicuous journalists. Television journalists positioned in an unfinished building overlooking the site of Arafat's funeral are highly visible because of their bright camera lights. *Source*: Amahl Bishara.

Figure 12 The acrobatics of vantage during Arafat's funeral. Palestinians gather on any elevated surface they can access in order to watch PA President Yasir Arafat's body return. *Source*: Amahl Bishara.

the funeral. Jawad cannily spotted a journalist's interpretation as it unfolded. An international journalist—it was not clear where he was from—was trailing an armed Palestinian police officer who was trying to convince people to climb down from the walls around the *Muqata'a*. The journalist was capturing what I read as an atmosphere of contained disorder. There was no sense of actual danger, but the general thrum of thousands of people's desires to mark the occasion the way they wanted to, to gather and to depict with some sense of autonomy, was a reminder to the authorities that they might not control the day. Jawad noticed what the journalist was doing. He remarked with consternation that the journalist was going to tell a story about Palestinian lawlessness. Like the character from *Taghriba Filastiniyya*, the Ramadan serial, shrewd Palestinians had their eyes out for negative coverage in the raw, reading headlines before they were written, even though those headlines were slated for an indistinct Western audience rather than a Palestinian one. Jawad was straining to watch U.S. television from the Palestinian street.[36]

Meanwhile, in the midst of the clamor, a PA official was using Palestinians' sense of being watched by the international press to keep order here. A few press accounts captured a PA official on the scene exhorting the crowds to calm down by invoking the international press. The *Boston Globe* quoted him as saying, "Our image to the world is very important. . . . No slogans, no chants,"[37] while the *Daily Telegraph* caught him insisting, "The whole world is watching us on television."[38] This official was using the idea of an international public, summoned by the Western press, to keep order at home. This weak quasi state did not have the power to survey and discipline its people, but it could piggyback on the many lenses and eyes of the immense international press presence. Anticipated representations-as-depicting were being used to strengthen the PA's efforts at representation-as-gathering. And this tableau was almost surely caught for the foreign correspondents by Palestinian fixers and translators with keen political sensibilities.

These moments epitomize Palestinian concern with and frequent sophistication about foreign representation. This is why processes of media production can have political consequences independent of any published media text. Despite institutional structures that would shape U.S. news narratives about Arafat's funeral, on the scene of media production Western journalists did not have the last word. Palestinians like Jawad and the PA official did their own interpretive work on these imagined texts, either critically or in the service of the PA. This initial elasticity contrasts with the structured forms of social and political power these media obtain as they circulate in their published forms, usually in relation to long-standing journalistic narratives, and quite out of reach of Jawad or the street-level PA official.

As the crowds waited for Arafat's body to arrive from abroad, police were endeavoring to prevent people from entering the *Muqata'a*. Standing on a rooftop we had staked out, we watched their ultimate failure. Palestinians had their own idea of what a legitimate form of representation-as-gathering was on this historic day, and they would not be kept from Arafat's grave. People poured over the retaining walls and into the open square of the *Muqata'a*, until there was little room for the helicopters that would bear Arafat's body to land. All of us—the mourners, the journalists, the curious internationals—braced ourselves when the two helicopters came roaring in. Wind and dust and dirt thrashed into our faces. But once the helicopters were on the ground, it seemed as though the two yellow giants had no advantage over the assembled masses. People were practically pressed up against the helicopters, making it difficult for officials to move Arafat's body to the grave. Former prime minister Ahmed Qurei, who had been on one of the helicopters, shooed them away with indignant swats of his hand. Quickly the officials saw their chance, and Arafat's body disappeared below the ground—without the crisp military salutes he had received in France, without the solemnity of the small funeral in Egypt, and without, most notably, any kind of funeral procession involving the tens of thousands of his compatriots who had come to carry him this last bit of the way. But by this point, Palestinians were standing on every surface of Arafat's compound, on every rooftop and slab of busted cement, in the trees, and on the outside walls (Figure 13). They were chanting, "*Arafat kul al-sha'b, wa-l-sha'b ma biymut*" (Arafat is all the people, and the people do not die). In comparison with the new Fatah leadership's ideological and physical distance from the people, this could be read as a defiant populist statement, even as it was also an indication of how much support this authoritarian leader had managed to maintain.

After the burial, even more people flooded into the *Muqata'a*. Militants' gunshots rang out into the air, in salute or threat or both. One freelance journalist who wrote features rather than breaking news told me that he was going to go home because he could just as well watch the rest on television without the risk of falling bullets. The real bullets used in salutes were another reminder of the potentially perilous material effects of symbolic action. While firing guns is a traditional form of tribute, there was no denying that the bullets posed a danger to everyone nearby. The day met no one's hopes for an honorable

Figure 13   Mourners fill Arafat's half-destroyed headquarters. PA officials were unable to prevent Palestinians from drawing close to Arafat's burial site. *Source*: Amahl Bishara.

funeral, and yet there was a sense that a small victory had been won in the midst—or perhaps by way—of the disarray, because Palestinians had insisted on involving themselves in this momentous gathering.

As Jawad had anticipated, the Western media did cover this event in part through an established narrative about the PA that tracked a particular question over time: In the face of growing Palestinian militancy and in the wake of Israeli destruction of PA institutions, is the PA in control of events on the Palestinian street? Like the debates about why peace negotiations had failed, this narrative centered on whether the PA was able to represent Palestinians effectively, and it had implications for whether negotiations would resume under the new Palestinian leadership. Journalists tended to depict a disorderly Palestinian public without attempting to explain why Palestinians had acted as they did. In U.S. news, the events were described as "chaotic," and people's actions as "frenzied." Several journalists wrote of Palestinians "swarming" the *Muqata'a*.[39] The *Washington Post* article began:

> The helicopter carrying Yasir Arafat's body touched the ground Friday, and the Palestinian leader's impassioned mourners surged forward. By the thousands,

they clambered over concrete walls, burst through police lines, trampled each other and flung themselves against the chopper's metal skin.

"He's here!" a man bellowed, his face contorted as he charged the helicopter.

Desperate and angry, Palestinian security forces fired wildly into the air. Black-masked gunmen answered with louder bursts. Momentarily panicked, people closest to the aircraft dived for the ground in a tangle of sweating bodies, intertwined limbs and lost shoes. Seconds later, they were back on their feet—chanting, screaming, cursing, demanding Arafat's coffin.[40]

Words like "swarming" and "angry" used to describe Palestinian crowds likely evoke entrenched preconceptions about an animalistic and senselessly violent Palestinian public for a U.S. audience that is less knowledgeable about the context of events. For example, it is not clear from the above passage in the *Washington Post* why Palestinians are so angry, if indeed anger was the best word to characterize the emotions of the day. These journalists had produced deft political analysis on other days. Perhaps this was deemed a day for drama rather than subtlety. Perhaps this language should be read as a submerged record of the anxiety they may have experienced that day, caught in the midst of events that were beyond official control. In any case, this coverage, at least as much as Palestinians' experience of the funeral, was politically significant. Whether or not Arafat's funeral would really bring a new era in Palestinian politics depended at least as much on what U.S. journalists said about the funeral and subsequent political events as it did on Palestinian actions.

A particular view of the Palestinian public—both as it constitutes itself in embodied forms at specific events and in the abstract—is in play in these news representations. Palestinian public opinion, and Arab public opinion more generally, is often glossed in U.S. press and political discourse as "the Arab [or Palestinian] street."[41] The expression carries the suggestion that Arab public opinion is irrational, unruly, and stagnant, and that it expresses itself only through violence.[42] This characterization of the Arab street draws on a familiar depiction of the orient as a space of barbarism and disorder. It paints the orient as a mirror image to liberal ideals of the public as a space for rational and disembodied discussion. In this way, it suggests a geographic distribution of norms of expression. According to some liberal ideologies, street gatherings produce dangerous passions, while indoor, ordered gatherings produce reasonable discussions. As Paul Manning writes, in liberal political thought "the passions of street oratory are the opposite of dispassionate, reasoned communication."[43] The coverage of Arafat's funeral discussed above evokes this view of the Arab street as a deeply flawed version of the public sphere. Most journalists did not try to explain why events had unfolded as they had, because the idea of a disorderly Arab street did not seem to require explanation. Yet, understanding why Arafat's funeral happened as it did underscores why the street should not be dismissed as illegitimate just because it stands outside of sanctioned forums for representation. In its planning, the PA had discounted Palestinian tradition and marginalized Palestinian participation. By breaching the walls of the *Muqata'a*, Palestinians were laying claim to their leader, their national space, and their own tradition. Their gathering was an instantiation of popular sovereignty shaped by a political system that has aimed to proscribe mass public presence.[44]

ELECTING PUBLICITY, MEDIATIZING AUTHORITY

A few months after Arafat's funeral, the first PA presidential elections since 1996 were underway to choose Arafat's successor. Although there were several major candidates, it was clear by Election Day on January 9, 2005, that Prime Minister Mahmoud Abbas, of Arafat's Fatah party, would win, especially because the strongest opposition party, Hamas, had declined to participate in these elections. Even though these were to be the first elections in nearly a decade, they were more a site for Palestinians' performance of themselves as a certain kind of political community than they were a forum for internal political change. These elections were taking place in the context of the U.S. campaign for democratization in the Middle East, an ancillary to the War on Terror that touted elections in Iraq and Afghanistan even as the United States continued to support dictatorships elsewhere in the region. Palestinian legitimacy was at stake after Arafat's extended physical and diplomatic isolation by Israel and the United States. Incumbent Palestinian officials' goals of conducting successful public relations with the Western media (a process of representation-as-depicting) and of winning the elections (a process of representation-as-gathering) overlapped with each other. Palestinian candidates and elections institutions aimed to promote not only themselves but also the Palestinian people as a whole, and at the same time to highlight the injustice of Israeli occupation. At times, it seemed that candidates aspired to win the international public relations campaign by way of winning the election, and at times it seemed they intended to win the election by way of winning a public relations campaign aimed at the Western press.

This dynamic was evident in the campaigns of the two leading candidates, Fatah candidate Mahmoud Abbas and progressive independent candidate Mustafa Barghouthi. Despite being the frontrunner, Abbas was not especially popular. During his 2003 stint as prime minister under Arafat's presidency, he had attained the moniker of "the Palestinian Karzai." Similar to Hamid Karzai, then the interim leader of Afghanistan, he was regarded as a lackey appointed to assuage the United States, which had stipulated that the PA should create the position of prime minister to minimize Arafat's power. In fact, after the elections, some Palestinians said that one reason Abbas had been such a successful candidate, eventually winning more than 60 percent of the vote, was that he had U.S. and Israeli support. Palestinians desperately needed a period of stability, and they knew that no leader without external support could negotiate with Israel, not even on relatively small issues like the removal of checkpoints or the release of prisoners. So, the argument went, some voted for stability by voting for the U.S. and Israeli candidate, Mahmoud Abbas.

The Western media also had a role to play for Mustafa Barghouthi, the progressive candidate and medical doctor who had established—and established himself in—a preeminent Palestinian health nonprofit organization. One way by which Barghouthi attracted attention during the campaign was to court Israeli arrest by entering Jerusalem illegally.[45] Soon after he would arrive in Jerusalem for a press conference, Israeli officials would detain him. Broadcast images of these arrests, handcuffs and all, were appealing to Palestinian voters. Moreover, Palestinian leftists and intellectuals, Barghouthi's core constituency, were sensitive to how Palestinians were represented abroad. I was with a Palestinian journalist watching BBC News on satellite television when we saw images of Barghouthi's arrest. Palestinians who saw this likely judged it a positive image that showed basic facts of Israeli occupation to foreign audiences—my journalist companion certainly did. Barghouthi's strategy thus seemed to include winning local votes by sending an international message about the occupation.

The Central Elections Committee (CEC), whose official role was to ensure that the elections ran smoothly and to disseminate information about elections results, also promoted a carefully crafted image of Palestinians to the foreign press during the elections. In an established and functioning democracy, this institution's job would be almost transparent, but in the Palestinian context its role was performative: to make possible a depiction of Palestinians as viable democratic subjects, or in other words to demonstrate for the assembled press that they could gather properly. As an elections official whom I interviewed told me, the elections were "an important opportunity to showcase Palestine." When states and state-like entities are weak, elections can take on a performative dimension with the international community as audience.[46] There were internal political stakes in this as well, because the CEC also highlighted the accomplishment of interim president Abbas in having established the guidelines for the CEC.

The CEC's elections headquarters were the Ramallah Cultural Palace, an upscale new theater in the PA's most cosmopolitan city. The Cultural Palace was accessible from the center of the city only by car, which, tellingly, meant that many of the usual constituents of the Palestinian "street" would have trouble making an appearance. During Arafat's life, I had become accustomed to attending press conferences at the *Muqata'a* in the center of town without having a press pass. I would simply walk in with another journalist, or sometimes just nod to the armed guards at the gates of the compound. However, in preparation for the elections, the CEC had been issuing laminated press passes with reporters' photographs on them, and they were checking these passes at the door of the Cultural Palace. Fortunately, I had been able to apply for and obtain the necessary passes. There were no restrictions on foreign press, no matter how small the organization, even though the Palestinian press faced considerable constraints from the PA. Upon registering, journalists received a packet of materials in either English or Arabic about the candidates and the procedures of the elections. The logo of the elections, printed on the folder of materials we all received and on banners inside the auditorium, was of a smiling, computer-generated cartoon figure wearing a kaffiyeh, holding a ballot, and stepping forward as though from offstage. The neat booths and brochures suggested that a new era of law and order had dawned in the PA.

On Election Day, the Cultural Palace was a tidy exhibition for foreign journalists of the strength of Palestinian democracy, the basic appeal of Palestinian society, and the injustice of Israeli occupation. The walls of the Cultural Palace were decorated with elections material that showcased the apparent burgeoning of "democratic culture" in the PA. Never mind that Palestinians' will to sovereignty substantially predated the computer-generated cartoons promoting voting, that minimalist democratic duty. Framed election posters encouraged Palestinians to register. One read "*filastin 'ala maw'id*" (Palestine on time) and contained an assembly of images of doctors, construction workers, painters, vegetable sellers, police officers, teachers, and families, all of whom together, the poster suggested, made up "Palestine." In the corner, a traditionally dressed man and woman—fellahin, or farmers, who iconically represent the Palestinian nation—placed a ballot in the box. Democracy was for everyone, the poster implied. The motto suggested that Palestinians were fulfilling the universal responsibility of democratic citizenship. The computer-generated graphics allowed for a clean control of images, a representation of precisely chosen segments of the Palestinian populace. There were no protesters or prisoners here. Citizenship was about economic production and voting. Another poster showed a photograph of an older hand passing a sapling tree to a child's hand, and read, "*yadan bi-yad, nasna' al-mustaqbal*" (Hand in hand, we build the future). Again, the image was closely cropped to promote a very specific message. The theme of the day was progress, literally hung on the wall for Western journalists' depiction.

Journalists also received a set of maps of the West Bank and Gaza. These maps, produced by the United Nations Office for the Coordination of Humanitarian Affairs (OCHA), provided the most detailed available information on the location and number of checkpoints, roadblocks, earth trenches, and other forms of Israeli closure, which at that time numbered 719 in the West Bank. Available in many restaurants and offices frequented by foreign visitors, they were clearly oriented toward visitors rather than local Palestinians, as they were in English and included photographs of what each of these kinds of barriers looked like. This was the first time I had seen a bound and complete set of the district maps, and it featured the logo of the CEC. The checkpoints had to do with the elections only peripherally. There had been debate in local and international press before the elections about whether the checkpoints would impede voting. However, the issue of the closures was arguably of greater consequence than the elections for Palestinian lives and prospects for sovereignty. The CEC had taken advantage of the presence of the hundreds of foreign journalists to distribute this information.

The CEC's headquarters also asserted the cultural richness and comfort of Palestinian society. The food was catered by a chic new Ramallah restaurant, Darna, discussed here in the interlude "An Innocent Evening Out?" and a favorite among PA and NGO elite. Along with the registration materials, CEC hosts were distributing a handsome DVD of photographs and music called "This Is Palestine," with photographs by Arab American photographer George Azar that showcased exuberant faces, rich traditions, and beautiful scenery from Palestinian society.[47] Between press conferences this DVD provided a striking slideshow in the auditorium that contained but a few hints of political conflict or occupation. Foreign correspondents who might have been discomfited by the crowds and gunshots fired in the air at Arafat's funeral could relax while watching the slideshow in cushioned seats.

In its press conferences, the CEC spokesperson reported on procedural matters, emphasizing the orderliness of the elections and presenting statistics about the relatively high turnout of women voters. One of Abbas's statements from the day also emphasized women's high levels of participation. Palestinians know that Western audiences have often judged the Arab world by the status of women.[48] However, for inquisitive journalists this did not obscure a more general issue: overall turnout was low. In a controversial move, the CEC kept the polls open for two extra hours. Unlike at Arafat's funeral, the presence of "the Palestinian people" was not just acceptable; it was imperative. This time, rather than having been cordoned off from politicized space, Palestinians had been recruited to perform the PA, but they had to do so on the PA's own terms. Officials tapped into established international norms regarding how to run elections, and these norms constituted the Palestinian people as a collective of individuals, each casting a ballot alone in a booth, as opposed to a crowd in the street with the potential to act together.

Palestinians' reactions to the day were mixed. Some were enthusiastic; others, amused. A Palestinian journalist I accompanied reported to his editor jauntily by phone that everyone was dressed in nice clothes, as though for a holiday. Some were cheerily testing the durability of the ink mark they received on their thumbs as a sign of having voted. Those who refused to participate did so quietly but maintained that elections under occupation were unproductive at best, and legitimizing of that very occupation at worst. None of the four men with whom I had attended Arafat's funeral, who had all hiked miles of desert hills to reach Ramallah from Bethlehem, voted in these elections, because they rejected the notion that anything significant could change while Israeli occupation continued. They regarded as spurious the kind of representation-as-gathering that was deemed most legitimate in U.S. news coverage.

This time, U.S. news narratives reflected the effectiveness of Palestinian public relations labor. The *New York Times* quoted Abbas as stating, "This process is taking place in a marvelous fashion, and is an illustration of how the Palestinian people aspire to democracy," and opposition candidate Barghouthi declared, "I felt my dream is coming true. This is a great step for the Palestinian people, a good test of our institutions and proof to the world that we can establish an independent state."[49] Headlines proclaimed that the elections "[stirred] hope for Mideast peace"[50] and constituted a "new start for the Palestinian people."[51] A *New York Times* editorial following the elections read, "There was much to celebrate about the way the Palestinians managed a free, fair, and democratic election in occupied territory, moving beyond mourning for Yasir Arafat and giving Mahmoud Abbas a broad mandate as the Arab world's sole democratically elected leader."[52] After years of uprising, the performance of statehood seemed to be back on track.

To a certain extent, the main message of the elections—that the PA was stable and democratic, and that the elections constituted a step forward—was one that satisfied both local Palestinians and the international community, just as Barghouthi's arrest "looked good" for him locally and for Palestinians internationally. Intifada-weary Palestinians thought that a positive image on the world stage might give Palestinians clout in minor negotiations that were in progress at that time. Palestinians were also anxious to see what would become of the PA after Arafat's death. However, this international message of progress affected local outcomes in a way that benefited some Palestinian sectors more than others. In promoting Palestinian progress and stability during the elections, the CEC, a PA institution closely linked to Fatah, Abbas's party, was also shoring up power for the PA and Abbas.

As it turns out, in the following months, the modest improvements Palestinians had expected Abbas's election to yield did not come to pass. There was no major prisoners' release, and the removal of checkpoints was minimal. Performing for the international media did not prove rewarding. Instead, a new crisis of representation arose. A year later, on January 25, 2006, PA parliamentary elections results startled many international and Palestinian observers. Hamas, the opposition Islamist party that Palestinians knew to be on the U.S. and Israel's lists of terrorist organizations, won a majority of seats and the right to appoint a prime minister to work alongside Abbas. Palestinian commentators have concluded that Hamas's success was in part a result of Fatah's inability to produce results in negotiations with Israel. Certainly Palestinians were not voting for the United States' favored candidate in these elections.

Even before Hamas formed a cabinet, Israel stopped handing over PA taxes that it collects. The United States and the European Union also quickly mobilized against Hamas, cutting off aid to the PA. Although there was some debate in U.S. media about how the United States could encourage democracy and then reject the result of elections, the notion that it was impossible to deal with "terrorists" remained powerful. It was another iteration of the "no partner" narrative. The New York Times editors, like other commentators, supported the isolation of the PA: "America cannot bankroll a Hamas government that preaches and practices terrorism, denies that Israel has any right to exist, and refuses to abide by peace agreements signed by previous Palestinian governments. That should be blindingly obvious. America is engaged in a global armed struggle against terrorism."[53] The ensuing crisis interrupted the PA's basic administrative functions and crippled the Palestinian economy. The PA was unable to administer its territory, and the thirteen-year-old negotiations process that had been designed to lead to Palestinian statehood continued to languish. The 2006 elections that brought Hamas into power yielded perhaps the starkest crisis of representation yet. Palestinians could represent themselves in that they carried out certifiably free and fair elections. They gathered themselves under the dome of electoral democracy through legitimate processes. Yet, the government that they chose went unrecognized. As a result, the PA could neither represent Palestinians effectively in the international arena nor govern its people. Palestinians could mobilize neither force nor fact in a methodical fashion.

CONCLUSIONS:
REPRESENTATIONAL CONTESTS ON/AND THE PALESTINIAN STREET

The U.S. press, the PA, and ordinary Palestinians depend on each other in their efforts to create media and establish polities, although they do not necessarily share concerns or goals. Arafat's funeral and the PA presidential elections stand as two distinct moments in Palestinians' struggle to represent themselves. Both officials and crowds anticipated that the Western press would be covering the funeral in terms of a narrative of law and order. PA officials appealed to the importance of Palestinians' global image to encourage crowds to follow their directions. Yet, for many Palestinians the struggle of the day was for the right to gather as they saw fit, a momentary democracy of assembly. Palestinians' determination to take part in the funeral of their leader was an expression of the lengths to which they would go to carry out an important social ritual in accordance with at least some of the cultural and political values surrounding that ritual, in this case, popular participation. As expected, though, the U.S. press coverage of Arafat's funeral portrayed Palestinians' failure to gather properly according to Western notions of public ritual decorum, and their unwillingness to abide by the processes set out for them by their government. Their overt use of their bodies in making a political statement was discrediting in these depictions. Their gathering was depicted to suggest that Palestinians exuded anger and chaos. In U.S. press accounts, the presidential elections, in contrast, seemed like a moment of progress. Key Palestinian elites were only too happy to promote images of well-dressed voters in orderly lines, because they, after all, were the ones being elected. But other Palestinians quietly rebuffed this story.

It has often been remarked that media always remediate, cite, or reframe older media. I want to add that representational projects intrude on one another while they are in progress, too. It is significant that journalists and Palestinians stood side by side on piles of rubble during Arafat's funeral so they each could watch events as they unfolded. At such sites, those involved with projects of depiction of all different scales and those who gather to make a political statement are susceptible in similar ways to the exigencies of the moment—bullets shot in the air, or just the emotional intensity of being part of a crowd—even though their representational projects are quite different. There is space for interaction at such sites; large media organizations do not consistently have the last word. As we saw in the case of Jawad, who was trying to watch U.S. television from the Palestinian street, journalists are subject to the interpretation and evaluation of those they depict.

Yet, once stories and photographs are published, media created in these Western news organizations trump local commentary on those media forms. As in Chapter 1, the acts of authoritative entextualization come at the end of long epistemic and political processes.[54] For Palestinians it is often a particular view of Palestinian actions, published the day after an event in outlets like the *New York Times* and the *Washington Post*, that influences Palestinian politics, at least as much as those Palestinian actions themselves, be they funerals or elections. The representations-as-depicting created by the U.S. media in some ways have greater effective status than the representations-as-gathering carried out by Palestinians, in terms of establishing conditions of possibility for future political actions. To a certain extent, press coverage of PA politics brings Palestinians and U.S. readers together so they are contemplating similar images and events, but at the same time it shapes the relationships among them in ways that reinforce global structures of power and local Palestinian hierarchies. There is generally no space for exchange between Palestinians and Americans, and exchanges among Palestinians can be colored by what Palestinians expect from foreign audiences.

Given journalistic practices that center on government officials and state institutions, and given Western liberal assumptions about political speech, the PA has more representational authority than the Palestinian street—but its authority is tenuous. Media practices can constitute the state in multiple ways, helping weak states and state-like entities to perform sovereignty, but for weak institutions like the PA, the success of the performance is not assured. The allegations of Barak and others with which I started this chapter, which held that Palestinian leaders were liars or that they were not true "partners for peace," were in some cases racist and in others merely politically expedient. Nonetheless, they do illustrate a larger truth. Statelessness is a problem of representation, in several meanings of this word. Most obviously, statelessness coincides with lacking institutions with which people can represent themselves to each other—a government—and also lacking positions from which people can represent themselves to the world—a seat at the United Nations, for example. Indeed, Palestinians have for decades struggled to have their leadership recognized. Statelessness—especially when compounded by the force of orientalist arguments—also results in a deep mistrust of what people have to say, and an inability of a leadership to communicate with the same ease as leadership that works from within effective state institutions. Viewing representation-as-gathering and representation-as-depicting next to each other allows us to analyze how states and state-like entities like the PA attempt to use depictions to substantiate themselves, to legitimize their forms of gathering. Media are key to producing the "state effect"[55] that is so critical in crystalizing state power for both domestic and international audiences. The global dominance of Western media means that these media can also be vehicles for spreading certain kinds of values and norms about what kinds of states and other gatherings are most legitimate.

Arafat's funeral was chaotic and harmful to Palestinians' world image in the short run. It was rowdy and male dominated. Palestinians themselves hardly see it as an ideal moment of self-determination or self-representation. However, during Arafat's funeral, people refused to bend themselves into neater public shapes for the sake of appearances. They insisted on trying to carry out Palestinian tradition even as their new leaders would have preferred they desist. Arafat's funeral urges us to consider what constitutes a legitimate representation-as-gathering, or a way of composing a public, without assuming that those publics that do arise are the ideal ones. Yet, recognizing the potential of these alternative political spaces is only a first step. People gathering in Palestinian streets may be able to bring together processes of gathering and depiction in creative and perhaps even emergently democratic ways, but Palestinians require the legitimization and amplification of the PA and U.S. media institutions to give these moments effective power in the world.

The state and the news media can be connected in myriad complex configurations: by a journalist's coveted inside source who can breed complicity, as in the case of *New York Times* reporter Judith Miller;[56] by an army's bullet or missile hitting a journalist or a news bureau; by journalists who promote the authority of a postcolonial state as they mobilize long-standing cultural values;[57] or even by an apparent lack of government regulation.[58] In Western media coverage of global issues, the possibilities are further compounded, such that the figure of the journalist might be called to stand in for powerful foreign governments by a weaker state or local authority. Global news institutions can mediate relationships between states and their publics, and they help to constitute the state itself, both for news audiences and for those on the scene of news production. Yet, such processes may spur dissent, as they did in the Palestinian case. In these instances, it is essential to study ethnographically the constellations of authority that are created and recreated in representational contests among media, governing institutions, and the publics they are representing. In doing ethnographies of journalism, we can examine the dynamics of participation and mediation as they solidify into fact.

A DISCERNING REPRESENTATION
OF MORE THAN "TWO SIDES"

"Bonded in Resistance to the Barrier, Palestinian Villagers, Jewish Neighbors Warily Join Forces"[1] was part of Scott Wilson's series "Two Peoples, Divided," which addressed the theme of the increased separation between Palestinians and Israelis. In this June 2007 article published in the Washington Post, *Wilson, then the Jerusalem bureau chief and later foreign editor and White House correspondent, explored how individuals from the Palestinian village of Wadi Fukeen and the Israeli town of Tzur Hadassah had tentatively come together in an alliance against the barrier, even as a nearby Israeli settlement, Betar Elit, further encroached upon the village's land. It was an unusual article for several reasons. Not only was it based in a rural context where no "breaking news" was occurring, but it also highlighted a partnership between Palestinians and Israelis even as it made clear that this partnership was difficult for all involved.*

The opening sentences set up this relationship:

WADI FUKIN, West Bank—The Palestinians of this village have long looked toward Tzur Hadassah, a neighboring Israeli town, for jobs building homes on land that decades ago belonged to them.

Now some Palestinians are looking to their Jewish neighbors for a different kind of help. Israel's separation barrier is slated to rise between the antique village and the modern suburb, replacing a stand of pines that marks the porous boundary here between the West Bank and Israel.

The characterization of Wadi Fukeen as antique in comparison to the modern Israeli suburb was more complicated than it seemed, as Wilson made clear in the rest of the text. While the suburb was decidedly new, the village was a new-old kind of place. Wadi Fukeen had been almost wholly rebuilt in 1972. As Wilson reported, the village, which was within the West Bank but very close to the armistice line, had been evacuated in 1948. Most of the villagers had taken refuge in Deheisheh Refugee Camp in Bethlehem. Five years after the 1967 War, these villagers had been allowed to rebuild their homes in their village. To my eye, the article did an unusually good job in presenting history and clarifying relations of power in the space of a feature article. I was curious what Palestinian readers would make of it, especially because partnerships between Israeli Jews and Palestinians were controversial in Palestinian society.

While sources were a point of Palestinian critique in other articles, in this case, the reporting struck readers as quite solid. Zayd, a math teacher, offered his praise. "My first impressions of this article were very good—excellent, really. I noticed that this journalist really made an effort. I get the sense that he really actually spent time with both sides, that he knows people there. He really listened. I got the sense that he was friendly with the people in his article." The mayor of Wadi Fukeen, Ghaleb Bader, who had also been interviewed for Wilson's article and who asked me to use his name here, suggested that while the journalist could have given more details about restrictions on his village, he generally had the right idea. Bader, who read the article in his Bethlehem office moments before the interview, seemed hesitant to offer any stringent critiques. "Maybe some things he didn't write because he wanted to avoid embarrassing Israelis. Maybe some things he didn't write because he wanted to avoid embarrassing Palestinians," he conceded, but overall the American journalist had been fair. Still, as indicated when, in the course of our conversation, Zayd casually characterized Tzur Hadassah—the Israeli town Wilson calls a "suburb"—as a "settlement," Palestinians did have a different perspective on the story. For many Palestinians, Israeli towns like Tzur Hadassah are hardly more legitimate than settlements in the West Bank because they too are built on Palestinian lands, as Wilson had acknowledged for this case.

Unlike many of the articles, this one won praise for addressing local histories and giving the kind of "color" that added important social and economic context. Said Lamis, a journalist from Bethlehem whom I interviewed in her office,

> *He talked about the war with Jordan and how [Wadi Fukeen] was on the line of fire, and how they lost half of their land. Also [the settlement of] Betar Elit took a lot of their lands. And he described how some of the land still actually owned by the villagers is inaccessible, because it is close to the settlement. On a practical level, this land is gone. Even if you own it, you cannot even get to it.*

Lamis appreciated how he described the village as well. Wilson wrote, "Natural springs water the patchwork of vegetable plots and olive groves that have sustained the village for centuries, even during the period when its people vanished" between 1948 and 1972. Lamis recalled still more details from his article: "They have a vegetable market in the spring. . . . You can feel and imagine the place while reading the article. When you have the five senses in the story, you can really sympathize with the people."

Rather than sparking a detailed dissection of the article, these readings spurred an open-ended discussion about the tribulations of Israeli-Palestinian interactions. For example, Wilson mentioned that Palestinians often labored to build Israeli houses on Palestinians' former lands. Lamis commented on this point: "One reason it's difficult to cut off our relationship with Israelis is that many men are employed in Israel as laborers, and many women work in Israel too." She added, "We cannot say all Palestinians who work in Israeli settlements are happy about their positions, but they need the work."

The article raised the question of whether Palestinians should normalize relations with Israelis and conduct regular dialogues with them. Wilson quoted a villager from Wadi Fukeen engaged in such dialogues who allowed, "I know there are those here who say [talking to Israelis] is like blowing into an open goatskin—that there is nothing there. And I know there is another group who says this is against our collective interest, against our religion—and our homeland." Zayd seemed torn about what could be accomplished when Palestinians worked with Israelis. On the one hand, he likened it to "making a deal with the devil" for pragmatic reasons, but he also voiced strong support for dialogue between Palestinians and Israelis as long as it happened within a framework that could lead to concrete progress, as he thought was the case with dialogue between residents of Wadi Fukeen and Tzur Hadassah. In a provisional way, he said, "they helped Palestinian refugees 'return' to their lands, giving them their rights as Palestinians. For example, one of the Israelis helped a Palestinian to pray in Jerusalem on a Friday. This was a very nice gesture, to take the Palestinian in his car. And there was even a kind of risk involved for the Israeli, right?" Israelis could be penalized for smuggling Palestinians into Israel.

Lamis acknowledged that each side approached the other with some degree of fear, or what Wilson called "mutual suspicion." She told me, "[Wilson] says that an Israeli woman buys vegetables from Wadi Fukeen, but that during the war with Lebanon, she was afraid to go down to the village. Nothing happened to her, but she was afraid. So there are obstacles." And she liked the image another Israeli in the article offered of a "mental barrier." As she explained, "It's like, even if I live in Lydd [a city inside Israel where many Palestinians live], and there is no [separation] wall there, there is a mental barrier. There is always fear. You count to three before you talk to your neighbor." She continued, "Even if there is no policy change regarding the wall, those Israelis who support us give us hope. This is the small change the Israeli talked about. We should break the mental barrier between us and move forward together." But Bader, the former mayor, had a darker perspective on this issue. "There is no trust in this relationship because in the end nothing has changed. . . . The personal barriers that were there are still present. You're an Israeli, and I'm a Palestinian. You're encroaching on my land; you're the aggressor; you're taking my rights. There is no openness or trust in our relationship. This group of friends [from Tzur Hadassah] has tried to foster a good relationship with us, but barriers remain."

Although this article seemed to reflect the difficulties of Palestinian lives more than many other articles, with its discussion of Palestinian land loss and settler aggression against Palestinians, Zayd still worried that the article encouraged American sympathy with Israelis. "The American people relate more to Israelis than to Palestinians. The average American thinks of Israel as having a rightful presence, and that's it, no discussion. And that the wall is there because of Palestinian aggression." This was one of the conclusions he had drawn from the decade or so when he had lived in the United States. Zayd continued, "They might think, this small group of Israelis, these respectable, clean people, sat down with those primitive, barbaric Palestinians in their own houses, and tried to help them." While this article sparked nuanced interpretations from Palestinians, Zayd feared that there was almost no way for Palestinians to be represented favorably in U.S. media. Was he correct that even the strongest reporting was often doomed to be read through an ethnocentric lens?

CONCLUSION

Framing Graffiti: Voice, Materiality, and Violence

Journalists arrived early to the Abu Dis demonstration, which was timed to coincide with the hearings against the separation wall at the International Court of Justice at The Hague. Television crews set up their communication equipment on an empty lot overlooking the wall. A small herd of goats grazed near the satellite dishes where Prime Minister Ahmed Qurei would later speak. Abu Dis was a familiar place for journalists, a place photojournalists based in Jerusalem could reach quickly to snap a photograph and return to their bureaus. In this village turned Jerusalem suburb, the wall truncated a road that had once been called the Jerusalem-Amman Road. When Amman became less accessible, people called it the Jerusalem-Jericho Road, referencing the city about an hour away near the Jordanian border. Now, it did not extend even that far.

The lower part of the wall had been painted a bright white, apparently to clear the way for new graffiti that the day of protests would surely yield. Immediately on the other side of the wall lay the charred metal remains of a bus destroyed in a Palestinian bombing the day before. It had been hauled there by Israeli authorities to make the point that such bombings necessitated the building of the wall. The bus might be regarded as the state's answer to graffiti, here the medium of the stateless, for it was the state's version of making things speak. On both sides, then, the stage was set. The journalists were chatting with each other and checking their equipment when a little event took shape. A girl of about twelve years, her long hair pulled back in a ponytail, stood at the barrier with a spray paint canister in hand. The photojournalists assembled around her with their cameras. Deliberately, in large, wavering spray paint handwriting, she wrote "Children Against the Wall" in English on the mammoth structure (Figure 14). When she finished, she turned around to an audience of several photojournalists, greeting them with a glowing smile.

Children at the wall were frequent subjects for journalists' contemplation. It was at this site that *New York Times* journalist James Bennet had spoken to a twelve-year-old boy who had been illegally crossing the wall wearing a T-shirt emblazoned with the slogan "Future Attack."[1] It was a passing detail in an article about the toll of the wall on Abu Dis, an area without enough schools, health clinics, and jobs to survive without Jerusalem. The allusion was unclear. Who could say what, if anything, the T-shirt meant? Did the boy know what the English writing said? Was there a graphic of a machine gun or a spaceship on the shirt? Was an attack promised in the future, or was perhaps the future itself attacking in some more existential sense? For some, Palestinian children represent a double threat of demographic shifts and political violence; for others, they represent hopes for a free and democratic future. The girl's graffito "Children Against the Wall" hinted at this latter possibility, evoking an orderly constituency unified against the barrier, a proper representation-as-gathering. The girl seemed like a perfect political subject for a liberal public sphere: English-speaking, nonviolent, and (apparently) secular. Dominant nar-

Figure 14 "Children Against the Wall." A girl inscribes her message of protest on the separation wall at Abu Dis before a group of journalists. *Source*: Amahl Bishara.

ratives about Palestinians in U.S. media might position her graffito in counter-point with the destroyed bus, suggesting that one side of the wall represented Palestinian aspirations to statehood and freedom of speech, while the other side referenced the dystopic option of violence, of past and future attacks. Yet, the girl's graffito was an election-style slogan at a time when there were no po-litically meaningful elections. Even more importantly, it was printed not on a traditional democratic medium like a handbill, placard, or button, but instead, on a wall that enclosed and restricted. The wall was an immense reminder of Israeli unilateralism, of Israel's disinterest in Palestinian concerns. In the eyes of many Palestinians, the utopic vision of democracy was as unrealistic as the dystopic one was grim.

This moment crystallized three contradictions: between the ideal of free-dom of speech and the fact of Palestinians stripped of many political rights; between a girl's act of expression and the confining separation barrier on which it was written; between the fantasy of plain language producing clear communication with imagined international audiences on the other side of the photographers' lenses, and the actual difficulties Palestinians have faced in translating their political experiences and aspirations to these audiences. In the next few years, as I watched the separation barrier fill with graffiti, much of them written not by Palestinians but by internationals, I came to see graf-fiti—and journalists' photography of graffiti—as exemplifying the problems Palestinians faced in expressing themselves to the amorphous international audiences they sought.

Like other forms of media, graffiti have undergone changes since the estab-lishment of the PA. During the first Intifada, roughly 1987–1993, a period when graffiti writing was especially important because Israeli authorities often shut down the newspapers, teenagers wrote graffiti under cover of night. Lookouts made sure that no one saw them, lest they be arrested by Israeli patrols.[2] The graffiti existed fleetingly: hours after they were written, Israeli soldiers might force other youth to erase them. It was not only the content of graffiti that was oppositional; the medium itself was, too. The audiences for graffiti—pass-ersby who had experience of military occupation—understood the risks graf-fiti writers were taking. People read graffiti both as they would a newspaper, for information, and also as an index of resistance. As one woman told anthro-pologist Julie Peteet at the time, "When I wake in the morning and see new graffiti I know that resistance continues. It tells me that people are risking their lives and that they live right here in this neighborhood."[3]

By the second Intifada, Israeli authorities did not generally arrest youth for writing graffiti. Israel's system of censorship of Palestinian media, in effect in the West Bank and Gaza Strip from 1967 to 1994, had long melted away. In fact, the separation barrier Israel built functions as a kind of invitation to discourse. It serves in some places as a prime billboard for graffiti writers. Graffiti on the wall epitomizes Palestinians' contemporary conundrum regarding free speech. From one perspective there is an atmosphere of apparent permissiveness to Palestinian speech, as discourses of state building flourish and as Israel tries to conceal its role as occupier. As I will argue, though, just as Israel has continued to control actions on the ground, so too does it have final say over Palestinian graffiti through its material practices.

The young girl's act of graffiti writing in Abu Dis was part of a wide spectrum of practices of writing on the wall, only some of which made the news. Visitors to the separation wall will find protesters' graffiti in Arabic, English, and other languages; writing commissioned by people who were never in the West Bank;[4] colorful murals done by delegations of solidarity activists; and clever artwork designed to comment on the wall as a structure. Those who venture beyond the wall into the heart of Palestinian communities will find other kinds of graffiti and murals: tributes to activists, lines of poetry, murals of Palestinian history, plainly written political slogans, and celebrations of pilgrims' return from Mecca.[5] Through photojournalism and other kinds of photography, the medium of graffiti—usually regarded as quintessentially local, grounded in place—has taken on a transnational scope, but as with other transnational media, this does not mean that Palestinian voices are communicated transparently. In the next few pages I want to examine what made some forms of visible protest more legible than others in the medium of news agency photography, and to explore how some of these graffiti might have seemed to represent Palestinian voices even when they did not. Some messages and forms of protest of Palestinians that are less clear are in fact more attuned to the political circumstances of their creation—but they are harder to represent in Western photojournalism.

The medium of graffiti does not easily fit into the dominant norms of Western news media. Liberal semiotic ideologies—normative ideas about how meaning should be made[6]—have favored disinterested and decontextualized speech.[7] By their nature, graffiti call attention to context, because they are written publicly on surfaces not generally intended for writing. When writing is so obviously located in the material world, as graffiti is, it can be seen to be constrained by this materiality, calling attention to limitations on expression and thought that the dominant liberal tradition has tried to disavow. Perhaps this is one reason that graffiti are an oppositional medium. They challenge ideas about meaning-in-context. Graffiti written on the separation barrier epitomize a tension between submitting to material constraints and seeming to overcome them. It might have seemed that the girl who wrote "Children Against the Wall" won a small victory when she completed her message because she exercised her right to free speech, but in fact she was still stranded on the West Bank side of the wall. Neither the authorities who built the wall nor those who elected the authorities would be likely to see her graffito. As we will see, news agency photographs that captured graffiti on the separation wall draw upon this tension, but they also necessarily decontextualize graffiti from their surroundings, just as quotations remove speech from context and thereby change its meaning (Chapter 1). In the published image, the constraints become less clear than the literal meaning the words send, thus obscuring the message that words and context might send together.

There has been extensive journalistic photography of graffiti on the separation wall, perhaps because it is so often visually compelling and it is easy to capture. News agency photographers often photograph graffiti that will be comprehensible to international audiences: English-language graffiti with a clear message that fits into news narratives. One photograph taken in Abu Dis on February 4, 2004, by Kevin Frayer, an award-winning photographer for the Associated Press, contained a graffito that read "Peace comes [by] agreement not separation" (Figure 15). The sentence, written in even blue writing, stretches across two panels of what looks like the separation barrier, and between these two panels peer a man and a boy, whose faces are only partially visible. The graffito is a critique of the barrier, and the photograph amplifies this message because we see people apparently trapped behind the wall. Thus the photograph's strength comes from a poetic relationship between the written message and its formal qualities. Still, both the graffito and the photograph conform to some aspects of the detached, plain-speaking style that liberal modernists have espoused. The graffito's language of "peace," "agreement," and "separation" is abstract; its handwriting is earnest and unadorned; the identity of the speaker is unclear. It is a statement that could aspire to universal truth. Even the people trapped behind the wall look calm and unemotional.

When I examined this photograph, I was sure because of its message and its location that the graffito had been written by an international solidarity activ-

Figure 15 "Peace Comes by Agreement Not Separation." This Associated Press image of a graffito on a temporary wall that would later be incorporated into the separation wall reads almost like a headline for an op-ed. *Source*: Kevin Frayer, Associated Press.

ist, and not by a Palestinian. Activists, political tourists, and pilgrims visited Abu Dis often, for the same reasons that journalists did. It was a convenient place from which to see the wall in all of its gray enormity. Moreover, Palestinians' language in barrier graffiti often took a different tone from this message about peace. By this point, "peace" as a theoretical term had little currency for many Palestinians. As the boy stated in the James Bennet article discussed in the interlude after Chapter 1, "Peace is a word that flies in the air." Instead, for Palestinians, the barrier is often a site for the assertion of rights that push more forcefully back on the wall as a technology of confinement. After the February demonstration, I could easily identify the graffiti that had been written by Palestinians. Many of these graffiti were written in both Arabic and English, as though direct translation would lead to the best possible communication. One read *"Al-jidar lan yabqa,"* translated into English as "The wall will not remain." Some graffiti used the barrier, which cut Abu Dis off from Jerusalem, to assert a connection to the city and its centrality to Palestinian politics: *"Nahnu fi al-Quds ila al-abad,"* and in English, "We will be in Jerusalem forever." Specificity of place was important. Some took advantage of the prominence of the wall to publicize neglected issues like that of prisoners: *"Hurriya li-asra al-hurriya,"* translated into English as "Freedom for the prisoners of freedom." Unlike the abstract statement Frayer captured, some of these graffiti are poetic, or they are explicitly written in a Palestinian voice, promising an eternal presence of "we." These kinds of graffiti were rarely photographed by international journalists.

In perusing my photo archive from Abu Dis, I found that I was right that the "Peace comes by agreement not separation" graffito had been written by internationals: it carried the signature "Ireland for Peace" (Figure 16). Moreover, it shows that the wall at this site was still a temporary, 2-meter structure. Had it been the full, completed 8-meter structure, no faces would have been visible on the other side of the wall. Frayer's message relied on this fortuitous material circumstance. This apparent critique of the barrier relied on the structure's incompleteness. This is important because it underscores the ways in which what the graffiti writers and the photographer can say depends on the material world. Meaning is not autonomous; it is highly contingent on the physical environment—and this environment is to a great extent shaped by state actors, in this case Israeli authorities.

My inelegant medium-shot photographs also display other kinds of graffiti that were not photographed by photojournalists. The graffito "God leads us to peace," likely written by an international staying at the convent that was just meters away from this site, could not be mistaken for the headline of an op-ed in the mostly secular discourse of foreign news as "Peace comes by agreement not separation" could. Even further outside the realm of possibility for inclusion in photojournalism is the advertisement for home heating oil scrawled in Arabic in red paint in the right half of the photograph followed by a phone number for contacting "Abu Ghulus."[8]

The barrier is also a canvas for paintings, often created by internationals. These too may be photographed by photojournalists. For example, an Associated Press photograph taken in Abu Dis in 2005 displays a giant mural that states, in Spanish, "*Paz con dignidad!*" (Peace with dignity!) over a background of a person calling out and a waving Palestinian flag. In the foreground of the photograph, a Palestinian shepherd stands in front of the wall. Other prominent paintings that have appeared in the news were created by the British graffiti artist Banksy, who has visited the West Bank more than once. More so than other graffiti or murals, Banksy's works exhibit a subversive playfulness regarding how to treat the barrier as an object. Most of his 2005 paintings dealt with the theme of escape or breaking through the wall. For example, in the same location where the girl wrote "Children Against the Wall," he painted in black and iridescent white a smiling child kneeling on the ground, paint-

Figure 16 Contextualizing "Peace." Patching together two photographs for a less elegant, wider-angle picture reveals that the "Peace" graffito was written by an Irish delegation. At this time, the

ing a ladder that rises to the top of the wall. Perhaps his most famous image, captured by photojournalists among others, is a silhouette of a girl in a short dress and formal shoes being lifted by a bouquet of balloons (Figure 17). It suggests that she will soon be liberated from the wall's constrictions. Unlike most other murals or graffiti, these images explicitly treat the wall as both a surface for writing *and* an oppressive barrier. However, these paintings remain Eurocentric in their iconography. The girl being lifted by the balloons sports a long braid with a bow on its end, a knee-length dress, and old-fashioned high-heeled shoes. She looks vaguely like a character out of a Victorian storybook. Generally, these images do not demonstrate any special knowledge about Palestinian society.[9]

Another feature of these news agency photographs is that they tend to feature a Palestinian in the foreground even though the message or image in the background was produced by internationals. The figures add visual depth, and they also serve to validate the images. Often these Palestinians represent Palestinian or Arab culture through clothing that indexes Arabs in the West: the kaffiyeh or the *hijab*. As Zeynep Gürsel has noted, photojournalists and their

wall was still under construction, and Palestinians found it easy to cross the temporary structure as long as no soldiers were nearby. *Source*: Amahl Bishara.

editors often favor images of people who will be recognizable as Palestinian to foreign audiences, rather than, say, a blond woman who to Western audiences looks dressed as though she is headed for an office.[10] Though Palestinians' presence is admissible and even desirable in photographs that would otherwise lack depth, a Palestinian voice is still attenuated by Western news organizations. Palestinians become part of the environment while others—graffiti writers and the photojournalists—speak about them. In some cases, Palestinians clearly were complicit in their own representation in this fashion (Figure 18). Does a Palestinian man sitting in front of the barrier in his kaffiyeh as though posing for the camera offer his endorsement of the graffiti behind him? Is he expressing his boredom? Might we imagine he is waiting for a buddy to arrive for a backgammon game? It is not clear. For the casual viewer of these photographs, the presence of a Palestinian may authenticate the words and images on the wall. But we can also read these as evidence of the environment for expression in the West Bank. These photographs were easy to take because, while in most cases the internationals who have written the graffiti have left, Palestinians have no choice but to live surrounded by the graffiti-covered wall.

Figure 17 Banksy's iconic mural of a girl being lifted over the wall by a bouquet of balloons. The original painting, near the Qalandia checkpoints in Ramallah, has been surrounded by other graffiti, some of which address Banksy's mural. *Source*: Mohammad Al-Azza.

Figure 18 Presence versus voice at/on the separation wall. When I arrived in Abu Dis with a group of political tourists, this man was sitting in front of the wall as though posing. Many of the tourists took head-on photographs of him. *Source*: Amahl Bishara.

Given that Palestinians were forced to live in its midst, we might wonder why there were few Palestinian murals painted on the separation wall. Murals *are* a prevalent Palestinian medium for decorating public space and producing popular history. Youth centers may produce them because they allow for collaborative work at multiple skill levels. For example, a set of murals in 'Aida Refugee Camp portrayed tableaus from each of the twenty-seven villages from which refugees in this camp came. Other murals in the camp memorialize martyrs, celebrate a holiday with a depiction of Jerusalem's gilded skyline, or pay tribute to prisoners (Figure 19). In the monotonous, overcrowded concrete jungle of Palestinian refugee camps, these murals enliven public space and commemorate community experiences and values.

Yet, these murals were located within the refugee camp, not on the wall around it. Many Palestinians have proscribed paintings on the barrier because they argue that the barrier should not be beautified; it should be torn down. As Fatin Farhat, cultural director of the prominent Sakakini Center, told an American journalist, "I get tens of [international] artists every day who want to work on the wall. I say, . . . Leave it ugly and terrible and call for its demoli-

Figure 19 A Palestinian mural located inside 'Aida Refugee Camp. This mural depicts a political prisoner breaking free from his chains. Note that the strategy of photographing a person along with a mural or graffito can give an image depth and a sense of movement or time. *Source*: Mohammad Al-Azza.

tion."[11] Banksy himself notes that he encountered this attitude from someone who walked by his work, as he recounts in his book:

Old man   You paint the wall, you make it look beautiful

Me   Thanks

Old man   We don't want it to be beautiful, we hate this wall, go home[12]

Just as when some Palestinians refused to be party to the pope's visit if they could not host him in their chosen location, many Palestinians found a self-restricting attitude to representation could better take into account the actual relations of power surrounding meaning making at the barrier. Rather than celebrate an appropriation of space on the barrier by painting on it, many Palestinians stuck to graffiti that did not aim to hide what they saw as the barrier's ugliness. Iyad Burnat, a leader of popular resistance in the village of Bil'in put it best when he told me during an interview in his home, "The flowers that are painted on the wall are not more beautiful than the olive trees that were uprooted to build the wall." As we spoke, I noticed a wall-hanging of Palestinian embroidery that quoted a popular saying of the Prophet Muhammad: "*Inna Allah jamil, yuhibb al-jamal*" (God is beautiful and loves beauty). Beauty has an esteemed place in Palestinian society. But when actual olive trees and painted flowers are so incommensurable, why even suggest otherwise?

THE WALL IS NOT A BLANK PAGE

The limitations of graffiti were brought into stark relief for me in Abu Dis, the same place where, in news agency photographs, graffiti seemed to reign. Though Israeli authorities did not regularly paint over graffiti or arrest people for writing graffiti on the wall, their control over space and movement impacted graffiti too. In an earlier phase of construction, the barrier in Abu Dis had been about 2 meters high—like the blocks on which "Peace comes by agreement not separation" was written. After the full-size, 8-meter wall was erected, some of these leftover blocks of cement remained scattered in an adjacent field, detritus of the barrier's progress. The graffiti on them was rendered fractured and non-sensical by the blocks' displacement. Halves of phrases lay on their side in the grass, signs quite literally disconnected from their original meanings. Some of these blocks had been reassembled as parts of new barriers nearby, thus remaking occupation barriers from the material of resistant graffiti. In Al-Ram, too, I saw one of the 2-meter concrete slabs repositioned to direct the line of cars at a checkpoint. Apparently, it previously had a memorial written on it, something like "The Intifada lives on in the memory of—" But as this slab was disconnected from the piece that had previously been adjacent to it, and it had been turned on its side, the phrase was incomplete. The words ran into the ground. I struggled to take a decent photograph of the graffito that had lost its writer's intended significance in a streetscape strewn with trash. This emphasizes a theme from throughout this book that in order to understand knowledge production under military occupation, we must attend to the material processes of the production of meaning. I never saw news agency photographs of these fractured graffiti in the news. These graffiti belied the clarity and sense of representational sovereignty of the intact graffiti I discussed above. In not photographing them, photojournalists probably made sound aesthetic judgments, but they tacitly upheld the illusion that speech and action occur in separate realms, that the built environment has no effect on our ability to speak.

As though understanding the tenuousness of their acts of resistance, Palestinians wrote graffiti even on surfaces that seemed to have only a peripheral or fleeting place in public view. When construction of the wall began in Al-Ram just north of Jerusalem, the barrier panels, shaped like elongated upside-down Ts, were lying down on the side of the main road. I noticed that graffiti had been scrawled on a few of the bottoms of these wall panels. One declared furtively, *"Al-Quds lana"* (Jerusalem is ours). Another attested, *"Allahu akbar la ilaha illa Allah"* (God is Great, There is no god but God). Riding by in a shared taxicab on my way from Jerusalem to Ramallah, I first thought this graffiti writer had chosen a degrading location for such weighty statements. It was as though she or he was writing on the bottom of a shoe. After all, the surfaces on which these graffiti were written would be underground once the wall was erected.

But construction of the wall in Al-Ram—as elsewhere in the West Bank— was a protracted enterprise. The barrier here was being built lengthwise down the middle of the road, and to build the wall the pavement on one side of the road had been destroyed, forcing two directions of traffic to sidle past each other on the remaining half of the street. Then this side of the road was closed, and cars sloshed through the mud on the other side. The process took months. Palestinians were living amidst a construction site for a project that had been designed without their consent and that would destroy economic, social, and other resources of their communities. For them, the disarray and violence of an extended construction period was further evidence that Israel was building the barrier with no consideration for local residents, to frustrate them and force them to submit to their own powerlessness.

The inconveniences and dangers of construction seemed to be part of the point, belying plainspoken Israeli assertions in the media that the wall was integral to Israeli security. Former Israeli prime minister Ehud Barak could declare in a *New York Times* op-ed, "Israel must embark on unilateral disengagement from the Palestinians and establish a system of security fences. Israel's very future depends on this."[13] But according to Louay Abu Shambiya, the boy in the "Future Attack" T-shirt interviewed by James Bennet at the wall in Abu Dis, the wall was there "to make people suffer."[14] In terms of representational authority, obviously Barak had Abu Shambiya beat. Barak's statement was authorized by the fact that he had at one time been elected to represent all Israelis. His full op-ed was published in the *New York Times*. In contrast, Abu Shambiya's quote—not even a full sentence—was produced in essence because of a gathering of interlopers at the wall, happened upon by a prominent journalist with an ear for evocative quotes. It was an illegal representation-as-gathering. Abu Shambiya was speaking to Bennet because he and others Bennet interviewed that day were crossing the wall to go to school or work. On top of that, Abu Shambiya was a child. Who would take seriously his assertion that the wall was there to make people suffer, alongside Barak's statement that the wall was there for security, at least if they did not already agree with the child? For Palestinians, though, the process of how Israel constructed the barrier informed how they construed Israeli intentions in building it.

As the cars moved more slowly on Al-Ram's compromised roads while the wall was being built, I found I had even more time for reading graffiti. The "Jerusalem is ours" graffito was visible for much of this period. Though its visual characteristics and its location would never have attracted the attention of a photojournalist, it turned out that it was presciently well suited to the circumstances of the building of the barrier. It was at eye level of those passengers in dusty taxis. Palestinians' means of protest express an urgency and local knowledge that exceed that of the eloquent and tidy graffiti written by foreign protesters. They reflect a keen sensitivity to the physical qualities of the barrier and to the processes of building it. Yet, these Palestinian protests were not always as legible to foreign audiences.

How else then did Palestinians visually articulate their rejection of the barrier? In Nablus and Gaza, protests of the barrier take place though the barrier is not nearby. Movement restrictions often prevent Palestinians from these areas from reaching protests that take place at the site of the barrier. Checkpoints thereby restrict both assembly and expression. Instead, protests in Nablus and Gaza can involve models of the barrier. In these protests, too, Palestinians write graffiti on the faux "wall" that they have constructed, but they do not pretend that *writing* on the barrier is the end goal of protest. First they write antibarrier graffiti on the mock barrier, and then they destroy it. These were also media performances, and images of these demonstrations were also published by news agencies. Yet, for American audiences they are probably less benign and less moving than the Frayer picture of "Peace comes by agreement not separation." Not only are the graffiti in Arabic rather than English, but they also might be read as reflecting a violent politics. In one Agence France-Presse photograph from Gaza, guns jut into the frame, and flags give the scene a nationalist and militarist air. Given associations between Arabs and violence, such an image might well be taken as a backhanded legitimation for the wall as much as it would a protest of it.

On the wall around 'Aida Refugee Camp, Bethlehem (Chapter 5), one can find straightforward Palestinian-authored graffiti like "*la li-l-jidar*" (No to the wall). One can also find complex statements that require a knowledge of Arab literature. Scrawled on the wall amidst a multicolored, multilingual pastiche of slogans, anarchy symbols, and landscape paintings—much of which were contributed by international visitors—is the line "*la budda li-l-layl an yanjali w-la budda li-l-qayd an yankasir*" (Inevitably the night will come to an end and the chains will be broken). The handwriting is a fluid but simple black cursive (Figure 20). This is a famous verse from the poem "*Lahn al-Haya*" (Melody of life) by the early twentieth-century Tunisian poet Abu Al-Qaasim Al-Shaabi. The line has great anticolonial resonance for Palestinians, as for other Arabs.[15] Elsewhere in the camp, on a wall that is not part of the separation barrier, one can read a famous line from the poetry of Mahmoud Darwish, "*'Ala hadha al-ard ma yastahiqq al-haya*" (On this earth is what is worth living).[16] With such graffiti, Palestinians inscribe their landscape with messages of resistance and steadfastness that evoke a rich Arab literary and political culture. Even those international visitors who can read these lines likely will not sense the succor they provide to Palestinians. Those interested in the Israeli-Palestinian conflict can scroll through online news photographs to see hundreds of images of the wall, graffiti, protests, and incursions, and bombings. It might seem that every inch of the separation wall has been covered by news agency photojournalists. But the apparent thoroughness of

Figure 20 "Inevitably the night will come to an end." This graffito on the wall at 'Aida Refugee Camp near Bethlehem quotes the Tunisian poet Abu Al-Qaasim Al-Shaabi. Note the juxtaposition with the graffito "Oh Little Star of Bethlehem," almost certainly written by an international visitor. *Source*: Amahl Bishara.

this coverage obscures all of the complexity and depth of a visual political culture that has sustained people through decades of oppression and violence.

Other forms of protest that leave their mark on the wall are even more enigmatic. Construction of the barrier in 'Aida Refugee Camp was drawn out over three years of recurrent conflict. In response to residents' protests, Israeli soldiers and barrier guards shot several Palestinian youth and arrested tens of others. In the summer of 2005, moments after the final guard tower was erected, signaling the completion of work in that area, youths set tires on fire on the ground next to the 8-meter concrete tower, staining the barrier and irritating any soldiers in the tower. The smoke obscured the faces of the protesters and thus helped Palestinians avoid arrest. This remained a symbolic action in that it posed little or no danger to either the barrier or to the soldiers, yet it also suggested that the violence of the barrier could not be answered with words alone. In the months that followed, residents saw the black mark on the barrier as an eloquent and fitting way to express their rejection of it (Figure 21). However, international audiences might see setting fire to tires next to the wall as reflecting a violence internal to Palestinian society rather than as a protest driven by a particular context.

Some symbolic protests left no trace for the news agency photographer to capture. In 2005, Ali, a teenaged boy in 'Aida Refugee Camp, built a wooden ladder and erected it next to the wall. Then he climbed the ladder and held up a Palestinian flag. This furtive protest was photographed—but by one of his

Figure 21 The mark of protest on the wall in 'Aida Refugee Camp. Visible are the spots where tires were burned and paint bombs hit the wall during protests. The graffiti pictured in Figure 20 are located at the corner of the wall in the lower right of this image. *Source*: Nidal Al-Azraq.

friends, not by a news agency photographer. A few days later, Israeli soldiers came to his house in the middle of the night to arrest the sixteen-year-old. He was sentenced to eight years in prison, though he was released early in a prisoner exchange.[17] The ladder was long gone when I returned to the camp months later, but a makeshift monument to Ali's protest had been installed. Youth had jammed wooden slats between the concrete slabs of the separation barrier to form a new, rough kind of ladder. The wood pieces were broken at one end, and I imagined they came from the dumping area that had taken shape next to the wall. They were unevenly spaced and jutting out at odd angles. No one had used this jagged ladder to scale the wall, and to do so would risk not only arrest but a violent response from a guard tower less than 50 meters away or a larger military base about 200 meters away. Still, youths took me to visit it in 2005 and 2007. The functionality of the structure as a means of actually penetrating the barrier was less important than its symbolic value. These teenagers' forms of protest did not reduce the wall to a flat surface as did much of the graffiti and murals. Instead, after months and years of living next to the wall, teenagers found its fissures and got to work. This ramshackle protest was not legible for news agency photographers, either. One had to know the story to decipher the meaning of these ragged pieces of wood.

MEDIATING WOOD AND WORDS, THE CONCRETE AND THE INSCRUTABLE

Stereotypes about the irrationality and violence of Palestinian political life reinforce orientalist ideas of an essential difference between "East" and "West." These stereotypes are also naturalized by dominant Euro-American semiotic ideologies that presume an essential difference between words and things, speech and action. According to these semiotic ideologies, "speaking with things" is dangerous and unproductive. Rational discussion is associated with liberal traditions in the United States and Europe, while violence and lesser ways of communication are located in the orient. These ideas about how Arabs use language affect discourse about Arab politics too. They naturalize the idea that "all they understand is force."[18]

But an alternative perspective suggests that Palestinians' experience with violence as people who have lived under military occupation for decades makes them especially aware of the relationship between words and violence. Watching their neighborhoods change, Palestinians discern that Israel is speaking—making its goals known—with things and militarized processes and not just with the public relations statements that make their way into mainstream news texts. Palestinians have different ways of reading and listening. Thus their own symbolic protests are sensitive to material processes. Protests closely attuned to their own material circumstances have unique logics that may not be translatable in media representations.[19] Palestinians' protests of the barrier address a context where movement is strictly controlled and violence is widespread, and both of these factors affect speech and assembly. Palestinians' semiotic practices take into account local histories of the relationship between language and violence. Recognizing these subaltern Palestinian expressions, even and perhaps especially in their most fragmentary forms—like the broken wood slats jammed into the concrete wall, or graffiti about God written on the bottom of the wall—is of critical importance if we aim to understand contemporary forms of Israeli military occupation and state violence from a Palestinian perspective.

A similar expertise about representational circumstances—not only about Israeli occupation but also about Palestinian society—is what makes Palestinian journalists such important partners for U.S. journalists. Their readings of the landscape can illuminate politics and history and also ensure that foreign correspondents arrive at their destinations safely. They know the back roads, the unlikely routes that knowledge must take when a territory is littered with obstacles. They know how to coax a story from a grieving mother or a high-level official. Without their work, U.S. news would include fewer glimpses into Palestinian life under occupation and fewer Palestinian voices. Photographers use skills of proximity that involve their bodies, their social proficiencies, and their geographical know-how to capture revealing and out-of-the-way images. Alternative understandings and reworkings of the relationship between words and things, like those evinced by a photojournalist's ability to talk himself out of Israeli army handcuffs, can be integral to producing news even if these understandings are not explicated in news texts. Palestinians' proximity to events and their investment in political outcomes are the conditions of possibility for their knowledge about the Israeli-Palestinian conflict. Their embodied presence makes them especially sensitive to political developments, whether they are at a checkpoint or listening to the sounds of weapons during an incursion. The vitality of press coverage of this conflict in the United States relies on the talents and sacrifices of Palestinian journalists who work with U.S. foreign correspondents to bring Americans the news each day.

Yet Palestinians' experiences as people living under military occupation are not only a foundation for their expertise; they are also a foundation for U.S. and Israeli skepticism about their ability to know and communicate properly.

Much collaboration between Palestinian and American journalists is hidden, largely because of the norms of U.S. news institutions that prefer to identify a single person, usually an American, as the carrier of news from distant places, and because the values of journalism favor disinterest, distance, and balanced objectivity as opposed to Palestinians' embedded values and knowledge. We might better conceive of news production as a process of accumulated authorship, since multiple actors' interpretations and information-moving labor are what bring ideas, quotes, or images to the fore, even if one perspective finally frames these media.

The images of graffiti on the separation barrier can be taken as metaphors for how Palestinian voices are written out of U.S. media because of the frames—figurative or, in the case of photography, literal—of U.S. news, because journalists and internationals tend to stay on the beaten path in places like Abu Dis, saying and recording things that they and their audiences readily understand. Even Palestinian presence or having a Palestinian photographer does not guarantee full-voiced Palestinian representation.

At the very least, understanding the process of producing news and the circuitous routes of knowledge should generate more humility about our understandings of the world. The "fantasy of immediation," that perfect communication is possible and mediation itself might leave no trace, is fed by globalization and new technologies.[20] The hundreds of news stories and photographs available about the Israeli-Palestinian conflict can allow American news audiences to imagine that they have the full story at their fingertips. Yet, meaning is not so easily transportable. The significance of graffiti, quotes, and even oppositional postures assumed during demonstrations shifts when these are removed from the flow of events and recontextualized in news texts. It can be impossible to trace—or even to imagine—these original meanings from succinct news articles or single photographs. Sometimes journalists do their audiences the best service when they leave feature articles open to multiple meanings, when they describe a scene but all of the details do not add up, when the quotes they record are a few steps away from the acknowledged frameworks of debate. Journalists who write such articles hint that they have not captured everything in their few hundred words.

The case of graffiti on the separation barrier also makes visual the complex ways in which state authorities provide and withhold forms of freedom of speech from citizens and subjects. In the Palestinian case, Israel seems not to stand in the way of free press. The cases when Israeli soldiers have shot journalists, ransacked media offices, or pulled broadcast towers to the ground are always, according to Israeli spokespeople, unintentional or exceptional measures taken in the name of security, if they are worthy of note at all. But the norm, it would seem, is freedom of expression. The wall seems to prove the point even as it restricts Palestinians in other ways, for Palestinians can say anything they want about the wall. They can even write anything they want on the wall. But in the final analysis, this space for discourse is nothing other than state space, provided and potentially dismantled by authorities.

Lest we think that this connection between expression and space or materiality is specific to Palestinians and Israelis, we might consider a case from the United States. As I make my final revisions, the protesters of Occupy Wall Street, Oakland, Boston, and other U.S. cities are staking their claims to public parks as spaces for expression. They display boisterous, wise, and poetic signs declaring their values and concerns. One strand of news coverage of the Occupy Wall Street and related protests has revolved around the cost to municipalities of the extra police duty required to regulate these protests.[21] These news reports effectively put a price on freedom of expression and even suggest that in an era of strict budget cuts perhaps our cities cannot afford a vibrant protest movement. During the Occupy protests, we have seen that police can endanger free expression by arresting protesters in large numbers, spraying protesters with pepper spray, and shooting at protesters. Police violence against protesters has become a major topic of concern. However, in some cases police presence can feel necessary for protesters' safety, especially when protesters are taking controversial stands or when they are physically vulnerable. Police presence at protests is not the ideal,[22] but it is the way in which our political culture operates today. As Warren Montag writes, "Behind reason, force."[23]

When we speak, the state—or more precisely our status within a state as citizens, migrants, the undocumented, or stateless people—is almost inevitably somewhere behind what we say, making us feel safe or threatened, feeding us information or hiding it from us, leading us down one route to knowledge or closing down such routes, letting us speak from one place or another, alone, in a fragmented fashion, or in gatherings we compose. For journalists, too, the state enables certain kinds of speech and disables others. Journalists working in Israel and the occupied Palestinian territories cultivate relationships with officials; they apply for government press cards; they negotiate movement with soldiers; they position themselves at an angle between tanks and protesters. Far from being the "free" mirror image of "state media" in authoritarian governments, journalists working for mainstream media in the U.S. have complex and often complicit relationships with state authorities, and the specifics of these relationships are conditioned by journalists' national statuses. This book asks us to broaden our understandings of the basic conditions required to create spaces of free expression. Commonsense understandings of freedom of the press see it as something secured by a lack of government action. First Amendment scholar Lee Bollinger offers a gloss of typical understandings of press freedom:

> In the United States, the government is forbidden by virtue of the First Amendment from censoring or punishing the press for what it chooses to say. The press is not licensed, as it was in the seventeenth-century England. It need not clear with the government what it proposes to publish. And, except under very limited circumstances, the government may not punish the press for what it has said.[24]

Yet, it is difficult to conceive of an instance in today's world in which speech is truly free of government involvement. Many consider freedom of speech to be the bedrock upon which other rights can be secured.[25] The arguments in this book demonstrate that a robust freedom of speech is interdependent with other rights as well.

Examination of graffiti on the separation wall also elucidates another key theme of this book, that news production has world-making effects quite independent from the resulting media. Journalists' cameras encourage writing of a particular style on the wall, just as they animate protests of a particular style near the wall. Palestinians may perform for journalists, as did the girl who wrote "Children Against the Wall." Who knows what she would have written had she imagined an Al-Jazeera crew posted behind her? As other examples of news photographs of graffiti demonstrate, Palestinians may also be marginalized by conversations among U.S. and European journalists and activists. Will artists like Banksy really listen to an old man who tells him to go home even when there is such a marvelous opportunity for poetic and public resistance for the taking? Even in their own communities, Palestinians may be pushed to the periphery and then compelled to live in the confines of the discourses that exclude them. But if there is anything we can learn from a long ethnographic project about a long struggle, it is that it is difficult to mark the end of a story. Some organizations that proscribe writing on the wall have bent their rules when a particularly compelling opportunity comes along. And sometimes, eloquence comes in forms inscrutable to outsiders. Acts of expression command attention and inspire other brave acts of expression. They are part of complex social and political processes and many long conversations.

When a girl wields a can of spray paint to send her message to the world, it is clear that Palestinians, too, sometimes share in a fantasy of immediation. She may have momentarily imagined that English-speaking audiences would hear her plea and that of others like her, and that something would change. Or Palestinians may self-consciously perform for the foreign media, shaping their messages for foreign consumption because the prospect of appealing to Palestinian or Israeli authorities seems so hollow. To the extent that event and coverage can be separated from each other, it is a fact of geopolitical power that U.S. coverage of events in the occupied Palestinian territories can matter as much or more than those events themselves. We cannot expect that U.S. journalism would be the best medium for Palestinian expression. After all, Palestinian voices go through layers of translation and multiple reframings before they reach an American audience. It is no surprise that it is frustrating for Palestinians to fit their political aspirations into the column inches allotted to them in the *New York Times*. Perhaps someday U.S. media will be less important to Palestinian politics. In the meantime, we can recognize how Palestinian activists and officials and U.S. and Palestinian journalists take part in a shared venture of representation that has serious implications for Palestinians.

Moreover, in acknowledging the ways Palestinians contribute to the vitality and variety of knowledge in the United States, perhaps we can better envision our world of interdependence, even as we remain aware of the pervasiveness of state and geopolitical power in shaping that interdependence. The production of U.S. news in the West Bank reveals that the information which is at the foundation of our public sphere is from its beginning produced by people who lack autonomy. This applies to both U.S. foreign correspondents and Palestinian journalists. The former, after all, cannot do their work without the support of Palestinian staff. As residents in Israel they are hardly removed from the context about which they write. During the second Intifada, they too heard the explosions of Palestinian bombings and the boom of Israeli warplanes overhead as they sat in their living rooms. Palestinian journalists have even higher stakes in the matters about which they report, as they live in occupied territory and seek self-determination. Yet, Palestinians' self-interests, like those of other journalists and knowledge producers, are multifaceted. Palestinian journalists' incentives are not only—and perhaps not even primarily—defined in terms of promoting national politics in print. They are also motivated by the goal of sustaining a livelihood, of building homes for themselves, and not only building a homeland. On many occasions, this imperative has compelled Palestinian journalists to sublimate nationalist ideology to preserve their jobs. On top of this, they must be concerned with their physical safety and that of their families. Not only is this a site of "situated knowledge,"[26] where knowledge is conditioned by its relationship to place; it is a site where knowledge is shared and its producers always vulnerable.

Examining collaboration among Palestinian and American journalists also challenges notions about the locus of fundamental human rights. Press freedom is a core value of American democracy. According to American media scholars Robert McChesney and Ben Scott, "It is in the United States, and the United States alone, that press freedom is the centerpiece of the entire political project. It is meant to be the shining star of a democratic political economy. Moreover it is an integral part of the vision of greatness the U.S. projects of itself in the global media system."[27] It is indeed widely assumed that the "West" (including the United States and Israel) is morally superior because it has freedoms that the Arab world lacks.[28] Freedom of expression is a vaunted export of the United States.[29] Yet, this book has demonstrated that U.S. press freedom is not "Made in America" in any simple way. An ethnographic perspective on news production reveals that Americans rely on Palestinian journalists—and by extension other journalists around the world, since the processes described in this book occur in other places, too, albeit in slightly different forms—for their news. Without the information about the world these journalists' labor provides, freedom of the press within the borders of the United States would be fragile and provincial. It is not only Americans who strive to maintain access to information for "the free world," but also Palestinians and others who struggle in repressive environments to produce knowledge and make it public for people beyond their borders. To put it slightly differently, while it has been widely recognized that our lives as consumers, tourists, and other kinds of thrill-seekers depend on global flows of money, labor, and commodities,[30] it is less widely acknowledged that our lives as citizens and thinkers depend on these global flows as well. It is not only that contemporary public spheres are transnational because issues like global warming, human rights, and terrorism draw the concern of people around the world, but also that our access to information about these crucial topics of international concern hinges on transnational collaborations among parties with profound disparities in effective rights and power.

REFERENCE MATTER

NOTES

Introduction

1. Hereafter, I refer to this area interchangeably as the occupied Palestinian territories, the occupied territories, or the West Bank and Gaza Strip. These terms have slightly different connotations, and none is ideal. Nor are alternatives such as Palestine. However, among the three of them, they refer to the areas under question clearly, indicate political status, and reference Palestinian residence in and claim to these areas.

2. Murphy 2002, 602.

3. Bishara 2002.

4. "Mazen Dana: 2001 Awardee, the Committee to Protect Journalists," Committee to Protect Journalists, http://cpj.org/awards/2001/dana.php, accessed June 4, 2010.

5. "About CPJ," Committee to Protect Journalists, http://www.cpj.org/about/#one, accessed Dec. 31, 2010.

6. Nader 1974.

7. Hannerz 2004, 3.

8. E.g., Bird 2010; Boyer 2010; Boyer and Hannerz 2006; Hasty 2010; Malkki 1997.

9. My conceptualization of what it means to "write alongside" journalists as an anthropologist emerges from conversations about other neighboring practices of media production, as between ethnographic film and aboriginal media (Ginsburg 1995). I also imagine writing alongside to be something akin to an "enunciatory community" as discussed by Fortun 2001, but I wish to emphasize the *process* of communicating, for in this case community may never form.

10. Hoyt and Palattella 2007.

11. Said 1978. Scholars have vigorously confirmed the relevance of Said's analysis today (e.g., Abu El-Haj 2005; McAlister 2005).

12. Arendt 1976, 302.

13. Said 1984.

14. E.g., Allen 2009; Davis 2011; Sayigh 1998; Slyomovics 1998; Swedenburg 1995.

15. Abu El-Haj 2001.

16. Fraser 2007.

17. See "The Iraq War: The Heaviest Death Toll for the Media Since World War II, March 2003–August 2010," Reporters Without Borders, Sept. 7, 2010, http://en.rsf.org/ iraq-the-iraq-war-the-heaviest-death-07-09-2010,38294.html, accessed Nov. 28, 2011; "The Press and the War on Terrorism: New Dangers and New Restrictions," Committee to Protect Journalists, May 5, 2004, http://www.cpj.org/reports/2004/05/the-press-and-the-war -on-terrorism.php, accessed Nov. 28, 2011; "Dateline Iraq—Five Years Later," Committee to Protect Journalists, Mar. 8, 2008, http://cpj.org/reports/2008/03/dateline-iraq-five-years -later.php, accessed Nov. 28, 2011; "For Sixth Straight Year, Iraq Deadliest Nation for Press," Committee to Protect Journalists, Dec. 18, 2008, http://www.cpj.org/reports/2008/12/for -sixth-straight-year-iraq-deadliest-nation-for.php, accessed Nov. 28, 2011.

18. See for example Joel Campagna, "Bloodied and Beleaguered," Committee to Protect Journalists, Oct. 20, 2000, http://cpj.org/reports/2000/10/is-pal-oct00.php, accessed Nov. 28, 2011; Joel Campagna, "Middle East Special Report: Picking up the Pieces," Committee to Protect Journalists, June 13, 2002, http://cpj.org/reports/2002/06/ west-bank-june02.php, accessed Nov. 28, 2011; Joel Simon, "Targeting Palestinian Media in Gaza," Committee to Protect Journalists, Jan. 7, 2009, http://cpj.org/blog/2009/01/ targeting-palestinian-media-in-gaza.php, accessed Nov. 28, 2011, "Israel: Allow Media and Rights Monitors Access to Gaza," Human Rights Watch, Jan. 5, 2009, http://www .hrw.org/news/2009/01/05/israel-allow-media-and-rights-monitors-access-gaza, accessed Nov. 28, 2011.

19. "Press Freedom Index 2003," Reporters Without Borders, http://en.rsf.org/spip .php?page=classement&id_rubrique=551, accessed Nov. 28, 2011.

20. Das and Poole 2004; see also Asad 2004.

21. Mbembe 2003, 39.

22. I join here a body of critical anthropological scholarship on democracy, such as Mitchell 2011 and Paley 2008, that critically analyzes the wide range of political forms regarded as democracies and is concerned with both how such democracies work, or do not work, in practice and how they are experienced.

23. Anthropologists have taken on the important task of expanding concepts of human rights by looking at how they function or fall short in specific situations (Goodale 2006; see also "Declaration on Anthropology and Human Rights," Committee for Human Rights, American Anthropological Association, 1999, available at: http://www .aaanet.org/stmts/humanrts.htm, accessed Nov. 11, 2011.)

24. For a parallel argument elsewhere in media anthropology, see Larkin 2008 for an approach to film theory through the lens of film in Nigeria rather than in Western locations.

25. E.g., Hannerz 2004; Pedelty 1995, 1993.

26. E.g., Bird 2010; Boczkowski 2005, 2010; Boyer 2010; Gürsel 2009; Russell 2010; Vesperi 2010.

27. E.g., Boyer 2005b; Hasty 2005; Hertsgaard 1988; Manzella and Yacher 2010; McChesney 2004, 98–137; Mermin 1999; Pedelty 1995, 85–98; Rao 2010; Roudakova 2010; Schiller 2011; Schwenkel 2010.

28. A few works that have addressed these journalists' roles include: Pedelty 1995, 203–218; and Salah Al-Nasrawi, "The Myth of Middle East Reporting," *Jadaliyya*, Mar. 20, 2012, http://www.jadaliyya.com/pages/index/4763/the-myth-of-middle-east-reporting, accessed May 21, 2012.

29. E.g., Herman and Chomsky 2002.

30. E.g., Gitlin 1980; Tuchman 1978.

31. E.g., Fanon 1965a, 69–98; Ginsburg 1989; Gitlin 1980; Rajagopal 2001; Sreberny-Mohammadi and Mohammadi 1994.

32. Haraway 1988.

33. E.g., Abu El-Haj 2001; Martin 1990, 1991; Shapin 1994, 2010, among many others.

34. Latour 1993.

35. Ginsburg, Abu-Lughod, and Larkin 2002, 6.

36. Hall 1980.

37. Abu-Lughod 2005; Dornfeld 1998.

38. Silverstein and Urban 1996.

39. Wahl-Jorgensen 2010.

40. Du Bois 2004.

41. For one set of definitions of terms like "off-the-record," "on-the-record," "background," and "deep background," see "Statement of News Values and Principles," Associated Press, http://www.ap.org/newsvalues/index.html, accessed Nov. 11, 2011.

42. To protect identities, I have also split identities of journalists, referring to the same journalist by different names so that if she or he is identified by peers in one anecdote, this will not carry over throughout the book. Writing about journalists and their published work while maintaining their confidentiality has also required care. Once in the book, in referring to a published article, I have changed very minor information so that the article and consequently its authors cannot be identified. In a handful of cases, I have generalized my description of an article so that it cannot be readily identified; for example, by not mentioning its location.

43. Participant-observation is a hallmark method of anthropology that involves observing social phenomena and invites the researcher's involvement in these phenomena as a complementary mode of inquiry.

44. I generally use the term "separation barrier" or, less frequently and following the International Court of Justice's terminology, "wall" to refer to the entirety of the 440-mile-long structure Israel has been building in the West Bank since 2002, ostensibly

to prevent Palestinians from entering Israel (see "Separation Barrier," B'Tselem, http://www.btselem.org/separation_barrier, accessed Nov. 11, 2011). This structure is made up of walls in many populated areas and fences in less populated areas, as well as barbed wire, trenches, roads, watchtowers, and combinations thereof. When I discuss parts of this structure that are made up of a concrete wall, I refer to it as a wall.

45. E.g., Basso 1996; Feld 1996b; Raffles 2002; Shehadeh 2007; Stewart 1996.

46. This reflexive phenomenological approach to embodied skills has benefited writing about such practices as *capoeira*, fishing, and boxing (Downey 2005; Harris 2005b; Wacquant 2003).

47. See Winegar 2006 for another example of how leisure time of cultural producers illuminates cultural production.

48. E.g., Coles 2004; Englund 2006; Graan 2010; Tate 2007.

49. On different elements of this dynamic, see Allen 2009 and Seitz 2003.

50. Especially as the second Intifada waned, more Israelis came to the West Bank in roles other than as soldiers. In particular, a vibrant protest movement against the wall has included Israelis and Palestinians. At least in some communities, this may have encouraged some Palestinians to regard Jewish Israelis as important interlocutors (Saunders 2011).

51. E.g., Abu-Lughod 1989, 267; Asch, Asch, and Conner 1981; Feld 1990, 239–268.

52. Abu-Lughod 1993.

53. Ginsburg 2002; Ginsburg and Myers 2006; Myers 2002; Lippard 1992; Prins 2002; Turner 2002.

54. Baisnée and Marchetti 2006; Boczkowski 2010; Hahn 2007; McChesney 1999.

55. Baisnée and Marchetti 2006.

56. McAlister 2001. Historically, Palestine figured prominently in Americans' imagination of the world (Davidson 2001; Obenzinger 1999).

57. Scholars and activists have made the valid point that the terms "first Intifada" and "second Intifada" overlook the fact that Palestinians have undertaken uprising (*intifada*) against Israeli occupation much more frequently than only during the periods generally referred to as the first and second Intifadas. I retain the use of the terms, however, because of their conventional value in referring to these two extended periods of resistance.

58. Hammami and Tamari 2001.

59. Esposito 2006, 195.

60. Hass 2002. See also B'Tselem's background on closure, "Restriction of Movement," B'Tselem, http://www.btselem.org/freedom_of_movement/closure, accessed Dec. 4, 2011; and the United Nations Office for the Coordination of Humanitarian Affairs' website on Access and Movements for the latest reports on closure, http://www.ochaopt.org/reports.aspx?id=105, accessed Dec. 4, 2011.

61. Naber 2007.

62. See Bakalian and Bozorgmehr 2009; Bayoumi 2008; Cainkar 2009.

63. The concept of semiotic ideologies, "basic assumptions about what signs are and how they function in the world" (Keane 2003, 419; see also Keane 2007), emerges from a literature on language ideologies, normative ideas about how language should function (Schieffelin, Woolard, and Kroskrity 1998; Kroskrity 2000).

64. Carr 2010b; Silverstein 1996; Woolard 1998. See Austin 1975 for an elaboration of other ways language is used to accomplish things.

65. Bauman and Briggs 2003.

66. Keane 2009, 58. See also Peterson 2007; Sakr 2010 on how modern liberal ideas of free speech have been interspersed with orientalism to sideline arguments about hate speech.

67. Keane 2007, 7.

68. Hirschkind 2006; Messick 1996; Sells 1999.

69. E.g., Larkin 2002; Masco 2004, 2008; Mazzarella 2003; Pinney 1997; Spitulnik 2002.

70. Keane 1997, 14.

71. Gupta 1992; Malkki 1992, 1995.

72. Nancy Fraser has argued persuasively that Habermas's classic concept of the public sphere (Habermas 1989) "conceived the participants in public sphere discussion as fellow members of a bounded political community" (Fraser 2007, 48).

73. Malkki 1996.

74. Between 1948 and 1966, the Palestinian press inside Israel was harshly restricted by the military rule over Palestinian communities and by such factors as licensing requirements based on Ottoman and British Mandate regulations (Jamal 2009, 39–60). During the period of direct military occupation of the West Bank and Gaza Strip, from 1967 to 1994, Israeli authorities exercised tight censorship over Palestinian media in these areas, while press from inside Israel had somewhat more freedom (CPJ 1988).

75. Boyer and Lomnitz 2005, 107.

76. Keith Brown discusses this stereotype in the context of U.S. training of armed forces in Iraq and Afghanistan (Brown 2008).

77. Comaroff 1998, 339; see also Wedeen 1999.

78. Carr 2010a, 26.

Does a Checkpoint Have Two Sides?

1. Moore 2004a.

2. For more on Palestinian citizens of Israel who serve in the Israeli army, see Kaananeh 2008.

Chapter 1. Balanced Objectivity and Accumulated Authorship

1. Mirzoeff 2005.

2. Ibid.

3. Daston and Galison 2007, 40–41.

4. See Hass 2002, B'Tselem's background on closure, "Restriction of Movement," http://www.btselem.org/freedom_of_movement/closure, accessed Dec. 4, 2011; and the United Nations Office for the Coordination of Humanitarian Affairs' website on Access and Movements for the latest reports on closure, available at: http://www.ochaopt.org/reports.aspx?id=105, accessed Dec. 4, 2011.

5. Mirzoeff 2005.

6. Ibid.

7. Mitchell 2002, 54.

8. E.g., Chakrabarty 2000; Englund 2006; Mitchell 2002; Shakry 2007; Tsing 2005.

9. Daston 1992.

10. Briggs 1986, 22.

11. Weber 1949, 60, his emphasis.

12. Ibid., 58.

13. Bateson and Mead 1977.

14. Daston and Galison 2007, 121.

15. Ibid., 254.

16. Mindich 1998, 95–112.

17. McChesney 2004, 64. In the first decades of the twentieth century, processes of professionalization also gave credibility to this new model of journalism. Professionalization in journalism coincided with professionalization of other fields, such as medicine and law; however, Robert McChesney points out ways in which the model of professionalization could not be seamlessly applied to journalism. For example, while medical and legal professionals were independent and self-employed, journalists were always employees. Moreover, while in other fields, professionalization was about mastery of a specific set of knowledge and skills, journalists did not have similarly specialized skills, as their goals were to communicate with a broad public (McChesney 2004, 67–68).

18. Schudson 1978, 157.

19. For example, journalist and author Mark Hertsgaard, writing about press during the Reagan era, cites a number of prominent journalists expressing their doubts about objectivity in journalism (Hertsgaard 1988). During the George W. Bush years, critics within the field of journalism also pointed out that the value of objectivity could preclude political analysis (Cunningham 2003). Objectivity is frequently problematized on the New York public radio show *On the Media* even as National Public Radio strives to appear as unbiased as possible (Gladstone 2011b,c).

20. Notably, objectivity is an especially central value in U.S. journalism as compared to European journalism (Chalaby 1996; Donsbach and Klett 1993; Schudson 2001).

21. Mindich 1998.

22. Schmemann 2002b.

23. Sontag 2001.

24. Moore 2004b.

25. Lynfield 2004.

26. Greenberg 2005.

27. Schudson 1978, 148.

28. For example, in coverage of the 2006 Palestinian parliamentary elections, the *New York Times* and the *Washington Post* were among the media outlets that indicated a clear preference for Fatah, the secular and U.S.-supported party that had been ruling the PA since its establishment, over Hamas, an Islamist party that the U.S. deems a terrorist organization. One gauge of how U.S. media represented Fatah and Hamas is in the phrases used to identify the two parties. In the weeks leading up to the elections, foreign correspondents glossed Hamas as opposed to Fatah in introductory passages such as: (1) a "militant Islamist faction" as opposed to the "long dominant" Fatah party (Myre 2006), (2) the "radical Islamic group dedicated to Israel's destruction" as opposed to the PA's "mainstay Fatah faction" (Erlanger 2006), (3) a party "dedicated to the destruction of Israel" and "a group labeled a terrorist organization" as opposed to the "ruling" Fatah (Kessler 2006). Hamas was characterized as "the people who helped make suicide bombing a household term" (Smith 2006), while Fatah was generally described only as corrupt. In these articles, the two parties were not described in equivalent ways: if Fatah was the "incumbent," Hamas was never just the challenger. If Hamas was "formally known as the Islamic Resistance Movement" (Wilson and Kessler 2006), Fatah was rarely if ever described by its full name, which if taken literally also has Islamic resonances. In Arabic, Fatah is an acronym for the Palestinian National Liberation Movement, and *fath* (literally, opening) is a term used to describe the Islamic expansion or conquering of other territories. This tendency to exhibit a preference for one party over another in foreign elections is consistent with findings that U.S. journalists covering foreign policy issues tend to stake their positions within the bounds of any existing U.S. official consensus in U.S. domestic coverage of foreign policy issues (Mermin 1999).

29. Bronner 2010.

30. Okrent 2005.

31. Erlanger 2005c.

32. Steven Erlanger, "Don't Blame the Messenger: A Response to Kathleen Christison," *CounterPunch*, May 1–3, 2005, http://www.counterpunch.org/2005/05/01/a-response -to-kathleen-christison/, accessed Dec. 17, 2011. Occasionally, journalists express their awareness that criticism from "both sides" is not the best measure of good journalism. For example, *New York Times* correspondent Ethan Bronner reflected in his Brandeis public lecture, "It's quite unsettling to be viewed as the source of evil in the way I am by two sides in this, not the broad middle, but certainly on both sides. I don't know how that's changed me, but I have lost sleep over it . . . I think it's very important not to be too self-satisfied or self-justifying and assume that the anger is unjustified and I'm doing it right. So the fact that everyone is yelling at you doesn't mean you're doing it right" (Bronner 2010).

33. Okrent 2005.

34. Similarly, Tuchman 1972 writes of objectivity as a "strategic ritual."

35. Bronner 2010. See also Myre 2003.

36. According to B'Tselem, in the first five years of the Intifada (Sept. 2000–Sept. 2005), 668 Israeli civilians and 305 Israeli soldiers and security forces were killed, while 3,288 Palestinians were killed by the Israeli Defense Forces (Esposito 2006, 196).

37. Friel and Falk 2007, 24. See Alessandrini ("Palestine in Scare Quotes: From the NYT Grammar Book," *Jadaliyya*, July 12, 2011, http://www.jadaliyya.com/pages/index /2109/palestine-in-scare-quotes_from-the-nyt-grammar-boo, accessed May 21, 2011) for more on *New York Times* coverage of this topic; and Zelizer et al. 2002 on why special attention to the *New York Times* is warranted.

38. See Philo and Berry 2004 for an excellent analysis of British news that analyzes how the journalistic value of balance can undermine readers' understanding of the conflict.

39. Boykoff and Boykoff 2003; Gladstone 2005a, 2005b.

40. "Finding Fault on Both Sides Can Be False Balance," FAIR, Fairness & Accuracy in Reporting, Sept. 30, 2004, http://www.fair.org/index.php?page=1985, accessed Dec. 17, 2011.

41. I take inspiration here from Summerson Carr's analysis of an image of President Clinton flanked by two African American women as he signed the Personal Responsibility and Work Opportunity Act of 1996 into law (Carr 2010b, 24). While they may seem to be routine, such images of political ceremonies are prime moments for the performance and reproduction of social and political norms.

42. McAlister 2005, 5.

43. Mimesis can function as a guiding value for journalists because they often believe their job is to reproduce facts found in the world (Peterson 2001). In this sense, journalism fits into the dominant liberal semiotic ideologies that privilege reference, as discussed in the Introduction.

44. Bourdieu 1993, 30.

45. In this regard, journalism is what Bourdieu calls a highly heteronomous field (Bourdieu 2005, 33). Building on Bourdieu, sociologists Rodney Benson and Erik Neveu characterize journalism's dependent relationship to politics thus: "The journalistic field is seen as part of the field of power; that is, it tends to engage with first and foremost those agents who possess high volumes of capital. Within this field of power, however, it lies within the 'dominated' field of cultural production" (Benson and Neveu 2005, 5). The logic of one dominant field, that of politics, seems to set the standards for the dependent one of journalism.

46. Mermin 1999.

47. In one famous example, Raymond Bonner, a *New York Times* journalist who exposed the massacre of hundreds of people in El Mozote, El Salvador, was removed from

the Central American desk because the Reagan administration maintained that no massacre had occurred. Later, his reporting was found to be accurate (Pedelty 1995, 85–98). Media scholar Robert McChesney identifies mainstream journalism's close relationship with government sources as a major influence on U.S. foreign correspondence: "Arguably the weakest feature of U.S. professional journalism has been its coverage of the nation's role in the world, especially when military action is involved. . . . Relying on official sources is the main culprit. Journalists who question agreed-upon assumptions by the political elite stigmatize themselves as unprofessional and political" (McChesney 2004, 74).

48. Geyer 1984; Gilboa 2005; Liebes and Kampf 2009.

49. Donovan 2000.

50. Bennet 2004b.

51. "New York Times Fails to Disclose Jerusalem Bureau Chief's Conflict of Interest," Electronic Intifada, Jan. 25, 2010, http://electronicintifada.net/content/new-york-times -fails-disclose-jerusalem-bureau-chiefs-conflict-interest/8644, accessed Dec. 17, 2011.

52. Hoyt 2010.

53. Bronner 2010.

54. Clark Hoyt with Bill Keller, "Bill Keller Takes Exception to 'Too Close to Home,'" Public Editor's Journal, *New York Times* online, Feb. 6, 2010, http://public editor.blogs.nytimes.com/2010/02/06/bill-keller-takes-exception-to-too-close-to -home/?scp=2&sq=bronner%20friedman%20jew&st=cse, accessed Dec. 17, 2011.

55. Ibid.

56. M. J. Rosenberg, "Why the Ethan Bronner Case Matters," *Talking Points Memo*, http://tpmcafe.talkingpointsmemo.com/2010/02/08/why_the_ethan_bronner_case_ matters/, accessed Nov. 6, 2011.

57. Ibid.

58. Jonathan Cook, "Do You Have to Be Jewish to Report on Israel from the New York Times?" Mondoweiss, Feb. 25, 2010, http://mondoweiss.net/2010/02/do-you-have -to-be-jewish-to-report-on-israel-for-the-new-york-times.html, accessed Dec. 31, 2011.

59. Hoyt 2010. For a historical perspective on Jewish foreign correspondents in Jerusalem for the *New York* Times, see Lewis 2012.

60. Hertsgaard 1988.

61. I am building here on Mark Allen Peterson's explication of the mimetic quality of U.S. journalism (Peterson 2001, 202).

62. Cf. Pedelty 1995, 41–59.

63. Ali Abunimah, "NY Times' Jerusalem Property Makes It Protagonist in Palestine Conflict," Electronic Intifada, Mar. 2, 2010, http://electronicintifada.net/v2/article11109 .shtml, accessed Dec. 17, 2011. See also Goodman 2008.

64. Mirzoeff 2005.

65. On houses as a ground for experience and perspective, see, e.g., Bachelard 1994; Bahloul 1996; and Bourdieu 1977, 89–95.

66. Okrent 2005.

67. "Victims of Palestinian Violence and Terrorism Since September 2000," Israel Ministry of Foreign Affairs, http://www.mfa.gov.il/MFA/Terrorism-+Obstacle+to+Peace/Palestinian+terror+since+2000/Victims+of+Palestinian+Violence+and+Terrorism+sinc.htm, accessed Nov. 6, 2011.

68. "Fatalities Since the Outbreak of the Second Intifada and Until Operation 'Cast Lead,'" B'Tselem, http://old.btselem.org/statistics/english/casualties.asp?sD=29&sM=09&sY=2000&eD=26&eM=12&eY=2008&filterby=event&oferet_stat=before, accessed Nov. 6, 2011.

69. Hannerz 1998, 566.

70. Bronner 2009; see also Ashley Bates, "The Perils of Reporting from Gaza," Behind the News blog, *Columbia Journalism Review*, Mar. 4, 2010, http://www.cjr.org/behind_the_news/the_perils_of_reporting_from_g.php?page=all, accessed Nov. 11, 2011; and "CPJ Urges Israel to Open Gaza to International Reporters," letter from Joel Simon to Ehud Barak, Committee to Protect Journalists, Jan. 6, 2009, http://www.cpj.org/2009/01/cpj-urges-israel-to-open-gaza-to-international-rep.php, accessed Nov. 11, 2011.

71. "Q. and A. with Taghreed El-Khodary in Gaza," The Lede, Blogging the News with Robert Mackey, *New York Times*, http://thelede.blogs.nytimes.com/2009/01/19/q-a-with-taghreed-el-khodary-in-gaza/, accessed Nov. 6, 2011.

72. Leys 2000 has written about how trauma can limit authoritative witnessing in certain historical contexts. Writing of the Palestinian case, Fassin 2008 shows how the traumatized voice of the professional eyewitness—rather than the primary victim—assumes a powerful place in public discourse.

73. Hirschkind 2006, 13–18.

74. See Morris 2002. For an analysis of orientalist views of "the Arab personality," see Moughrabi 1978, especially 103.

75. Davis 2010, 307.

76. Appadurai 1988, 37. Many other fields of cultural production have posited the "native" as the source of "raw" information which must be shaped, selected, or otherwise processed by a Western expert to become authoritative, whether in the fields of archaeology (Smith 2005), ethnobotany (Hayden 2003), fine art (Clifford 1988), or music (Feld 1996a), and the final products have obscured the contributions of those other than the Western expert. While these fields have failed to recognize—financially, intellectually, or publicly—the contributions of subaltern parties, ethnographies have begun to uncover these sometimes unwitting collaborations. Nevertheless, anthropology as a discipline has not systematically recognized the contributions of anthropological "interlocutors," and this has served to reinforce colonialist assumptions about who is capable of reflexive intellectual work (Sanjek 1993).

77. Suskind 2006, 138; see also Dan Schulman, "What Happened at Al-Jazeera's Kabul Bureau?" *Columbia Journalism Review*, June 23, 2006, http://www.cjr.org/politics/

what_happened_at_aljazeeras_ka.php, accessed Nov. 11, 2011; and "Author Suskind Alleges Afghan Bombing of Al-Jazeera Was Deliberate," Committee to Protect Journalists, June 21, 2006, http://cpj.org/2006/06/author-suskind-alleges-afghan-bombing-of-al jazeera.php, accessed Dec. 12, 2011.

78. This phrase is from his September 21, 2001, address to a joint session of Congress. Transcript available at: http://archives.cnn.com/2001/US/09/20/gen.bush.transcript/, accessed Dec. 26, 2010.

79. Gladstone 2010.

80. Fraser 2007.

81. Bauman and Briggs 2003. John Locke and Francis Bacon, for example, were among those Enlightenment philosophers who believed intertextuality was problematic. Locke even avoided quotations and tried to hide his own citations (Bauman and Briggs 2003, 38–40).

82. Use of "contrib." lines or the granting of bylines to high-level fixers is becoming somewhat more common owing to the limitations foreign correspondents have faced in circumstances of conflict. During the most violent parts of the Iraq War, for instance, the security situation prevented the vast majority of U.S. foreign correspondents from conducting extensive reporting (Gladstone 2006; Hoyt and Palattella 2007). Other factors, including scandals, have also shifted norms of attribution within some news organizations. The Jayson Blair scandal of 2003, in which a domestic *New York Times* reporter falsified datelines and used the reporting of others as his own, precipitated a new emphasis on "coherent, consistent byline policies" in which "bylines should be freely given for substantial work by reporters, stringers, freelancers, and clerical staff members" (Siegal 2003, 11), with the goal that, as *New York Times* executive editor William Keller put it, bylines and datelines should "disclose clearly to readers who is responsible for an article, and from what location" (Siegal 2003, 2). Still, none of these adjustments consistently mandate the acknowledgment of the collaborative, multinational labor that goes on behind most international news articles, and the privileges of authorship continue to lie in bylines at the top of the article rather than in contribution lines at the foot of the article.

83. For the Reuters news agency, more complex attributions are now a matter of policy. The end of an article makes note of who has done additional reporting, the writing, and the editing. This change serves subscribers (i.e. other media institutions that buy their reports) by giving them a better sense of whom to contact with questions; it also may assuage internal conflicts over attribution. For the specifics of this policy, see Reuters' "Handbook of Journalism," especially the sections Bylines and Sign-offs, http://handbook.reuters.com/index.php/News_Presentation, Reuters, accessed Nov. 6, 2011. The Associated Press's recently revised attribution guidelines are somewhat more flexible, but again, a byline signals that a journalist was at the datelined location. For the Associated Press, "If multiple staffers report the story, the byline is the editor's judgment

call. In general the byline should go to the staffer who reported the key facts. Or, one staffer can take the byline for one cycle, and another for the following cycle." See the section on bylines in Associated Press, "What's New," http://www.ap.org/newsvalues/index .html, accessed Nov. 6, 2011.

84. See Philo and Berry 2004, 105–125, for an analysis of how the language used to represent violence in this conflict can impact audience understanding.

85. Edited transcript of "Covering Conflict in Palestine: A Panel Discussion," Part 1, Palestine Center, Washington, D.C., http://www.thejerusalemfund.org/ht/display/Content Details/i/14064/pid/897.

86. Edited transcript of "Covering Conflict in Palestine: A Panel Discussion," Part 2, Palestine Center, Washington, D.C., http://www.thejerusalemfund.org/ht/display/Content Details/i/14066/pid/897, accessed Sept. 7, 2011. For more on this topic, see Lewis 2012.

87. Poovey 1998, 9.

88. I take infrastructure here to be the "totality of both technical and cultural systems that create institutionalized structures" (Larkin 2008, 6).

89. To protect the identities of those with whom I spoke, I have changed names of those involved; however, the information I present regarding the circumstances of his death is, of course, accurate.

90. Barthes 1972, 127.

91. Hannerz 1998, 564.

92. Sennott 2003, xxx.

93. Ibid., xxx–xxxi. The notion that the Bible would serve as a good introduction to the conflict for journalists also resonates with Abu El-Haj's analysis of how biblical narratives served as starting points for archaeological analysis (Abu El-Haj 2001).

94. Israeli leaders have compared Palestinians to animals—including cockroaches, grasshoppers, snakes, and ants—on various occasions. See Beinart 2010; Newsweek 1988; Rubin 1983. Palestinians' complaints that the Israeli occupation treats them as subhuman reverberate in popular culture, too, as in the Palestinian hip-hop song "Meen Irhabi?" (Who's the terrorist?) by the group DAM. The Palestinian rappers recount Palestinian deaths under the rubble of a destroyed home, and then say, "Our blood is like that of dogs. No, not even that valuable, because when a dog dies they remember them. So our blood is cheaper than that of dogs? No, my blood is dear" (Ma hu damna dam kilab. La hata la, lama kalb biymut, fi al-rifq bi-l-haywan. Ya'ni damna arkhas min dam al-kilab? La, dami ghali). A video produced for this song by Jackie Salloum, with English subtitles as translated here, is available on YouTube at: http://www.youtube.com/ watch?v=CXDRoFboGHo, accessed Nov. 6, 2011.

The metaphor of the native as animal is common in colonialist and anticolonial discourse. Fanon writes that the Manicheism of colonialism "dehumanizes the native, or to speak plainly, it turns him into an animal. In fact, the terms the settler uses when he mentions the native are zoological terms. He speaks of the yellow man's reptilian motions, of the stink of the native quarter, of breeding swarms, of foulness, of spawn, of gesticulations. When the settler seeks to describe the native fully in exact terms he constantly refers to the bestiary" (Fanon 1965b, 42). As in the Palestinian context, this is not lost on the native: "The native knows all this, and laughs to himself every time he spots an allusion to the animal world in their other's words. For he knows that he is not an animal; and it is precisely at the moment he realizes his humanity that he begins to sharpen the weapons with which he will secure its victory" (Fanon 1965b, 43).

95. "Fatalities Since the Outbreak of the Second Intifada and Until Operation 'Cast Lead,'" B'Tselem, http://old.btselem.org/statistics/english/casualties.asp?sD=29 &sM=09&sY=2000&eD=26&eM=12&eY=2008&filterby=event&oferet_stat=before, accessed Nov. 6, 2011.

96. The series of events leading to Jamal's death was not unique to this incident. The IDF often demanded that Palestinians remove clothing in public in order to search them during the widespread detentions of this period (Sissons 2002), and the IDF also repeatedly delayed ambulances from reaching wounded Palestinians (Bouckaert, Sissons, and Bjorken 2002).

97. In another case when a single quote from a victim circulated in international media, rather than remaining a kind of gripping ambiguity, the phrase heightened the tragedy of what had happened (Bishara 2010b). One key difference between the two cases is that while this victim's case was never reported in detail by any journalist, the other, the death of a professor in Nablus, received extensive publicity.

98. This sense of authorship as a means of attributing responsibility has historical precedents, as when authorship was a way for authorities to hold an individual accountable for voicing unorthodox views (Foucault 1984, 108).

99. Pulitzer 1989, 193–194.

100. This returns us to Mary Poovey's argument about the dual nature of a fact as standing alone and always being in relation to an argument (Poovey 1998).

101. Silverstein and Urban 1996.

102. Ibid., 11.

103. Biagioli 1999, 13.

104. Silverstein and Urban 1996, 1.

105. Abu-Lughod 1989.

106. Roy 2007, 54–55. As discussed in Roy 2010, changes in academic standards of writing on the conflict are likewise also related to developments in politics and civil society.

107. See Kabha 2007, 135, 189, for more on how collaboration among Jewish and Palestinian journalists benefited all under the British Mandate. Similar practices continued in the Israeli state, as well.

108. Writing about "big science," Mario Biagioli makes a similar point that this would "introduce not a graduated credit scale, but an incommensurability between two classes of contributors" (Biagioli 1999, 24).

Words That Fly in the Air

1. Bennet 2003a.

Chapter 2. Arming State Speech, Constraining Journalists' Work

1. Naylor 2002b.

2. "CPJ Names World's Worst Places to Be a Journalist," Committee to Protect Journalists, May 3, 2002, http://www.cpj.org/enemies/worst_places_02/worst_places_02.html; "World's Worst Places to Be a Journalist," Committee to Protect Journalists, May 3, 2003, http://www.cpj.org/enemies/worst_places_03/worst_places_03.html; "World's Worst Places to Be a Journalist," Committee to Protect Journalists, May 3, 2004, http://cpj.org/reports/2004/05/worlds-worst-places-to-be-a-journalist.php, all accessed Nov. 11, 2011.

3. "CPJ Names World's Worst Places to Be a Journalist," Committee to Protect Journalists, May 3, 2002, http://www.cpj.org/enemies/worst_places_02/worst_places_02.html, accessed Nov. 11, 2011.

4. In addition, two Hamas-affiliated Palestinian journalists were killed by Fatah PA operatives following the Hamas-Fatah split of 2007. Mohammad Matar Abdo, distributor for *Palestine*, the Hamas-affiliated daily, and Suleiman Abdul-Rahim al-Ashi, economics editor for *Palestine*, were beaten and shot by PA gunmen wearing Presidential Guard uniforms on May 13, 2007, in Gaza City. Al-Ashi died on the scene, while Abdo died the next day in a hospital. See "Suleiman Abdel-Rahim al-Ashi," Committee to Protect Journalists, http://cpj.org/killed/2007/suleiman-abdul-rahim-al -ashi.php/, accessed Sept. 11, 2010.

5. "Israel/Palestinian Territories, In the Line of Fire, March 2003, Archived Conversations," Frontline/World, http://www.pbs.org/frontlineworld/react/archived/israel .palestine/react.html, accessed Nov. 7, 2011.

6. Ibid.

7. Mbembe 2003, 28.

8. Campagna 2001, 262.

9. Campagna 2000, 384.

10. Campagna 2001, 261.

11. As of this writing, the GPO issues press cards only to those in international journalism working for larger media organizations, covering what they call "real time news." For example, a newspaper must be sold in national circulation and be published at least once a week with a circulation of at least ten thousand copies. For more information on these policies, see the link to criteria on the GPO's website, http://www.pmo.gov.il/ PMO/Templates/General.aspx?NRMODE=Published&NRNODEGUID=%7b5D4088 2A-0DD3-4F7D-9CA5-C1A829ACF9F2%7d&NRORIGINALURL=%2fPMOEng%2fPM %2bOffice%2fDepartments%2fGPO%2ehtm&NRCACHEHINT=Guest#two, accessed Nov. 5, 2011.

12. The U.S. Department of State's 2007 Country Reports on Human Rights Practices for Israel and the Occupied Territories describes this Israeli system of censorship:

> The law authorizes the government to censor material regarded as sensitive reported from Israel or occupied Palestinian territories. Under an agreement between the government and media representatives, all media organizations must submit to military censors materials that deal with specific military issues as well as strategic infrastructure issues such as oil and water supplies. The censor's decisions may be appealed to the Supreme Court, and media cannot be closed by the military censor for censorship violations. The censor cannot appeal a court judgment. Foreign journalists must submit sensitive articles and photographs to the military censor but in practice rarely complied.

See "Israel and the Occupied Territories," U.S. Department of State, http://www.state .gov/g/drl/rls/hrrpt/2007/100597.htm, accessed Nov. 18, 2011. See also Nossek and Limor 2010.

13. The GPO website accurately notes, "The press card facilitates entrance to Government buildings, press conferences, and access across IDF checkpoints and Police lines." See website of the Government Press Office, available at: www.pmo.gov.il/PMO/ Templates/General.aspx?NRMODE=Published&NRNODEGUID={5D40882A-0DD3 -4F7D-9CA5-C1A829ACF9F2}&NRORIGINALURL=%2fPMOEng%2fPM%2bOffice %2fDepartments%2fGPO.htm&NRCACHEHINT=Guest#twox, accessed Nov. 18, 2011.

14. See map, "West Bank Closures, January 2004," UN Office for the Coordination of Humanitarian Affairs.

15. Bishara 2002.

16. Appadurai 1988, 37.

17. Saif v. Government Press Office, HCJ 5627/02 2004, 4.

18. 2003 Statements, Foreign Press Association, available at: http://www.fpa.org.il/ ?categoryId=74730, under the dropdown menu for 2003 Statements, accessed Nov. 15, 2011.

19. See, for example, Ha'aretz's interview with Rashid Khalidi, in which Khalidi observes, "there is only one state between the Jordan River and the Mediterranean, in which there are two or three levels of citizenship or non-citizenship within the borders of that one state that exerts total control" (Shalev 2011). Also see Philip Weiss's approving quotation of Peter Beinart's assertion, "When I say Israel, I mean all the territory under Israeli domain. Some parts of which I wish were not under Israeli sovereignty. That is Israel. The people there might not be Israeli citizens, but that's Israel. We have to take ownership of the fact that until a Palestinian state is created, that's Israel" (quoted in Philip Weiss, "Beinart Says Israel Must Give Citizenship to Palestinians Under Occupation," Mondoweiss, http://mondoweiss.net/2011/12/beinart-says-israel-must-give -citizenship-to-palestinians-under-occupation.html, accessed Dec. 12, 2011).

20. Quoted in CPJ 1988, 100.

21. Ibid., 101.

22. For a similar argument, see Gutmann 2005, 251–252.

23. Staff 2005.

24. Cook, Hanieh, and Kay 2004, 7.

25. See Statistics on Administrative Detention, http://www.btselem.org/administrative_detention/statistics, B'Tselem, accessed Nov. 11, 2011.

26. Kaplan 2000; Weiss 2002.

27. Schmemann 2002a.

28. "Divergent Israeli Views: Interview with Danny Seaman," conducted by Patricia Naylor, available at: http://www.pbs.org/frontlineworld/stories/israel.palestine/seaman.html, accessed Nov. 5, 2011.

29. Saif v. Government Press Office, HCJ 5627/02 2004, 4.

30. Austin 1975.

31. Butler 2004, 80.

32. Ibid., 56.

33. Gutmann 2005, 252.

34. Austin 1975, 14.

35. Butler 1997.

36. Butler 2004, 80.

37. It is, in J. L. Austin's terms, a perlocutionary speech act, "what we bring about or achieve *by* saying something" (Austin 1975, 108).

38. Austin might consider this to be the illocutionary or indirect dimension of these speech acts (Austin 1975, 116): they promote, rather than in themselves accomplish, prejudice against Palestinian journalists that limits Palestinians' ability to speak.

39. Quoted in Saif v. Government Press Office, HCJ 5627/02 2004, 3.

40. Izenberg 2003.

41. Brown 2007, 207.

42. Ibid., 128

43. As Bush declared on September 21, 2001, "[The attackers of 9/11] hate our freedoms: our freedom of religion, our freedom of speech, our freedom to vote and assemble and disagree with each other. . . . These terrorists kill not merely to end lives, but to disrupt and end a way of life" (transcript available at: http://archives.cnn.com/2001/US/09/20/gen.bush.transcript/, accessed Nov. 5, 2011).

44. Lahav 1985, 299.

45. Ibid., 298.

46. Quoted in Schmemann and Brinkley 2002.

47. Friedman 2002.

48. Gutmann 2005, 248.

49. Quoted in Arenson 2002.

50. As Judith Butler argues, by identifying Jewishness with the state of Israel, Summers's formulation also severely constricted the meaning of Jewishness in a way that in fact echoes anti-Semitic tactics (Butler 2004, 123).

51. Leith 2001.

52. Quoted in Editors, *Ha'aretz* 2000.

53. Carol Greenhouse suggests that when authorities deploy the tactic of discursive fracture, they can "control the significance of opposition . . . by means of selective appropriation and recomposition" of a variety of arguments (Greenhouse 2008, 196).

54. Campagna 2005, 181.

55. Available through link to criteria for press cards at: www.pmo.gov.il/PMO/Templates/General.aspx?NRMODE=Published&NRNODEGUID={5D40882A-0DD3-4F7D-9CA5-C1A829ACF9F2}&NRORIGINALURL=%2fPMOEng%2fPM%2bOffice%2fDepartments%2fGPO.htm&NRCACHEHINT=Guest#twox, accessed Nov. 18, 2011.

56. Campagna 2003, 342–343.

57. Lynfield 2002b.

58. Attitudes toward the "enemy" in Israel are shaped not only by the military conflict but also by long-standing orientalist assumptions and by relations between Jews and Palestinians in domestic life inside Israel, where Palestinians are on the margins of Israeli Jewish society and experience racism in many institutions (Rouhana 1997; Torstrick 2000; Willen 2010). Ariella Azoulay describes the naturalized quality of Jewish Israeli distrust of Palestinians: "[L]ooking at the Palestinian as a suspect requires no particular skills, nor does it result from a gaze that is in any way exceptional. On the contrary, this is the normal gaze of any Israeli citizen. . . . This gaze is shared by both the citizen and the ruling power—the citizen who recognizes the Palestinian as a threat" (Azoulay 2008, 416). For a telling series of reports on Palestinians inside Israel, see Mada Al-Carmel's periodic Israel and the Palestinian Minority: Political Monitoring Report (PMR), http://www.mada-research.org/?LanguageId=1&System=Category&MenuId=88&PMenuId=3&MenuTemplateId=3&CategoryId=65, Mada Al-Carmel, accessed Nov.11, 2011.

59. Goodman 2003.

60. Naylor 2002b. Because Nitzan had been in the army, he had the rare opportunity of meeting with the soldier who had shot him. The soldier apologized to him in the hospital, and later told him that he thought Nitzan was a Palestinian. See interview with Patricia Naylor by Stephen Talbot, http://www.pbs.org/frontlineworld/stories/israel.palestine/naylor.html, accessed Nov. 28, 2011.

61. Naylor 2002b.

62. "At Risk: Covering the Intifada," Committee to Protect Journalists, June 26, 2001, http://cpj.org/reports/2001/06/israeljun01.php, accessed Nov. 18, 2011.

63. "Divergent Views: Interview with Gideon Levy," conducted by Patricia Naylor, http://www.pbs.org/frontlineworld/stories/israel.palestine/levy.html, accessed Nov. 28, 2011.

64. Because Israel does not often declare its intent to assassinate a leader, it is difficult to count these events; along with these "confirmed" assassinations and attempts,

the *Journal of Palestine Studies* counted another 109 "possible" assassinations, in which 28 bystanders were killed (Esposito 2006, 195–196).

65. "27 December 2009: One Year Since Operation Cast Lead, Still No Accountability," B'Tselem, http://www.btselem.org/English/Gaza_Strip/20091227_A_year_to_Castle ad_Operation.asp/, accessed Dec. 27, 2010.

66. "Nazeh Darwazeh," Committee to Protect Journalists, http://cpj.org/killed/2003/nazih-darwazeh.php, accessed Nov. 28, 2011.

67. According to Naylor TTA, there were roughly 150,000 Palestinians and some 400 Jewish settlers in the late 1990s.

68. In this account, I draw both upon the documentary *In the Line of Fire* (Naylor 2002a) and on CPJ's report of the incident (Campagna 1999, 325–326).

69. Naylor 2002a.

70. Ibid.

71. Ibid.

72. The Israeli spokesperson's response to Nazeh Darwazeh's death similarly defied material evidence. Two Reuters journalists, Hasan Titi and Abed Qusini, were present and said the area had been free of Palestinian gunfire at the time Darwazeh was shot, although some Palestinian gunfire had occurred in the vicinity earlier. Video evidence also demonstrated that Darwazeh had been shot from the direction of the Israeli soldiers. Nevertheless, IDF spokesperson Sharon Feingold maintained that Darwazeh was among Palestinian militants armed with explosives and guns, and that it was unclear from whence the shot that killed him came. See "Nazeh Darwazeh," Committee to Protect Journalists, http://cpj.org/killed/2003/nazih-darwazeh.php, accessed Nov. 28, 2011.

73. Struck 1998.

74. The *New York Times* coverage of the incident followed a similar rubric (Schmemann 1998). As with the *Washington Post* article, the journalist does not draw a clear conclusion, and instead presents two opposing sets of evidence.

75. "At Risk: Covering the Intifada," Committee to Protect Journalists, June 26, 2001, http://cpj.org/reports/2001/06/israeljun01.php, accessed Nov. 18, 2011.

76. I benefit here from Yurchak 2005's analysis of the workings of authoritative discourse in the Soviet context. In that case, as well, the constative, or referential, meanings of official statements were less important than their performative dimensions.

77. "CPJ Requests Information on Status of Investigation into Journalists' Deaths," Committee to Protect Journalists, http://cpj.org/2004/02/cpj-requests-information-on -status-of-investigatio.php, accessed Nov. 6, 2011.

78. Naylor 2002b.

79. Lynfield 2002a.

80. Sheraz Sadiq, "More Fire—And More Fallen," *Frontline*, June 4, 2003, http://www.pbs.org/frontlineworld/stories/israel.palestine/update.html, accessed Dec. 30, 2011. Seaman's preference of protecting soldiers rather than civilians in the battlefield has

been buttressed by Israeli military scholarship. Leading Israeli military scholars have even argued that protecting the lives of Israeli soldiers is a higher priority than protecting civilians who are not "under the effective control of the state" (Kasher and Yadlin 2005, cited in Khalidi 2010, 10). They define many Palestinians in the West Bank and Gaza to be outside of Israel's effective control. This stance contravenes international law regarding the imperative to protect civilians.

81. "No Criminal Charges Against IDF Soldier in Journalist's Shooting Death," Committee to Protect Journalists, Mar. 9, 2005, http://cpj.org/2005/03/no-criminal-charges-against-idf-soldier-in-journal.php, accessed Dec. 18, 2011.

82. Tate 2007, 216.

83. Greenhouse 2008.

An Innocent Evening Out?

1. Mitnick 2004.

Chapter 3. Working from Home

1. That year, Israeli repression of the protests had led to six unarmed demonstrators' deaths and hundreds of arrests (King-Irani 2000).

2. I echo here Jessica Cattelino's observation that in circumstances of constraint and especially entrenched settler colonialism, sovereignty can be temporarily reconfigured in domestic terms that hardly make up for the lack of fuller kinds of sovereignty but that still make a difference. She writes that traditional Seminole houses erected next to European-style Floridian ones stand for "a distinctly Seminole way of viewing the world" (Cattelino 2008, 127). As one Seminole woman said, "Sometimes you gotta sleep in a chickee—you can't always sleep in the white man's house" (ibid.). As with the Seminoles, for Palestinians homes can at least provisionally stand in lieu of fuller kinds of sovereignty, even as they exceed any reductive political meaning.

3. McChesney 2004, 57–97.

4. Shapin 1994.

5. Here I think of politics as "the continuation of war by others means," drawing on Foucault's reversal of Clausewitz's famous declaration (Foucault 2003, 15). This definition seems especially apt in the Israeli-Palestinian context since the movement between politics and war is so fluid. I qualify politics here as state politics or the politics of sovereignty to distinguish them from other politics more centrally oriented around other forms of power, though obviously I recognize the ways in which state power is interwoven with other forms of power.

6. Asad 2003.

7. See Agrama 2012 for a similar argument regarding secularism and politics in Egypt before and during the Arab Spring.

8. E.g., MacKinnon 1989.

9. Quoted in Benvenisti 1983, 38.

10. Quoted in ibid., 43.

11. For comparisons with other media associated with liberation movements, see Fanon 1965a, 69–98; Schwenkel 2010.

12. E.g., Hannerz 2004, 173; Pedelty 1995, 117.

13. Armenians were on the forefront of photography in many Middle East locations during the Ottoman Empire and in its aftermath (El-Hage 2007).

14. In this regard, Palestinian journalists have something in common with many of their colleagues around the world. U.S. journalists are also ambivalent about the need for professional training in journalism and often assert that on-the-job experience or topical knowledge is more important to their success than a degree in journalism (Hannerz 2004, 73); Hasty reports another kind of disconnect between training and practice in Ghana (Hasty 2006).

15. Jamal 2005, 72–106, 139–164; see also "Journalist, Media Worker Killed in Gaza City," Committee to Protect Journalists, May 14, 2007, http://cpj.org/2007/05/journalist-media -worker-killed-in-gaza-city.php, accessed Dec. 29, 2011; "Al-Jazeera Suspended in the West Bank," Committee to Protect Journalists, July 15, 2009, http://www.cpj.org/2009/07/al-jazeera -suspended-in-the-west-bank.php, accessed Dec. 29, 2011.

16. For more on how NGOs were transforming Palestinian politics and society, see Hanafi and Tabar 2005; and Allen, unpublished manuscript.

17. Cf. Sacco 2001, 5–6.

18. Some have alleged that Palestinian hospitality is so enthralling as to present a political danger. One journalist writing in *Commentary* warned that foreign journalists form overly romantic impressions of Palestinian society at the most famous Palestinian hotel in Jerusalem, which is also a legendary hangout for the best funded of the foreign journalists. As she writes, the American Colony seduces its guests "with its reassuring air of Arab refinement, the plashing of the fountain in the hotel's paradisiacal little garden where breakfast is served amid jasmine and roses, its white and blue Armenian titles, its Eastern touches adjusted to Western tastes, the friendliness of its staff cloaked in cour- tesy and dignity" (Nirenstein 2001, 56). Her argument rests on orientalist tropes that the "East" can make "Westerners" lose touch with rationality, and obviously the American Colony hotel is not a location of vernacular Palestinian culture. Yet, in a sense Nirenstein recognizes the power of experiencing a dimension of Palestinian society outside of press conferences and sites of violence.

19. Hammer 2003, 68.

20. Ibid., 70–71.

21. See Abu-Lughod 2005, 138–161, for another analysis of the cultural currency of *ibn al-balad* as represented in Egyptian television.

22. Yazan and Kareem's names have been changed, though those of Rachel Corrie's family have not.

23. "Rachel Corrie's Parents Speak at Nablus Demonstration to Remember Those Killed in Gaza," International Solidarity Movement, Mar. 20, 2008, http://palsolidarity .org/2008/03/rachel-corries-parents-speak-at-nablus-demonstration-to-remember -those-killed-in-gaza/, accessed Nov. 5, 2011.

24. AP 2008.

25. Garfield 2011a, 2011b.

26. Allen 2008.

27. Daston and Galison 2007.

A Reliable Source?

1. McGirk 2007.

Chapter 4. The Embodied and Up-Close Work of Journalism

1. Bachelard 1994; Feld and Basso 1996.

2. Ingold 2000, 1993.

3. Loïc Wacquant's study of boxing in the South Side of Chicago offers an interesting parallel about the skills of managing societal violence being honed and redirected into boxing, something potentially fulfilling, prestigious, and productive (Wacquant 2003).

4. Harris 2005b, 199.

5. Bishara 2010b. Compare with the radically different auditory knowledge of place explicated by Feld 1996b in Bosavi, Papua New Guinea.

6. Goodman 2003.

7. Naylor 2002a.

8. For more on settler violence in Hebron, see B'Tselem 2001; Gish 2001; HRW 2001; Levin 2005; Swisa 2003.

9. These values and embodied practices of masculinity are obviously quite different than the dominant and stereotypical views of Arab masculinity that tend to circulate in the United States (Massad 2007). Ethnographic examinations can reveal local iterations of masculinities that not only contradict but also dismiss the centrality of such stereo-types (Inhorn and Wentzell 2011).

10. "RSF Condemns String of Violent Attacks Against Palestinian Journalists," Re-porters Without Borders and the International Freedom of Expression Exchange, June 21, 2004, available at: http://www.ifex.org/palestine/2004/06/21/rsf_condemns_string_ of_violent/, accessed Nov. 11, 2011.

11. Butler 1997, 40.

12. As B'Tselem reports, Muhammad Mahmoud Abu Qaber Diriya, thirty-five, was killed on Nov. 4, 2004, in the village of 'Aqraba, by gunfire. He was not participating in fighting at the time when he was killed. They detail that he was "Killed during the arrest of his brother, who [was] Wanted by Israel." See "Palestinians Killed by Israeli Security

Forces in the West Bank, 29.9.2000–3.9.2011," B'Tselem, http://old.btselem.org/statistics/english/Casualties_Full_Data.asp?Category=1&region=WB&order=InjuryTypeEng, accessed Nov. 11, 2011.

13. Zelizer 2007.

14. Hass 2002.

15. See map, "West Bank Closures, January 2004," UN Office for the Coordination of Humanitarian Affairs.

16. Bishara 2002.

17. Chu 2010.

18. Stewart 1996, 6.

19. Hirschkind 2006, 8, drawing on Hannah Arendt.

20. "CPJ International Press Freedom Awards 2001: Covering a Dangerous Beat," Committee to Protect Journalists, https://cpj.org/awards01/dana.html, accessed Nov. 11, 2011.

21. Schneider 2005.

22. My argument here is in part inspired by Saba Mahmood in her ethnography of the Egyptian mosque movement. Mahmood shows that for a group of pious Egyptians, moral cultivation is an embodied discipline nurtured through repeated performance (Mahmood 2006, 136).

23. Klinenberg 2007; McChesney 2004.

24. Velthuis 2006.

25. Baisnée and Marchetti 2006.

26. This problem has been addressed by scholars including Boyer 2005a; Corrigan 1988; Latour 1999. Some recent ethnographic challenges to these assumptions include analyses of the dexterity involved with bench work in the laboratory sciences (Knorr-Cetina 1999, 97). Others have examined embodied knowledge as "habituated epistemic order" embedded in intellectuals' gestures and ticks (Boyer 2005a, 260) or even as people's memories and rituals (Fassin 2007; Shaw 2002).

Locating the Foreign Correspondent at a Demonstration

1. Erlanger 2005b.

Chapter 5. The Separation Wall as Stage for Refugee Identities

An earlier version of parts of this chapter was published as "Covering the Barrier in Bethlehem: The Production of Sympathy and Reproduction of Difference," in *The Anthropology of News and Journalism: Global Perspectives* (Bloomington: Indiana University Press, 2009), 54–69.

1. "Separation Barrier," B'Tselem, http://www.btselem.org/separation_barrier, accessed Nov. 11, 2011.

2. See Lynch 2003 for more on how this Arab public sphere has functioned despite authoritarian governments.

3. According to a study by the Palestinian organization MIFTAH, "The percentage of the news and translated materials from international, Arabic- and Hebrew-language journals on average comprise 55% of the editorial copy, i.e. of the newspapers' content minus advertisements" (MIFTAH 2005, 3).

4. Du Bois 2004, 2.

5. Warner 2002, 90.

6. Azoulay 2008.

7. I conceive of performance here along the lines of Kelly Askew's conception, which emphasizes that "performance is best viewed as active dialogic interaction between and among performers and audience," and also that "the distinction between the communicators and the communicatees is highly fluid" (Askew 2002, 23).

8. Hacking 1999, 2000. Hacking argues that social processes can create categories of people, and then the people defined by these categories can respond in various ways to them. He characterizes these as looping processes of social construction. His argument bears some similarities with that of Stuart Hall, who describes how media production influences society and then is influenced by society (Hall 1980), though each scholar is most interested in a different part of this circuit of cultural production.

9. "Aida Refugee Camp," United Nations Relief and Works Agency (UNRWA), http://www.unrwa.org/etemplate.php?id=104, accessed Nov. 11, 2011.

10. Ibid.

11. Baumgarten-Sharon 2011; Bishara and Al-Azraq 2010; Cook, Hanieh, and Kay 2004.

12. I have changed the name of the youth center in order to protect individuals involved with it.

13. As Joseph Massad observed writing of an earlier era in Palestinian nationalism, "struggling against the Israeli occupiers and colonizers [was] not only an affirmation of Palestinian nationalist agency, it [was] also a masculinizing act enabling the concrete pairing of nationalist agency and masculinity" (Massad 1995, 480).

14. Peteet 1994, 31.

15. Allen 2006, 2009; Khalili 2007.

16. Hammami and Tamari 2000; Johnson and Kuttab 2001.

17. Norman 2010.

18. Massad 2007; Shaheen 2008.

19. Johnson and Kuttab 2001, 34.

20. Rashid Khalidi summarizes this irony: "In 1967, the adjective 'Palestinian,' if used at all, served primarily as a modifier for 'refugees.' . . . A precondition for any achievements on the levels of international legality and world public opinion was that the Palestinians change the image of themselves as refugees" (Khalidi 1987, 7).

21. Johnson and Kuttab 2001.

22. E.g., Barr 2002; Cohen 2002; Dao 2002; Frankel 2003.

23. I am inspired here by Ted Swedenburg's analysis of how a polysemic Israeli pop song likewise crossed Middle Eastern borders (Swedenburg 2000).

24. According to Guy Debord, media spectacles occur when "the real world changes into simple images" and the image "escapes reconsideration" (Debord 1983 [1967], sec. 18).

25. This echoes Mark Pedelty's suggestion that photojournalists' work can be more ethnographic than reporters' because they are required to be close to the events they are covering (Pedelty 1995, 166; see also Woodward 2012).

26. Major international news institutions have not covered the anti-wall movement extensively. In general, the coverage of protest movements in mainstream news is often fraught because protesters are presumed to be instigators of social and political unrest. In other locations, scholars of journalism have noted that there can be a tension between journalists' (institutionally situated) proclivity to view protests as spectacles or sites of potential disorder and protest organizers' will to communicate a political message (Gitlin 1980; Pedelty 1993; Wolfsfeld, Avraham, and Aburaiya 2000).

27. The B'Tselem listing notes about Salamah Hamadan that he "Did not participate in hostilities when killed. Additional information: Killed in his house." According to B'Tselem, Salameh Hamdan was one of three people who were not participating in hostilities killed in 'Aida Refugee Camp that month. See "Statistics: Palestinians Killed by Israeli Security Forces in the West Bank, 29.9.2000–26.12.2008," http://old.btselem .org/statistics/english/Casualties_Data.asp?Category=1&region=WB&sD=29&sM= 09&sY=2000&eD=26&eM=12&eY=2008&filterby=event&oferet_stat=before, accessed Nov. 11, 2011.

28. Malkki 1996; Moeller 1999.

29. Starrett 2003, 400.

30. Edwards 2006, 31.

31. Pedelty 1993.

32. Ulf Hannerz has found that foreign correspondents cover the world through regional narratives that reflect their existing conceptions of a particular place (Hannerz 2004). Catherine Lutz and Janet Collins suggest that photography in popular media like National Geographic also works on this model (Lutz and Collins 1993). These news narratives are linked with much older kinds of cultural production. In nineteenth-century travelogues and fairs (Davidson 2001; McAlister 2001; Obenzinger 1999; Shepherd 1987) and in early twentieth-century anthropology (Rabinowitz 2001), Palestinians were represented as relics of biblical times. This is another example of what Johannes Fabian identified as a tendency of those in the West to think of other places in the world as existing in their own past (Fabian 1983).

33. Launch Speeches, Open Bethlehem, http://openbethlehem.org/index.php ?option=com_content&task=view&id=61&Itemid=7, accessed Nov. 11, 2011.

34. Ibid.

35. E.g., Harris 2005a; Morris 2005.

36. Farrell 2005.

37. See Greenberg 2005. Statistics on this matter are difficult to find, but according to research commissioned by Open Bethlehem, four hundred Christian families emigrated from Bethlehem between 2001 and 2006, and 16 percent of Christians were in the process of emigrating (see Bethlehem Opinion Polls, Open Bethlehem, http://openbethlehem. org/index.php?option=com_content&task=view&id=122&Itemid=80, accessed Dec. 17, 2011). The Christian population is in a clear decline from the mid–twentieth century. In 1946, Christians were about 78 percent of the population of Bethlehem and Beit Jala, while in the 1990s they were only 52 percent of the population (Lybarger 2002, 412).

38. The 2006 Palestinian census found that in the West Bank and Gaza as a whole, 38.6 percent of camp residents lived in poverty, compared to 29.3 percent of urban residents (PCBS 2007, 29).

39. Bowman 2000; Lybarger 2002.

40. Feldman 2007.

41. For more on road access, see "Checkpoints, Physical Obstructions, and Forbidden Roads," B'Tselem, http://www.btselem.org/freedom_of_movement/checkpoints_and_forbidden_roads, accessed May 30, 2012.

42. In the Palestinian case as elsewhere, T-shirts are everyday, material items that can signal political and social affiliation (Glass 2008).

43. Khalili 2007.

44. For example, the Associated Press remarked on the unveiling in a sentence out of a six-hundred-word report on Israel's sixtieth anniversary: "In Bethlehem, some 500 marchers followed a flatbed truck carrying a huge key, meant to symbolize the hope of refugees to return one day to their villages, most of them leveled, in what is now Israel" (Gutkin 2008). After its unveiling, the key did become an iconic image of 'Aida Refugee Camp in progressive internet media. In early 2012, though, the key was removed for exhibition in Europe. The decision to move the key generated further controversy among camp residents.

45. Though they did not say so, another source of resentment might have been that the UNRWA school was regarded as another outside institution the refugees had to manage. For all it had provided to refugees over the last decades, UNRWA was viewed as strictly avoiding politics. Even the schoolyard—one of few open spaces in the camp—was off-limits after school hours. To hold the ceremony in the school was effectively holding it in private space.

46. Said 2009.

47. Ibid.

48. Malti 2009.

49. Hall 1980.

50. Hacking 1999, 2000.

51. E.g., Abu-Lughod, 2012; Guss 2000.

Parsing "Chaos"

1. Ephron and Hirsch 2004; interviewees read first two paragraphs plus a sentence.

2. Stone and Chabin 2004; interviewees read entire article.

Chapter 6. Watching U.S. Television from the Palestinian Street

An earlier version of this article was published as "Watching U.S. Television from the Palestinian Street: The Media, the State, and Representational Interventions," *Cultural Anthropology* 23 (3): 488–530.

1. Morris 2002.

2. See Moughrabi 1978 for an analysis of this and other stereotypes of Arabs in academic writing.

3. For example, one of the key texts making such assertions, Raphael Patai's *The Arab Mind* (2002), originally published in 1973, was reissued with a new foreword by the director of Middle East Studies at the JFK Special Warfare Center and School at Fort Bragg. It has been used widely in military circles (Gonzalez 2007). See Davis 2010, 304, for a sense of how these stereotypes might have played out in Iraq.

4. Barry Rubin, "The Reason There Is No Palestinian State Today: Arafat," *Jerusalem Post*, Nov. 14, 2010, http://www.jpost.com/Opinion/Columnists/Article.aspx?id=195323, accessed Nov. 10, 2011.

5. Andrew McCarthy, "The Father of Modern Terrorism; The True Legacy of Yasir Arafat," Nov. 12, 2004, http://www.defenddemocracy.org/media-hit/the-father-of-modern-terrorism-the-true-legacy-of-yasser-arafat/, accessed Nov. 10, 2011.

6. DPA 2000; Weymouth 2000.

7. Friedman 2000; see also Will 2000.

8. Barak 2001.

9. E.g., Ephron 2002.

10. Neve Gordon, "The No-Partner Myth," *In These Times*, Nov. 12, 2004, http://www.inthesetimes.com/article/1685/, accessed Dec. 17, 2011.

11. Spivak 2010, 30. She writes about the contrast between representation as "a proxy" or as "a portrait."

12. Latour 2005, 16. See also, e.g., Comaroff and Comaroff 1992, 176; Subramanian 2009, 15.

13. The normative form of governmental representation corresponds to what Bruno Latour calls "the ways to *gather* the legitimate people around some issue" (my italics; Latour 2005, 16). Acts of representations-as-gathering constitute a polity. They assert a connection among people by bringing them together in some act, like voting, protest-

ing, or public mourning. Media representation corresponds to Latour's description of a second basic kind of representation that "presents or rather *represents* what is the object of concern to the eyes and ears of those who have been assembled around it" (ibid.), as do media. The distinction Latour draws between these two kinds of representation in "From Realpolitik to Dingpolitik" is similar to that which he draws between scientific and political representation in *We Have Never Been Modern* (Latour 1993, 27–29).

14. This returns us to linguistic anthropological arguments that the dominant language ideology of Euro-Americans emphasizes the role of language as a means of transparently representing the world, and diminishes other ways of using language (Silverstein 1996).

15. Austin 1975; Butler 1997.

16. Rosen 1999.

17. Mansour 2005, 162; see also Said 2000, 51–52.

18. Khalidi and Kattan 2011.

19. Geertz 1980; see also Coronil 1997; Hasty 2006; Wedeen 2003. Palestinian prime minister Salam Fayyad's declared plan to build a state even under occupation, outlined in August 2009, has arguably been a continuation of this trajectory.

20. Ackerman 2001.

21. Fishman 1980, 51; Gans 1979, 283; Mermin 1999; Pedelty 1995, 87.

22. For a parallel example, see Velthuis 2006, 142.

23. Mitchell 1991.

24. Ferguson and Gupta 2002.

25. Cook 1998, 5; see also Fishman 1980, 84.

26. Bishara 2010; Johnson and Kuttab 2001.

27. It is no coincidence that I attended the funeral with a bunch of men from the camp, even though many women in the refugee camp were deeply involved with national politics. However, these women did not have, or felt compelled to suppress, that desire to be on the scene of action. Whether as mothers or daughters, many had family responsibilities that prevented them from leaving Bethlehem on a whim, though they regularly attended rallies and protests they deemed important. This is how it happened that I spent the funeral with a group of male contacts, and this informs why the funeral itself was a male-dominated space. For an analysis of a similar dynamic during the Egyptian Revolution, see Winegar 2012.

28. Ramadan serials are a prominent form of entertainment media in the Arab world (Abu-Lughod 2005; Salamandra 1998), and the West Bank is no exception. While in countries like Egypt national productions have dominated this media form, PA television does not have the resources for such undertakings, so Palestinians tend to watch serials produced in other parts of the Arab world on satellite television.

29. Palestinians are not unique in their regard for a foreign media; e.g., Froehling 1997; Graan 2010; Manning 2007.

30. Palestinians who dealt with foreign media frequently, including Palestinians employed by foreign media institutions and also activists and officials, had sharp analyses of different media organizations. They evaluated Fox News differently than CNN and the BBC, judging Fox News to be more conservative and more pro-Israel than CNN. Those who worked closely with journalists or in public relations also had impressions of individual journalists and their politics. A handful of prominent European journalists were recognized as being unusually critical of Israel. Palestinians did not as commonly imagine the Israeli public to be an important audience for their narratives. During the second Intifada, Palestinians did not regularly encounter Israeli journalists working independently in Palestinian areas. Many Israeli journalists would not go to the occupied territories on their own out of concern for their safety. As of 2003, there was only one Israeli journalist working on Palestinian affairs living in the West Bank or Gaza. Amira Hass, a columnist for *Ha'aretz*, is widely known and admired among politically active Palestinians. However, for most Israelis and Palestinians, the second Intifada was a period of extreme separation, quite distinct from the decades that preceded it.

31. For more on the development of Palestinian police apparatuses and the trend toward authoritarianism that has only intensified since Arafat's death, see Sayigh 2011.

32. A poll conducted by Khalil Shikaki's Palestinian Center for Policy and Survey Research indicated renewed approval of Arafat following his death. See "Results of Poll #14," Policy and Survey Research, Dec. 1–5, 2004, http://www.pcpsr.org/survey/polls/2004/p14a.html#postarafat, accessed Dec. 30, 2011.

33. Palestinians generally regard anyone who dies struggling for the nation, or who is killed by Israeli forces, to be a martyr. Arafat was considered a martyr because of his eminence and his life of struggle for the Palestinian people.

34. Hannerz 2004, 82; Pedelty 1995, 109–112.

35. Full text of speech available at: http://www.monde-diplomatique.fr/cahier/proche-orient/arafat74-en, accessed Nov. 11, 2011.

36. It is worth considering whether Jawad could actually watch U.S. television and, if U.S. television was out of reach, what his other options were. In recent years, Palestinians' media landscape has grown much richer. After the establishment of the PA in 1994, Palestinians for the first time obtained their own public and private broadcast media, having previously watched in on Israeli, Jordanian, Egyptian, Syrian, and Lebanese broadcasts that happened to reach Palestinian televisions (Batrawi 2001). Over the past decade and a half, Palestinians have benefited from the flourishing of satellite media in the Middle East. According to a 2003 survey by the Jerusalem Media and Communications Center (JMCC), Palestinians watch more satellite television than local television (cited in Maiola and Ward 2007, 98–99). CNN International is available on major Palestinian satellite services, but other U.S. news networks are less accessible. However, CNN International is not a popular source of news, first because of most people's lack

of fluency in English, and second because most Palestinians believe that stations like Al-Jazeera offer high-quality news.

37. Radin 2004.

38. Bishop 2004.

39. Radin 2004; Bennet 2004a; Bishop 2004.

40. Moore and Anderson 2004.

41. The expression is used in Arabic as well. However, in the Arab world it is more likely to be used in a positive sense when people who have few formal routes by which to influence autocratic governments take to the streets to express populist and Arabist sentiments.

42. Bayat 2003; Lynch 2003; Regier and Khalidi 2009.

43. Manning 2007, 193.

44. See Chakrabarty 2007 for a discussion of Indian popular sovereignty shaped by colonial histories.

45. Palestinians carrying identity cards from the West Bank and Gaza, like Mustafa Barghouthi, are not allowed to enter Israeli-annexed east Jerusalem without a permit. Moreover, Israel prohibited campaigning inside Jerusalem because it claims sovereignty over the entire city.

46. Kimberly Coles's article on elections in Bosnia-Herzegovina also analyzes how the procedural and technical sides of an election communicate both to the international community and to a citizenry about a nation's democratic values and strength (Coles 2004); whereas Lisa Wedeen analyzes the performative aspects of elections in Yemen that actually foreclosed democratic possibilities (Wedeen 2003).

47. This project, sponsored by the UN Development Programme, is available at: http://thisispalestine.yvod.com/, accessed Nov. 11, 2011.

48. Abu-Lughod 2002; Hirschkind and Mahmood 2002.

49. Erlanger 2005a.

50. Ephron 2005.

51. MacIntyre 2005.

52. Editors, *New York Times* 2005.

53. Editors, *New York Times* 2006.

54. Silverstein and Urban 1996.

55. Mitchell 1991.

56. Garfield 2005; Van Natta Jr., Liptak, and Levy 2005.

57. Hasty 2005.

58. McChesney 2004; Schiller 2011.

A Discerning Representation of More Than "Two Sides"

1. Wilson 2007.

Conclusion. Framing Graffiti

1. Bennet 2003b.

2. Peteet 1996.

3. Ibid., 151.

4. See Send a Message, http://www.sendamessage.nl/, accessed Nov. 4, 2009. See also Bishara 2010a and Sauders 2011a regarding graffiti on the wall and analysis of Send a Message.

5. A few books have featured Palestinian graffiti (Gröndahl 2009; Krohn and Lager-weij 2010), and a volume of Banksy's street art contains a section on his graffiti in the occupied territories (Banksy 2006).

6. Keane 2007.

7. Bauman and Briggs 2003.

8. The same advertisement is visible in the "Children Against the Wall" image. It serves as a reminder that there is a diversity of Palestinian norms governing what is appropriate to write on the wall.

9. His later images do address occupation more incisively. In murals made in a return trip to the West Bank in 2007, Banksy painted on military themes. Some of these murals nevertheless to a certain extent maintain Eurocentric iconography.

10. Gürsel 2009.

11. Kalman 2006.

12. Banksy 2006, 142.

13. Barak 2002.

14. Bennet 2003b.

15. This line of poetry provided power to the revolutionaries of the Arab revolts of 2011 as well (Saad 2012). The photograph of the graffito on the separation wall was taken in 2009, before these revolts.

16. Darwish 2003, 6.

17. The documentary *Ali Wall*, produced by Mohammad Al-Azza, narrates this story. It is available at: http://www.youtube.com/watch?v=ahap7fXRP10, accessed Dec. 17, 2011.

18. Brown 2008.

19. Cf. Aretxaga 1995.

20. Mazzarella 2006, 299; see also Allen 2009.

21. For example, see Katie Rodgers, "Occupy DC by the Numbers: Protest Cost Nears $1 Million," *Washington Post* online, Nov. 21, 2011, http://www.washingtonpost.com/blogs/the-buzz/post/occupy-dc-by-the-numbers-protest-cost-nears-1-million/2011/10/31/gIQAEShBiN_blog.html, accessed Nov. 22, 2011; and Susanna Kim, "Occupy Protests Across the Country Take Toll on City Budgets," ABC News online, Nov. 18, 2011, http://abcnews.go.com/Business/occupy-wall-street-protests-cost-cities-millions/story?id=14975940#.TsvDtHGi10w, accessed Nov. 22, 2011.

22. Indeed, the presence of police at protests even when they are not being repressive of protesters can be seen as an element of the prerogative dimension of the masculinist state that asserts that women and others require the state's protection to speak (Brown 1992).

23. Montag 2000, 144.

24. Bollinger 1991, 1.

25. Ishay 2008, 80–81. See also "About CPJ," Committee to Protect Journalists, http://www.cpj.org/about/#four, accessed Dec. 4, 2011.

26. Haraway 1988.

27. McChesney and Scott 2004, 1.

28. For analyses of this dynamic, see Abu-Lughod 2002; Asad 2007; Hirschkind and Mahmood 2002.

29. For example, in that the U.S. State Department often stipulates that countries institute legislation similar to the U.S. Freedom of Information Act as a condition of receiving aide (Gladstone 2011a).

30. Kincaid 1988; Ong 1987; Ortner 1999, for just a few examples.

WORKS CITED

Abu El-Haj, Nadia. 2001. *Facts on the Ground: Archaeological Practice and Territorial Self-Fashioning in Israeli Society*. Chicago: University of Chicago Press.

———. 2005. "Edward Said and the Political Present." *American Ethnologist* 32 (4):538–555.

Abu-Lughod, Lila. 1989. "Zones of Theory in the Anthropology of the Arab World." *Annual Review of Anthropology* 18:267–306.

———. 1993. *Writing Women's Worlds: Bedouin Stories*. Berkeley: University of California Press.

———. 2002. "Do Muslim Women Really Need Saving? Anthropological Reflections on Cultural Relativism and Its Others." *American Anthropologist* 104 (3):783–790.

———. 2005. *Dramas of Nationhood: The Politics of Television in Egypt*. Chicago: University of Chicago Press.

———. 2012. "Living National Spaces: The Revolt from/in the Egyptian Countryside." *American Ethnologist* 39 (1):21–25.

Ackerman, Seth. 2001. "Al-Aqsa Intifada and the U.S. Media." *Journal of Palestine Studies* 30 (2):61–74.

Agrama, Hussein. 2012. "Reflections on Secularism, Democracy, and Politics in Egypt." *American Ethnologist* 39 (1):26–31.

Allen, Lori. 2006. "The Polyvalent Politics of Martyr Commemorations in the Palestinian Intifada." *History and Memory* 18 (2):107–138.

———. 2008. "Getting by the Occupation: How Violence Became Normal During the Second Palestinian Intifada." *Cultural Anthropology* 23 (3):453–487.

———. 2009. "Martyr Bodies in the Media: Human Rights, Aesthetics, and the Politics of Immediation in the Palestinian Intifada." *American Ethnologist* 36 (1):161–180.

———. Forthcoming 2013. *The Rise and Fall of Human Rights: Cynicism and Politics in Occupied Palestine*. Stanford: Stanford University Press.

AP (Associated Press). 2008. "Parents of US Peace Activist Mark Fifth Anniversary of Death with Memorial in West Bank." Associated Press report, March 20.

Appadurai, Arjun. 1988. "Putting Hierarchy in Its Place." *Cultural Anthropology* 3 (1):36–49.

Arendt, Hannah. 1976. *The Origins of Totalitarianism*. New York: Harcourt.

Arenson, Karen. 2002. "Harvard President Sees Rise in Anti-Semitism on Campus." *New York Times*, September 21.

Aretxaga, Begoña. 1995. "Dirty Protest: Symbolic Overdetermination and Gender in Northern Ireland Ethnic Violence." *Ethos* 23 (2):123–148.

Asad, Talal. 2003. *Formations of the Secular: Christianity, Islam, Modernity*. Stanford: Stanford University Press.

———. 2004. "Where Are the Margins of the State?" In *Anthropology in the Margins of the State*, edited by V. Das and D. Poole. Santa Fe: School of American Research Press, 279–288.

———. 2007. *On Suicide Bombing*. New York: Columbia University Press.

Asch, Timothy, Patsy Asch, and Linda Conner. 1981. *Jero on Jero*. Documentary. Instructional Resources Unit.

Askew, Kelly. 2002. *Performing the Nation: Swahili Music and Cultural Politics in Tanzania*. Chicago: University of Chicago Press.

Austin, J. L. 1975. *How to Do Things with Words: The William James Lectures Delivered in Harvard University in 1955*. New York: Oxford Paperbacks.

Azoulay, Ariella. 2008. *The Civil Contract of Photography*. New York: Zone Books.

B'Tselem. 2001. "Free Rein: Vigilante Settlers and Israel's Non-Enforcement of the Law." Jerusalem: B'Tselem, Israeli Information Center for Human Rights in the Occupied Territories.

Bachelard, Gaston. 1994. *The Poetics of Space*. Boston: Beacon Press.

Bahloul, Joëlle. 1996. *The Architecture of Memory: A Jewish-Muslim Household in Colonial Algeria 1937–1962* [La maison de mémoire]. Translated by C.D.P. Ménagé. Cambridge: Cambridge University Press.

Baisnée, Olivier, and Dominique Marchetti. 2006. "The Economy of Just-in-Time Television News Casting: Journalistic Production and Professional Excellence at Euronews." *Ethnography* 7 (2):99–123.

Bakalian, Anny, and Mehdi Bozorgmehr. 2009. *Backlash 9/11: Middle Eastern and Muslim Americans Respond*. Berkeley: University of California Press.

Banksy. 2006. *Banksy: Wall and Piece*. London: Century.

Barak, Ehud. 2001. "Israel Needs a True Partner for Peace." *New York Times*, July 30.

———. 2002. "Israel's Security Requires a Sturdy Fence." *New York Times*, April 14.

Barr, Cameron W. 2002. "After 21 Months of Intifada, A Wall Is Born." *Christian Science Monitor*, July 10.

Barthes, Roland. 1972. *Mythologies*. Translated by A. Lavers. New York: Hill and Wang.

Basso, Keith. 1996. *Wisdom Sits in Places: Landscape and Language Among the Western Apache.* Albuquerque: University of New Mexico Press.

Bateson, Gregory, and Margaret Mead. 1977. "Margaret Mead and Gregory Bateson on the Use of the Camera in Anthropology." *Studies in the Anthropology of Visual Communication* 4 (2):78–80.

Batrawi, Walid. 2001. "Private Television in Palestine." Master's thesis, Mass Communications, Leicester University.

Bauman, Richard, and Charles L. Briggs. 2003. *Voices of Modernity: Language Ideologies and the Politics of Inequality.* Cambridge: Cambridge University Press.

Baumgarten-Sharon, Naama. 2011. *No Minor Matter: Violation of the Rights of Palestinian Minors Arrested by Israel on Suspicion of Stone Throwing.* Jerusalem: B'Tselem, Israeli Information Center for Human Rights in the Occupied Territories.

Bayat, Asif. 2003. "The 'Street' and the Politics of Dissent in the Arab World." *Middle East Report* 226:10–17.

Bayoumi, Moustafa. 2008. *How Does It Feel to Be a Problem? Being Young and Arab in America.* New York: Penguin Press.

Beinart, Peter. 2010. "The Failure of the American Jewish Establishment." *New York Review of Books,* June 10, 16–20.

Bennet, James. 2003a. "Al Shati Journal; Rising Above, with Sticks, Paper and String." *New York Times,* July 18.

———. 2003b. "Small Town on West Bank Stands as an Epitaph to Dashed Dreams." *New York Times,* September 14.

———. 2004a. "An Emotion-Driven Flock Storms the Burial Ceremony." *New York Times,* November 13.

———. 2004b. "In Mideast, a Soldier's Duty Is to His Father, Too." *New York Times,* January 24.

Benson, Rodney, and Erik Neveu. 2005. "Introduction: Field Theory as a Work in Progress." In *Bourdieu and the Journalistic Field,* edited by R. Benson and E. Neveu. Cambridge, UK, and Malden, MA: Polity Press, 1–25.

Benvenisti, Meron. 1983. *Israeli Censorship of Arab Publications: A Survey.* New York: Fund for Free Expression.

Biagioli, Mario. 1999. "Aporias of Scientific Authorship: Credit and Responsibility in Contemporary Biomedicine." In *The Science Studies Reader,* edited by M. Biagioli. New York and London: Routledge, 12–30.

Bird, Elizabeth. 2010. "Introduction, The Anthropology of News and Journalism: Why Now?" In *The Anthropology of News and Journalism: Global Perspectives,* edited by E. Bird. Bloomington: Indiana University Press, 1–20.

Bishara, Amahl. 2002. *Across Oceans, Among Colleagues.* Documentary. New York: Culture and Media Program, New York University.

———. 2010a. "New Media and Political Change in the Occupied Palestinian Territories: Assembling Media Worlds and Cultivating Networks of Care." *Middle East Journal of Culture and Communication* 3:63–81.

———. 2010b. "Weapons, Passports, and News: Palestinian Perceptions of U.S. Power as a Mediator of War." In *Anthropology and Global Counterinsurgency*, edited by J. Kelly, B. Jauregui, S. T. Mitchell, and J. Walton. Chicago: University of Chicago Press, 125–136.

Bishara, Amahl, and Nidal Al-Azraq. 2010. *Degrees of Incarceration*. Documentary. Palestinian West Bank and Somerville, MA, United States.

Bishop, Patrick. 2004. "Scenes of Chaos as Arafat Is Buried." *Daily Telegraph*, November 13.

Boczkowski, Pablo. 2005. *Digitizing the News: Innovation in Online Newspapers*. Boston: MIT Press.

———. 2010. *News at Work: Imitation in an Age of Information Abundance*. Chicago: University of Chicago Press.

Bollinger, Lee C. 1991. *Images of a Free Press*. Chicago: University of Chicago Press.

Bouckaert, Peter, Miranda Sissons, and Johanna Bjorken. 2002. "Jenin: IDF Military Operations." New York: Human Rights Watch.

Bourdieu, Pierre. 1977. *Outline of a Theory of Practice*. Cambridge: Cambridge University Press.

———. 1993. *The Field of Cultural Production*. New York: Columbia University Press.

———. 2005. "The Political Field, the Social Science Field, and the Journalistic Field." In *Bourdieu and the Journalistic Field*, edited by E. Neveu and R. Benson. Cambridge, UK, and Malden, MA: Polity Press, 29–47.

Bowman, Glenn. 2000. "Two Deaths of Basem Rishmawi: Identity Constructions and Reconstructions in a Muslim-Christian Palestinian Community." In *Perplexities of Identification: Anthropological Studies in Cultural Differentiation and the Use of Resources*, edited by H. Driessen and T. Otto. Aarhus: Aarhus University Press, 56–94.

Boyer, Dominic C. 2005a. "The Corporeality of Expertise." *Ethnos* 70 (2):243–266.

———. 2005b. *Spirit and System: Media, Intellectuals, and the Dialectic in Modern German Culture*. Chicago: University of Chicago Press.

———. 2010. "Digital Expertise in Online Journalism (and Anthropology)." *Anthropological Quarterly* 83 (1):73–96.

Boyer, Dominic C., and Ulf Hannerz. 2006. "Introduction: Worlds of Journalism." *Ethnography* 7 (1):5–18.

Boyer, Dominic C., and Claudio Lomnitz. 2005. "Intellectuals and Nationalism: Anthropological Engagements." *Annual Review of Anthropology* 34:105–120.

Boykoff, Maxwell, and Jules M. Boykoff. 2003. "Balance as Bias: Global Warming and the U.S. Prestige Press." *Global Environmental Change* 14 (2):125–136.

Briggs, Charles. 1986. *Learning How to Ask: A Sociolinguistic Appraisal of the Role of the Interview in Social Science Research*. Cambridge: Cambridge University Press.

Bronner, Ethan. 2009. "Israel Puts Media Clamp on Gaza." *New York Times*, January 6.

———. 2010. "Covering the Middle East in 2010: A Report from the Field." Public lecture, February 2, Brandeis University, International Lounge, Usdan Student Center.

Brown, Keith. 2008. "'All They Understand Is Force': Debating Culture in Operation Iraqi Freedom." *American Anthropologist* 110 (4):443–453.

Brown, Wendy. 1992. "Finding the Man in the State." *Feminist Studies* 18 (1):7–34.

———. 2007. *Regulating Aversion: Tolerance in the Age of Identity and Empire*. Princeton: Princeton University Press.

Butler, Judith. 1997. *Excitable Speech: A Politics of the Performative*. New York: Routledge.

———. 2004. *Precarious Life: The Powers of Mourning and Violence*. London and New York: Verso.

Cainkar, Louise A. 2009. *Homeland Insecurity: The Arab American and Muslim American Experience After 9/11*. New York: Russell Sage Foundation.

Campagna, Joel. 1999. "The Middle East and North Africa." In *Attacks on the Press 1998*, edited by A. Chasan. New York: Committee to Protect Journalists, 311–370.

———. 2000. "The Middle East and North Africa." In *Attacks on the Press in 1999*, edited by R. Murphy. New York: Committee to Protect Journalists, 366–418.

———. 2001. "The Middle East and North Africa." In *Attacks on the Press in 2000*, edited by R. Murphy. New York: Committee to Protect Journalists, 248–276.

———. 2003. "The Middle East and North Africa." In *Attacks on the Press in 2002*, edited by S. Ellingwood. New York: Committee to Protect Journalists, 298–352.

———. 2005. "The Middle East and North Africa." In *Attacks on the Press in 2004*, edited by B. Sweeny. New York: Committee to Protect Journalists, 166–196.

Carr, E. Summerson. 2010a. "Enactments of Expertise." *Annual Review of Anthropology* 39:17–32.

———. 2010b. *Scripting Addiction: The Politics of Therapeutic Talk*. Princeton: Princeton University Press.

Chakrabarty, Dipesh. 2000. *Provincializing Europe: Postcolonial Thought and Historical Difference*. Princeton: Princeton University Press.

———. 2007. "'In the Name of Politics': Democracy and the Power of the Multitude in India." *Public Culture* 19 (1):35–57.

Chalaby, Jean K. 1996. "Journalism as an Anglo-American Invention." *European Journal of Communication* 11 (3):23.

Chu, Julie. 2010. *Cosmologies of Credit: Transnational Mobility and the Politics of Destination in China*. Durham: Duke University Press.

Clifford, James. 1988. *The Predicament of Culture: Twentieth-Century Ethnography, Literature, and Art*. Cambridge: Harvard University Press.

Cohen, Richard. 2002. "Build a Fence." *Washington Post*, April 16.

Coles, Kimberley A. 2004. "Election Day: The Construction of Democracy Through Technique." *Cultural Anthropology* 19 (4):551–580.

Comaroff, John. 1998. "Reflections on the Colonial State, in South Africa and Elsewhere: Factions, Fragments, Facts and Fictions." *Social Identities* 4 (3):321–361.

Comaroff, J. L., and J. Comaroff. 1992. *Ethnography and the Historical Imagination.* Boulder: Westview Press.

Cook, Catherine, Adam Hanieh, and Adah Kay. 2004. *Stolen Youth: The Politics of Israel's Detention of Palestinian Children.* London: Sterling Press.

Cook, Timothy E. 1998. *Governing with the News: The News Media as a Political Institution.* Chicago: University of Chicago Press.

Coronil, Fernando. 1997. *The Magical State: Nature, Money, and Modernity in Venezuela.* Chicago: University of Chicago Press.

Corrigan, Philip. 1988. "The Body of Intellectuals/The Intellectuals' Body (Remarks for Roland)." *Sociological Review* 36 (2):368–380.

CPJ. 1988. *Journalism Under Occupation: Israel's Regulation of the Palestinian Press.* New York: Committee to Protect Journalists.

Cunningham, Brent. 2003. "Re-thinking Objectivity." *Columbia Journalism Review,* July–August, http://www.cjr.org/feature/rethinking_objectivity.php?page=all.

Dao, James. 2002. "Redefining an Idea as Old as Civilization Itself." *New York Times,* April 21.

Darwish, Mahmoud. 2003. *Unfortunately, It Was Paradise.* Translated by M. Akash, C. Forche, S. Antoon, and A. El-Zein. Berkeley: University of California Press.

Das, Veena, and Deborah Poole. 2004. "State and Its Margins: Comparative Ethnographies." In *Anthropology in the Margins of the State,* edited by V. Das and D. Poole. Santa Fe: School of American Research Press, 3–34.

Daston, Lorraine. 1992. "Objectivity and the Escape from Perspective." *Social Studies of Science* 22 (4):597–618.

Daston, Lorraine, and Peter Galison. 2007. *Objectivity.* New York: Zone Books.

Davidson, Lawrence. 2001. *America's Palestine: Popular and Official Perceptions from Balfour to Israeli Statehood.* Gainesville: University Press of Florida.

Davis, Rochelle. 2010. "Cultural Sensitivity in a Military Occupation: The U.S. Military in Iraq." In *Anthropology and Global Counterinsurgency,* edited by J. Kelly, B. Jauregui, S. T. Mitchell, and J. Walton. Chicago: University of Chicago Press, 297–310.

———. 2011. *Palestinian Village Histories: Geographies of the Displaced.* Stanford: Stanford University Press.

Debord, Guy. 1983 [1967]. *Society of the Spectacle.* Detroit: Black and Red.

Donovan, John. 2000. "Holy Land, Moment of Crisis; Panelists Made Up of Israelis and Palestinians Discuss Conflict in Middle East." ABC News, *Nightline,* October 10.

Donsbach, Wolfgang, and Bettina Klett. 1993. "Subjective Objectivity: How Journalists in Four Countries Define a Key Term of Their Profession." *International Communication Gazette* 51:53–83.

Dornfeld, Barry. 1998. *Producing Public Television, Producing Public Culture.* Princeton: Princeton University Press.

Downey, Greg. 2005. *Learning Capoeira: Lessons in Cunning from an Afro-Brazilian Art.* Oxford and New York: Oxford University Press.

DPA (Deutsche Presse-Agentur). 2000. "Failure to Make Peace Would Be Tragic for Palestinians: Barak." News agency report, September 1.

Du Bois, W.E.B. 2004. *The Souls of Black Folk.* Boulder and London: Paradigm.

Editors. 2000. "Palestinian Journalists Forced to Be One-Sided." *Ha'aretz,* November 7.

——. 2005. "Signs of Life After Arafat." *New York Times,* January 11.

——. 2006. "Underwriting Hamas." *New York Times,* March 4.

El-Hage, Badr. 2007. "The Armenian Pioneers of Middle Eastern Photography." *Jerusalem Quarterly* 31:22–26.

Englund, Harri. 2006. *Prisoners of Freedom: Human Rights and the African Poor.* Berkeley: University of California Press.

Ephron, Dan. 2002. "Arafat Cancels Session with New Cabinet." *Boston Globe,* June 11.

——. 2005. "Abbas Declares Win, Stirs Hopes for Mideast Peace." *Boston Globe,* January 10.

Ephron, Dan, and Michael Hirsch. 2004. "Life After Arafat." *Newsweek,* November 22.

Erlanger, Steven. 2005a. "Abbas Declares Victory in Vote by Palestinians." *New York Times,* January 10.

——. 2005b. "At Israeli Barrier, More Sound than Fury." *New York Times,* October 8.

——. 2005c. "Israel, on Its Own, Is Shaping the Borders of the West Bank." *New York Times,* April 19.

——. 2006. "Israel's Hamas Problem: The Danger Begins Next Door." *New York Times,* January 15.

Esposito, Michele K. 2006. "Various Organizations, Losses on the Five-Year Anniversary of the Al-Aqsa Intifada, Comparative Statistical Table." *Journal of Palestine Studies* 35 (2):194–199.

Fabian, Johannes. 1983. *Time and the Other: How Anthropology Makes Its Object.* New York: Columbia University Press.

Fanon, Frantz. 1965a. *A Dying Colonialism.* New York: Grove Press.

——. 1965b. *The Wretched of the Earth.* New York: Grove Press.

Farrell, Stephen. 2005. "Today's Joseph and Mary Would Face 15 Checkpoints." *The Times* [London], December 23.

Fassin, Didier. 2008. "The Humanitarian Politics of Testimony: Subjectification Through Trauma in the Israeli-Palestinian Conflict." *Cultural Anthropology* 23 (3):531–558.

Feld, Steven. 1990. *Sound and Sentiment: Birds, Weeping, Poetics, and Song in Kaluli Expression.* Philadelphia: University of Pennsylvania Press.

——. 1996a. "Pygmy POP: A Genealogy of Schizophonic Mimesis." *Yearbook for Traditional Music* 28:1–35.

————. 1996b. "Waterfalls of Song: An Acoustemology of Place Resounding in Bosavi, Papua New Guinea." In *Senses of Place*, edited by K. Basso and S. Feld. Santa Fe: School of American Research Press, 91–136.

Feld, Steven, and Keith Basso. 1996. *Senses of Place*. Santa Fe: School of American Research Press.

Feldman, Ilana. 2007. "Difficult Distinctions: Refugee Law, Humanitarian Practice, and Political Identification in Gaza." *Cultural Anthropology* 22 (1):129–169.

Ferguson, James, and Akhil Gupta. 2002. "Spatializing States: Toward an Ethnography of Neoliberal Governmentality." *American Ethnologist* 29 (4):981–1002.

Fishman, Mark. 1980. *Manufacturing the News*. Austin: University of Texas Press.

Fortun, Kim. 2001. *Advocacy After Bhopal: Environmentalism, Disaster, New Global Orders*. Chicago: University of Chicago Press.

Foucault, Michel. 1984. "What Is an Author?" In *The Foucault Reader*, edited by P. Rabinow. New York: Pantheon Books, 101–120.

————. 2003. *Society Must Be Defended: Lectures at the Collège de France, 1975–76*. New York: Picador.

Frankel, Glenn. 2003. "Jerusalem Borders Are Usually ..." *Washington Post*, June 22.

Fraser, Nancy. 2007. "Transnationalizing the Public Sphere: On the Legitimacy and Efficacy of Public Opinion in a PostWestphalian World." In *Identities, Affiliations, and Allegiances*, edited by S. Benhabib, I. Shapiro, and D. Petranovich. Cambridge: Cambridge University Press, 45–66.

Friedman, Thomas L. 2000. "Arafat's War." *New York Times*, October 13.

————. 2002. "The Core of Muslim Rage." *New York Times*, March 6.

Friel, Howard, and Richard Falk. 2007. *Israel-Palestine on Record: How the New York Times Misreports Conflict in the Middle East*. London and New York: Verso.

Froehling, Oliver. 1997. "The Cyberspace 'War of Ink and Internet' in Chiapas, Mexico." *Geographical Review* 87 (2):291–307.

Gans, Herbert. 1979. *Deciding What's News: A Study of 'CBS Evening News,' 'NBC Nightly News,' 'Newsweek,' and 'Time.'* New York: Pantheon Books.

Garfield, Bob. 2005. "Former New York Times Staffer Judith Miller." *On the Media*. Radio broadcast, WNYC, November 11, http://www.onthemedia.org/transcripts /2005/11/11/04.

————. 2011a. "(More) Controversy at NPR." *On the Media*. Radio broadcast, WNYC, October 28, http://www.onthemedia.org/2011/oct/28/more-controversy-npr/.

————. 2011b. "Public Radio Journalists and Political Expression." *On the Media*. Radio broadcast, WNYC, November 4, http://www.onthemedia.org/2011/nov/04/public -radio-journalists-and-political-expression/.

Geertz, Clifford. 1980. *Negara: The Theatre State in Nineteenth-Century Bali*. Princeton: Princeton University Press.

Geyer, Georgie Anne. 1984. "Journalists: The New Targets, the New Diplomats, the New

Intermediary People." In *The Responsibilities of Journalism,* edited by R. Schmuhl. Notre Dame: University of Notre Dame Press.

Gilboa, Eytan. 2005. "Media-Broker Diplomacy: When Journalists Become Mediators." *Critical Studies in Media Communication* 22 (2):99–120.

Ginsburg, Faye D. 1989. *Contested Lives: The Abortion Debate in an American Community.* Berkeley: University of California Press.

———. 1995. "The Parallax Effect: The Impact of Aboriginal Media on Ethnographic Film." *Visual Anthropology Review* 11 (2):64–76.

———. 2002. "Screen Memories: Resignifying the Traditional in Indigenous Media." *Media Worlds: Anthropology on New Terrain,* edited by F. D. Ginsburg, L. Abu-Lughod, and B. Larkin. Berkeley: University of California Press, 39–57.

Ginsburg, Faye D., Lila Abu-Lughod, and Brian Larkin, eds. 2002. *Media Worlds: Anthropology on New Terrain.* Berkeley: University of California Press.

Gish, Arthur G. 2001. *Hebron Journal: Stories of Nonviolent Peacemaking.* Scottdale: Herald Press.

Gitlin, Todd. 1980. *The Whole World Is Watching: Mass Media in the Making and the Unmaking of the New Left.* Berkeley: University of California Press.

Gladstone, Brooke. 2005a. "Evolving Debate." *On the Media.* Radio broadcast, WNYC, August 26, http://www.onthemedia.org/2005/aug/26/evolving-debate/.

———. 2005b. "Political Science." *On the Media.* Radio broadcast, WNYC, April 8, http://www.onthemedia.org/2005/apr/08/political-science/.

———. 2006. "Iraq's New Journalism." *On the Media.* Radio broadcast, WNYC, October 20, http://www.onthemedia.org/transcripts/2006/10/20/05.

———. 2010. "Al-Jazeera Now." *On the Media.* Radio broadcast, WNYC, August 6, http://www.onthemedia.org/transcripts/2010/08/06/06.

———. 2011a. "Freedom of Information Laws Around the World." *On the Media.* Radio broadcast, WNYC, November 18, http://www.onthemedia.org/2011/nov/18/freedom-information-laws-around-world/.

———. 2011b. "Journalists Are People Too." *On the Media.* Radio broadcast, WNYC, November 4, http://www.onthemedia.org/2011/nov/04/journalists-are-people-too/.

———. 2011c. "The Objectivity Bias." *On the Media.* Radio broadcast, WNYC, July 29, http://www.onthemedia.org/2011/jul/29/reporting-extreme-positions/.

Glass, Aaron. 2008. "Crests on Cotton: 'Souvenir' T-Shirts and the Materiality of Remembrance Among the Kwakwaka'wakw of British Columbia." *Museum Anthropology* 31 (1):1–18.

Gonzalez, Roberto. 2007. "Patai and Abu Ghraib." *Anthropology Today* 23 (5):23.

Goodale, Mark. 2006. "Introduction to 'Anthropology and Human Rights in a New Key.'" *American Anthropologist* 108 (1):1–8.

Goodman, Amy. 2003. "Darwazeh: No Immunity for Palestinian Journalists." *Democracy Now.* Radio broadcast, New York City, April 21.

————. 2008. "As Palestinians Mark 60th Anniversary of Their Dispossession, a Conversation with Palestinian Writer and Doctor Ghada Karmi." *Democracy Now*. Radio broadcast, New York City, May 15, http://www.democracynow.org/2008/5/15/as_palestinians_mark_60th_anniversary_of.

Graan, Andrew. 2010. "On the Politics of *Imidž*: European Integration and the Trials of Recognition in Postconflict Macedonia." *Slavic Review* 69 (4):835–858.

Greenberg, Joel. 2005. "Wall Casts Shadow on Arabs in Bethlehem." *Chicago Tribune*, December 21.

Greenhouse, Carol. 2008. "Fractured Discourse: Rethinking the Discursivity of States." In *Democracy: Anthropological Approaches*, edited by J. Paley. Santa Fe: School for Advanced Research Press, 193–218.

Gröndahl, Mia. 2009. *Gaza Graffiti: Messages of Love and Politics*. Cairo: The American University in Cairo Press.

Gupta, Akhil. 1992. "The Song of the Nonaligned World: Transnational Identities and the Reinscription of Space in Late Capitalism." *Cultural Anthropology* 7 (1):63–79.

Gürsel, Zeynep. 2009. "U.S. Newsworld: The Rule of Text and Everyday Practices of Editing the World." In *Anthropology of News and Journalism: Global Perspectives*, edited by E. Bird. Bloomington: Indiana University Press, 35–53.

Guss, David. 2000. *The Festive State: Race, Ethnicity, and Nationalism as Cultural Performance*. Berkeley: University of California Press.

Gutkin, Steven. 2008. "Israel Celebrates Its 60th with Pride, but also Uncertainty." Associated Press, May 8.

Gutmann, Stephanie. 2005. *The Other War: Israelis, Palestinians, and the Struggle for Media Supremacy*. San Francisco: Encounter Books.

Habermas, Jürgen. 1989. *The Structural Transformation of the Public Sphere*. Translated by T. Burger. Cambridge: MIT Press.

Hacking, Ian. 1999. "Making Up People." In *The Science Studies Reader*, edited by M. Biagioli. New York: Routledge, 161–171.

————. 2000. *The Social Construction of What?* Cambridge: Harvard University Press.

Hahn, Oliver. 2007. "Cultures of TV News Journalism and Prospects for a Transcultural Public Sphere." In *Arab Media and Political Renewal*, edited by N. Sakr. London, New York: I.B. Tauris, 13–27.

Hall, Stuart. 1980. "Encoding/Decoding." In *Culture, Media, Language*, edited by S. Hall, D. Hobson, A. Lowe, and P. Willis. London: Hutchinson.

Hammami, Rema, and Salim Tamari. 2000. "Anatomy of Another Rebellion." *Middle East Report* 216:2–15.

————. 2001. "The Second Uprising: End or New Beginning?" *Journal of Palestine Studies* 30 (2):5–25.

Hammer, Joshua. 2003. *A Season in Bethlehem: Unholy War in a Sacred Place*. New York: Free Press.

Hanafi, Sari, and Linda Tabar. 2005. *The Emergence of Palestinian Globalized Elite: Donors, International Organizations, and Local NGOs*. Jerusalem: Institute of Jerusalem Studies.

Hannerz, Ulf. 2004. *Foreign News: Exploring the World of Foreign Correspondents*. Chicago: University of Chicago Press.

Haraway, Donna. 1988. "Situated Knowledges: The Science Question in Feminism and the Privilege of Partial Perspective." *Feminist Studies* 14 (3):575–599.

Harris, John. 2005a. "Marooned: Bethlehem." *The Guardian*, November 5.

Harris, Mark. 2005b. "Riding a Wave: Embodied Skills and Colonial History on the Amazon Floodplain." *Ethnos* 70 (2):197–219.

Hass, Amira. 2002. "Israel's Closure Policy: An Ineffective Strategy of Containment and Repression." *Journal of Palestine Studies* 31 (3):5–20.

Hasty, Jennifer. 2005. *The Press and Political Culture in Ghana*. Bloomington: Indiana University Press.

———. 2006. "Performing Power, Composing Culture: The State Press in Ghana." *Ethnography* 7 (1):69–98.

———. 2010. "Journalism as Fieldwork: Propaganda, Complicity, and the Ethics of Anthropology." In *The Anthropology of News and Journalism: Global Perspectives*, edited by E. Bird. Bloomington: Indiana University Press, 132–148.

Hayden, Cori. 2003. *When Nature Goes Public: The Making and Unmaking of Bioprospecting in Mexico*. Princeton: Princeton University Press.

Herman, Edward, and Noam Chomsky. 2002. *Manufacturing Consent: The Political Economy of the Mass Media*. New York: Pantheon.

Hertsgaard, Mark. 1988. "A Palace Court Press." In *Our Unfree Press: 100 Years of Radical Press Criticism*, edited by R. McChesney and B. Scott. New York: New Press, 412–429.

Hirschkind, Charles. 2006. *The Ethical Soundscape: Cassette Sermons and Islamic Counterpublics*. New York: Columbia University Press.

Hirschkind, Charles, and Saba Mahmood. 2002. "Feminism, the Taliban, and the Politics of Counter-Insurgency." *Anthropological Quarterly* 75 (2):339–354.

Hoyt, Clark. 2010. "Too Close to Home." *New York Times*, February 7.

Hoyt, Mike, and John Palattella. 2007. *Reporting Iraq: An Oral History of the War by the Journalists Who Covered It*. Hoboken: Melville House.

HRW (Human Rights Watch). 2001. *Center of the Storm: A Case Study of Human Rights Abuses in Hebron District*. Chicago: Human Rights Watch.

Ingold, Tim. 1993. "The Temporality of the Landscape." *World Archaeology* 25 (2):152–174.

———. 2000. *The Perception of the Environment: Essays on Livelihood, Dwelling and Skill*. London and New York: Routledge.

Inhorn, Marcia C., and Emily A. Wentzell. 2011. "Embodying Emergent Masculinities: Men Engaging with Reproductive and Sexual Health Technologies in the Middle East and Mexico." *American Ethnologist* 38 (4):801–815.

Ishay, Micheline R. 2008. *The History of Human Rights From Ancient Times to the Globalization Era*. Berkeley: University of California Press.

Izenberg, Dan. 2003. "GPO Head Calls Palestinian Journalists Security Risks." *Jerusalem Post*, April 25.

Jamal, Amal. 2005. *Media, Politics and Democracy in Palestine*. Sussex: Academic Press.

———. 2009. *The Arab Public Sphere in Israel: Media Space and Cultural Resistance*. Bloomington: Indiana University Press.

Johnson, Penny, and Eileen Kuttab. 2001. "Where Have All the Women (and Men) Gone? Reflections on Gender and the Second Palestinian Intifada." *Feminist Review* 69 (1):21–43.

Kabha, Mustafa. 2007. *The Palestinian Press as Shaper of Public Opinion, 1929–1939*. London and Portland: Vallentine Mitchell.

Kalman, Matthew. 2006. "Barrier-Wall Art Divides Palestinians: Most Want Structure to Remain Ugly Symbol of Strife, Oppression." *San Francisco Chronicle*, April 23.

Kanaaneh, Rhoda. 2008. *Surrounded: Palestinian Soldiers in the Israeli Military*. Stanford: Stanford University Press.

Kaplan, Danny. 2000. "The Military as a Second Bar Mitzvah: Combat Service as Initiation to Zionist Masculinity." In *Imagined Masculinities: Male Identity and Culture in the Modern Middle East*, edited by M. Ghoussoub and E. Sinclair-Webb. London: Saqi Books, 127–144.

Kasher, Asa, and Amos Yadlin. 2005. "Military Ethics of Fighting Terror: An Israeli Perspective." *Journal of Military Ethics* 4:3–32.

Keane, Webb. 1997. *Signs of Recognition: Powers and Hazards of Representation in an Indonesian Society*. Berkeley: University of California Press.

———. 2003. "Semiotics and the Social Analysis of Material Things." *Language and Communication* 23:409–425.

———. 2007. *Christian Moderns: Freedom and Fetish in the Mission Encounter*. Berkeley: University of California Press.

———. 2009. "Freedom and Blasphemy: On Indonesian Press Bans and Danish Cartoons." *Public Culture* 21 (1):47–76.

Kessler, Glenn. 2006. "Vote Complicates Area's Diplomacy; Hamas Emerges as Significant Force Despite U.S. Efforts." *Washington Post*, January 26.

Khalidi, Muhammad Ali. 2010. "'The Most Ethical Army in the World': The New 'Ethical Code' of the Israeli Military and the War on Gaza." *Journal of Palestine Studies* 39 (3):6–23.

Khalidi, Rashid. 1987. "The Palestinians Twenty Years After." *Middle East Report* (146):6–14.

Khalidi, Rashid, and Victor Kattan. 2011. "A Reset for U.S. Policy? Not Now, but Watch the Base, Interview by Victor Kattan with Rashid Khalidi." Al-Shabaka: Palestinian Policy Network.

Khalili, Laleh. 2007. *Heroes and Martyrs of Palestine: The Politics of National Commemoration.* Cambridge: Cambridge University Press.

Kincaid, Jamaica. 1988. *A Small Place.* New York: Farrar, Straus and Giroux.

King-Irani, Laurie. 2000. "Land, Identity and the Limits of Resistance in the Galilee." *Middle East Report* 216:40–44.

Knorr-Cetina, Karin. 1999. *Epistemic Cultures: How the Sciences Make Knowledge.* Cambridge: Harvard University Press.

Krohn, Zia, and Joyce Lagerweij. 2010. *Concrete Messages: Street Art on the Israeli-Palestinian Separation Barrier.* Årsta, Sweden: Dokument Press.

Kroskrity, Paul, ed. 2000. *Regimes of Language: Ideologies, Polities, and Identities.* Santa Fe: School of American Research Press.

Lahav, Pnina. 1985. "Israel's Press Law." In *Press Law in Modern Democracies,* edited by P. Lahav. New York: Longman, 265–314.

Larkin, Brian. 2002. "The Materiality of Cinema Theaters in Northern Nigeria." In *Media Worlds: Anthropology on New Terrain,* edited by F. D. Ginsburg, L. Abu-Lughod, and B. Larkin. Berkeley: University of California Press, 319–336.

———. 2008. *Signal and Noise: Media, Infrastructure, and Urban Culture in Nigeria.* Durham: Duke University Press.

Latour, Bruno. 1993. *We Have Never Been Modern.* Translated by C. Porter. Cambridge: Harvard University Press.

———. 1999. *Pandora's Hope: Essays on the Reality of Science Studies.* Cambridge: Harvard University Press.

———. 2005. "From Realpolitik to Dingpolitik, Or How to Make Things Public." In *Making Things Public: Atmospheres of Democracy,* edited by B. Latour and P. Weibel. Cambridge: MIT Press, 4–41.

Leith, Sam. 2001. "Palestinian Journalists Told It's No-Go." *Daily Telegraph,* August 29.

Levin, Jerry. 2005. *West Bank Diary: Middle East Violence as Reported by a Former American Hostage.* Pasadena: Hope.

Lewis, Neil. 2012. "The *Times* and the Jews." *Columbia Journalism Review* January/February, http://www.cjr.org/feature/the_times_and_the_jews.php?page=all.

Leys, Ruth. 2000. *Trauma: A Genealogy.* Chicago: University of Chicago Press.

Liebes, Tamar, and Zohar Kampf. 2009. "Performance Journalism: The Case of Media's Coverage of War and Terror." *Communication Review* 12 (3):239–249.

Lippard, Lucy, ed. 1992. *Partial Recall.* New York: New Press.

Lutz, Catherine, and Jane L. Collins. 1993. *Reading National Geographic.* Chicago: University of Chicago Press.

Lybarger, Loren D. 2002. "Between Sacred and Secular: Religion, Generations, and Collective Memory Among Muslim and Christian Palestinians in the Post-Oslo Period." PhD Dissertation, University of Chicago.

Lynch, Marc. 2003. "Beyond the Arab Street: Iraq and the Arab Public Sphere." *Politics and Society* 31 (1):55–91.

Lynfield, Ben. 2002a. "Israel Launches 'Image Management' Campaign." *Christian Science Monitor*, April 2.

———. 2002b. "Reporters on the Job." *Christian Science Monitor*, April 19.

———. 2004. "Israeli Women Keep Eyes on Army." *Christian Science Monitor*, February 24.

MacIntyre, Donald. 2005. "A New Start for the Palestinian People; Hopes Rise of End to Armed Conflict as Abbas Heads for Landslide." *The Independent* [London], January 10.

MacKinnon, Catharine. 1989. *Toward a Feminist Theory of the State.* Cambridge: Harvard University Press.

Mahmood, Saba. 2006. *Politics of Piety: Islamic Revival and the Feminist Subject.* Princeton: Princeton University Press.

Maiola, Giovanna, and David Ward. 2007. "Democracy and the Media in Palestine: A Comparison of Election Coverage by Local and Pan-Arab Media." In *Arab Media and Political Renewal: Community, Legitimacy, and Public Life*, edited by N. Sakr. London: I.B. Tauris, 96–117.

Malkki, Liisa. 1992. "National Geographic: The Rooting of Peoples and the Territorialization of National Identity Among Scholars and Refugees." *Cultural Anthropology* 7 (1):24–44.

———. 1995. "Refugees and Exile: From 'Refugee Studies' to the National Order of Things." *Annual Review of Anthropology* 24 (1995):495–523.

———. 1996. "Speechless Emissaries: Refugees, Humanitarianism, and Dehistoricization." *Cultural Anthropology* 11 (3):377–404.

———. 1997. "News and Culture: Transitory Phenomena and the Fieldwork Tradition." In *Anthropological Locations: Boundaries and Grounds of a Field Science*, edited by A. Gupta and J. Ferguson. Berkeley: University of California Press, 86–101.

Malti, Djallal. 2009. "Pope Calls for Palestinian Homeland, Laments 'Tragic' Wall." Agence France Press report, May 13.

Manning, Paul. 2007. "Rose-Colored Glasses? Color Revolutions and Cartoon Chaos in Postsocialist Georgia." *Cultural Anthropology* 22 (2):171–213.

Mansour, Camille. 2005. "The Palestinian Perception of America After 9/11." In *With Us or Against Us: Studies in Global Anti-Americanism*, edited by T. Judt and D. Lacorne. New York: Palgrave Macmillan, 157–171.

Manzella, Joseph, and Leon I. Yacher. 2010. "News and Myth in Venezuela: The Press and the Chavez Revolution." In *The Anthropology of News and Journalism: Global Perspectives*, edited by E. Bird. Bloomington: Indiana University Press, 71–85.

Martin, Emily. 1990. "Toward an Anthropology of Immunology: The Body as Nation State." *Medical Anthropology Quarterly* 4 (4):410–426.

————. 1991. "The Egg and the Sperm: How Science Has Constructed a Romance Based on Stereotypical Male-Female Roles." *Signs* 16 (3):485–501.

Masco, Joseph. 2004. "Nuclear Technoaesthetics: Sensory Politics from Trinity to the Virtual Bomb in Los Alamos." *American Ethnologist* 31 (3):349–373.

————. 2008. "'Survival Is Your Business': Engineering Ruins and Affect in Nuclear America." *Cultural Anthropology* 23 (2):361–398.

Massad, Joseph Andoni. 1995. "Conceiving the Masculine: Gender and Palestinian Nationalism." *Middle East Journal* 49 (3):467–483.

————. 2007. *Desiring Arabs.* Chicago: University of Chicago Press.

Mazzarella, William. 2003. *Shoveling Smoke: Advertising and Globalization in Contemporary India.* Durham: Duke University Press.

————. 2006. "Internet X-Ray: E-Governance, Transparency, and the Politics of Immediation in India." *Public Culture* 18 (3):473–505.

Mbembe, Achille. 2003. "Necropolitics." *Public Culture* 15 (1):11–40.

McAlister, Melani. 2001. *Epic Encounters: Culture, Media, and U.S. Interests in the Middle East, 1945–2000.* Berkeley: University of California Press.

————. 2005. *Epic Encounters: Culture, Media, and U.S. Interests in the Middle East Since 1945.* Berkeley: University of California Press.

McChesney, Robert. 1999. *Rich Media, Poor Democracy: Communication Politics in Dubious Times.* New York: New Press.

————. 2004. *The Problem of the Media: U.S. Communication Politics in the 21st Century.* New York: Monthly Review Press.

McChesney, Robert, and Ben Scott. 2004. "Introduction." In *Our Unfree Press: 100 Years of Radical Media Criticism,* edited by R. McChesney and B. Scott. New York: New Press, 1–30.

McGirk, Tim. 2007. "Palestinian Moms Becoming Martyrs." *Time,* May 5.

Mermin, Jonathan. 1999. *Debating War and Peace: Media Coverage of U.S. Intervention in the Post-Vietnam Era.* Princeton: Princeton University Press.

Messick, Brinkley. 1996. *The Calligraphic State: Textual Domination and History in a Muslim Society.* Berkeley: University of California Press.

MIFTAH, Media Monitoring Unit. 2005. "Public Discourse and Perceptions: Palestinian Media Coverage of the Palestinian-Israeli Conflict." Ramallah: MIFTAH.

Mindich, David T.Z. 1998. *Just the Facts: How "Objectivity" Came to Define American Journalism.* New York: New York University Press.

Mirzoeff, Sacha. 2005. *Shooting Under Fire.* Documentary. Berlin: Context TV.

Mitchell, Timothy. 1991. "The Limits of the State: Beyond Statist Approaches and Their Critics." *American Political Science Review* 85 (1):77–96.

————. 2002. *Rule of Experts: Egypt, Techno-Politics, Modernity.* Berkeley: University of California Press.

———. 2011. *Carbon Democracy: Political Power in the Age of Oil.* London and New York: Verso.

Mitnick, Joshua. 2004. "Palestinians Take Back the Night in Ramallah." *Christian Science Monitor*, August 31.

Moeller, Susan. 1999. *Compassion Fatigue: How the Media Sell Disease, Famine, War, and Death.* New York: Routledge.

Montag, Warren. 2000. "The Pressure of the Street: Habermas's Fear of the Masses." In *Masses, Classes, and the Public Sphere*, edited by M. Hill and W. Montag. New York: Verso, 132–145.

Moore, Molly. 2004a. "Checkpoints Take Toll on Palestinians, Israeli Army." *Washington Post*, November 29.

———. 2004b. "Refuge Is Prison for Hunted Palestinian." *Washington Post*, August 22.

Moore, Molly, and John Ward Anderson. 2004. "Amid Gunfire and Chaos, Palestinians Bury Arafat; Thousands Storm Leader's Ramallah Compound." *Washington Post*, November 13.

Morris, Benny. 2002. "Camp David and After: An Exchange (1. An Interview with Ehud Barak)." *New York Review of Books*, June 13, 42–46.

Morris, Harvey. 2005. "Isolated Bethlehem Struggles for Its Survival." *Financial Times*, December 24.

Moughrabi, Fouad. 1978. "The Arab Basic Personality: A Critical Survey of the Literature." *International Journal of Middle East Studies* 9:99–112.

Murphy, Richard McGill, ed. 2002. *Attacks on the Press in 2001: A Worldwide Survey by the Committee to Protect Journalists.* New York: Committee to Protect Journalists.

Myers, Fred R. 2002. *Painting Culture: The Making of an Aboriginal High Art.* Durham: Duke University Press.

Myre, Greg. 2003. "Fencing Off: In the Middle East, Even Words Go to War." *New York Times*, August 3.

———. 2006. "Palestinians Wrap Up Campaigns as Vote Nears." *New York Times*, January 24.

Naber, Nadine. 2007. "Arab Americans and U.S. Racial Formations." In *Race and Arab Americans Before and After 9/11: From Invisible Citizens to Visible Subjects*, edited by N. Naber and A. Jamal. Syracuse: Syracuse University Press, 1–45.

Nader, Laura. 1974. "Up the Anthropologist—Perspectives Gained from Studying Up." In *Reinventing Anthropology*, edited by D. Hymes. New York: Vintage Books, 284–311.

Naylor, Patricia. 2002a. *In the Line of Fire.* Documentary. New York: Filmakers Library.

———. 2002b. "In the Line of Fire (20–minute version)." Frontline, http://www.pbs.org/frontlineworld/watch/player.html?pkg=201_israel&seg=1&mod=0.

Newsweek. 1988. "Overheard." *Newsweek*, April 11, p. 21.

Nirenstein, Fiamma. 2001. "The Journalists and the Palestinians." *Commentary*, 55–58.

Norman, Julie. 2010. *The Second Palestinian Intifada: Civil Resistance.* London and New York: Routledge.

Nossek, Hillel, and Yehiel Limor. 2010. "Fifty Years in a 'Marriage of Convenience': News Media and Military Censorship in Israel." *Communication Law and Policy* 6 (1):1–35.

Obenzinger, Hilton. 1999. *American Palestine: Melville, Twain, and the Holy Land Mania.* Princeton: Princeton University Press.

Okrent, Daniel. 2005. "The Hottest Button: How the Times Covers Israel and Palestine." *New York Times,* April 24.

Ong, Aihwa. 1987. *Spirits of Resistance and Capitalist Discipline: Factory Women in Malaysia.* Albany: State University of New York Press.

Ortner, Sherry. 1999. *Life and Death on Mt. Everest: Sherpas and Himalayan Mountaineering.* Princeton: Princeton University Press.

Paley, Julia, ed. 2008. *Democracy: Anthropological Approaches.* Santa Fe: School for Advanced Research Press.

Patai, Raphael. 2002. *The Arab Mind.* Long Island City: Hatherleigh Press.

PCBS (Palestinian Central Bureau of Statistics). 2007. "Poverty in the Palestinian Territory, 2006: Main Findings Report." Ramallah: PCBS.

Pedelty, Mark. 1993. "News Photography and Indigenous Peoples: An 'Encounter' in Guatemala." *Visual Anthropology* 6 (3):285–301.

———. 1995. *War Stories: The Culture of Foreign Correspondents.* New York: Routledge.

Peteet, Julie. 1994. "Male Gender and Rituals of Resistance in the Palestinian 'Intifada': A Cultural Politics of Violence." *American Ethnologist* 21 (1):31–49.

———. 1996. "The Writing on the Walls: The Graffiti of the Intifada." *Cultural Anthropology* 11 (2):139–159.

Peterson, Mark Allen. 2001. "Getting to the Story: Unwriteable Discourse and Interpretive Practice in American Journalism." *Anthropological Quarterly* 74 (4):201–211.

———. 2007. "Making Global News: 'Freedom of Speech' and 'Muslim Rage' in U.S. Journalism." *Contemporary Islam* 1 (3):247–264.

Philo, Greg, and Mike Berry. 2004. *Bad News from Israel.* London: Pluto Press.

Pinney, Christopher. 1997. *Camera Indica: The Social Life of Indian Photographs.* Chicago: University of Chicago Press.

Poovey, Mary. 1998. *A History of the Modern Fact: Problems of Knowledge in the Sciences of Wealth and Society.* Chicago: University of Chicago Press.

Prins, Harold. 2002. "Visual Media and the Primitivist Perplex: Colonial Fantasies, Indigenous Imagination, and Advocacy in North America." In *Media Worlds: Anthropology on New Terrain,* edited by F. D. Ginsburg, L. Abu-Lughod, and B. Larkin. Berkeley: University of California Press, 58–74.

Pulitzer, Joseph. 1989. "Selections from the College of Journalism." In *Killing the Messenger: 100 Years of Media Criticism,* edited by T. Goldstein. New York: Columbia University Press, 190–200.

Rabinowitz, Dan. 2001. "Natives with Jackets and Degrees: Othering, Objectifiction, and the Role of Palestinians in the Co-existence Field in Israel." *Social Anthropology* 9 (1):65–80.

Radin, Charles. 2004. "Arafat Laid to Rest Amid Tumult, Grief; Throngs Rush Burial Site in West Bank." *Boston Globe*, November 13.

Raffles, Hugh. 2002. *In Amazonia: A Natural History.* Princeton: Princeton University Press.

Rajagopal, Arvind. 2001. *Politics After Television: Hindu Nationalism and the Reshaping of the Public in India.* Cambridge: Cambridge University Press.

Rao, Ursula. 2010. *News as Culture: Journalistic Practices and the Remaking of Indian Leadership Traditions.* New York and Oxford: Berghahn Books.

Regier, Terry, and Muhammad Ali Khalidi. 2009. "The Arab Street: Tracking a Political Metaphor." *Middle East Journal* 63 (1):11–29.

Rosen, Jay. 1999. *What Are Journalists For?* New Haven: Yale University Press.

Roudakova, Natalia. 2010. "Journalism as 'Prostitution': Understanding Russia's Reactions to Anna Politkovskaya's Murder." *Political Communication* 26 (4):412–429.

Rouhana, Nadim. 1997. *Palestinian Citizens in an Ethnic Jewish State: Identities in Conflict.* New Haven: Yale University Press.

Roy, Sara. 2007. "Humanism, Scholarship, and Politics: Writing on the Palestinian-Israeli Conflict." *Journal of Palestine Studies* 36 (2):54–65.

———. 2010. "Reflections on the Israeli-Palestinian Conflict in U.S. Public Discourse: Legitimizing Dissent." *Journal of Palestine Studies* 39 (2):23–38.

Rubin, Trudy. 1983. "City on a Hill: Israel Dedicates Settlement Overlooking Arabs." *Christian Science Monitor*, April 19.

Russell, Adrienne. 2010. "Salon.com and New-Media Professional Journalism Culture." In *The Anthropology of News and Journalism: Global Perspectives*, edited by E. Bird. Bloomington: Indiana University Press, 270–282.

Saad, Reem. 2012. "The Egyptian Revolution: A Triumph of Poetry." *American Ethnologist* 39 (1):63–66.

Sacco, Joe. 2001. *Palestine.* Seattle: Fantagraphics Books.

Said, Edward W. 1978. *Orientalism.* Vintage Books ed. New York: Random House.

———. 1984. "Permission to Narrate." *Journal of Palestine Studies* 8 (3):27–48.

———. 2000. "America's Last Taboo." *New Left Review* 6:45–53.

Said, Ezzedine. 2009. "Palestinian Refugees Want Pope Against the Wall." Agence France Presse report, May 11.

Saif v. Government Press Office, HCJ 5627/02. 2004. Israeli High Court of Justice.

Sakr, Naomi. 2010. "Enriching or Impoverishing Discourse on Rights? Talk About Freedom of Expression on Arab Television." *Middle East Journal of Culture and Communication* 3:101–119.

Salamandra, Christa. 1998. "Moustache Hairs Lost: Ramadan Television Serials and the Construction of Identity in Damascus, Syria." *Visual Anthropology* 10 (2–4):227–246.

Sanjek, Roger. 1993. "Anthropology's Hidden Colonialism: Assistants and Their Ethnographers." *Anthropology Today* 9 (2):13–18.

Sauders, Robert. 2011a. "Whose Place Is This Anyway? The Israeli Separation Barrier, International Activists, and Graffiti." *Anthropology News* 53 (3):16.

———. 2011b. "Partners for Peace: Cooperative Popular Resistance and Peacebuilding
in the Israeli-Palestinian Conflict." In *Nonviolent Resistance in the Second Intifada:
Activism and Advocacy*, edited by M. C. Hallward and J. M. Norman. New York: Palgrave Macmillan, 53–68.

Sayigh, Rosemary. 1998. "Palestinian Camp Women as Tellers of History." *Journal of Palestine Studies* 27 (2):42–58.

Sayigh, Yezid. 2011. "Policing the People, Building the State: Authoritarian Transformation in the West Bank and Gaza." Washington: Carnegie Endowment for International Peace.

Schieffelin, Bambi, Kathryn Woolard, and Paul Kroskrity, eds. 1998. *Language Ideologies:
Practice and Theory*. Oxford: Oxford University Press.

Schiller, Naomi. 2011. "Catia Sees You: Community Television, Clientalism, and the State
in the Chávez Era." In *Venezuela's Bolivarian Democracy: Participation, Politics, and
Culture Under Chávez*, edited by J. Buxton and M. Lopez Maya. Durham: Duke University Press, 104–130.

Schmemann, Serge. 1998. "Militant Jews Start Melee by Marching in Hebron." *New York
Times*, March 14.

———. 2002a. "A Breach Prompts Israel to Bar Foreign Media from Ramallah." *New
York Times*, April 1.

———. 2002b. "Up Close, Too Close, to a Suicide Bombing." *New York Times*, March 22.

Schmemann, Serge, and Joel Brinkley. 2002. "At Least 8 Killed in Suicide Bombing on a
Bus in Israel." *New York Times*, April 10.

Schneider, Uri. 2005. *One Last Shot: The Life and Death of Mazen Dana*. Documentary.
Tel Aviv: Tele Aviv Productions.

Schudson, Michael. 1978. *Discovering the News: A Social History of American Newspapers*.
New York: Basic Books.

———. 2001. "The Objectivity Norm in American Journalism." *Journalism* 2 (2):21.

Schwenkel, Christina. 2010. "'The Camera Was My Weapon': Reporting and Representing War in Socialist Vietnam." In *The Anthropology of News and Journalism: Global
Perspectives*, edited by E. Bird. Bloomington: Indiana University Press, 86–99.

Seitz, Charmaine. 2003. "ISM at the Crossroads: The Evolution of the International Solidarity Movement." *Journal of Palestine Studies* 32 (4):50–67.

Sells, Michael. 1999. *Approaching the Qur'an: The Early Revelations*. Ashland: White
Cloud Press.

Sennott, Charles M. 2003. *The Body and the Blood: The Middle East's Vanishing Christians and the Possibility for Peace*. New York: Public Affairs.

Shaheen, Jack. 2008. *Guilty: Hollywood's Verdict on Arabs After 9/11.* New York: Olive Branch Press.

Shakry, Omnia. 2007. *The Great Social Laboratory: Subjects of Knowledge in Colonial and Postcolonial Egypt.* Stanford: Stanford University Press.

Shalev, Chemi. 2011. "Leading Palestinian Intellectual: We Already Have a One-State Solution." *Ha'aretz,* December 5.

Shapin, Steven. 1994. *A Social History of Truth: Civility and Science in Seventeenth-Century England.* Chicago: University of Chicago Press.

———. 2010. *Never Pure: Historical Studies of Science as If It Was Produced by People with Bodies, Situated in Time, Space, Culture, and Society, Struggling for Credibility and Authority.* Baltimore: Johns Hopkins University Press.

Shaw, Rosalind. 2002. *Memories of the Slave Trade: Ritual and the Historical Imagination in Sierra Leone.* Chicago: University of Chicago Press.

Shehadeh, Raja. 2007. *Palestinian Walks: Forays into a Vanishing Landscape.* New York: Scribner.

Shepherd, Naomi. 1987. *The Zealous Intruders: The Western Rediscovery of Palestine.* San Francisco: Harper and Row.

Siegal, Allan M. 2003. "Report of the Committee on Safeguarding the Integrity of Our Journalism." New York: New York Times Corporation.

Silverstein, Michael. 1996. "Monoglot 'Standard' in America: Standardization and Metaphors of Linguistic Hegemony." In *The Matrix of Language: Contemporary Linguistic Anthropology,* edited by D. Brenneis and R.K.S. Macaulay. Boulder: Westview Press, 284–306.

Silverstein, Michael, and Greg Urban. 1996. "The Natural History of Discourse." In *Natural Histories of Discourse,* edited by M. Silverstein and G. Urban. Chicago: University of Chicago Press, 1–17.

Sissons, Miranda. 2002. "In a Dark Hour: The Use of Civilians During IDF Arrest Operations." New York: Human Rights Watch.

Slyomovics, Susan. 1998. *Object of Memory: Arab and Jew Narrate the Palestinian Village.* Philadelphia: University of Pennsylvania Press.

Smith, Craig S. 2006. "Warm and Fuzzy TV, Brought to You by Hamas." *New York Times,* January 18.

Smith, Kimbra L. 2005. "Looting and the Politics of Archeological Knowledge in Northern Peru." *Ethnos* 70 (2):149–170.

Sontag, Deborah. 2001. "What Terror Keeps Teaching Us; Bringing Jerusalem Home." *New York Times,* September 23.

Spitulnik, Debra. 2002. "Mobile Machines: Zambian Radio Culture." In *Media Worlds: Anthropology on New Terrain,* edited by F. Ginsburg, L. Abu-Lughod, and B. Larkin. Berkeley: University of California Press, 337–354.

Spivak, Gayatri Chakravorty. 2010. "Can the Subaltern Speak? Revised Edition." In *Can the Subaltern Speak?: Reflections on the History of an Idea*, edited by R. C. Morris. New York: Columbia University Press, 21–79.

Sreberny-Mohammadi, Annabelle, and Ali Mohammadi. 1994. *Small Media, Big Revolution: Communication, Culture, and the Iranian Revolution*. Minneapolis: University of Minnesota Press.

Staff, *Jerusalem Post*. 2005. "Where Reporting Stops." *Jerusalem Post*, January 18.

Starrett, Gregory. 2003. "Violence and the Rhetoric of Images." *Cultural Anthropology* 18 (3):398–428.

Stewart, Kathleen C. 1996. *A Space by the Side of the Road: Cultural Poetics in an 'Other' America*. Princeton: Princeton University Press.

Stone, Andrea, and Michele Chabin. 2004. "Arafat Death Sparks Anger, Grief and Relief." *USA Today*, November 12.

Struck, Doug. 1998. "West Bank Simmers in Wake of Shootings." *Washington Post*, March 15.

Subramanian, Ajantha. 2009. *Shorelines: Space and Rights in South India*. Stanford: Stanford University Press.

Suskind, Ron. 2006. *The One Percent Doctrine*. New York: Simon & Schuster.

Swedenburg, Ted. 1995. *Memories of Revolt: The 1936–1939 Rebellion and the Palestinian National Past*. Minneapolis: University of Minnesota Press.

———. 2000. "Saʿida Sultan/Danna International: Transgender Pop and the Polysemiotics of Sex, Nation, and Ethnicity on the Israeli-Egyptian Border." In *Mass Mediations: New Approaches to Popular Culture in the Middle East and Beyond*, edited by W. Armbrust. Berkeley: University of California Press, 88–119.

Swisa, Shlomi. 2003. "Hebron, Area H-2, Status Report," edited by Y. Stein. Jerusalem: B'Tselem, Israeli Information Center for Human Rights in the Occupied Territories.

Tate, Winifred. 2007. *Counting the Dead: The Culture and Politics of Human Rights Activism in Colombia*. Berkeley: University of California Press.

Torstrick, Rebecca. 2000. *The Limits of Coexistence: Identity Politics in Israel*. Ann Arbor: University of Michigan Press.

Tsing, Anna. 2005. *Friction: An Ethnography of Global Connection*. Princeton: Princeton University Press.

Tuchman, Gaye. 1972. "Objectivity as Strategic Ritual: An Examination of Newsmen's Notions of Objectivity." *American Journal of Sociology* 77:660–679.

———. 1978. *Making News: A Study in the Construction of Reality*. New York: Free Press.

Turner, Terence. 2002. "Representation, Politics, and Cultural Imagination in Indigenous Video: General Points and Kayapo Examples." In *Media Worlds: Anthropology on New Terrain*, edited by F. D. Ginsburg, L. Abu-Lughod, and B. Larkin. Berkeley: University of California Press, 75–89.

Turner, Victor. 1986. *The Anthropology of Performance*. New York: PAJ Publications.

Van Natta Jr., Don, Adam Liptak, and Clifford J. Levy. 2005. "The Miller Case: A Notebook, a Cause, a Jail Cell and a Deal." *New York Times*, October 16.

Velthuis, Olav. 2006. "Inside a World of Spin." *Ethnography* 7 (1):125–150.

Vesperi, Maria D. 2010. "When Common Sense No Longer Holds: The Shifting Locus of News Production in the United States." In *The Anthropology of News and Journalism: Global Perspectives*, edited by E. Bird. Bloomington: Indiana University Press, 257–269.

Wacquant, Loïc. 2003. *Body and Soul: Notebooks of an Apprentice Boxer*. Oxford: Oxford University Press.

Wahl-Jorgensen, Karin. 2010. "News Production, Ethnography, and Power: On the Challenges of Newsroom-Centricity." In *The Anthropology of News and Journalism: Global Perspectives*, edited by E. Bird. Bloomington: Indiana University Press, 21–34.

Warner, Michael. 2002. *Publics and Counterpublics*. New York: Zone Books.

Weber, Max. 1949. "'Objectivity' in Social Science and Social Policy." In *The Methodology of the Social Sciences*, edited by E. A. Shils and H. Finch. New York: Free Press, 49–112.

Wedeen, Lisa. 1999. *Ambiguities of Domination: Politics, Rhetoric, and Symbols in Contemporary Syria*. Chicago: University of Chicago Press.

———. 2003. "Seeing Like a Citizen, Acting Like a State: Exemplary Events in Unified Yemen." *Comparative Studies in Society and History* 75 (3):680–713.

Weiss, Meira. 2002. *The Chosen Body: The Politics of the Body in Israeli Society*. Stanford: Stanford University Press.

Weymouth, Lally. 2000. "Ariel Sharon on Arafat, Barak and the Temple Mount." *Newsweek*, October 16.

Will, George F. 2000. "No Partners for Peace." *Washington Post*, October 22.

Willen, Sarah. 2010. "Citizens, 'Real' Others, and 'Other' Others: The Biopolitics of Otherness and the Deportation of Unauthorized Migrant Workers from Tel Aviv, Israel." In *The Deportation Regime: Sovereignty, Space, and the Freedom of Movement*, edited by N. De Genova and N. Peutz. Durham: Duke University Press, 262–294.

Wilson, Scott. 2007. "Bonded in Resistance to the Barrier, Palestinian Villagers, Jewish Neighbors Warily Join Forces." *Washington Post*, June 8.

Wilson, Scott, and Glenn Kessler. 2006. "Palestinian Candidates Condemn U.S. Program; Events Boosted Government." *Washington Post*, January 24.

Winegar, Jessica. 2006. *Creative Reckonings: The Politics of Art and Culture in Contemporary Egypt*. Stanford: Stanford University Press.

———. 2012. "The Privilege of Revolution: Gender, Class, Space, and Affect in Cairo." *American Ethnologist* 39 (1):67–70.

Wolfsfeld, Gadi, Eli Avraham, and Issam Aburaiya. 2000. "When Prophecy Always Fails: Israeli Press Coverage of the Arab Minority's Land Day Protests." *Political Communication* 17 (2):115–131.

Woodward, Michelle. 2012. "After the Decisive Moment: Moving Beyond Photojournalism's High-Risk Mode." In *Film and Risk*, edited by M. Hjort. Detroit: Wayne State University Press, 227–244.

Woolard, Kathryn. 1998. "Introduction: Language Ideology as a Field of Inquiry." In *Language Ideologies: Practice and Theory*, edited by B. Schieffelin, K. Woolard, and P. Kroskrity. Oxford: Oxford University Press.

Yurchak, Alexei. 2005. *Everything Was Forever, Until It Was No More: The Last Soviet Generation*. Princeton: Princeton University Press.

Zelizer, Barbie. 2007. "On 'Having Been There': 'Eyewitnessing' as a Journalistic Key Word." *Critical Studies in Media Communication* 24 (5):408–428.

Zelizer, Barbie, David Park, and David Gudelunas. 2002. "How Bias Shapes the News: Challenging *The New York Times'* Status as a Newspaper of Record on the Middle East." *Journalism* 3 (3):283–307.

INDEX

Abbas, Mahmoud: as PA president, 123, 192, 193, 203, 205, 221, 224; during presidential elections of 2005, 219–20, 223, 224

ABC News, 95

Abdo, Mohammad Matar, 272n4

Abu Allan, Hussam, 158

Abu Dis, 40, 141–42, 152, 154, 177; graffiti on separation barrier at, 233–35, 236, 237, 238–39, 243, 245, 247, 252

Abu El-Haj, Nadia, 270n93

Abu Halima, Mohamed, 77

Abu-Lughod, Lila, 12

Abu Shambiya, Louay, 246–47

Abu Zahra, Imad, 76, 96

accumulated authorship, 57–59, 64–65, 66–67, 252

advocacy journalism, 204

Afghanistan: Al-Jazeera's Kabul office, 1, 51; journalists in, 2, 3, 6, 8, 219; Karzai, 220

Agence France-Presse (AFP), 18, 167, 168, 247

'Aida Refugee Camp, 16, 146, 162, 163, 178, 180, 184, 188, 189, 190–94, 198, 283n44, 285n27; and Benedict XVI's visit, 191–94; Salameh Hamdan killed in, 178–79, 282n27; history of, 171–72; murals in, 243, 244; protests against separation barrier at, 172–76, 181, 247–50

Ajarmeh, Adnan, 192–93

Al-Bishawi, Muhammad, 76, 95, 178

Al-Jazeera, 121, 287n36; Baghdad office, 51; GPO card policy challenged by, 81, 88; Kabul office, 1, 51

Al-Jazeera English, 20, 51

Al-Qaeda, 1, 23, 51, 86

Al-Quds, 179

Al-Ram, 136–37, 138, 245–46, 247

Al-Walaja, 137

anthropology, 25, 37, 160–61, 259n9, 260nn22–24, 268n76, 285n14; ethnography in, 8, 17–18, 67, 130; vs. journalism, 5–6, 13–14, 67; participant-observation method, 14, 136, 261n43

AP. *See* Associated Press

Appadurai, Arjun, 51, 80

Arab revolts of 2011, 167, 288n15

Arafat, Yasir: compound in Ramallah, 103; funeral of, 14, 24, 141, 197–201, 207–19, 222, 223, 225, 227; Nobel Peace Prize of, 199, 211; Palestinian attitudes regarding, 199–201, 207–8, 210–11, 286n32, 286n33; as PA president, 76, 77, 102, 197, 202, 206, 207, 220; as PLO chairman, 21, 43, 197, 207

Arendt, Hannah, 6

Asad, Talal, 110

Ashi, Suleiman Abdul-Rahim al-, 272n4

Askew, Kelly, 281n7

Associated Press (AP), 18, 52, 123, 160, 168, 177, 237, 239, 283n44; attribution guidelines, 269n83. *See also* Darwazeh, Nazeh

Austin, J. L.: on speech acts, 85, 86, 274nn37,38

315